AF538349

HORSES

IN LIVING COLOR

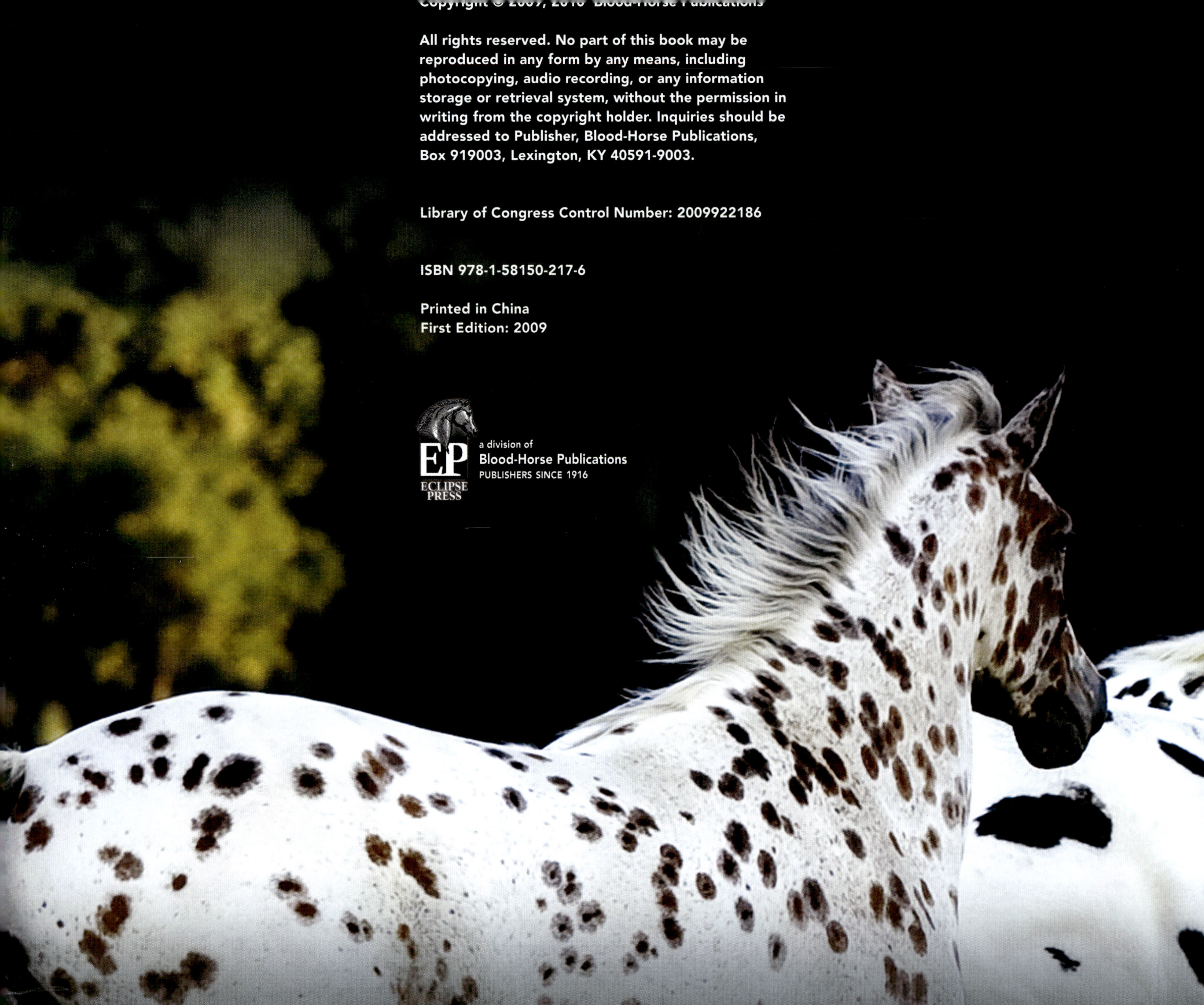

Library of Congress Control Number: 2009922186

ISBN 978-1-58150-217-6

Printed in China
First Edition: 2009

EP
ECLIPSE PRESS
a division of
Blood-Horse Publications
PUBLISHERS SINCE 1916

HORSES

IN LIVING COLOR

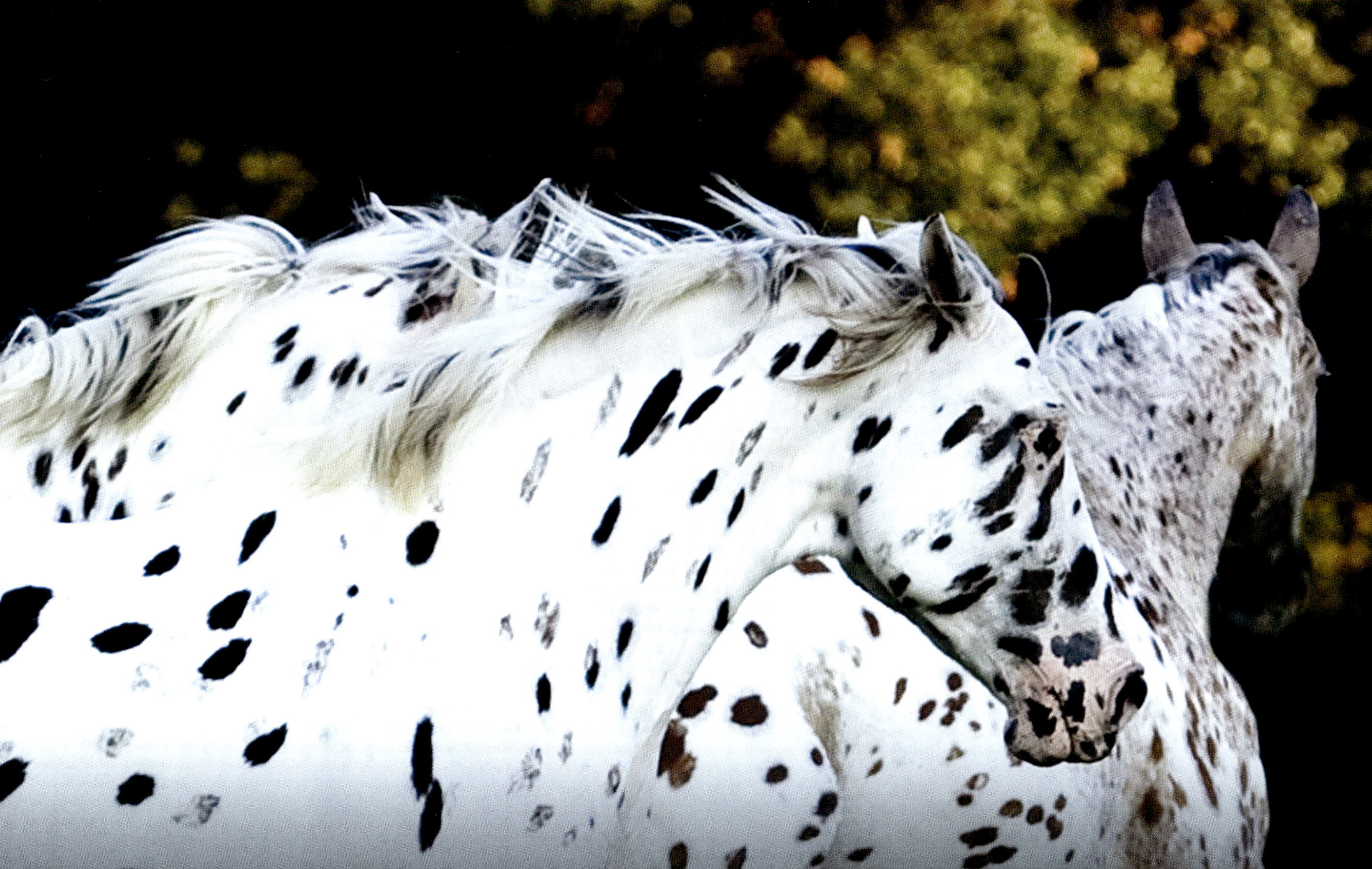

FOREWORD

The Lone Ranger's Silver galloped alongside Tonto's Scout, and Roy Rogers and Dale Evans rode Trigger and Buttermilk. Gene Autry shared the silver screen with Champion, Tom Mix with Tony, and William S. Hart with Fritz.

General Robert E. Lee rode Traveller, and Alexander the Great's colorful mount was Bucephalus, said to be black with a large white star and blue eye.

John Steinbeck penned *The Red Pony*, Walter Farley *The Black Stallion*, and Anna Sewell *Black Beauty*.

And there were Fury of Broken Wheel Ranch, Flicka, Thunderhead, and, of course, the lovable Mr. Ed.

History is richly painted with these and other colorful, heroic steeds, both real and fictionalized. Yet why does a flashy horse so stir the emotions?

My first regular mount was an aged white gelding named Pete. The kindly old boy willingly let me slip twine through his halter loop and hop aboard bareback. Off we would tear at speeds that — in hindsight — were perhaps not entirely safe.

The farm's legend held that, decades earlier, Pete had been a circus horse. To this pre-teen girl, Pete was magic.

And then I encountered Clarence Stewart, a New York-bred Thoroughbred, and the first colt registered as white by The Jockey Club. When he cut through a foggy homestretch at Saratoga in 1979, his alabaster coat glowing, I was thunderstruck.

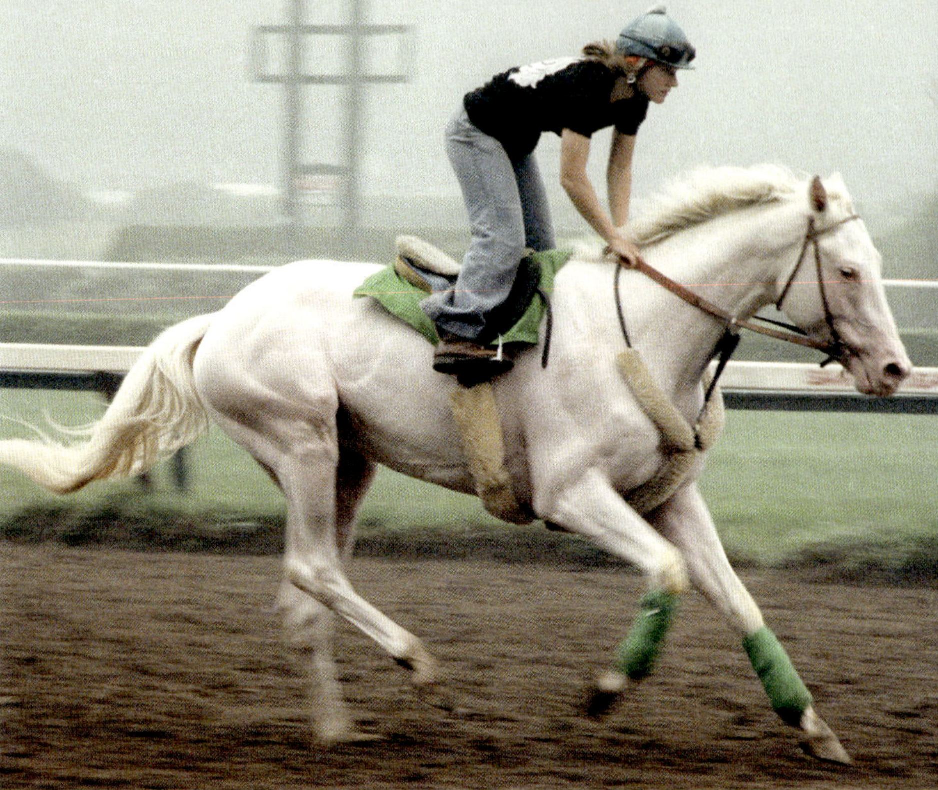

Clarence Stewart inspired my love of colored Thoroughbreds.

While I'd loved colorful horses as long as I could remember (what young girl doesn't?), thus began my passion for unusually colored Thoroughbreds, too. That passion is celebrated in *Horses In Living Color*, a project that transported me beyond the Thoroughbred realm and into the universe of colored horses. It led me across the country and into the presence of some of the most enchanting and unusual horses I had ever seen.

Clarence Stewart's color was a shocking accident. His sire was brown and dam chestnut, and no one expected them to produce a white horse. But nowadays, many breeders strive to produce eye-catching horses, recognizing the power of color, and "flash" or "bling." Farms hawk such beauties in terms of being "the icing on the cake!" or, for instance, "the world's first buckskin and white sabino Thoroughbred."

Advances in the study of equine genetics are creating a new appreciation for the beauty, and inheritability, of color. Labs now test blood for various genotypes, the results of which can sometimes guarantee a horse will produce — or not produce — offspring of certain colors.

New terms seem to spring up daily to describe various color combinations and patterns. In a recent book by leading researcher D. Phillip Sponenberg, nine variations of the color "bay" are categorized.

On Web sites such as one devoted exclusively to equine color genetics, people compare photos, pedigrees, and possibilities: Is that white horse a maximum sabino or a dominant white? Is this a true roan, a rabicano, or something else? What causes dapples? What's the difference between a sooty buckskin and a dusty buckskin?

Here's an owner's description of her horse who, to most of us, might simply seem a flashy chestnut mare (see photos, pp. 108-109):

Color: Flaxen Chestnut Overo

Her genotype is:

Extension (red factor): e/e (red based)

Agouti (bay): A/A (homozygous dominant for agouti and thus she can never produce a foal that is any variant of black, only bay bases and chestnut bases)

Champagne: n/n

Cream: n/n

Dun: n/n

Pearl: n/n

Silver: n/n

Frame overo (LWO): O/n (one copy, making her a genetic frame overo)

Sabino1: n/n (she is another, as of yet unlocated, sabino)

Tobiano: n/n

She carries frame, and appears to carry splash white and sabino as well. As of now there is no test for splash white and no all-inclusive test for sabino so this belief is based solely on her phenotype.

I strongly believe that she carries a white suppression gene, which would explain how a genetic frame overo has no obvious body white as it "should." This suppressor is believed to be the cause of the spots on her face and legs.

Visually she appears to be diluted, but she has tested negative for every dilution gene for which we can currently test. The dun test is a haplotype (marker) test and as such there is some room for error. Taking that into account, it is possible she is a red dun. The majority of my peers, and even some researchers, believe that to be the case as there is no other known explanation for her clearly diluted color and prominent dun factor.

To be sure, there is more to color than meets the eye. It is such a convoluted, controversial, and changeable topic, that this book does not attempt to delve into genetics; the knowledge and terminology are advancing too rapidly. These photographs are not in-depth studies of the "hows" and "whys" of horse appearance. They simply celebrate the captivating and sometimes shocking world of colorful horses.

Captions accompany the photos when an explanation seems necessary. Otherwise, the pictures tell the story. Either way, if possible, horses are identified in the back of the book.

Whatever the scientific reason for these animals' appearances, it is easily understood how horses whose manes flow white or whose eyes reflect blue bewitch the senses. Like Silver, Trigger, Clarence Stewart, and Pete, they are magic.

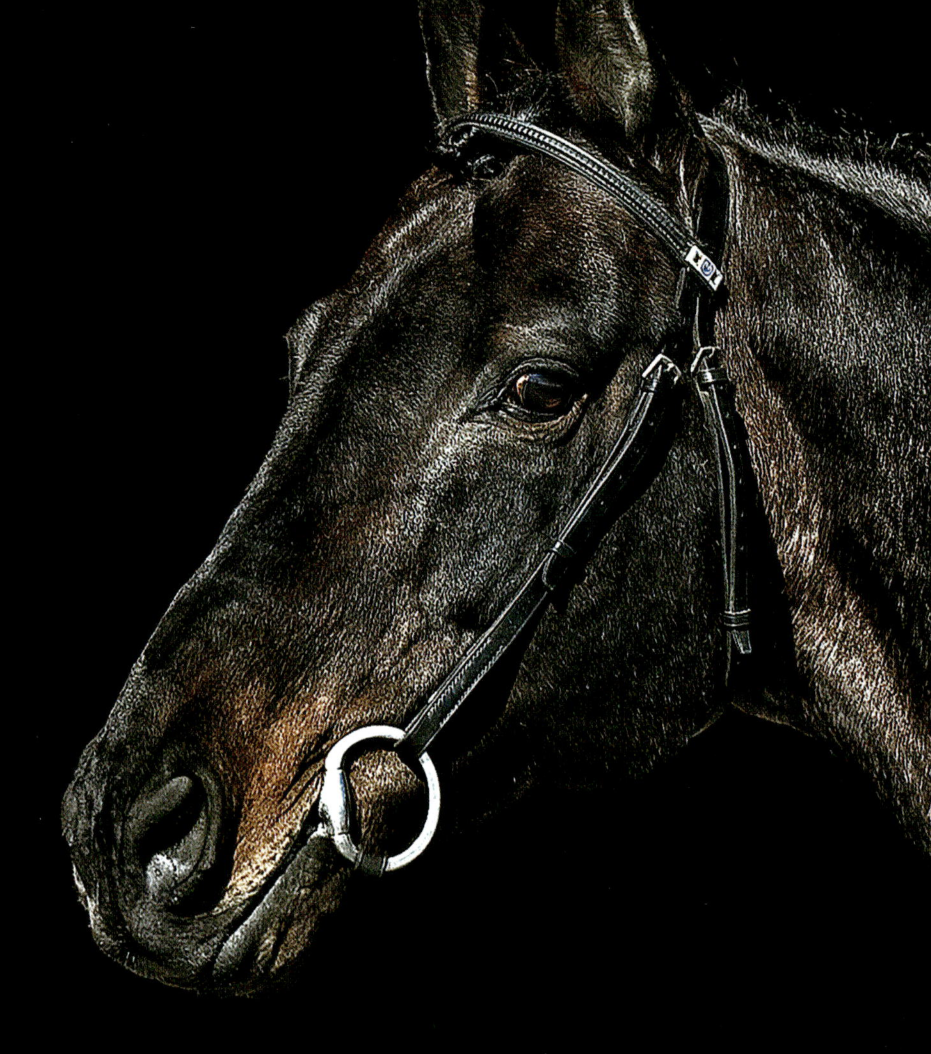

Brindle horses, such as this Brazilian Warmblood stallion (also pictured on p. 104), exhibit truly remarkable coloration.

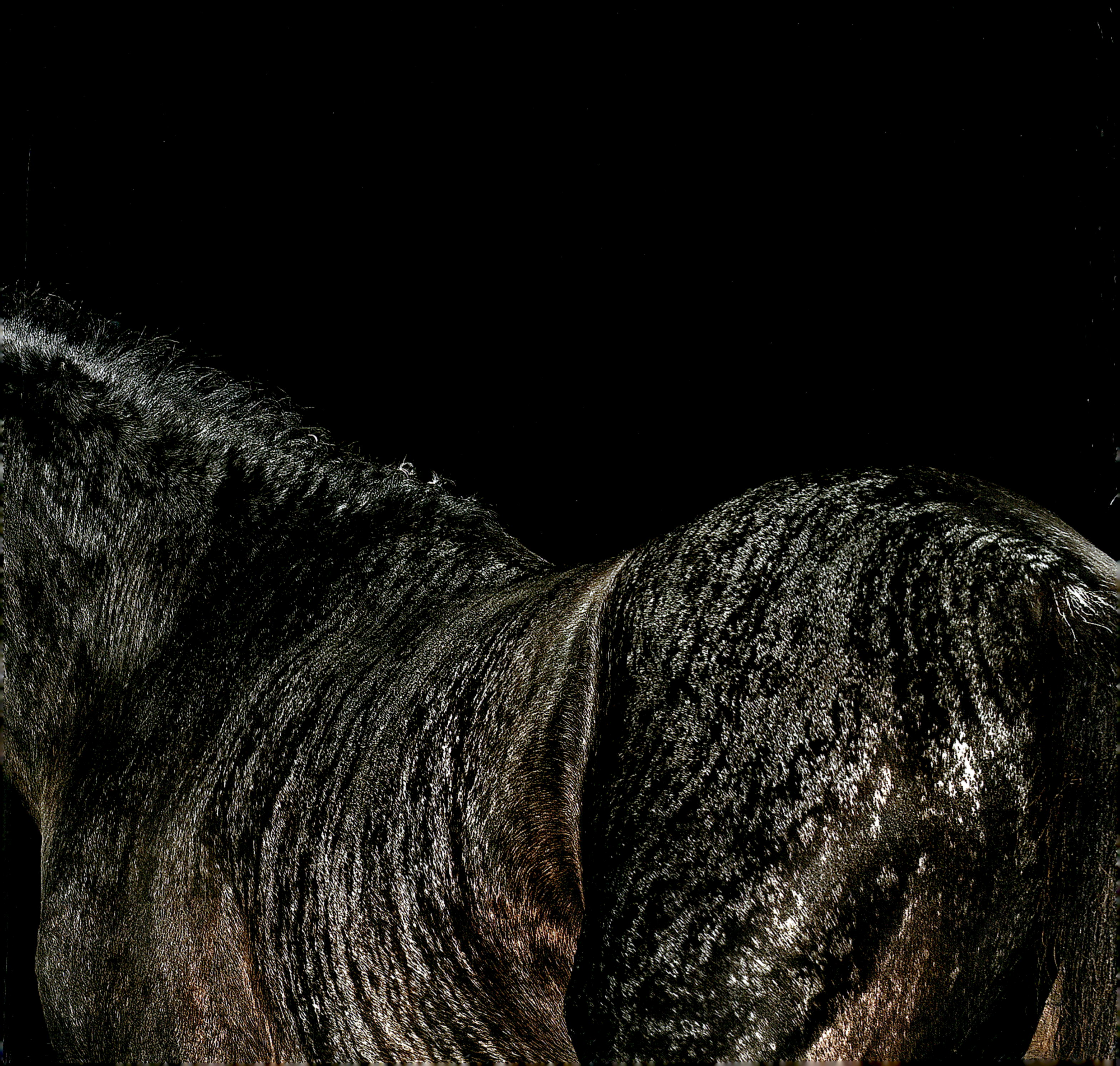

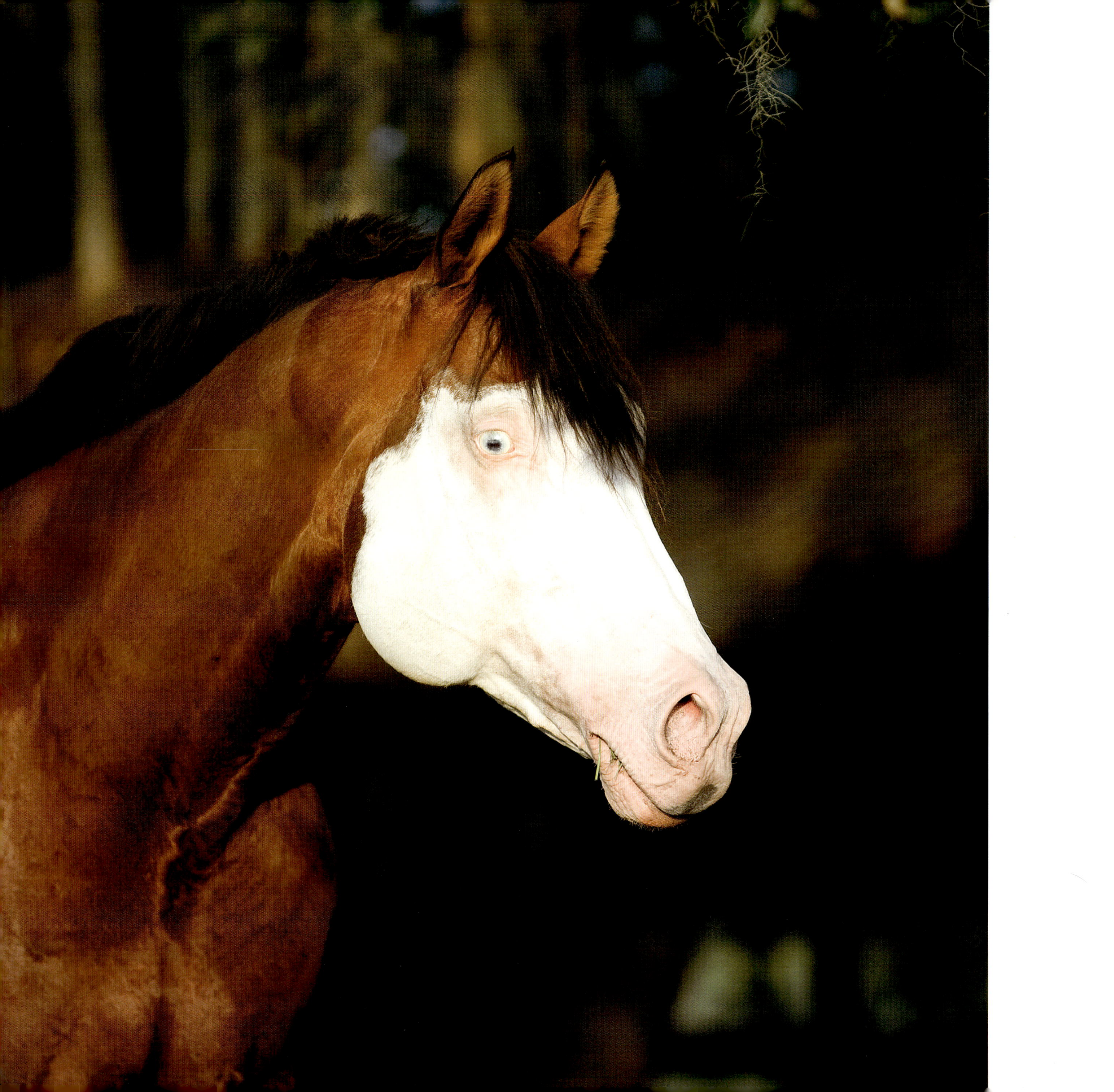

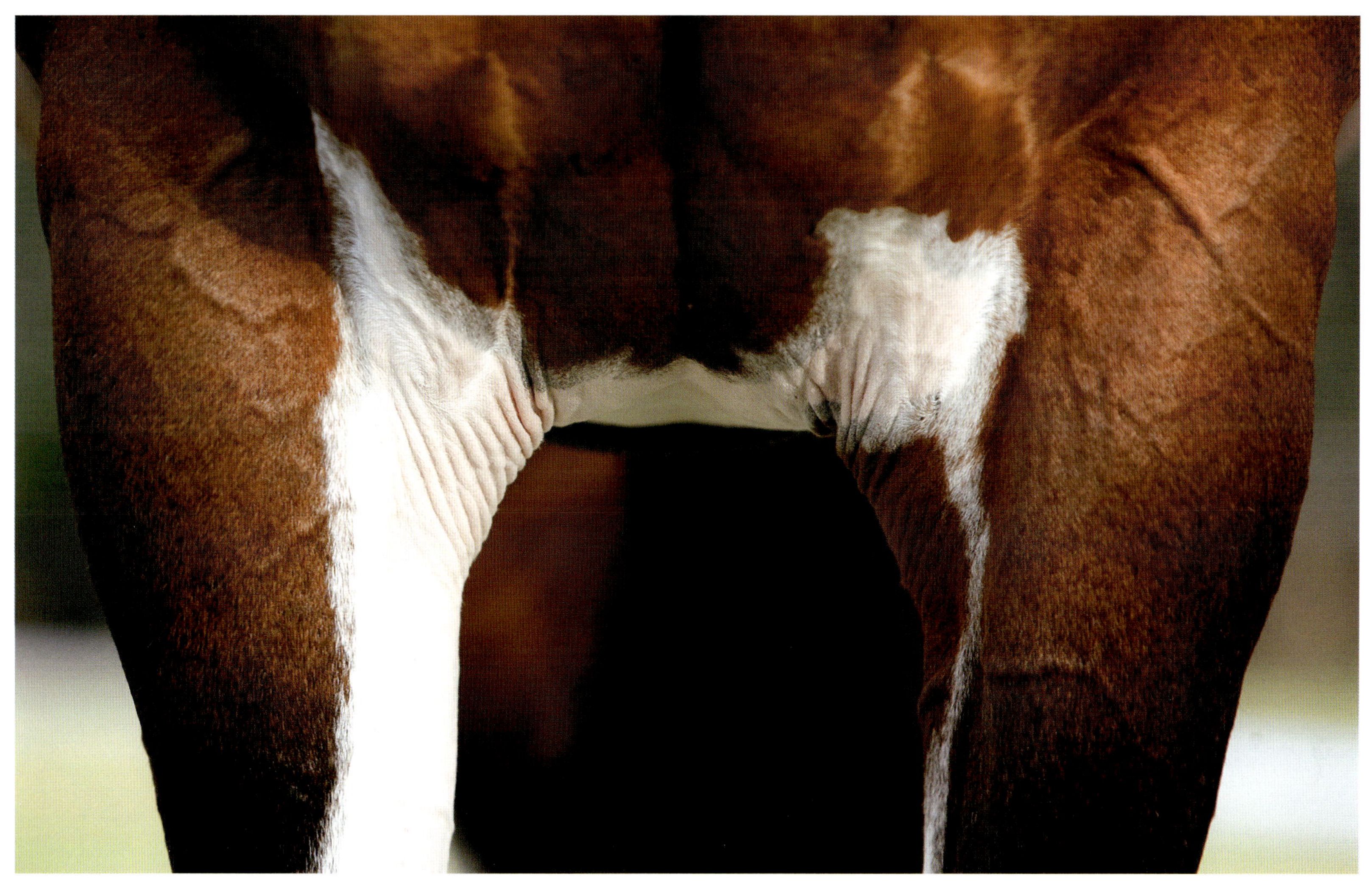

Splash, or splash white, is a pattern often marked by indicators such as a head that appears to have been dipped in milk.

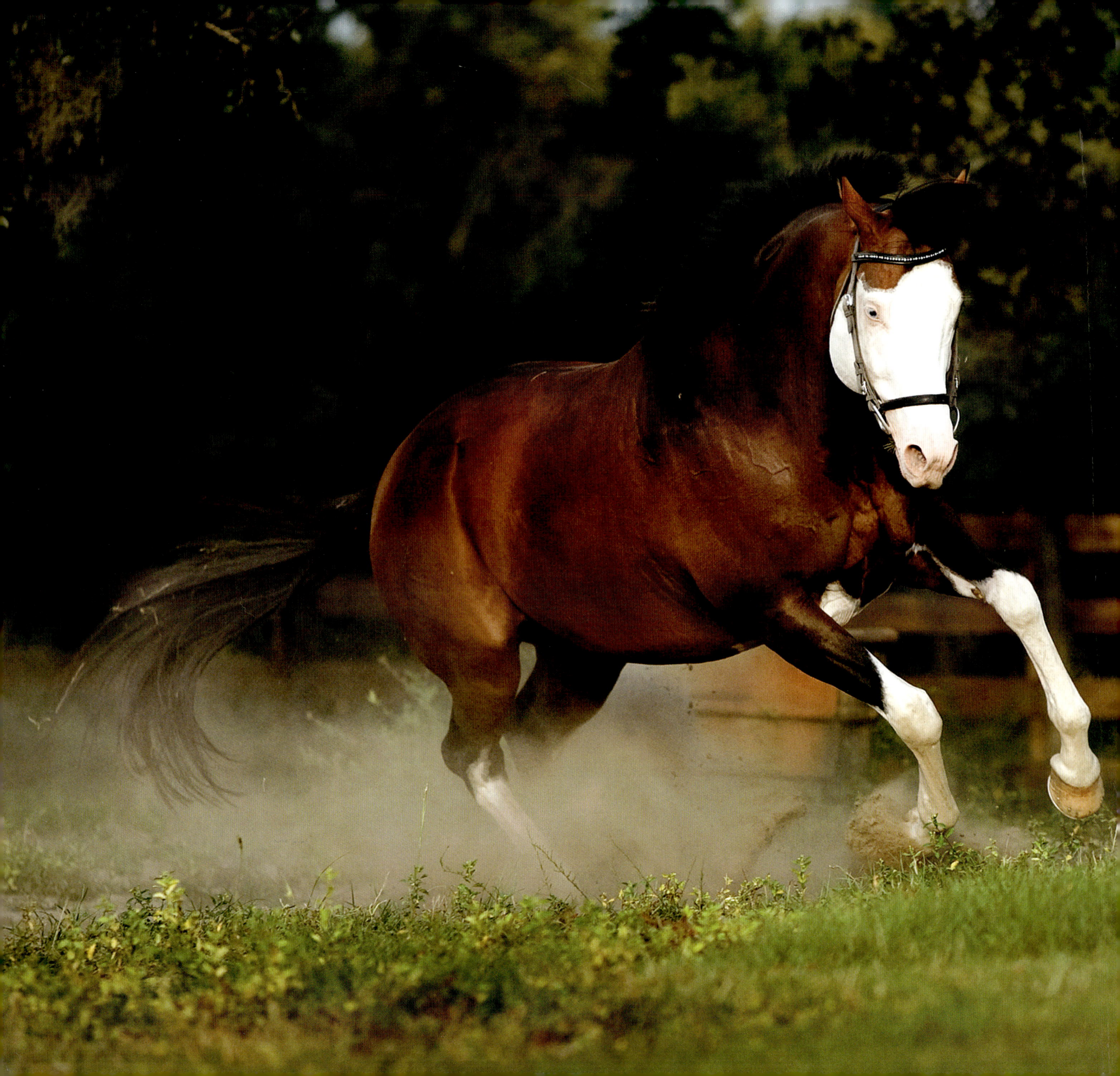

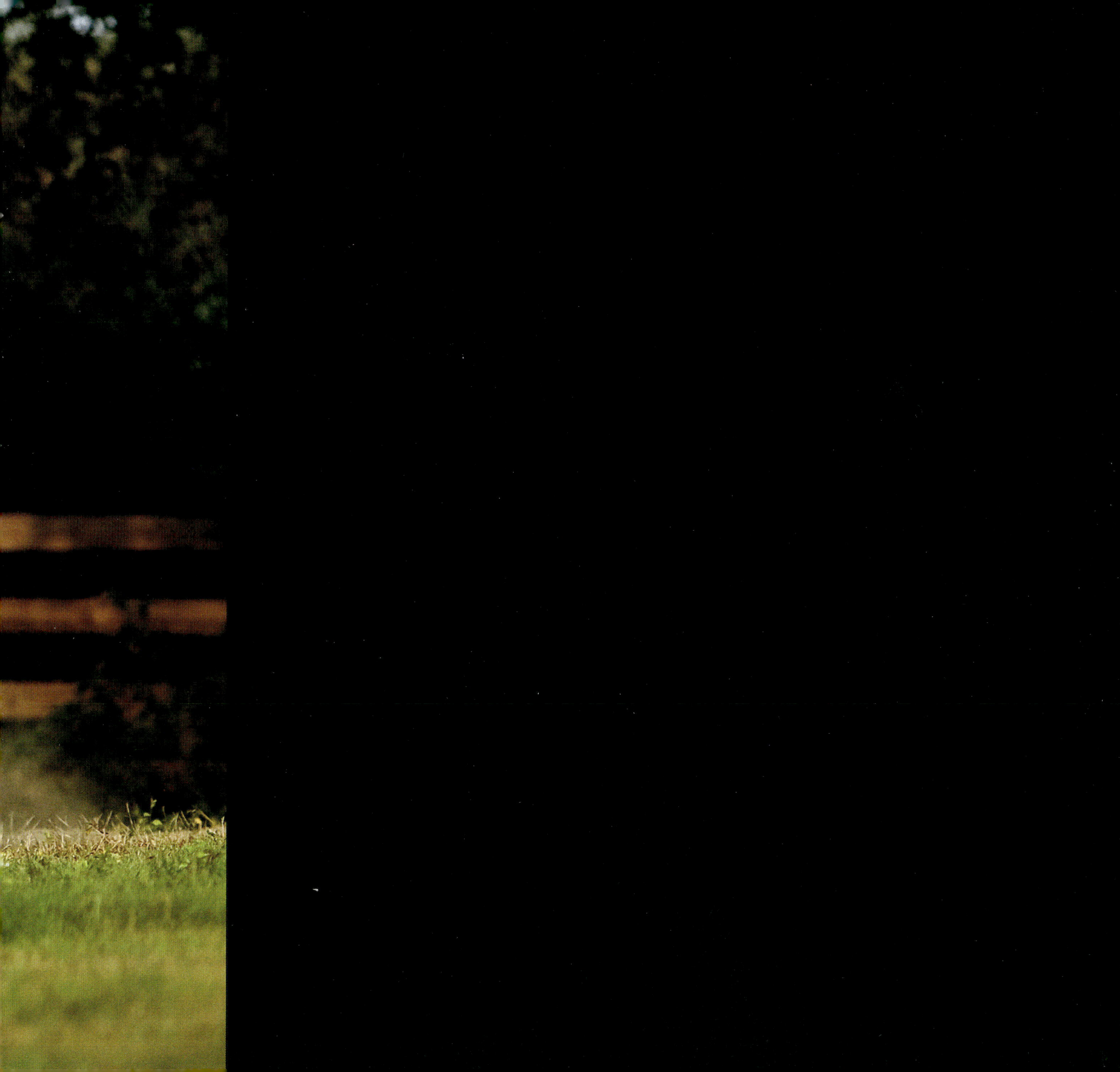

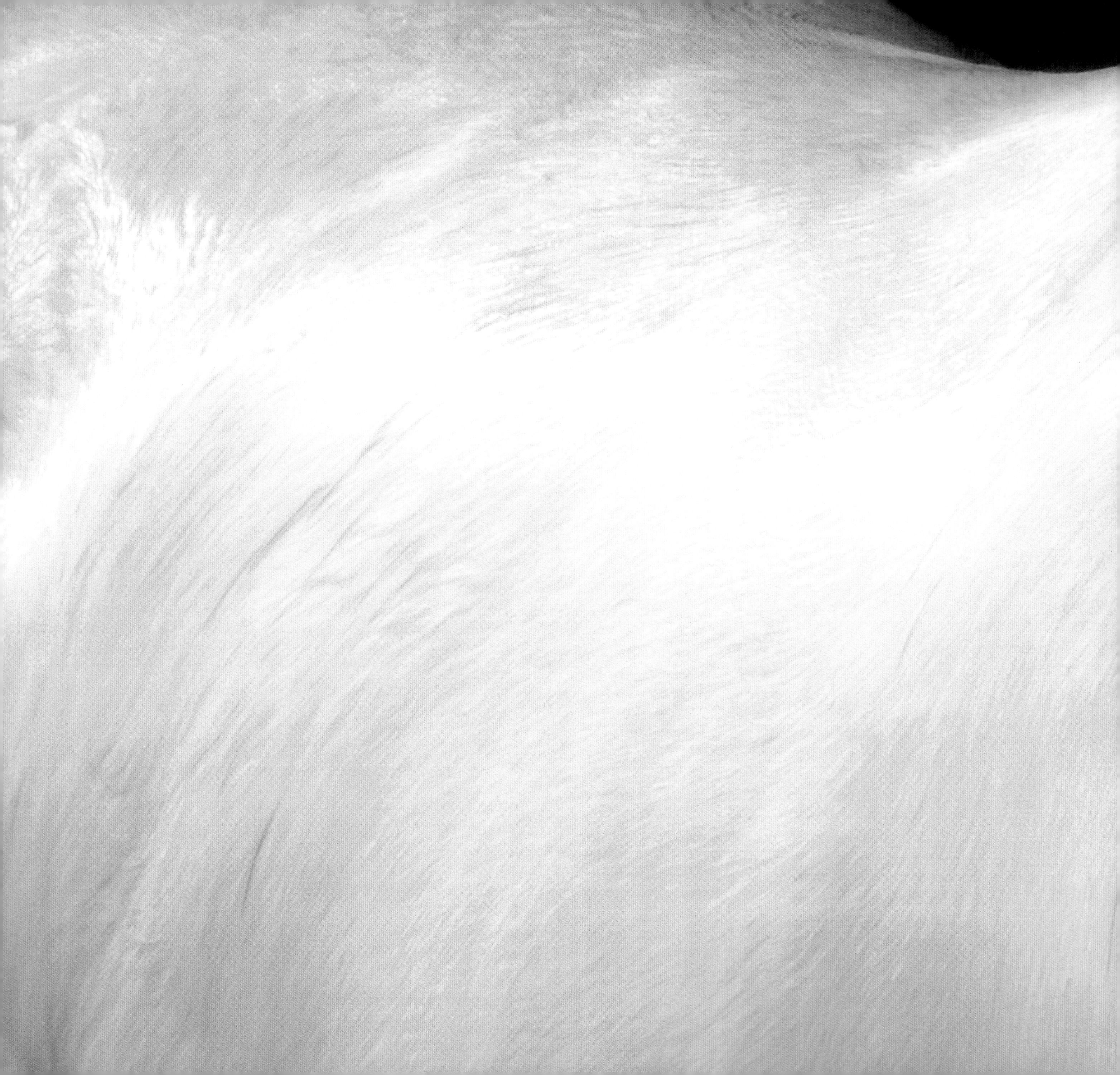

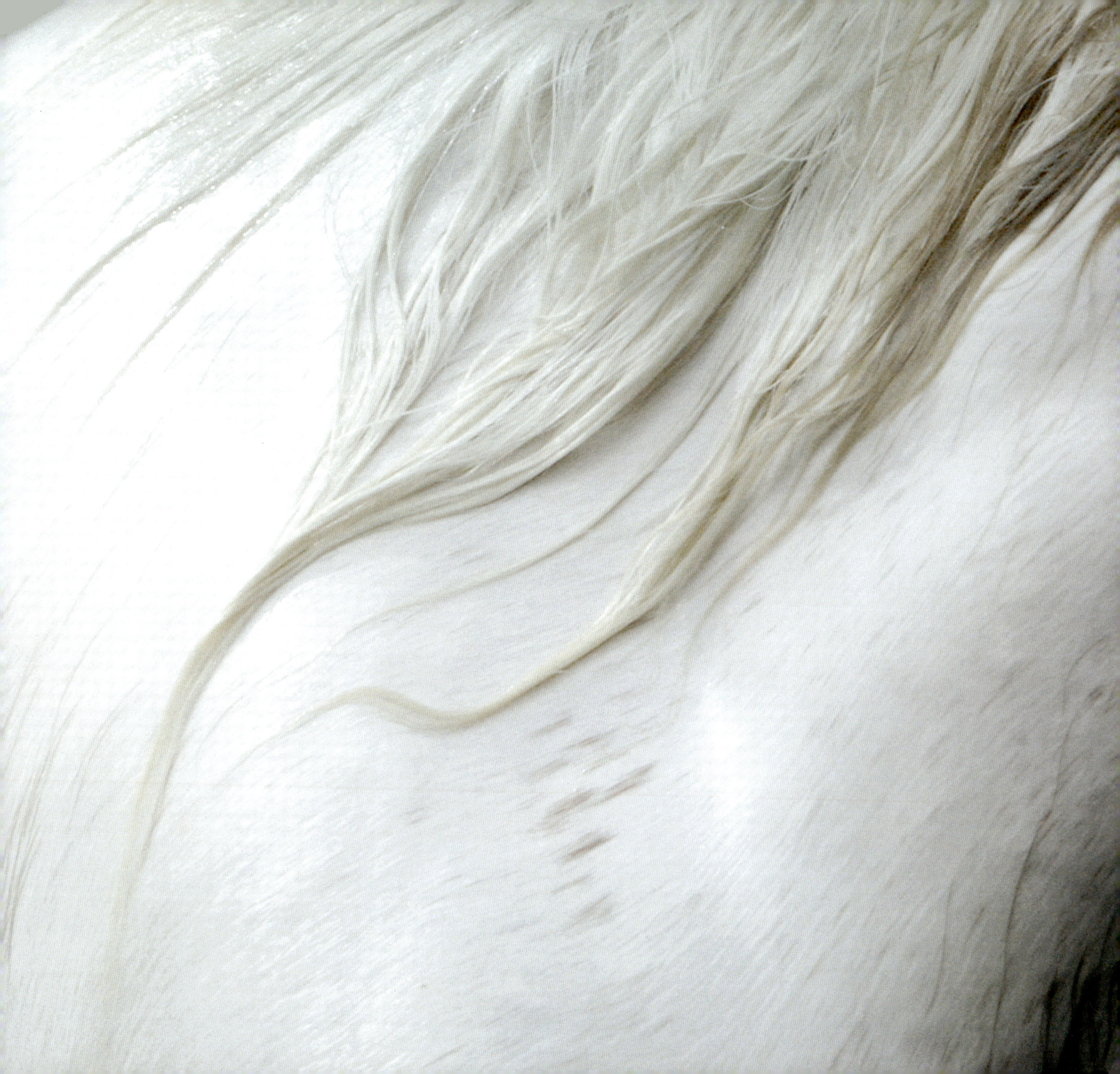

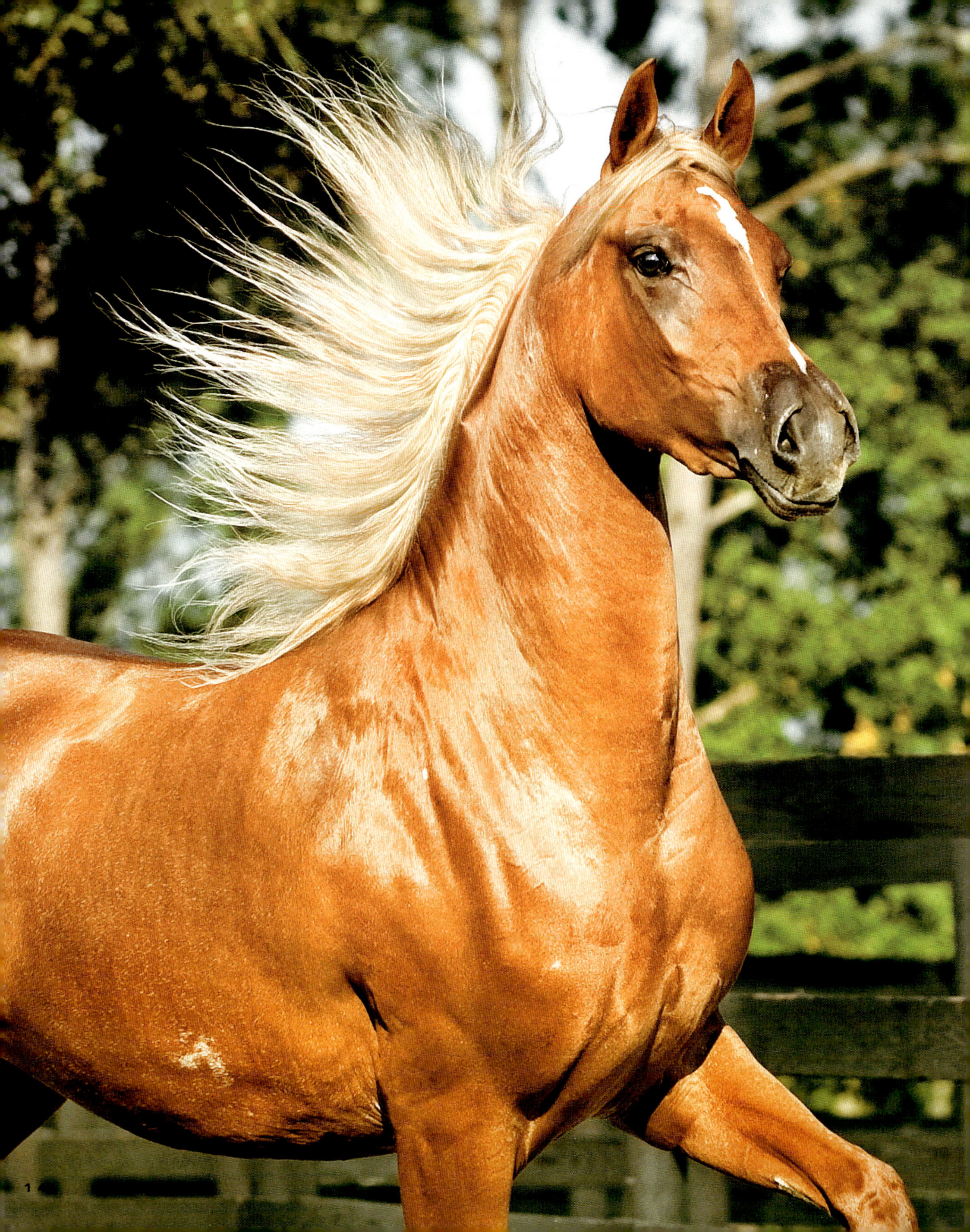

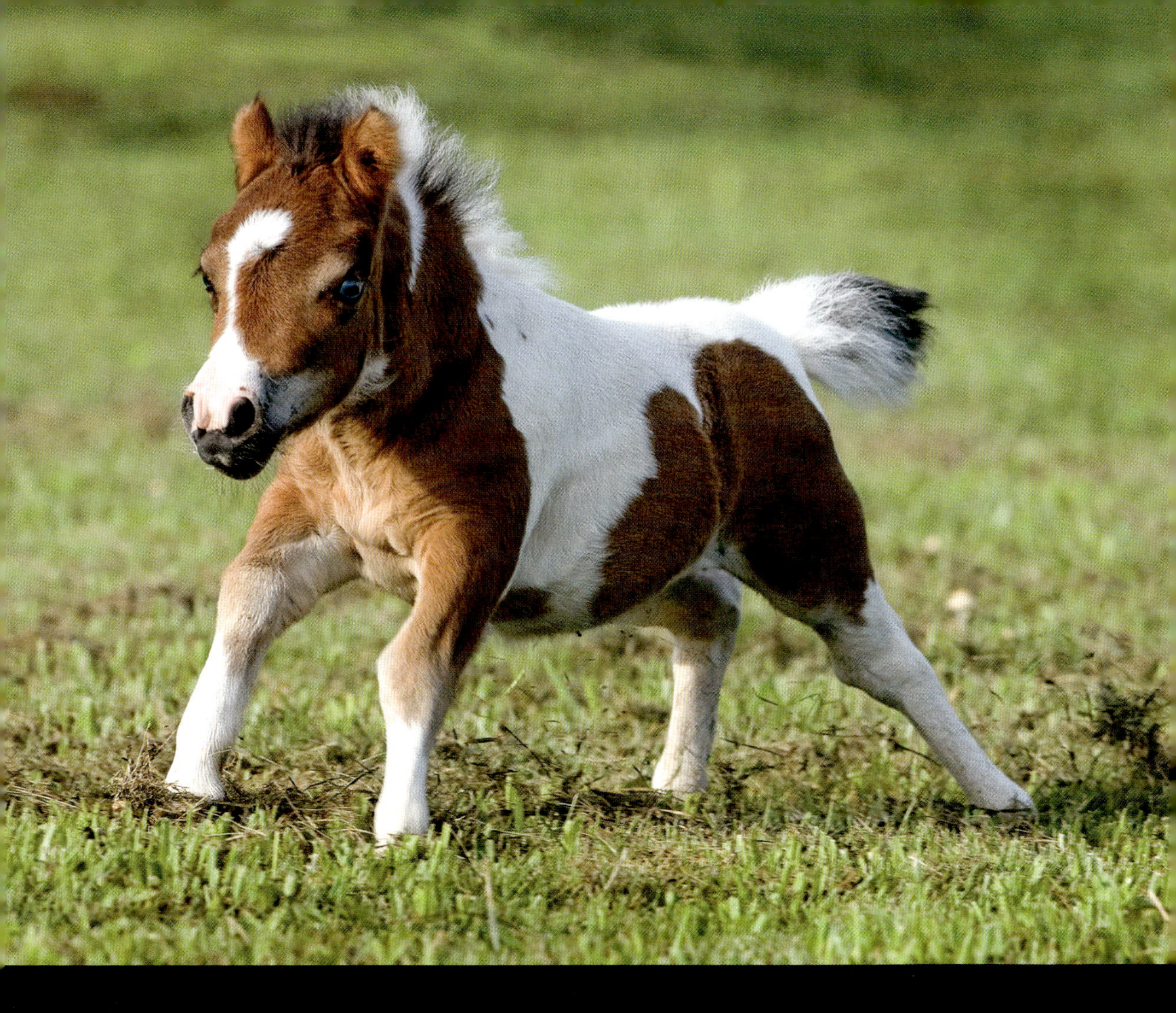

Left, this filly is compelling evidence, as some believe, that the Arabian is the most beautiful breed of horse. Above, the adorable American Miniature Horse was 13½ inches tall at birth, and she has matured to a height of 24 inches

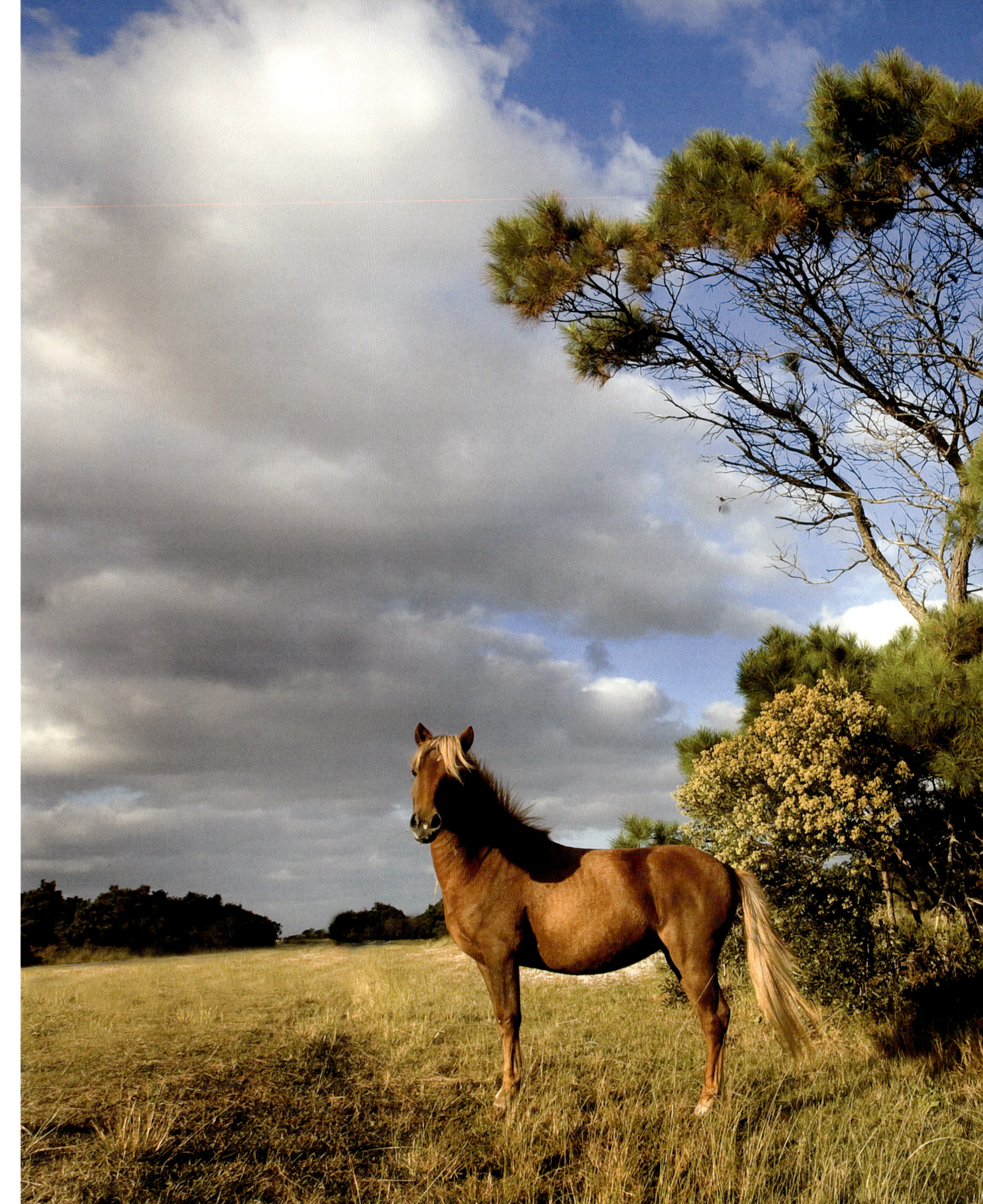

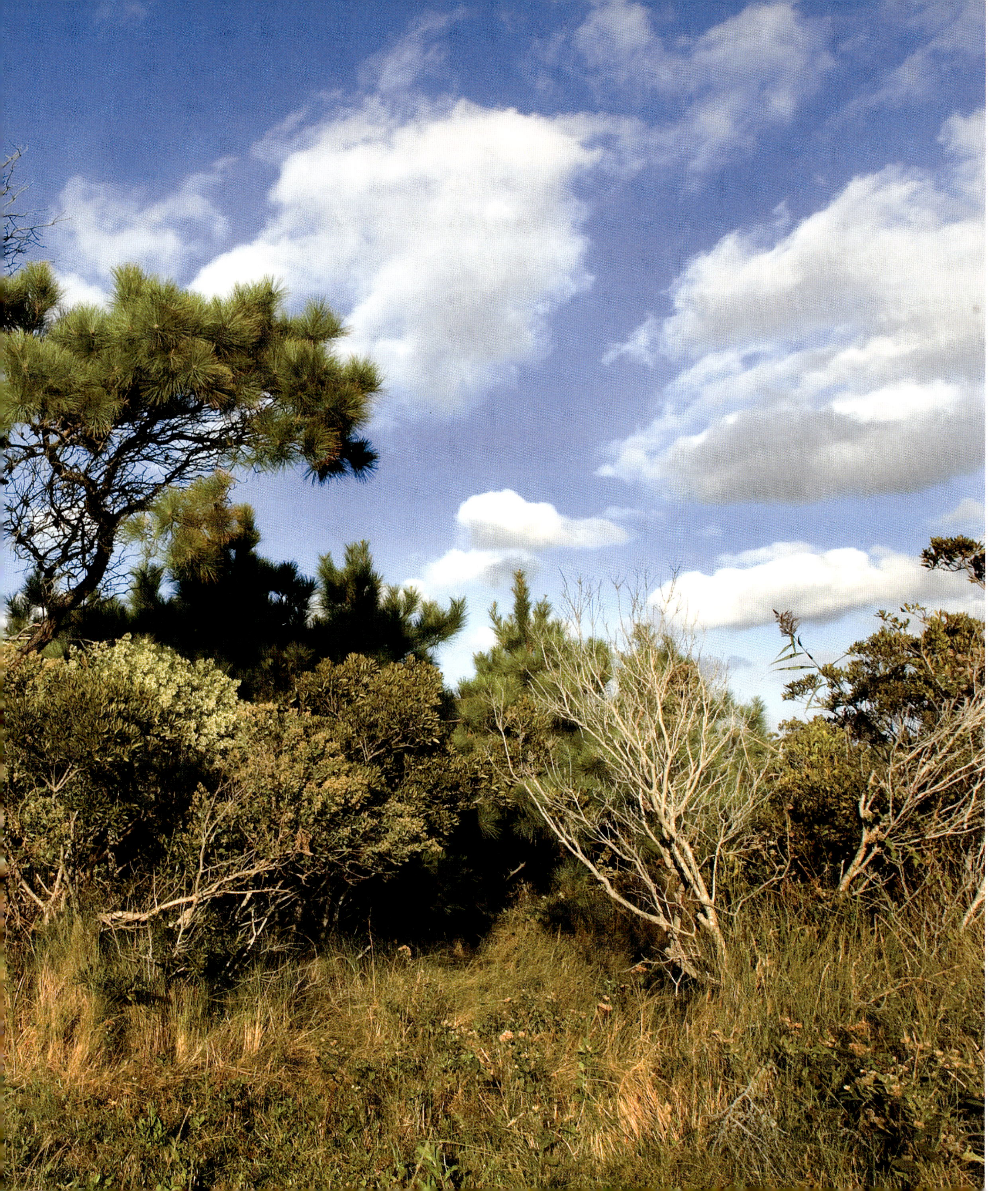

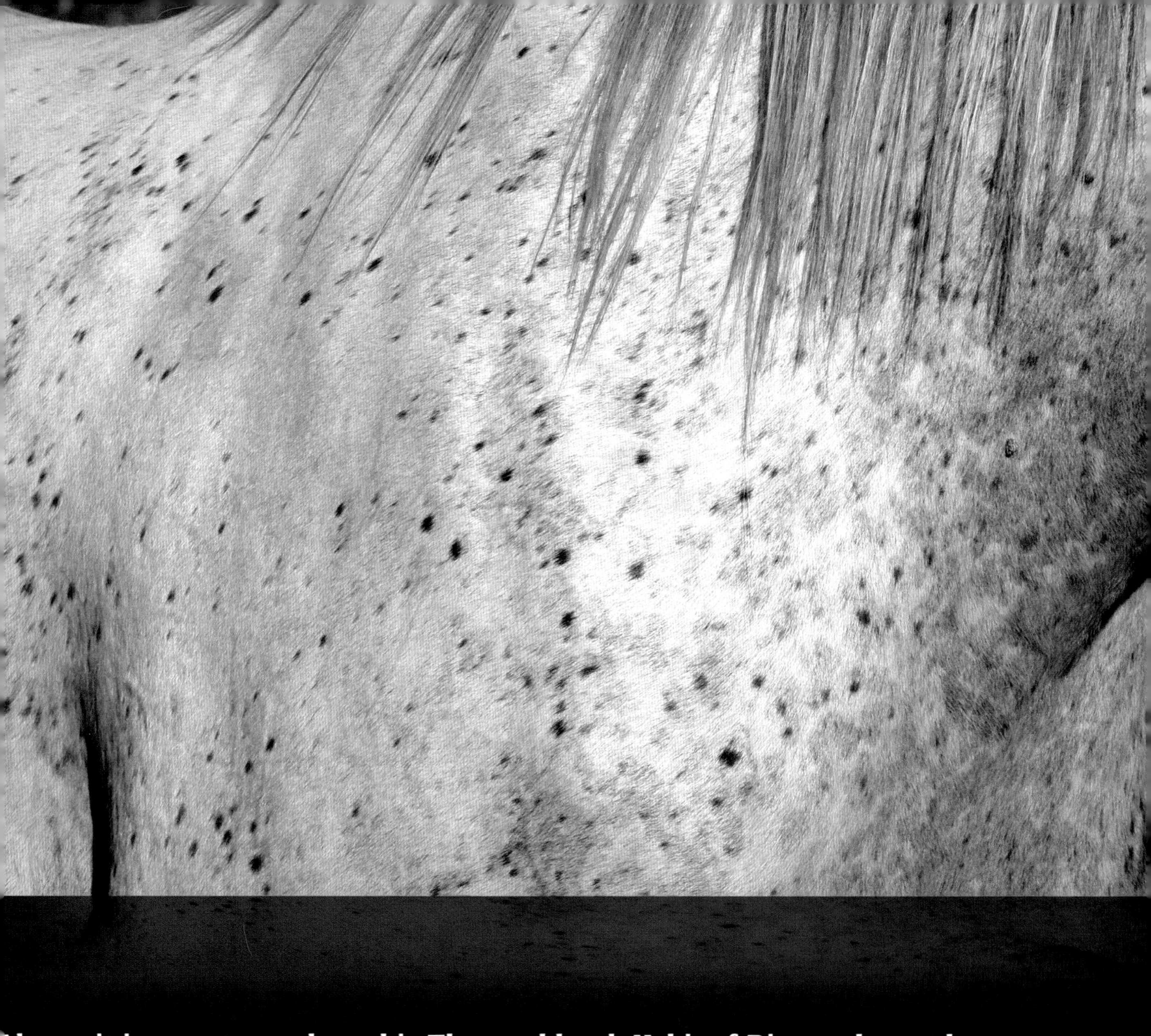

Above, it is easy to see how this Thoroughbred, Habit of Diamonds, got her name. And it's easy to see how the horse's face marking, right, is called a bald face.

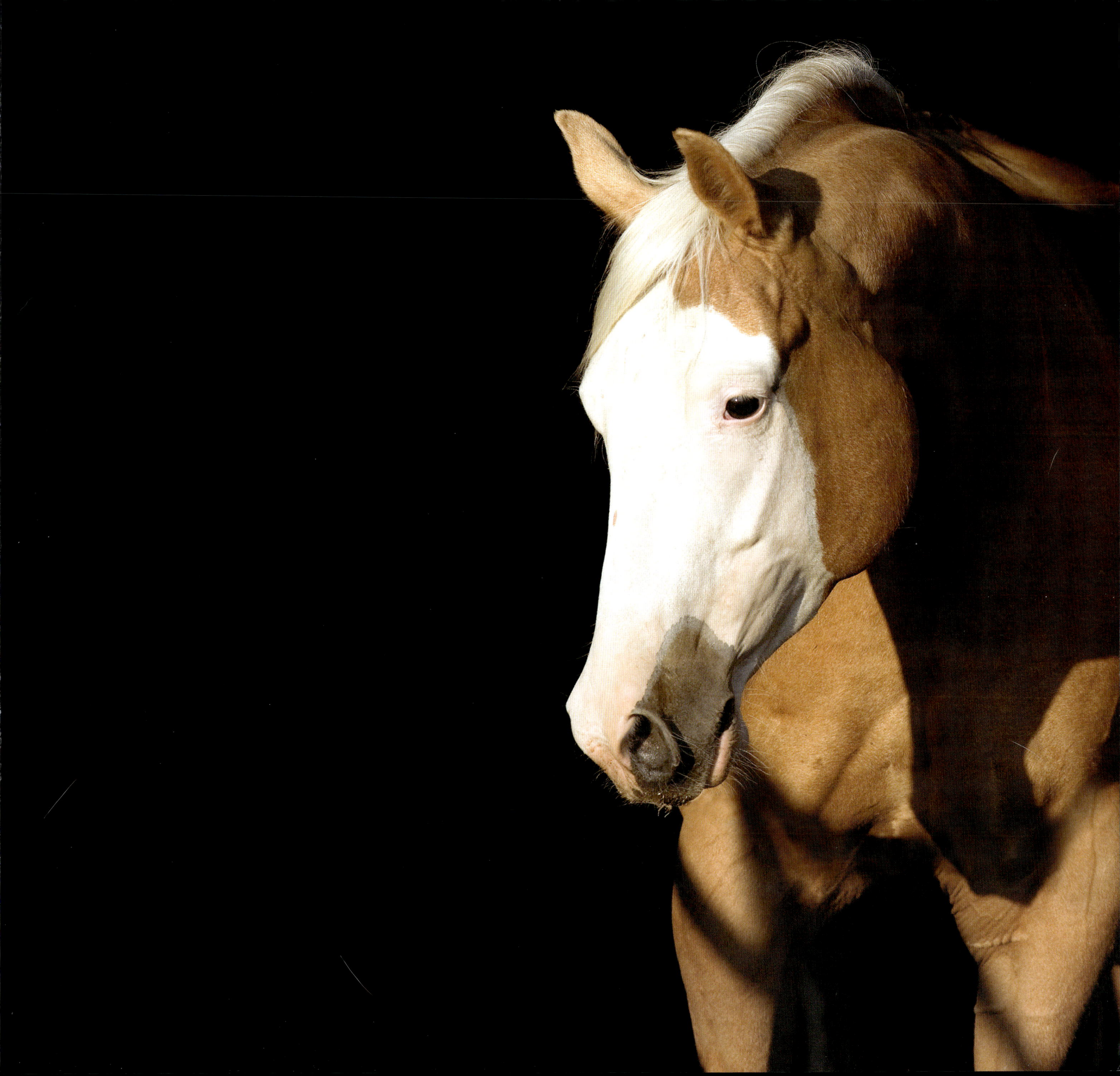

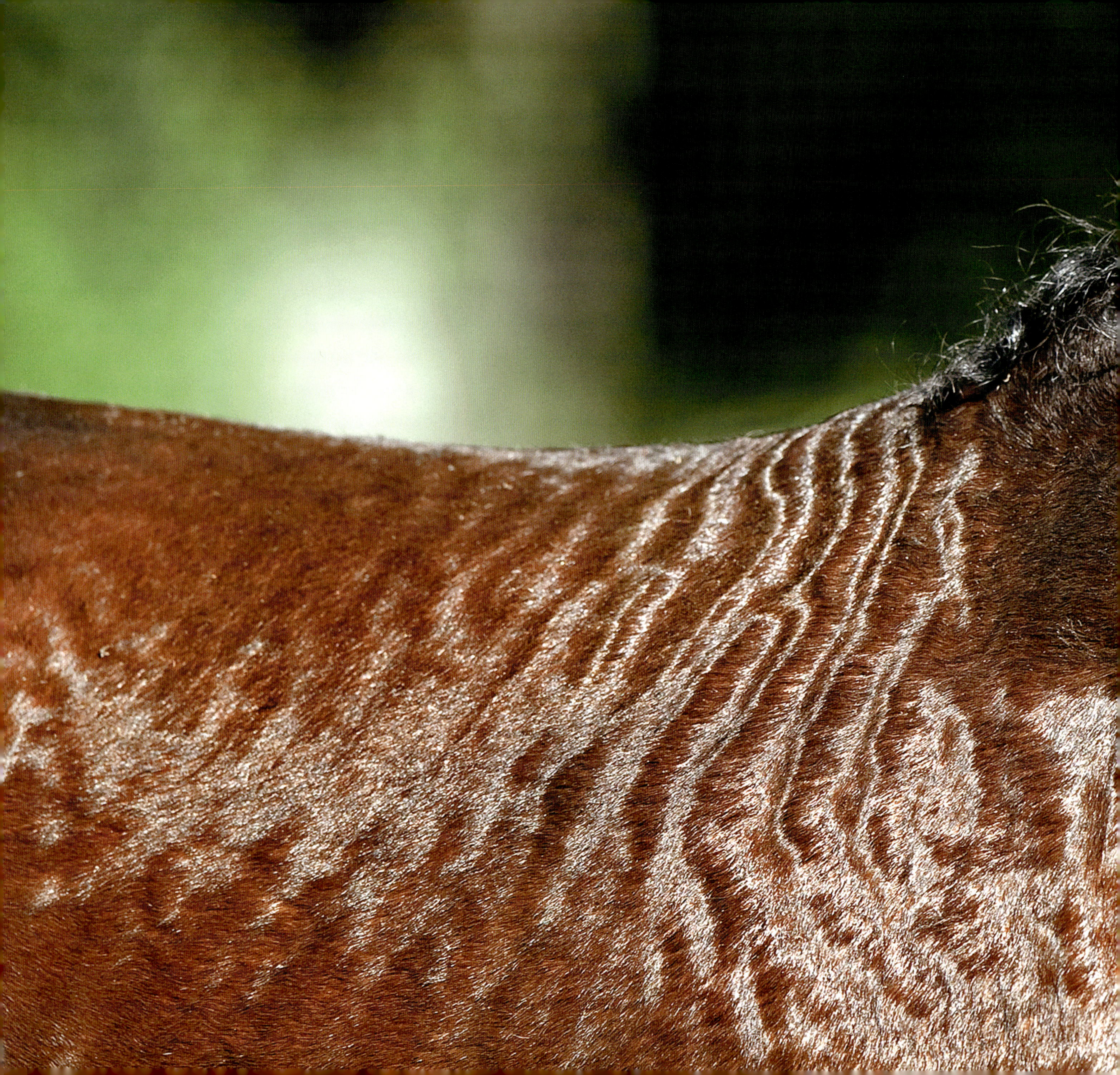

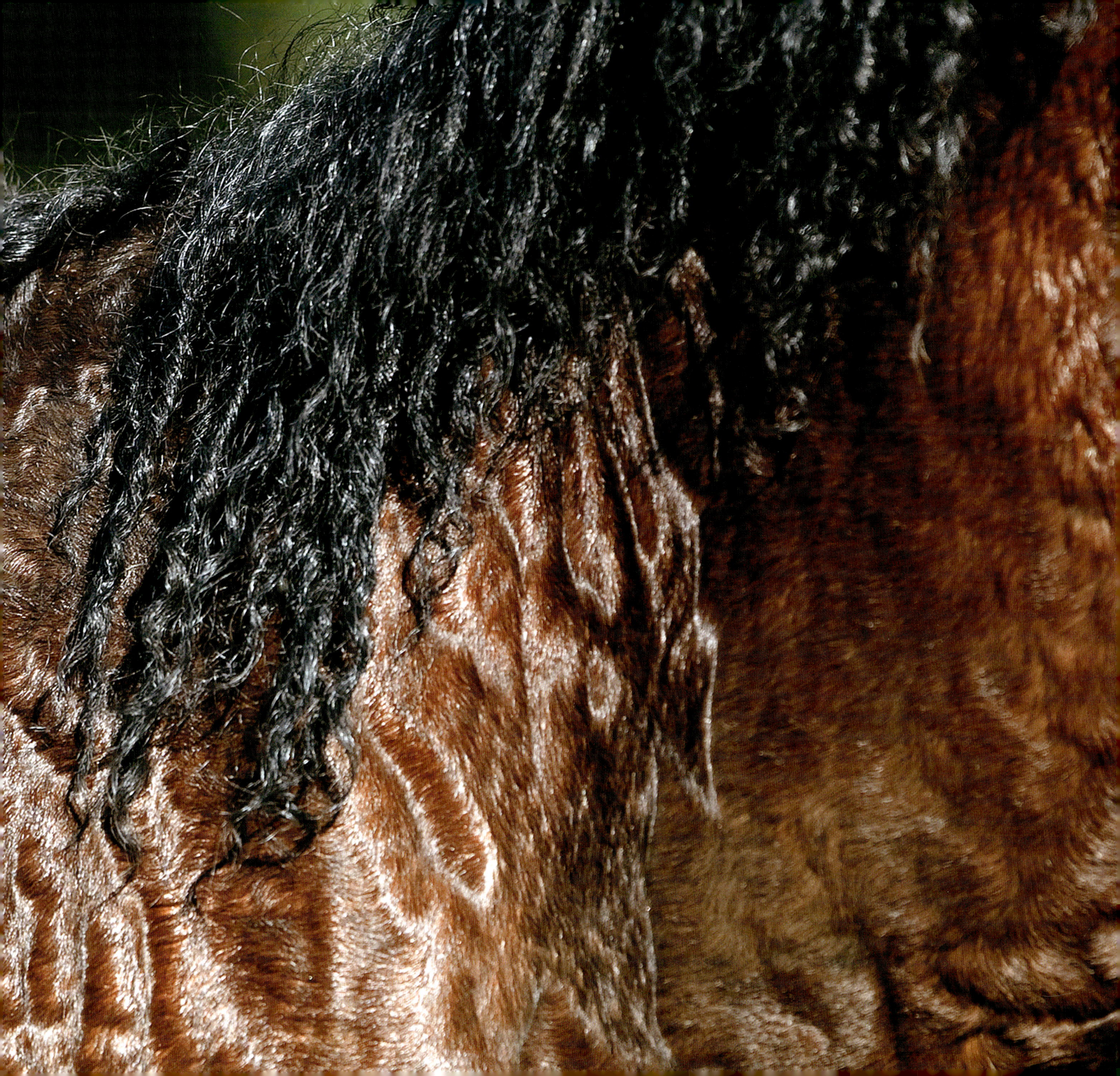

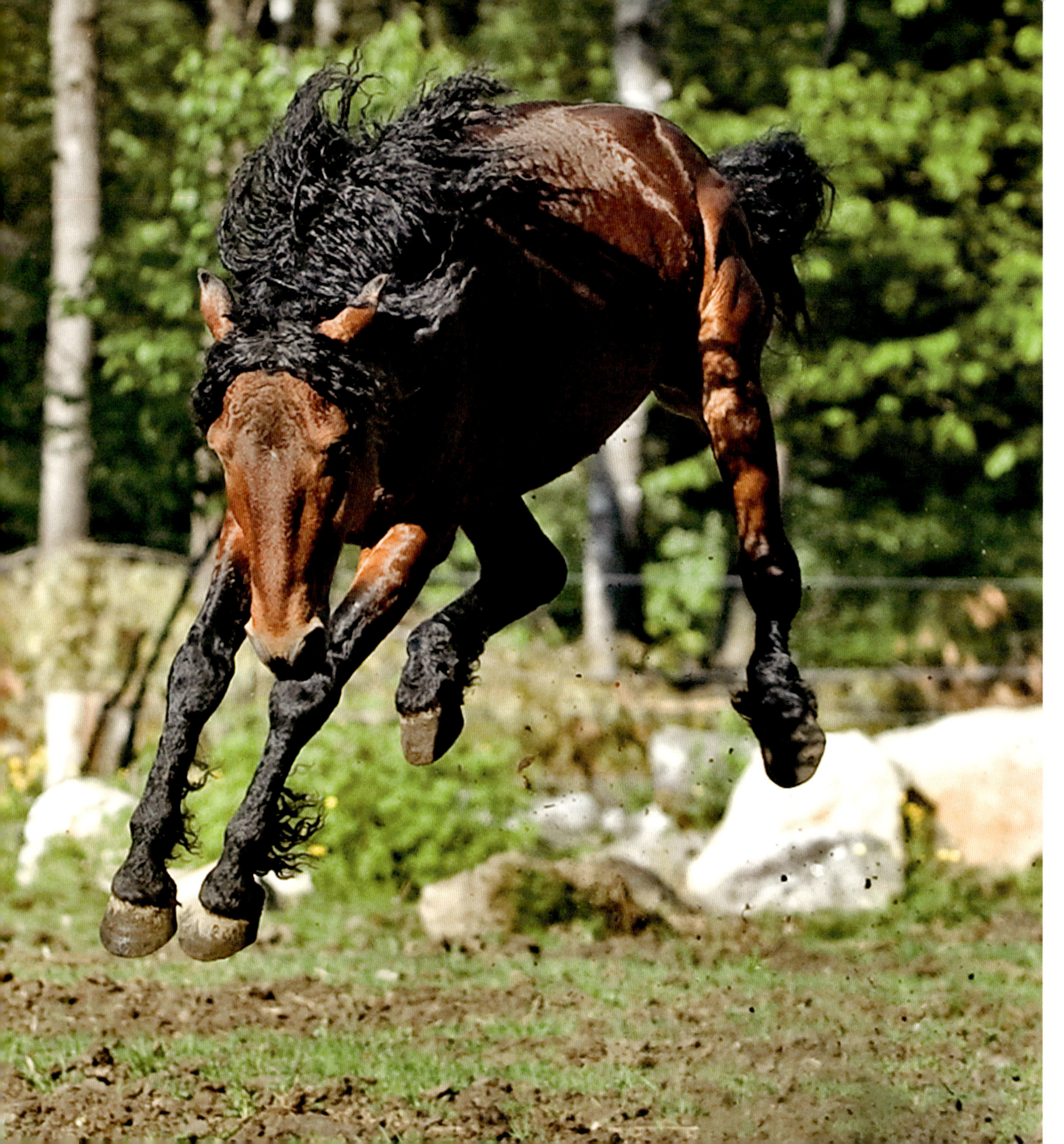

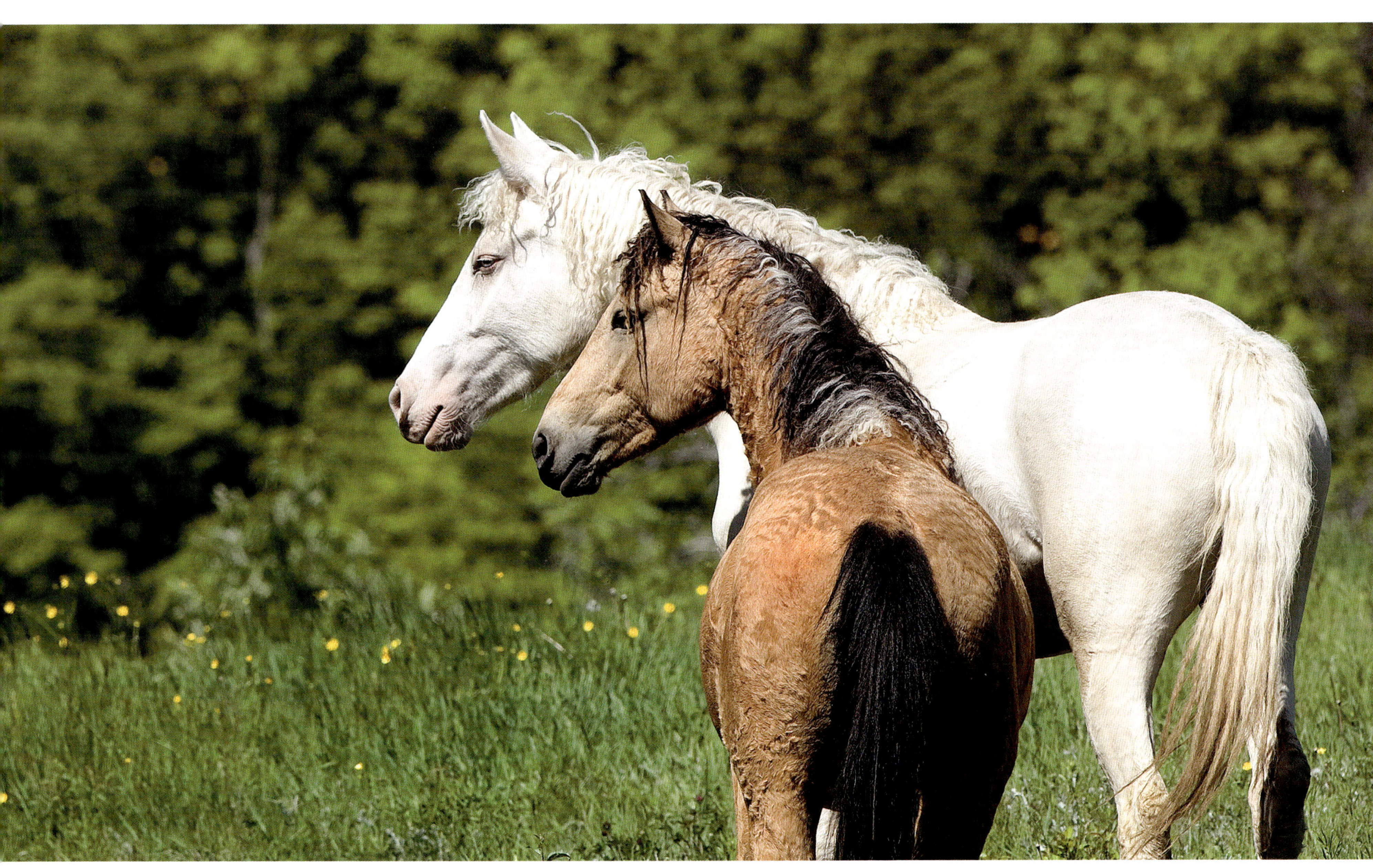

The North American Curly Horse, which comes in many colors, often features a very curly coat that makes for a most unusual sight (this and previous spread).

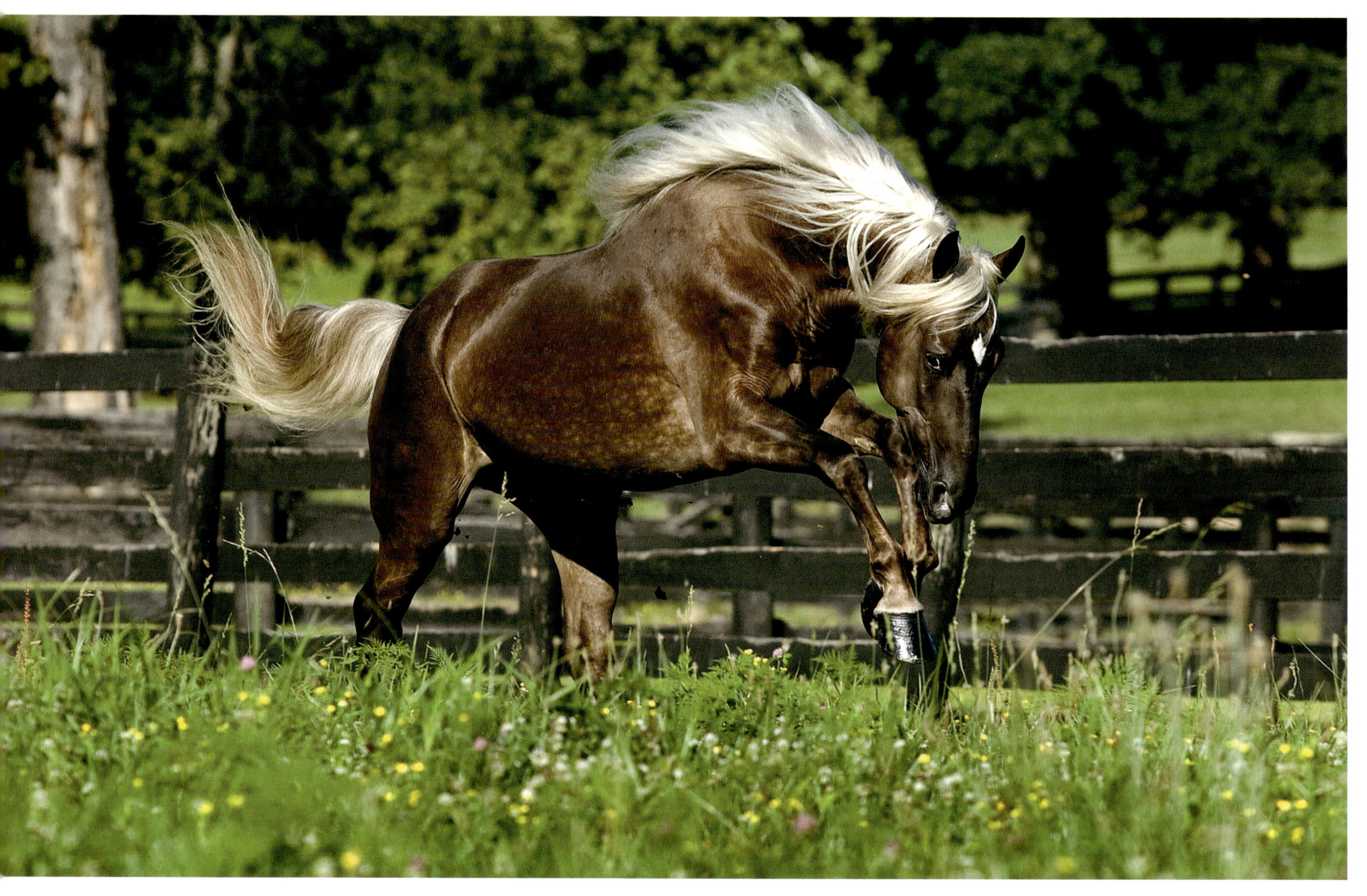

The hardy and beautiful Rocky Mountain Horse is often chocolate in color.

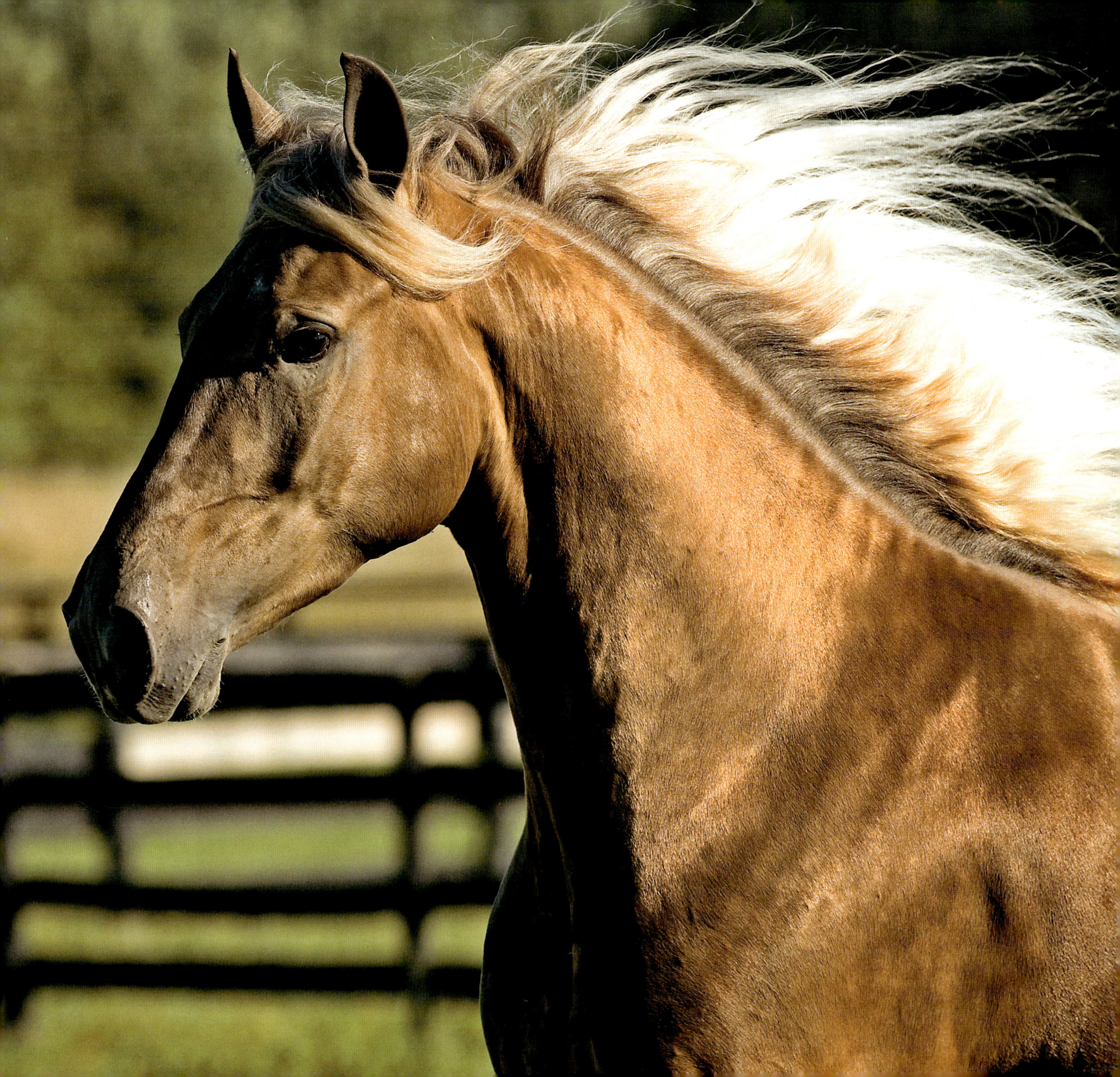

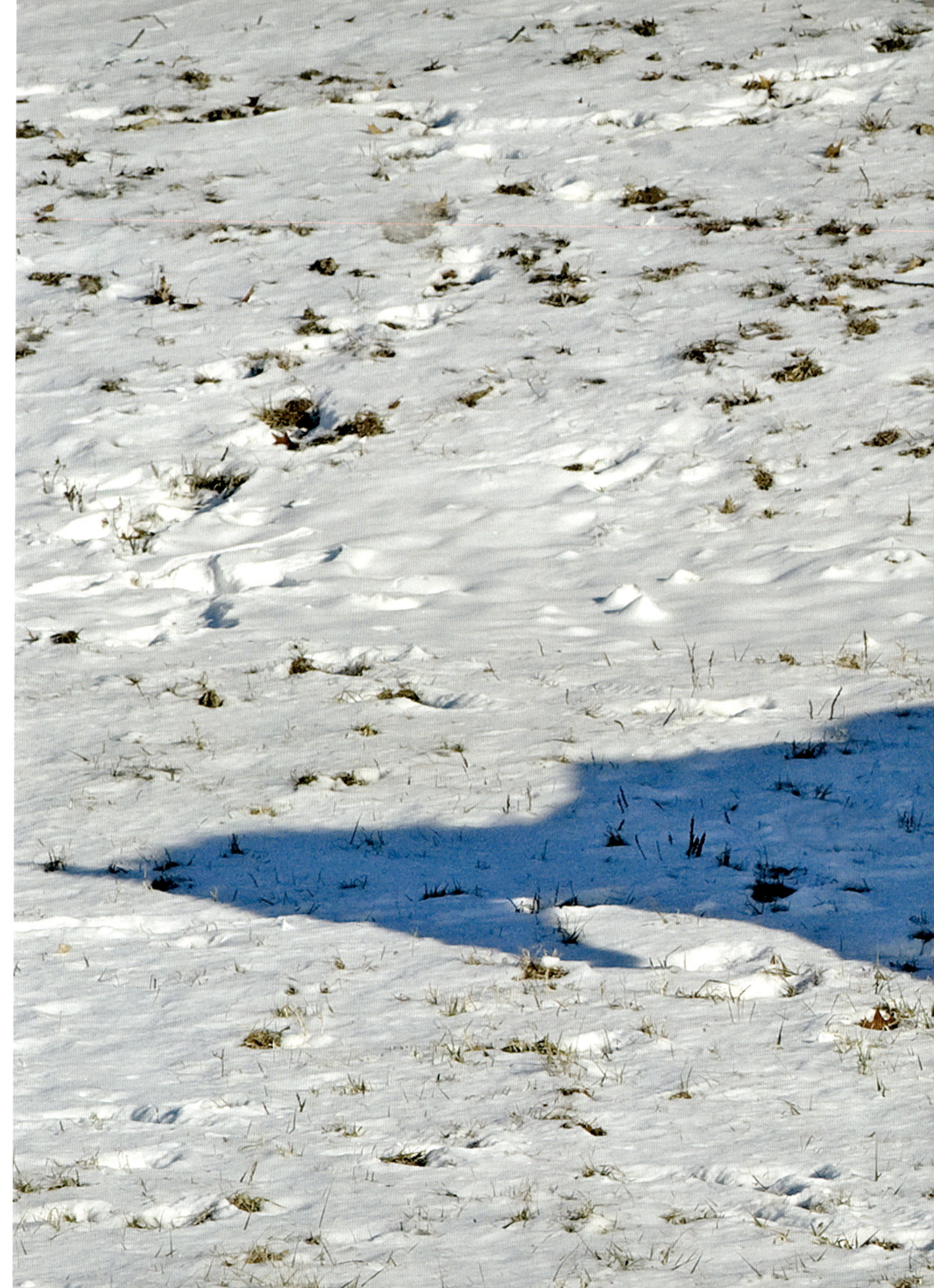

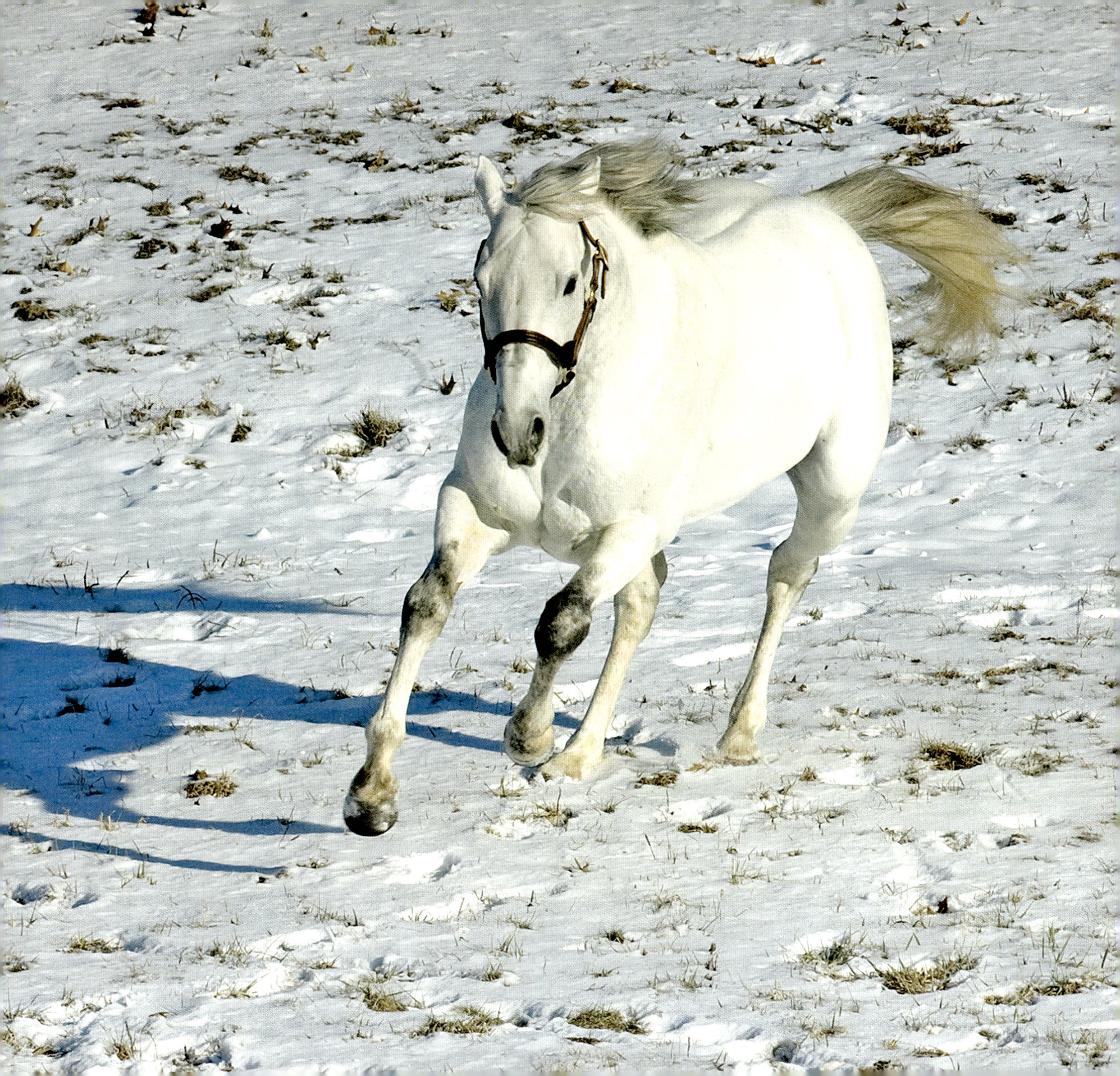

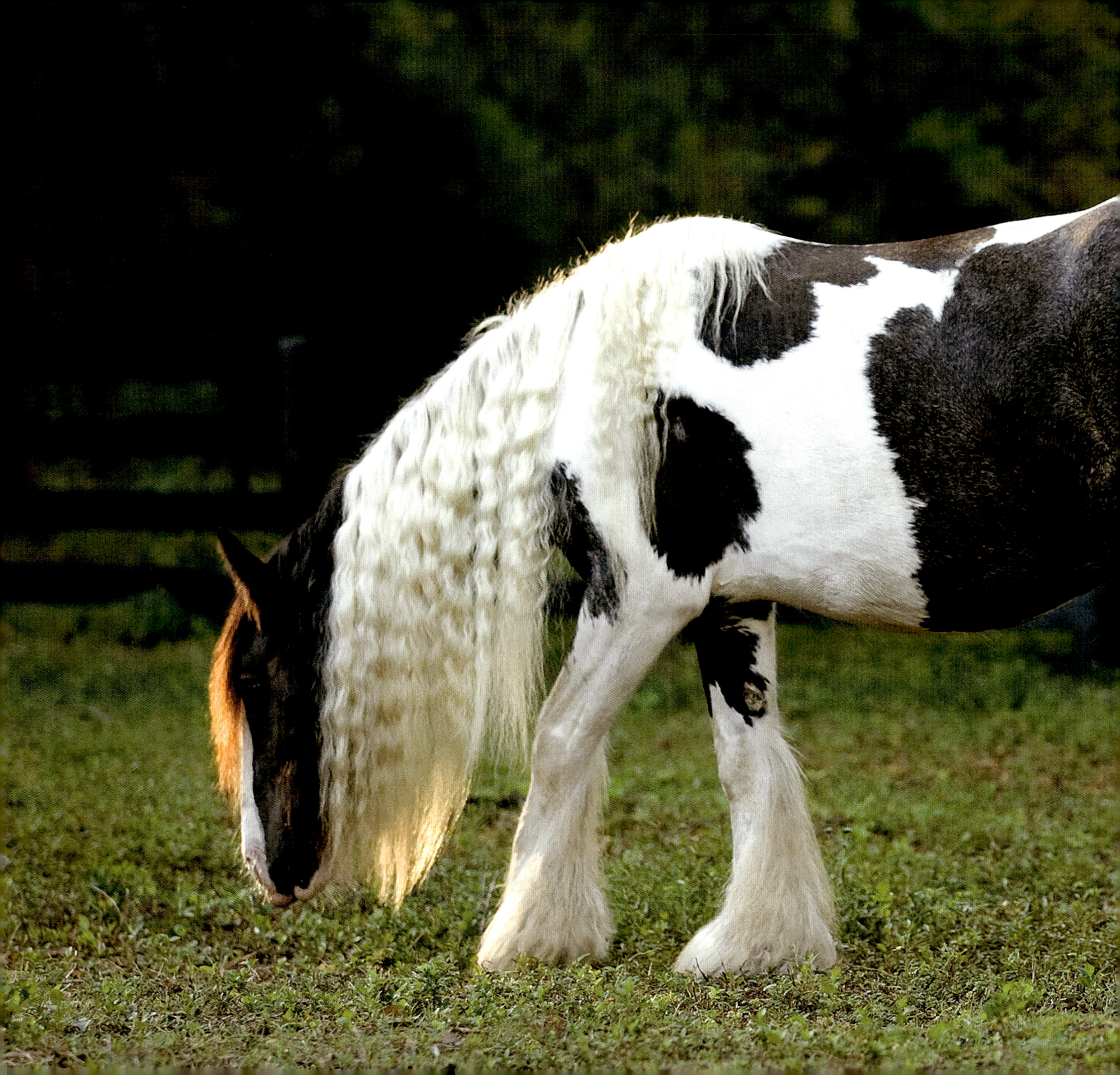

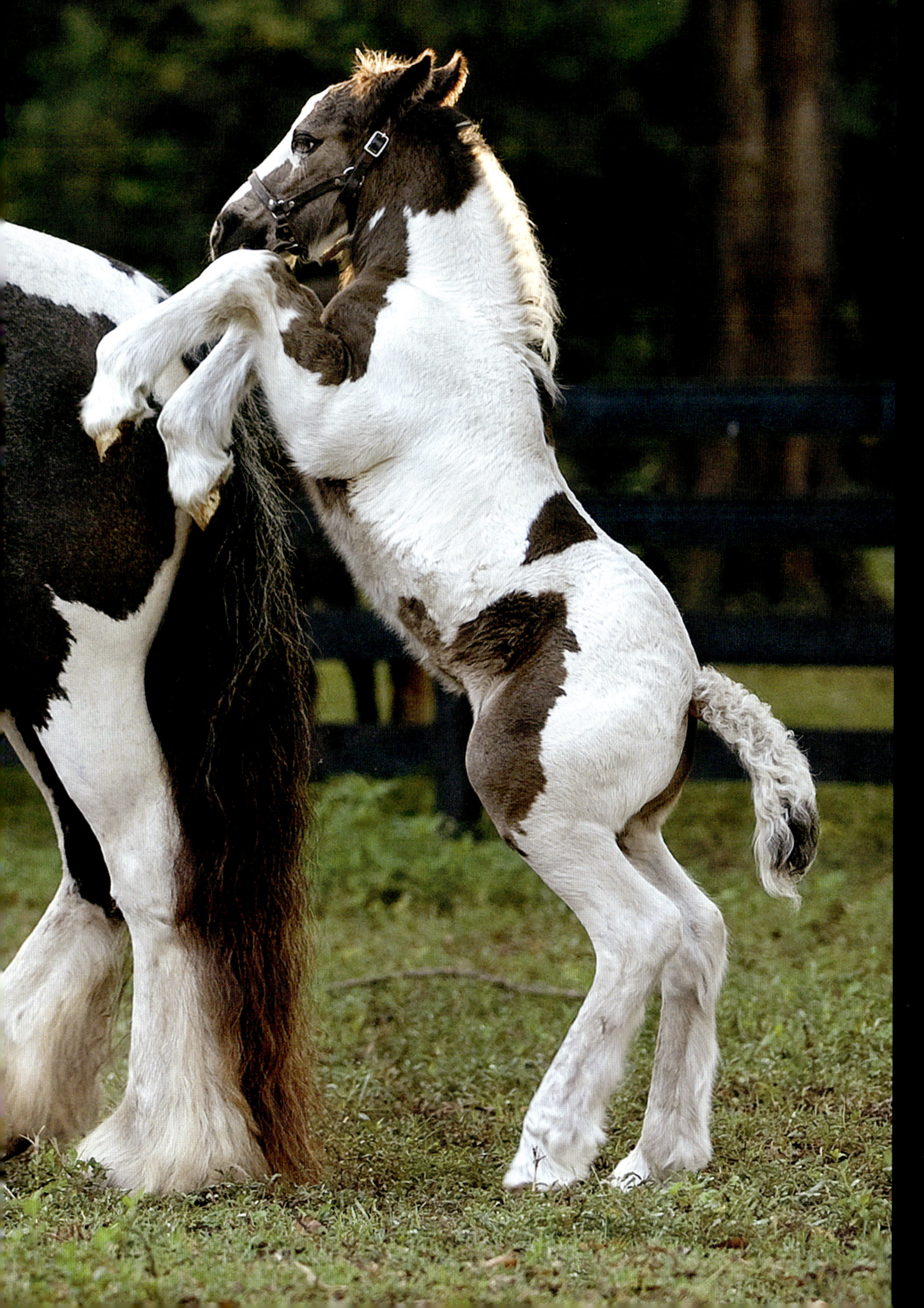

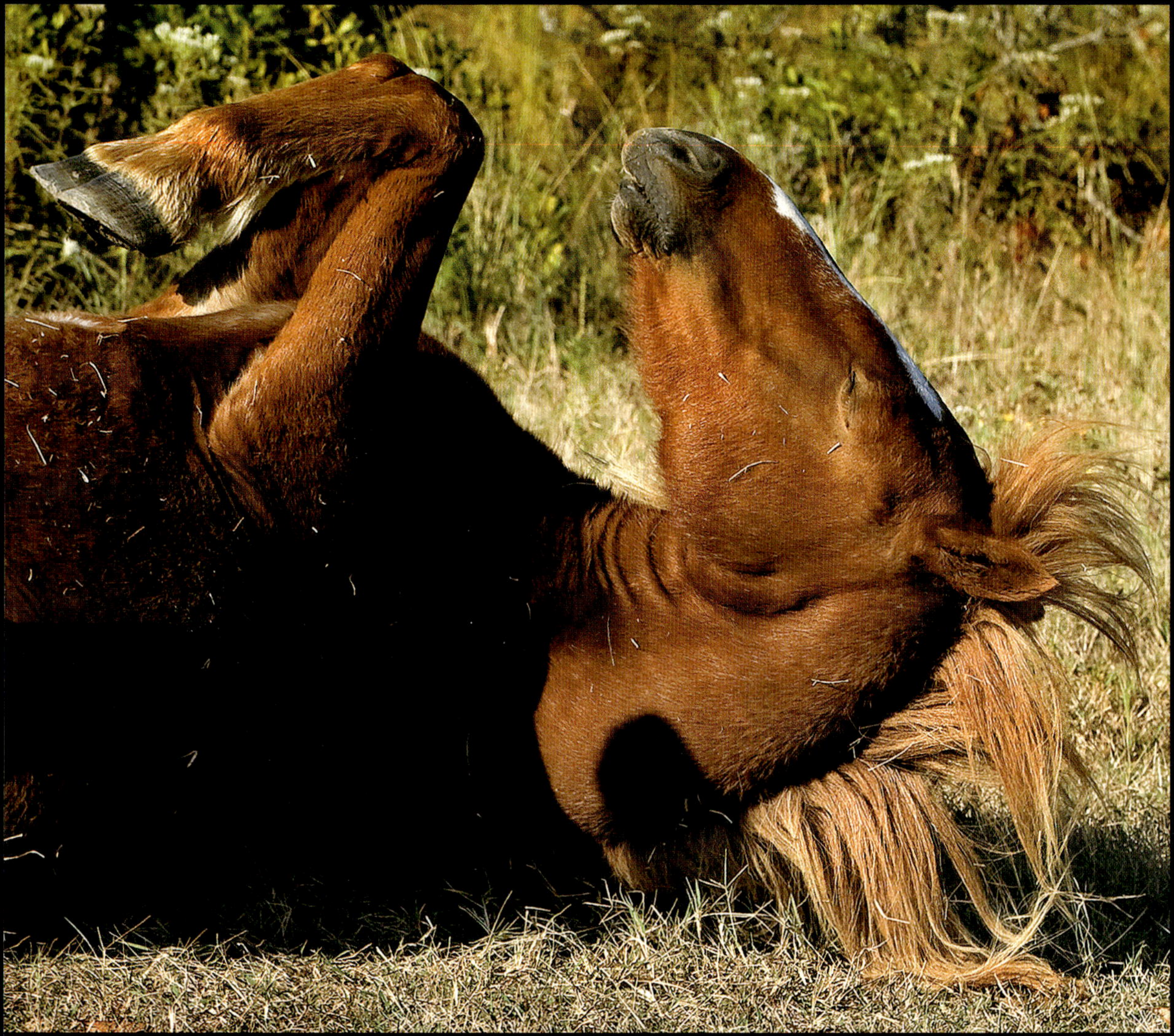

Assateague Island, in Maryland and Virginia, is home to a variety of colorful feral ponies. Many are used to tourists, and some will even poke their head into car windows looking for treats.

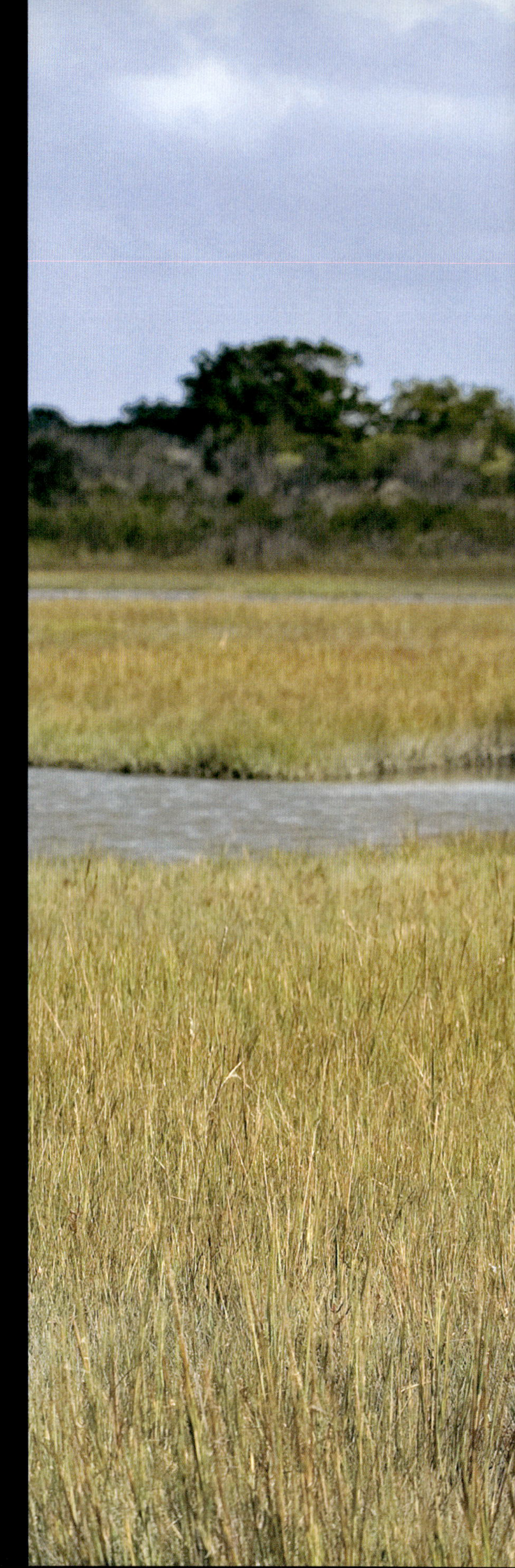

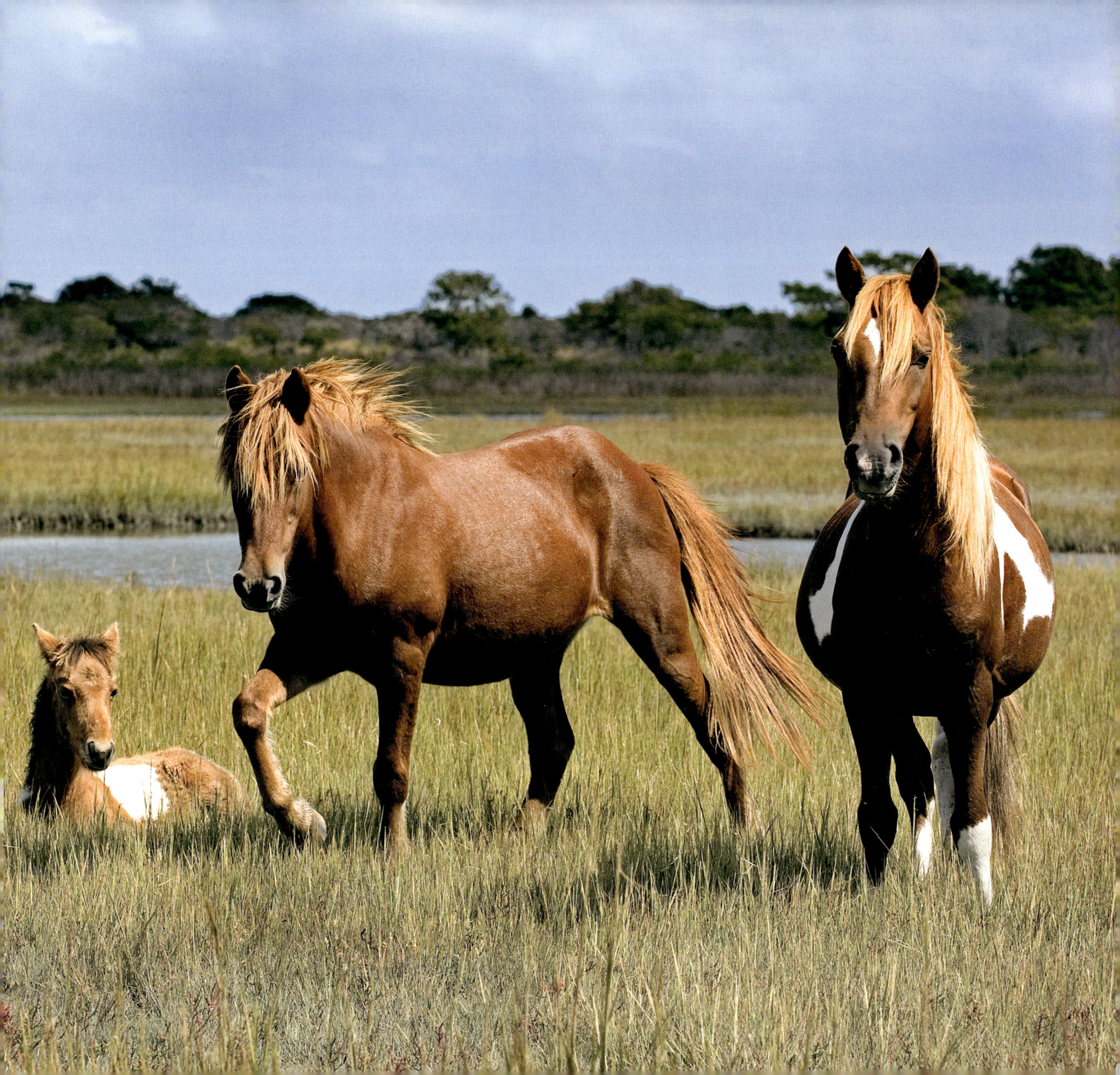

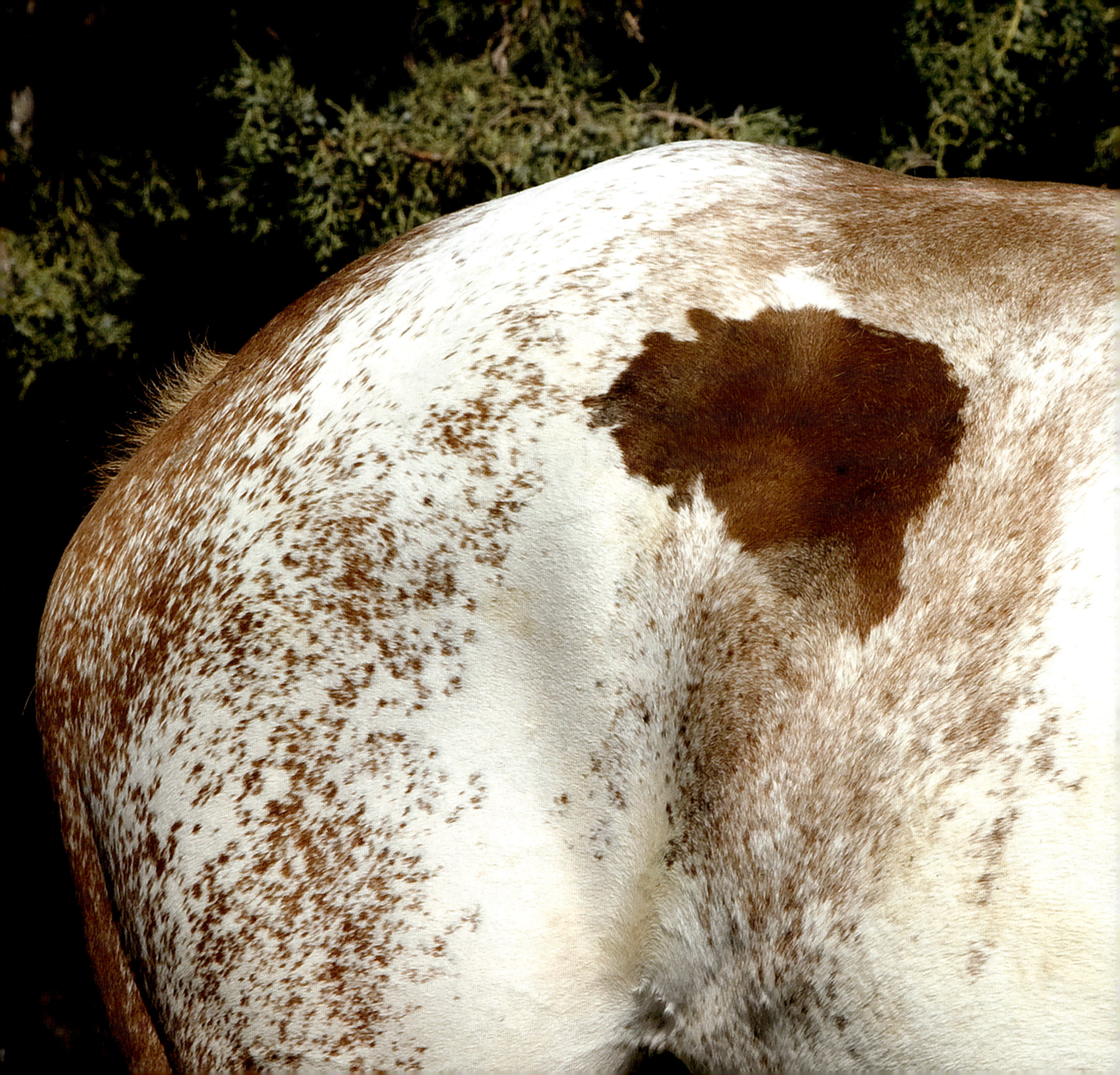

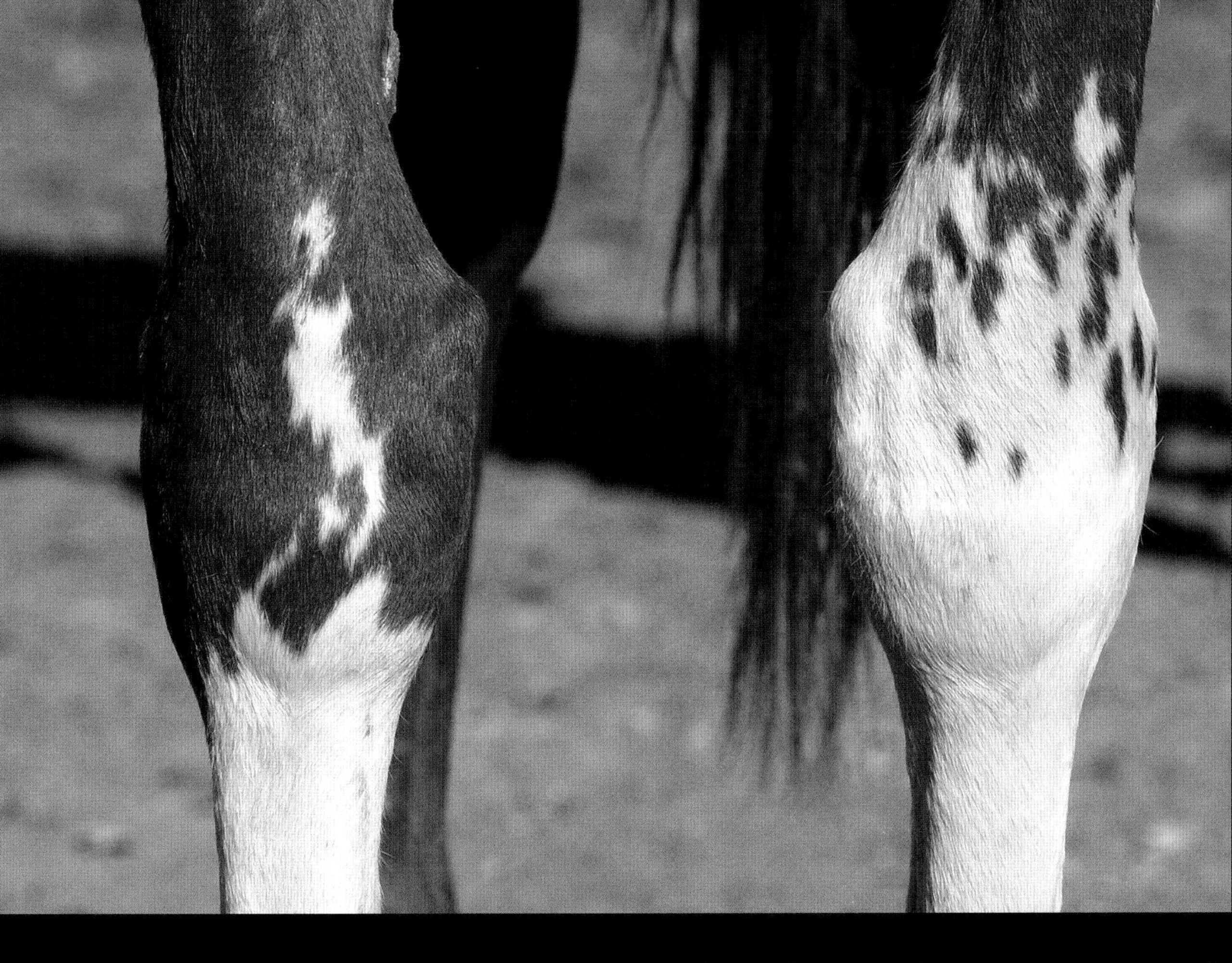

The Thoroughbreds of Painted Desert Farm, in Redmond, Oregon, are some of the most colorful and unique in the country.

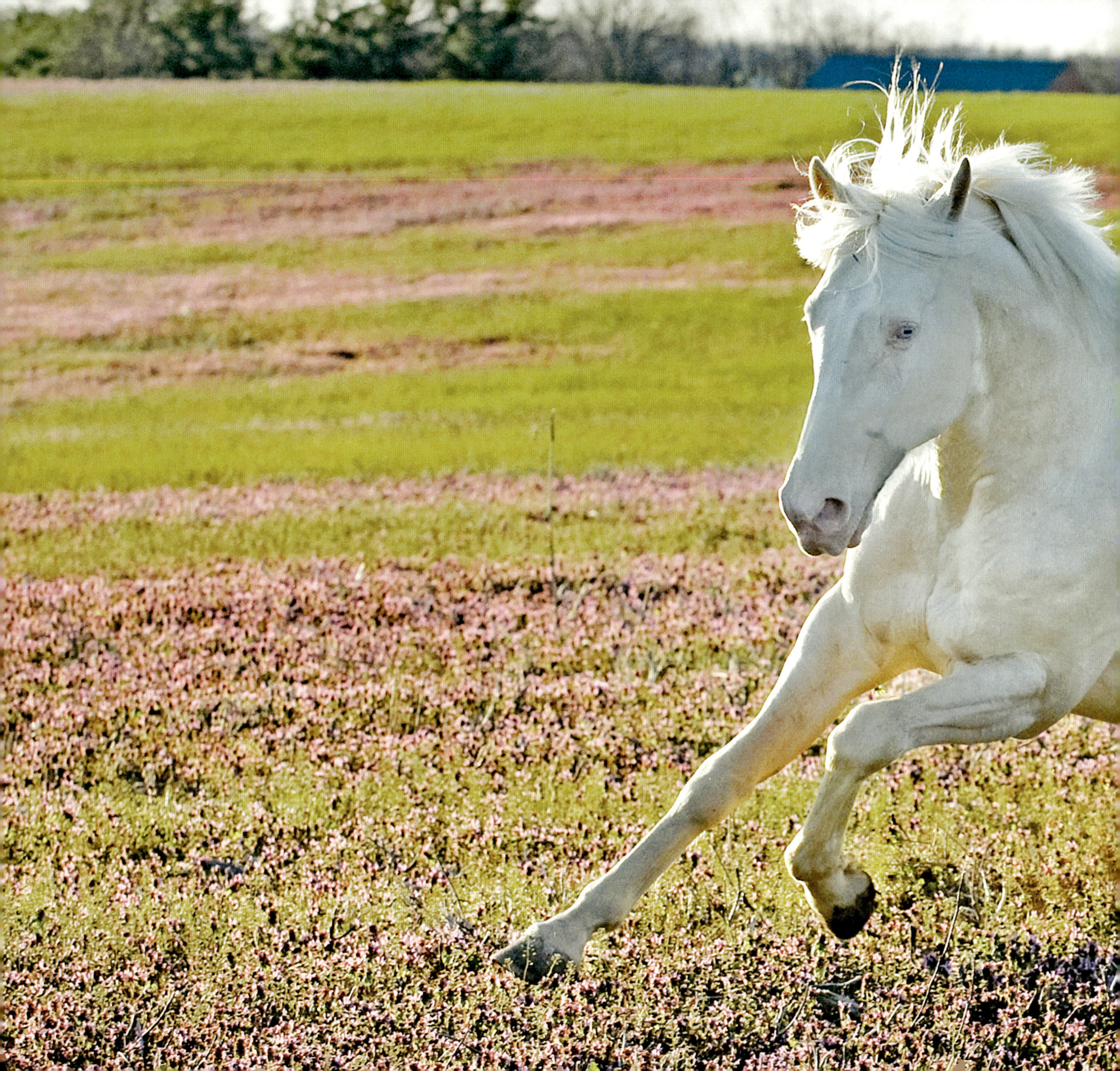

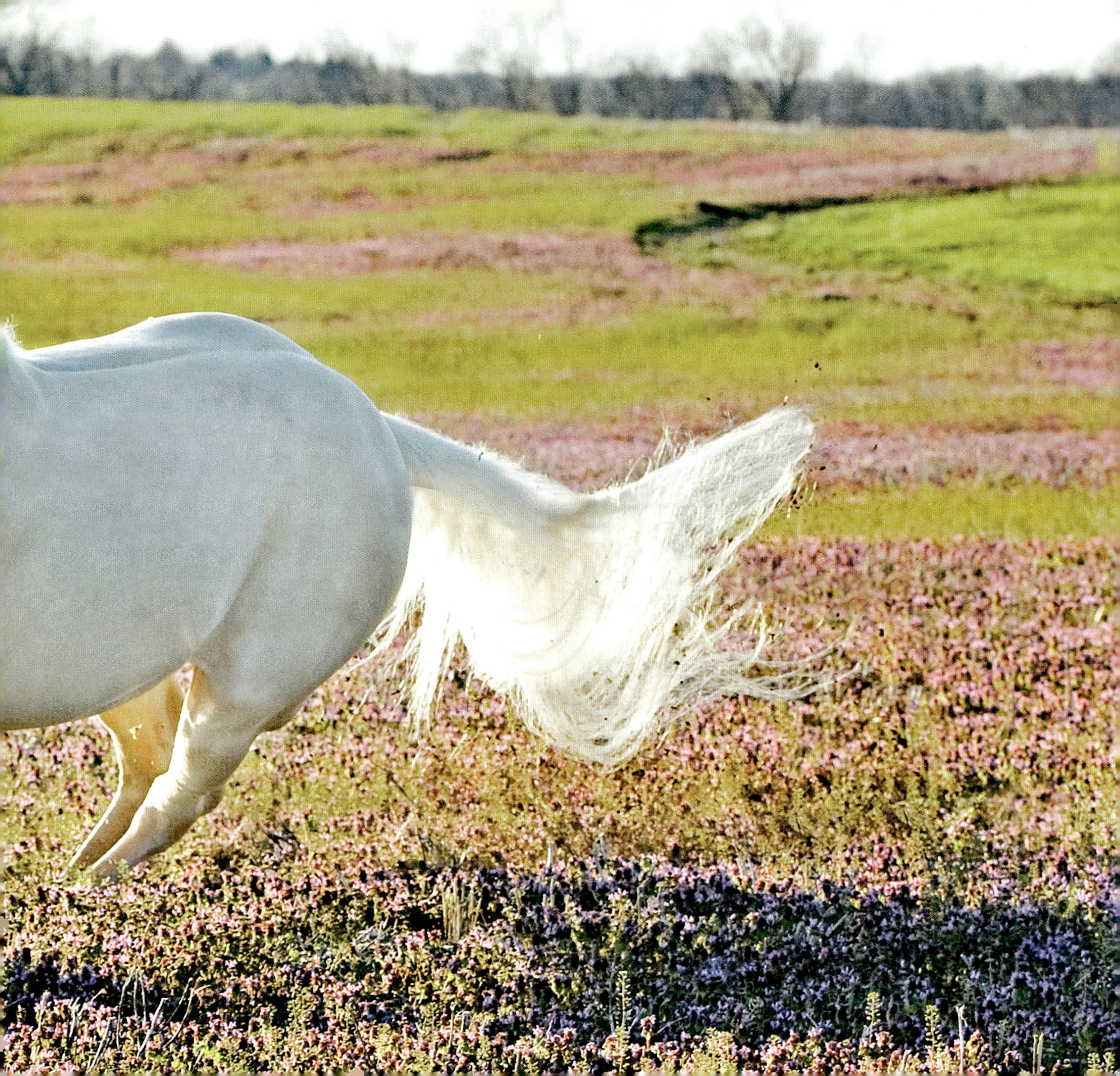

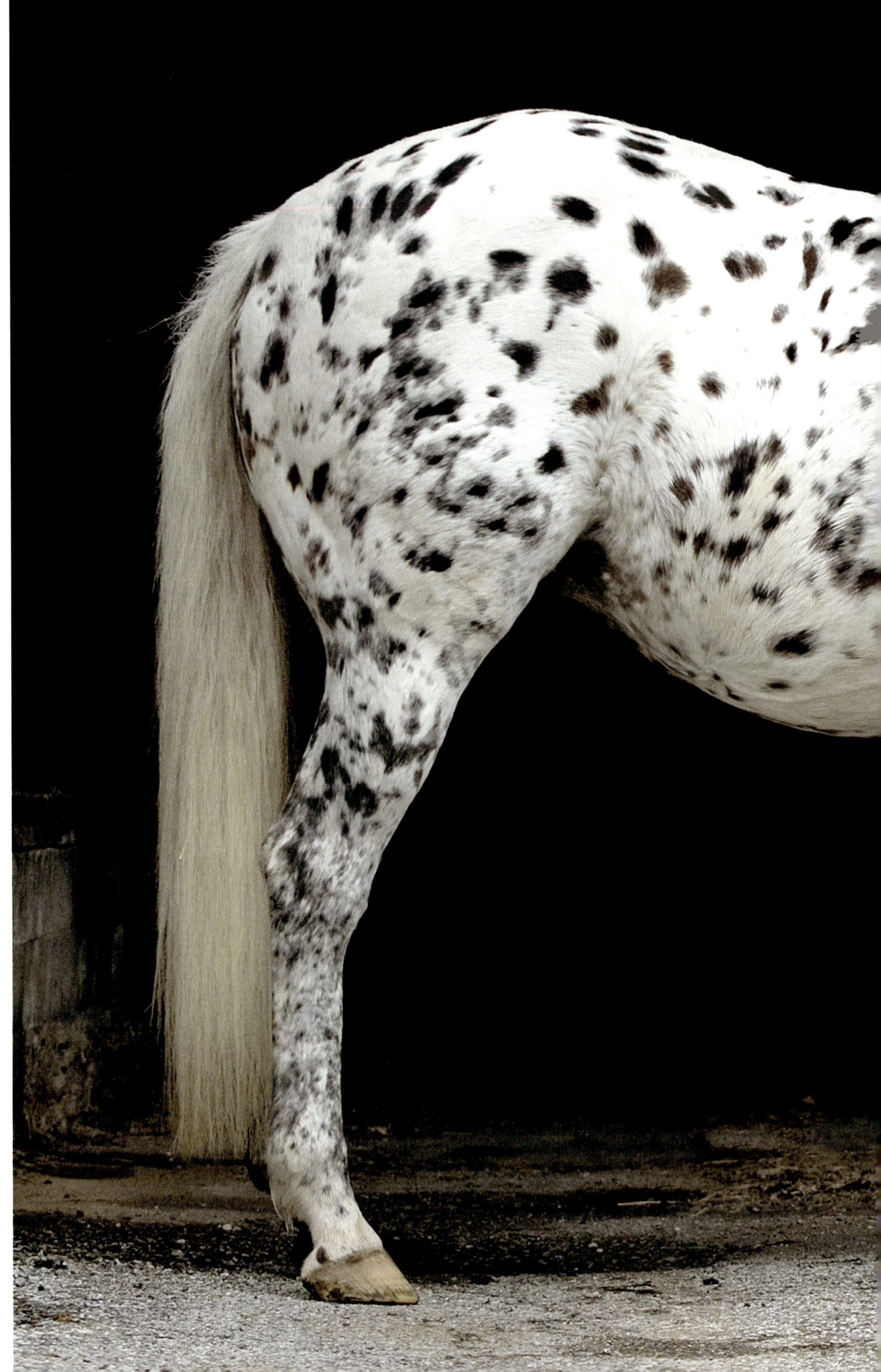

A top-notch polo pony in her day, this spotted mare is a Kentucky retiree now.

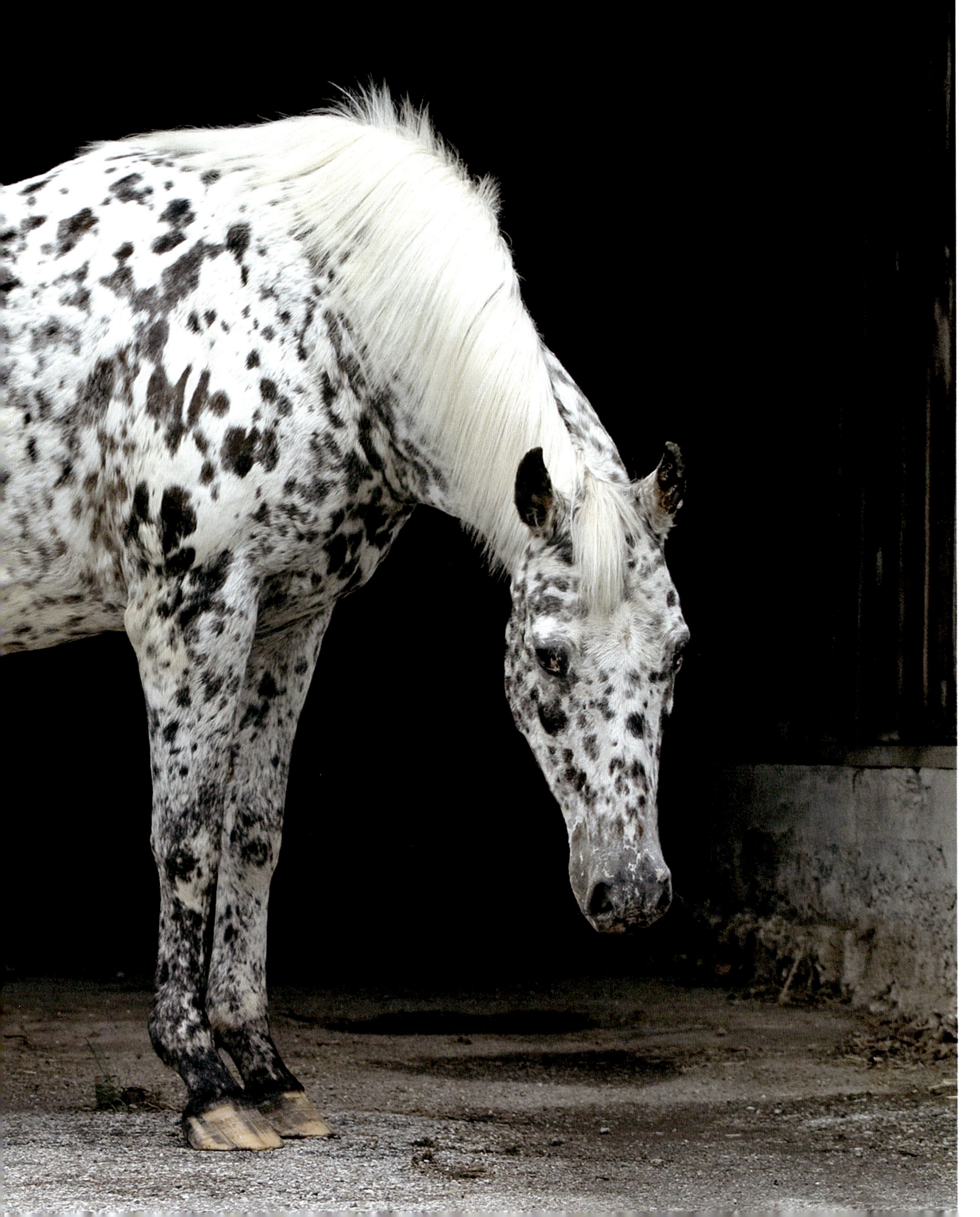

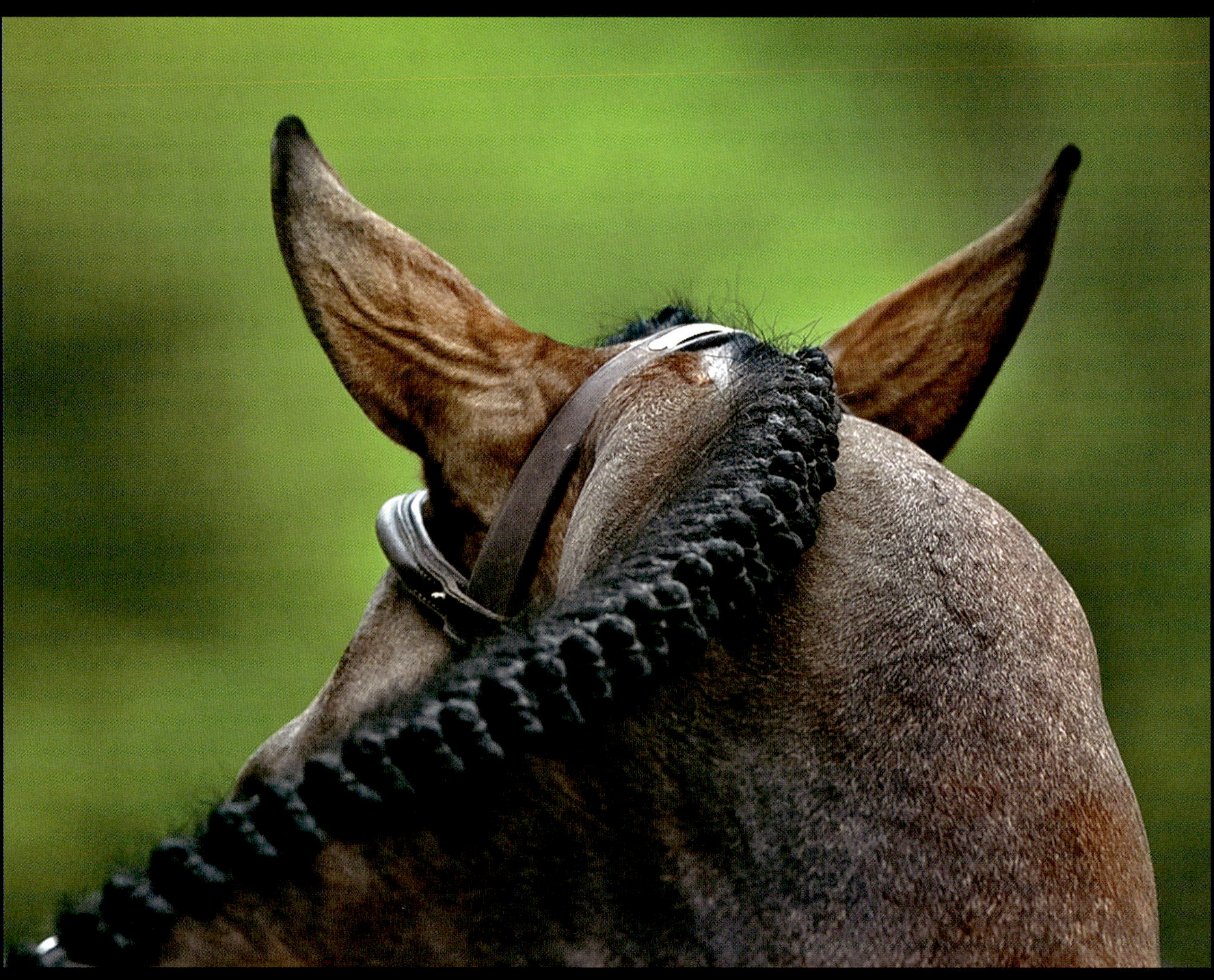

Right, Norwegian Fjords, such as this horse cleverly called Harrison Fjord, have unusual manes. Their dorsal stripe runs through the mane, and the sides consist of lighter hairs called guard hairs. Fjords' manes are cut to accentuate the look.

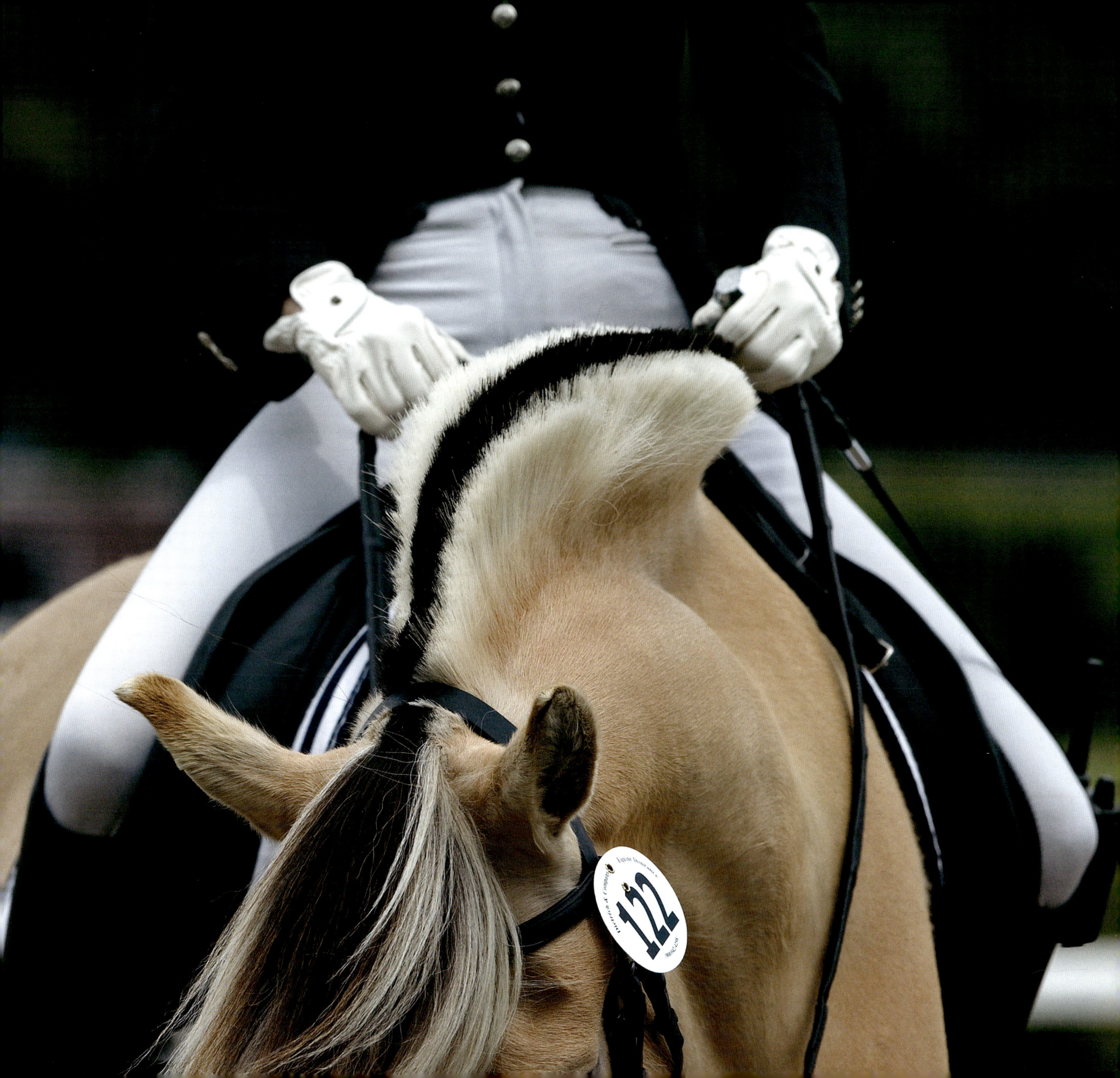
122

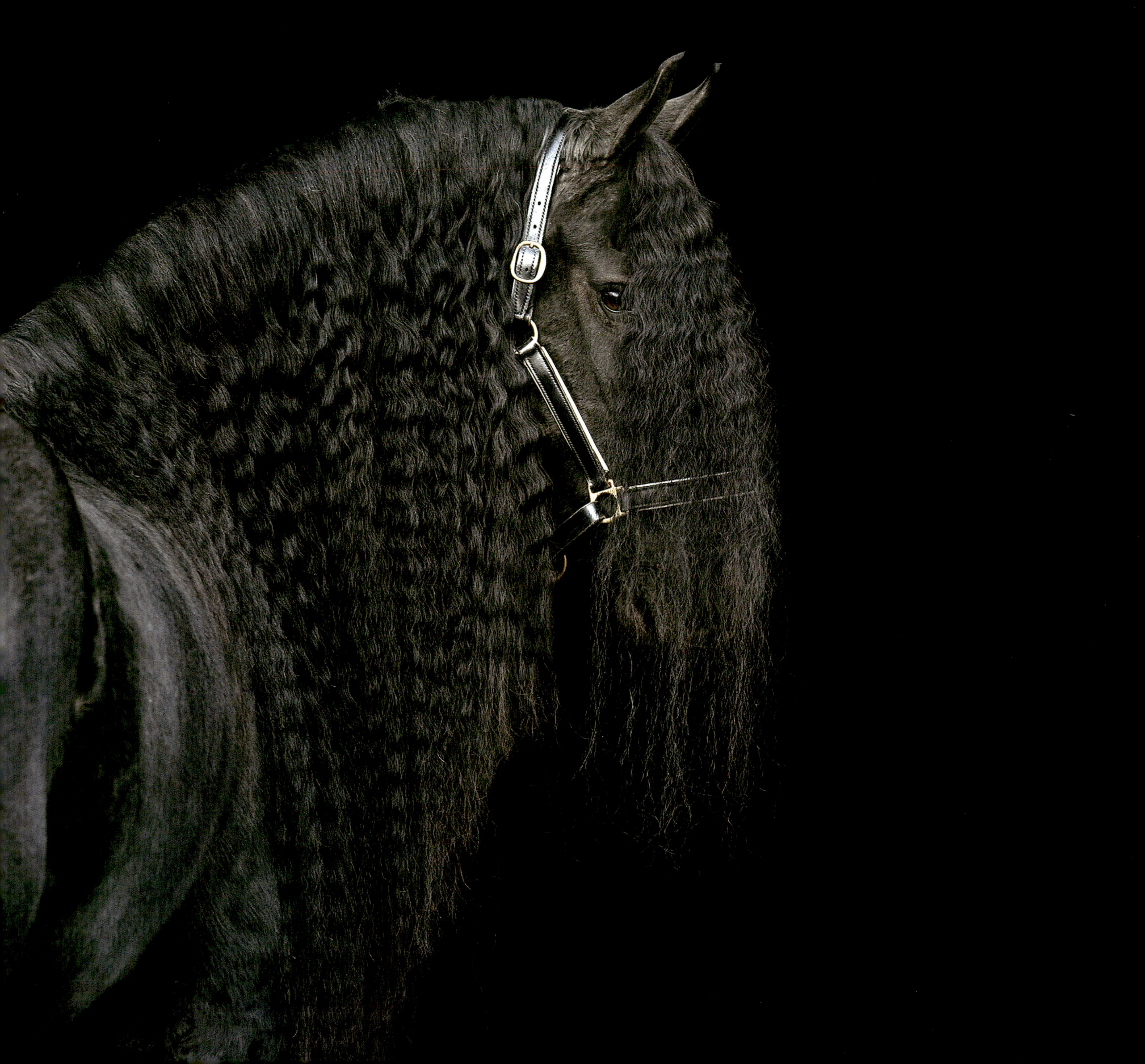

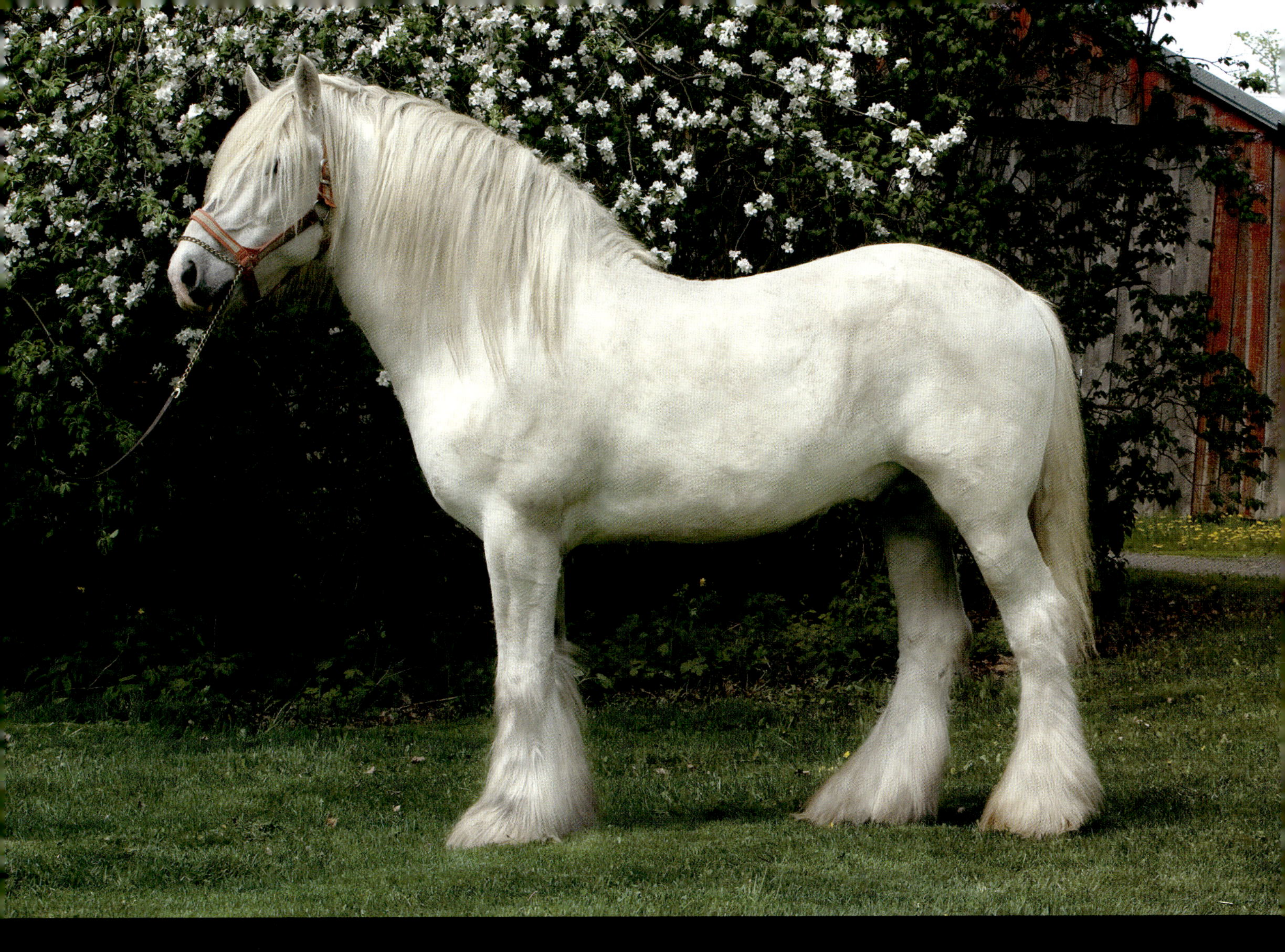

Left, the waves in this black Friesian mare's mane are due to braiding. Above, the 19-hand stallion is a Shire, the tallest modern breed of horse.

When it comes to color, it doesn't get much more interesting than the Knabstrupper, a breed still extremely rare in the United States.

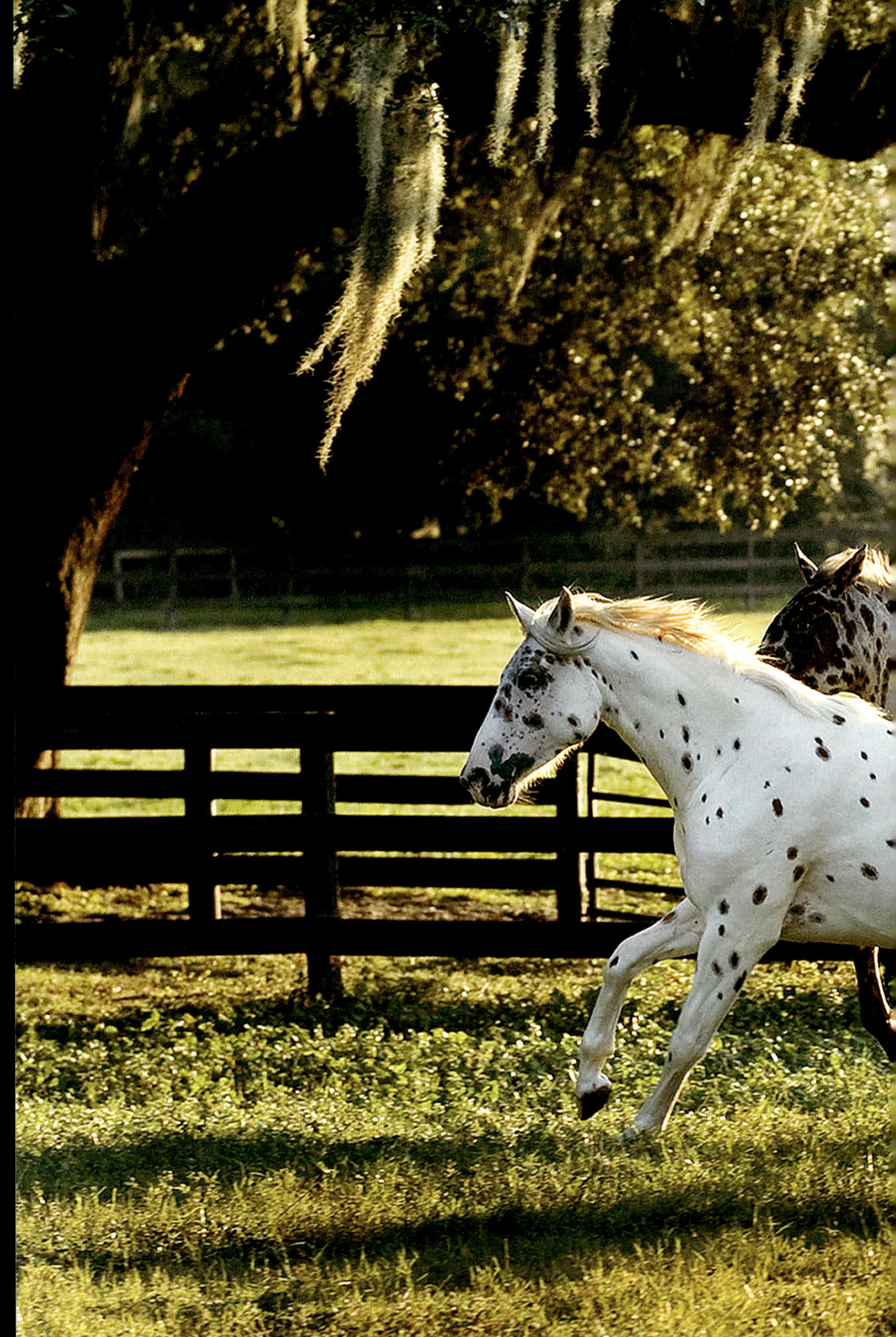

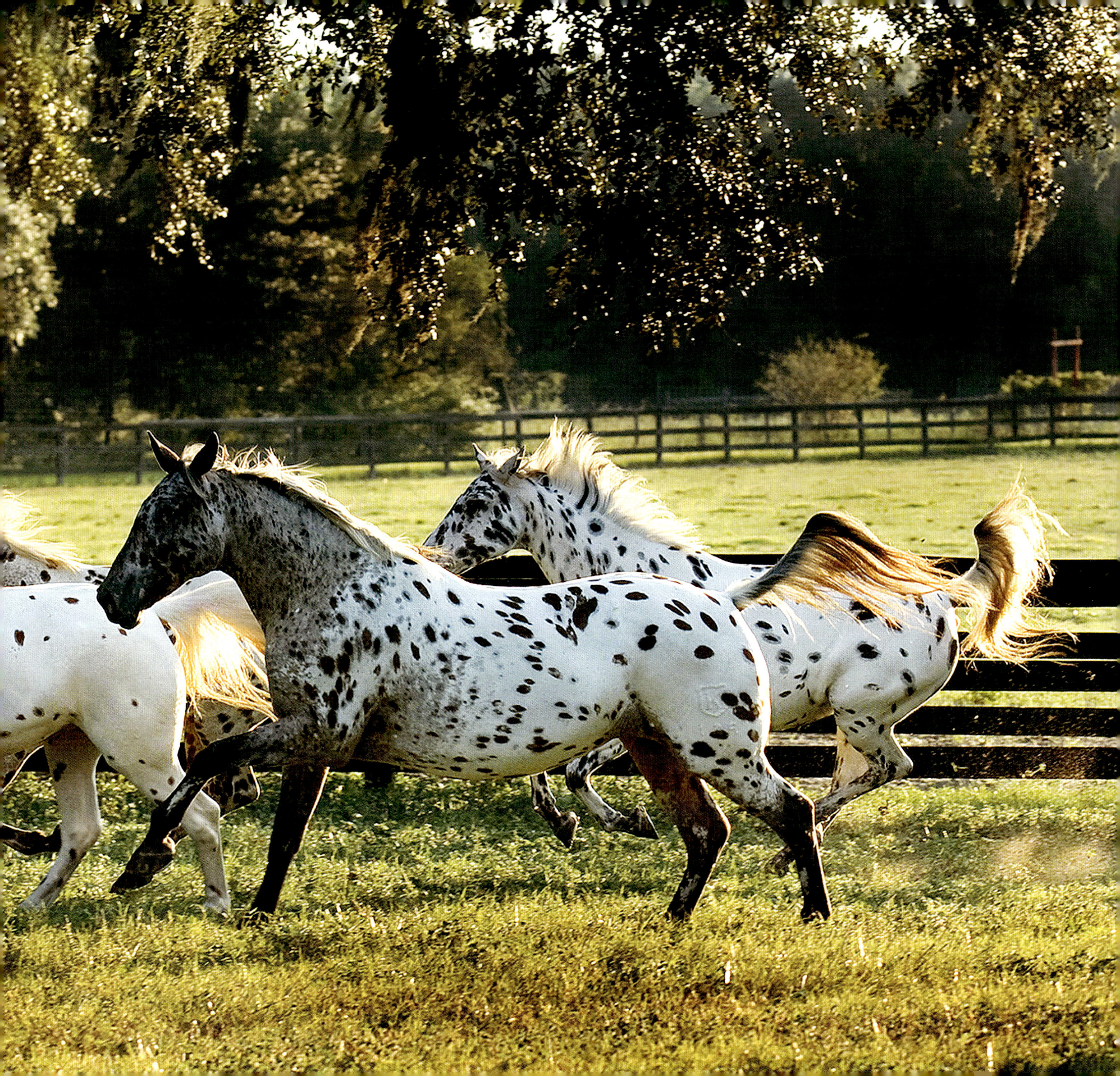

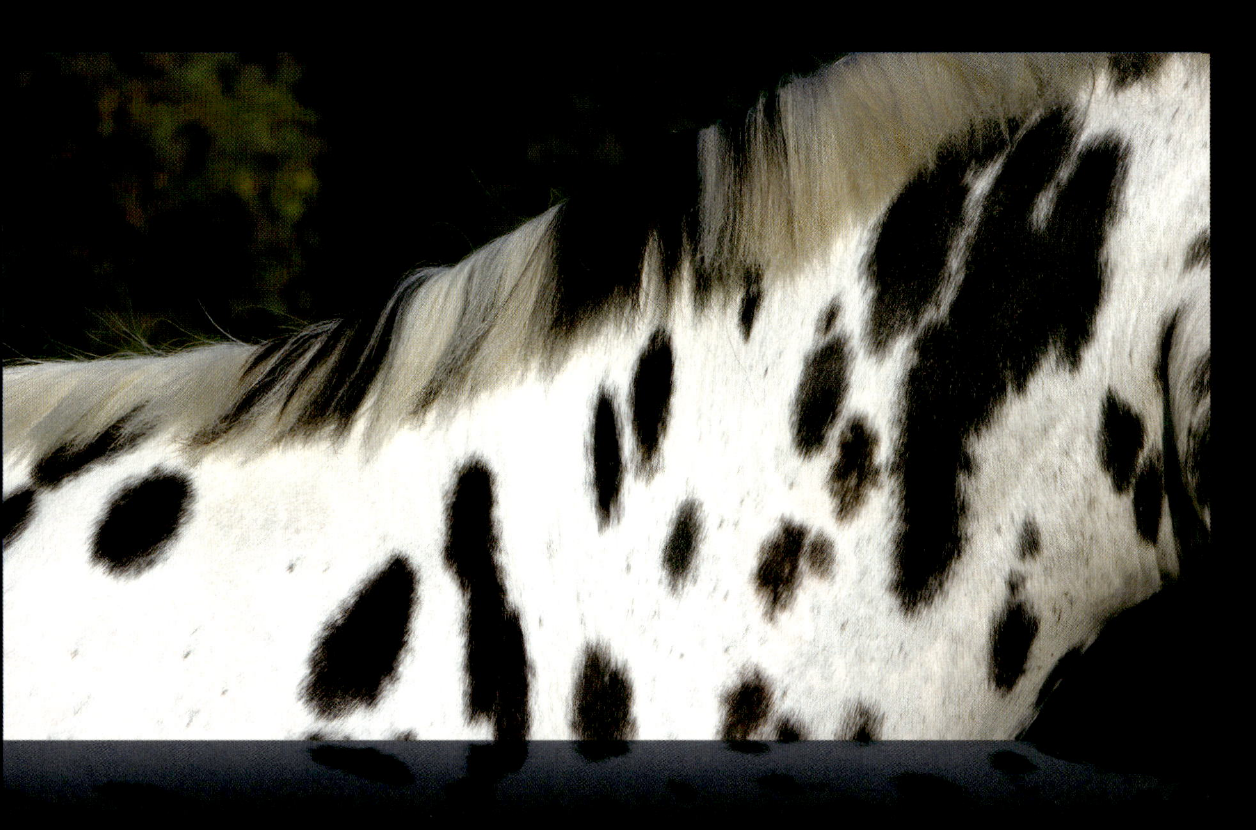

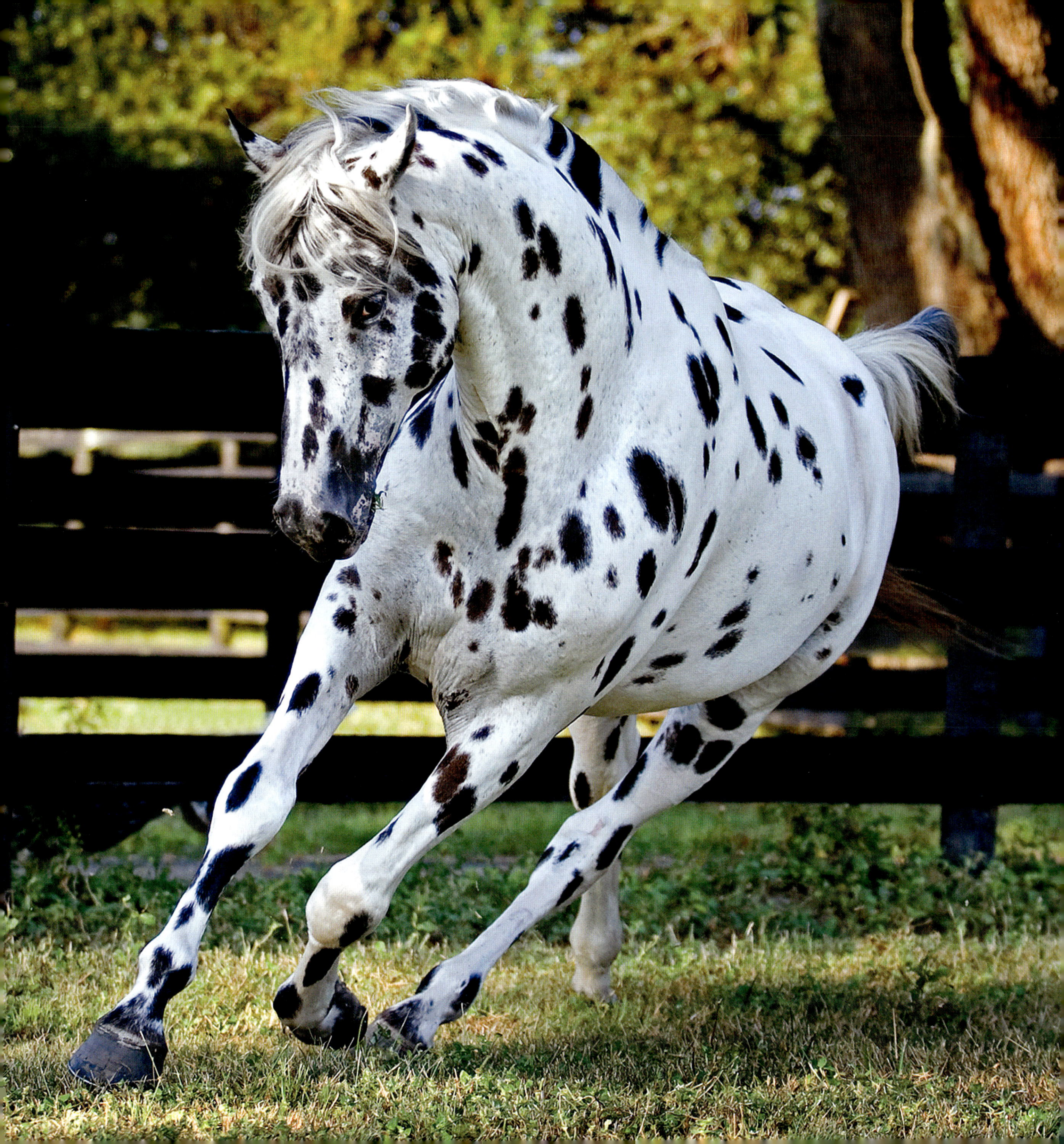

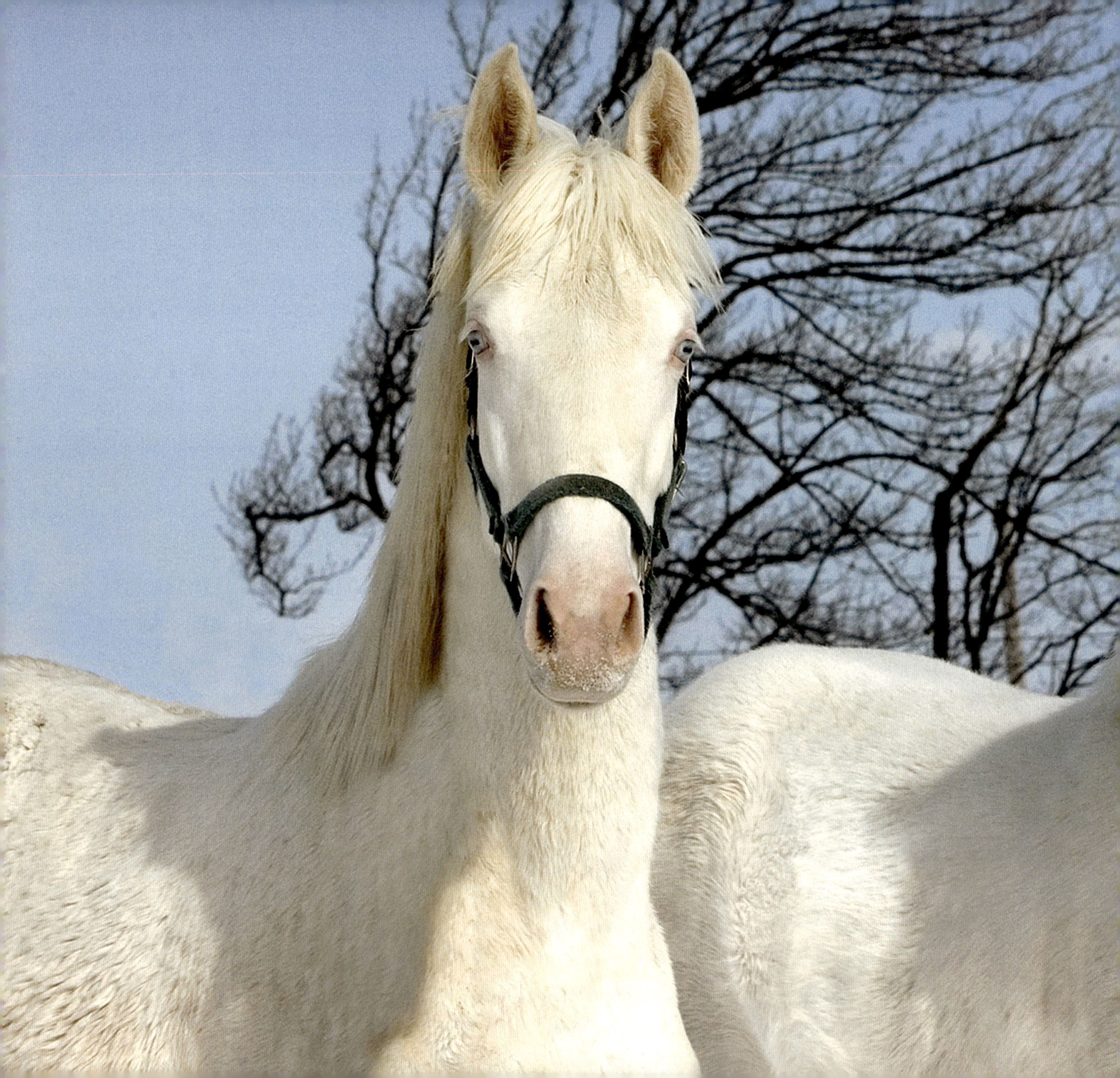

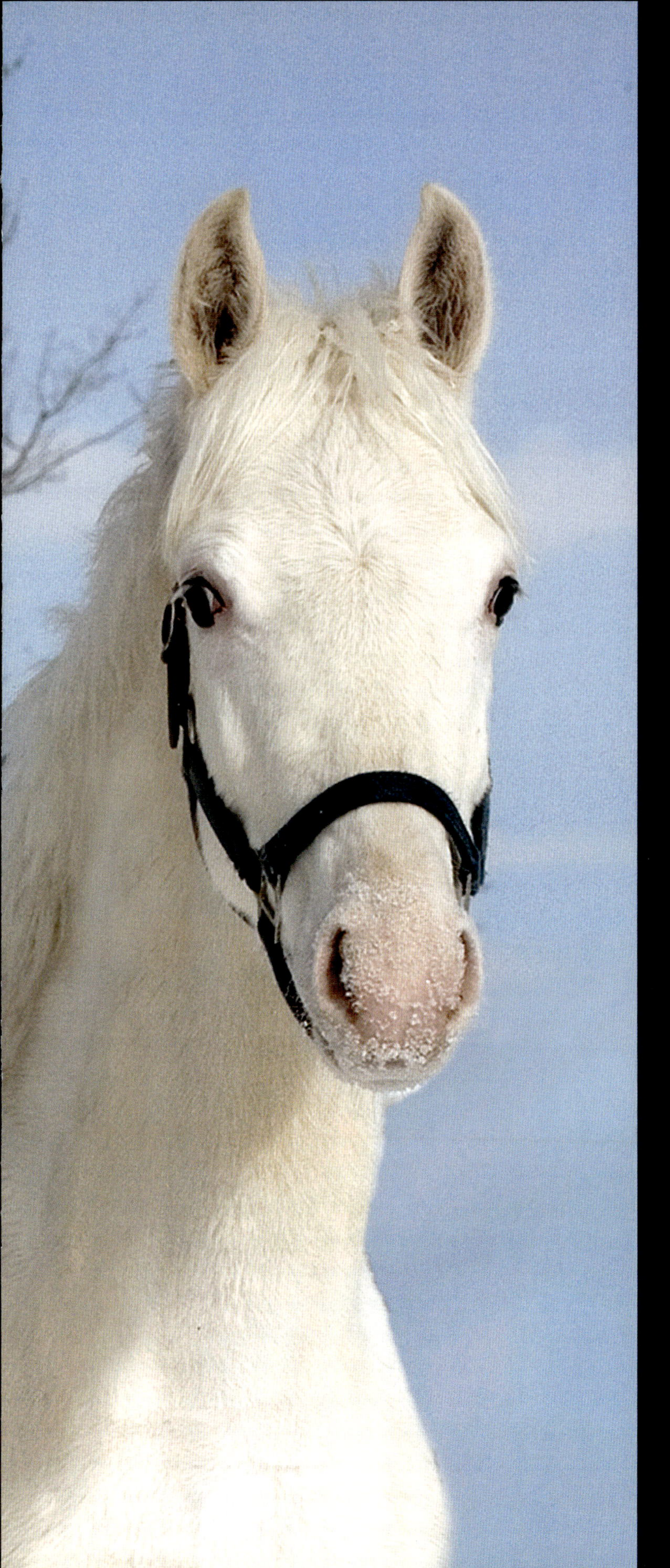

This seemingly matching set of yearlings is anything but. The filly on the left is a cremello with blue eyes, while the colt on the right is a palomino with dark eyes.

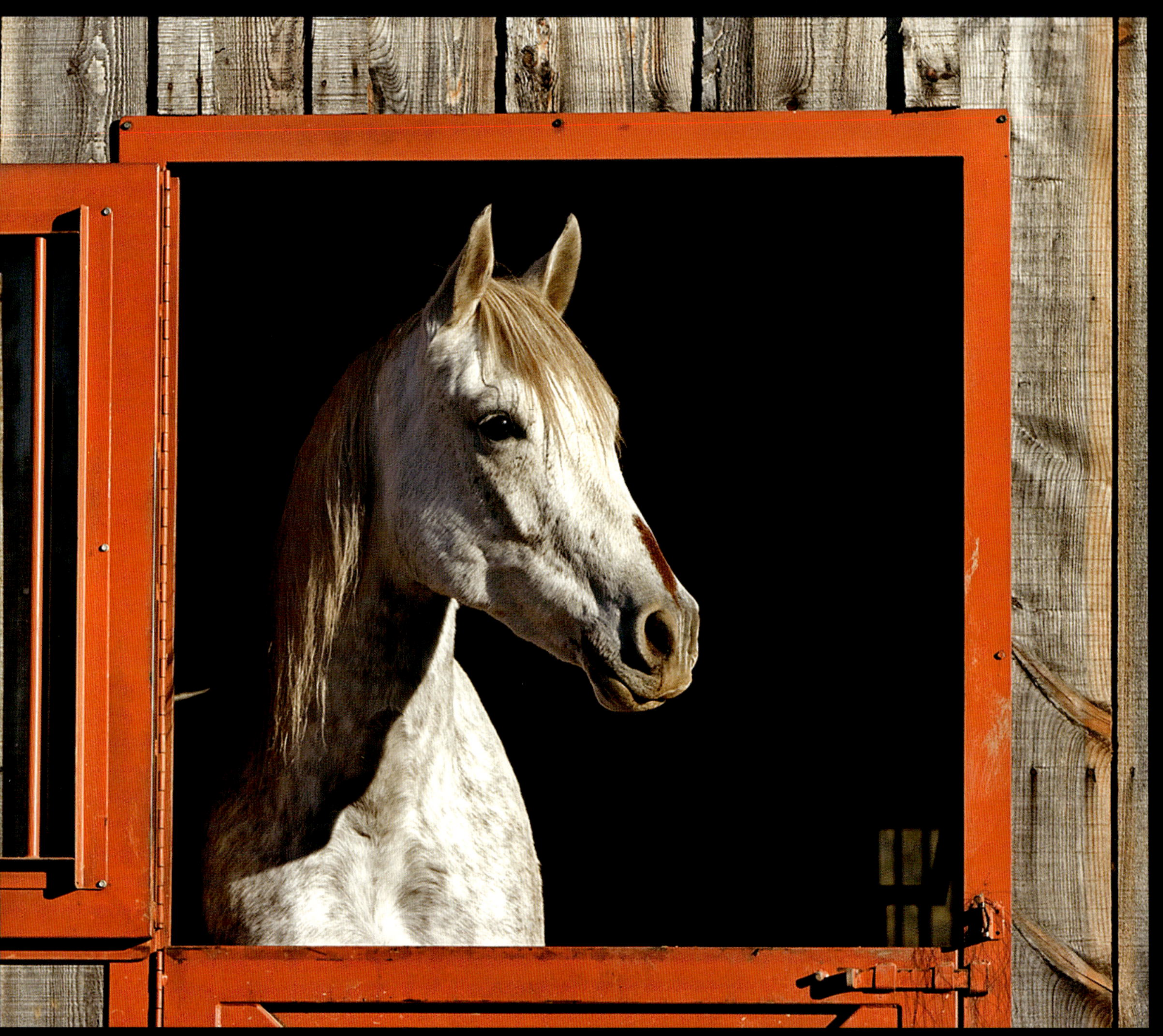

Grey horses occasionally have random red patches called blood marks, such as the marking above the nose of this Andalusian/Arabian cross. Opposite, a zorse's front legs (detail)

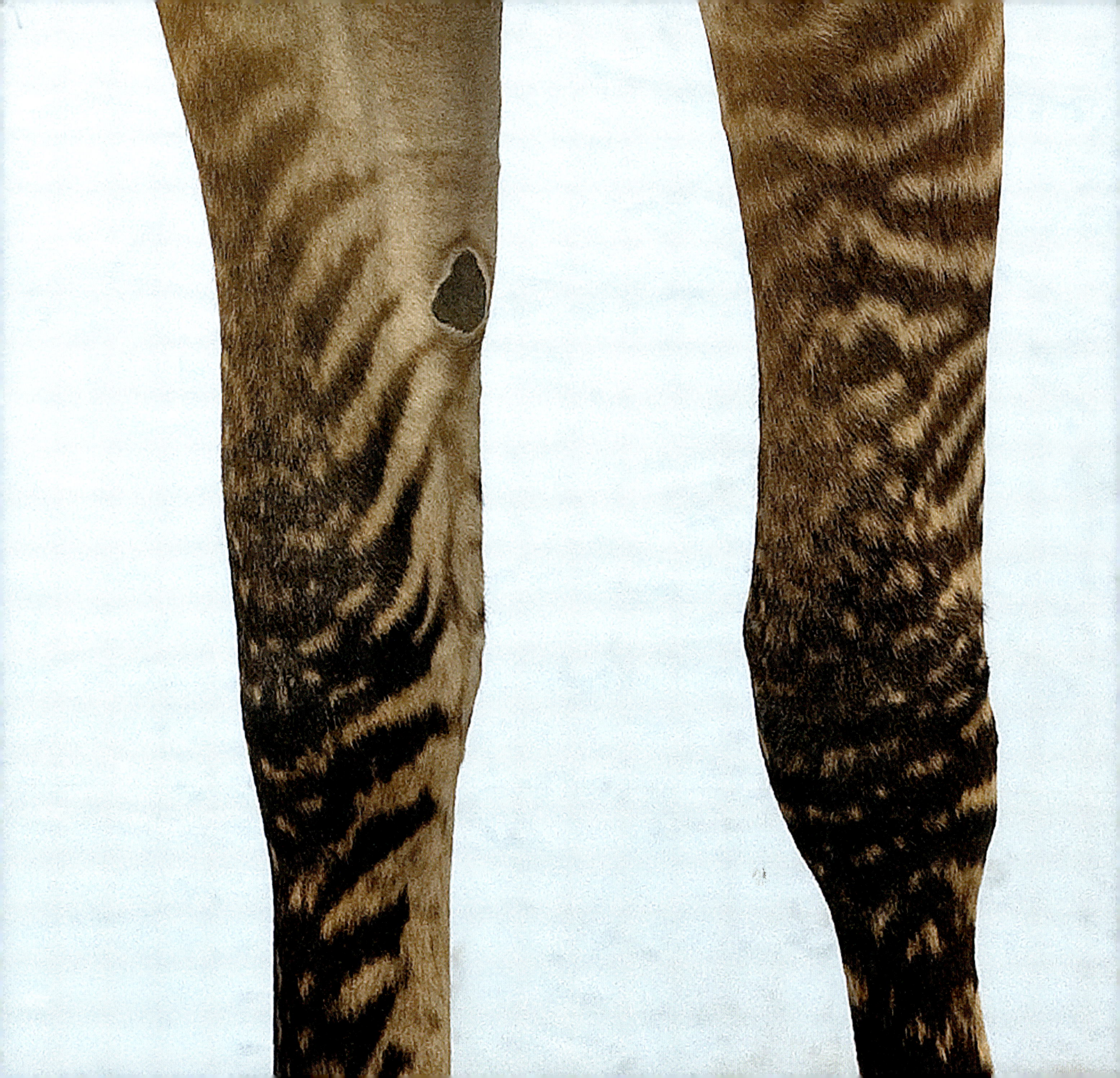

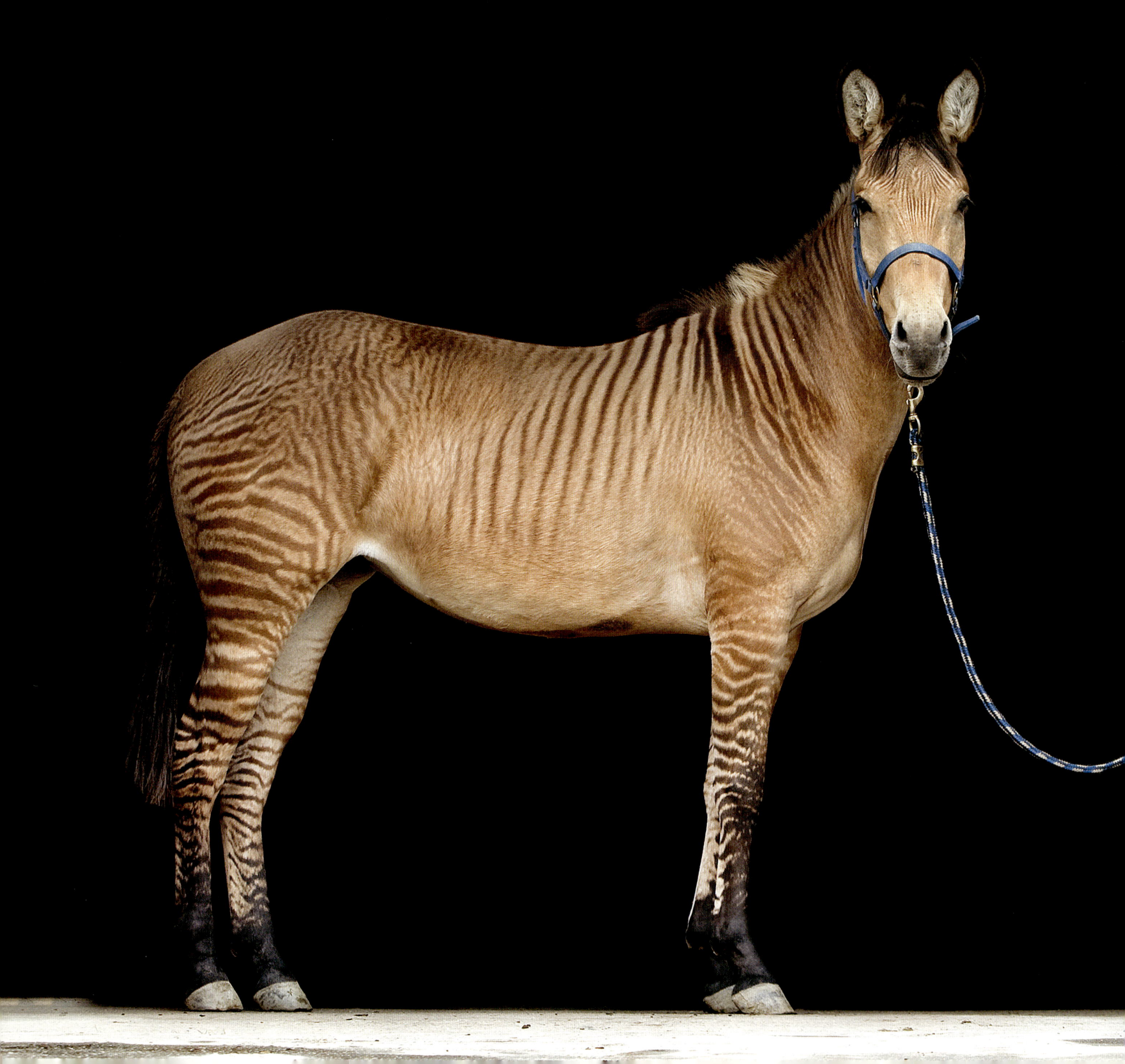

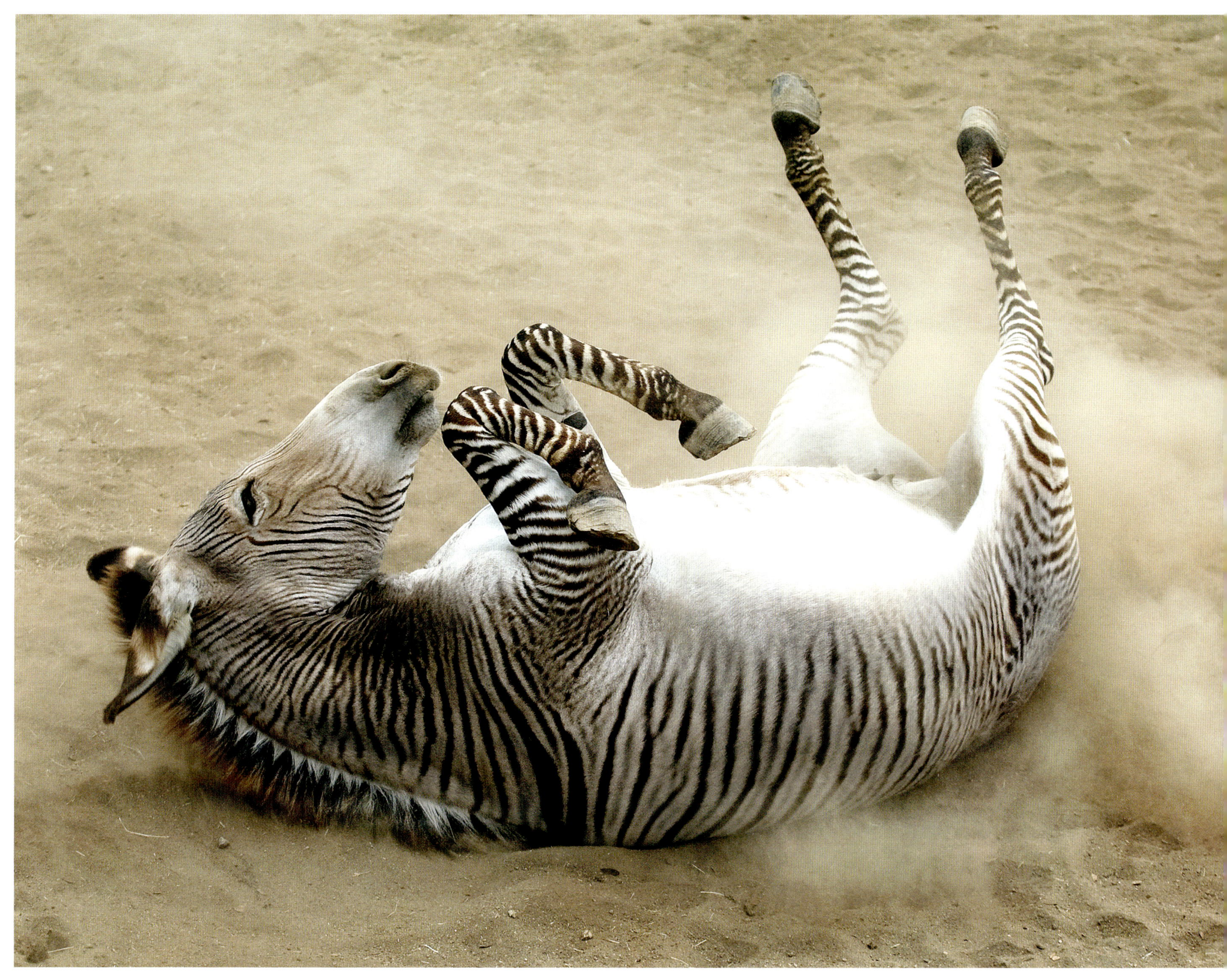

Left, the zorse is a product of a zebra sire and a red dun Quarter Horse mare, while a zonkey, above, is a cross between a zebra and a donkey.

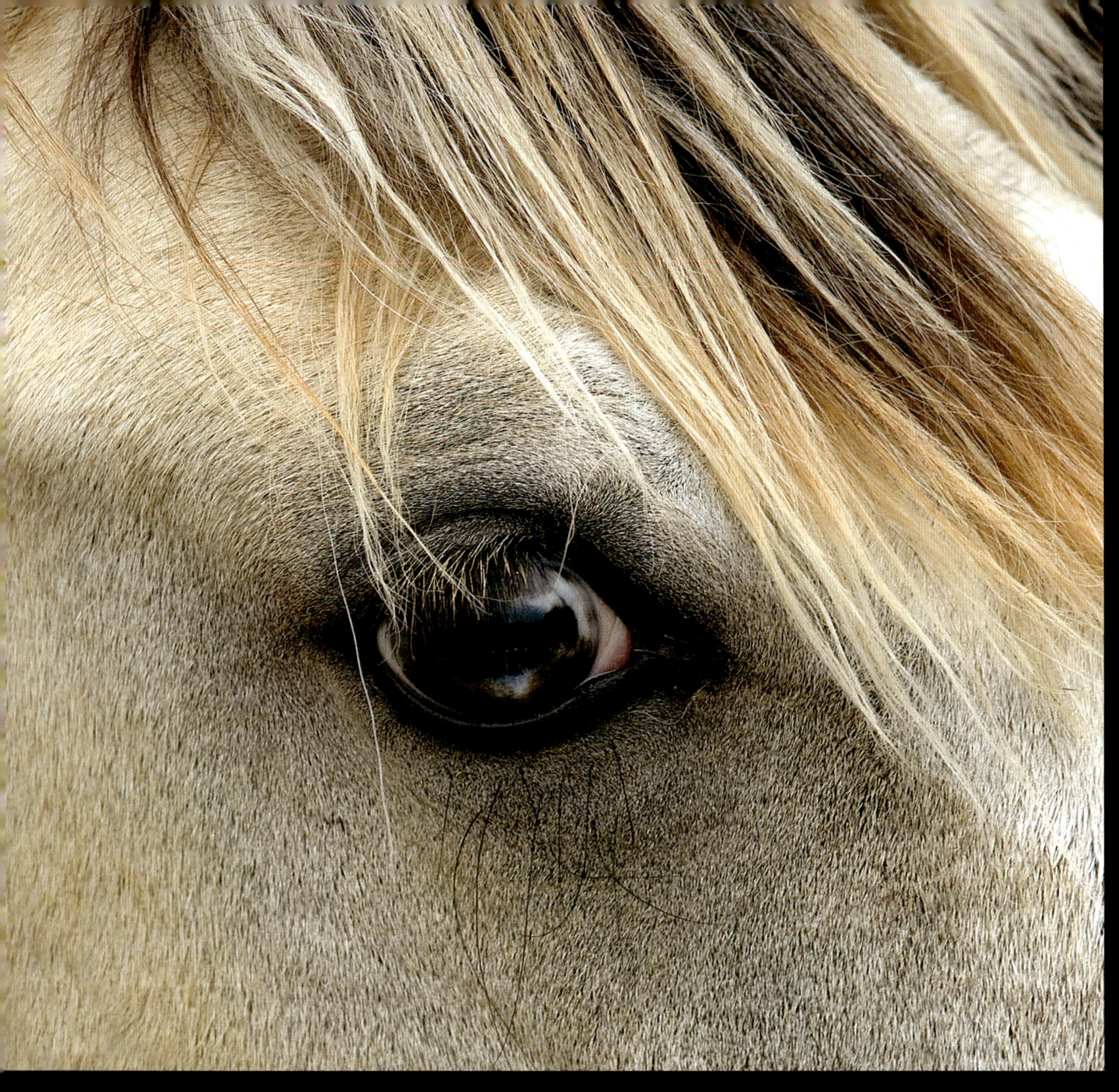

The close-up of this Colonial Spanish Horse seems a virtual artist's palette, from the touch of sky blue in her eye to her multi-colored forelock. Right, Mirabeau is a proud cremello German Warmblood.

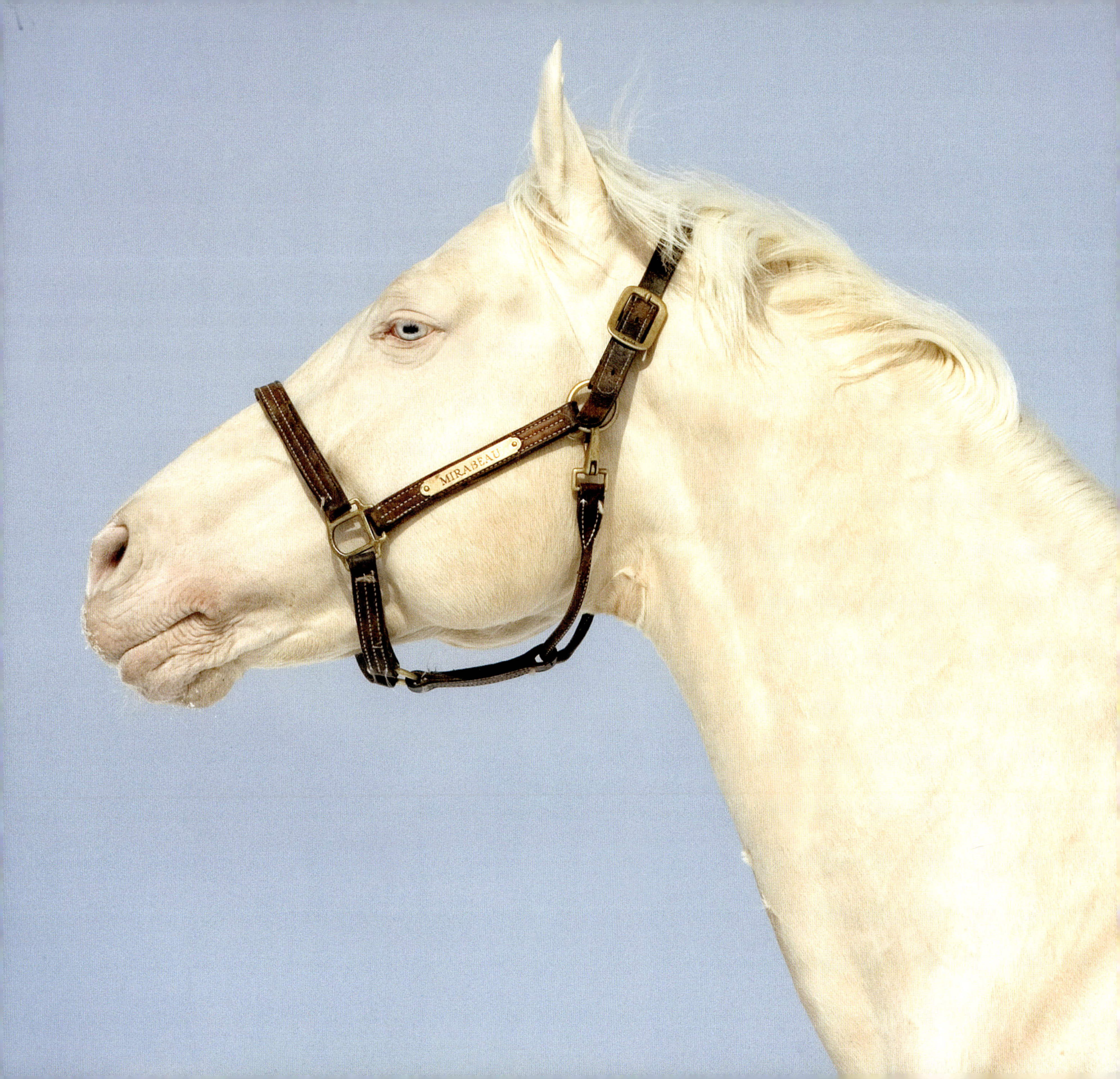
MIRABEAU

Among this outstanding reining horse's unusual traits are abundant dapples, a hind end that is darker than his front end, one blue eye, high leg markings, and a light mane with scattered dark hairs.

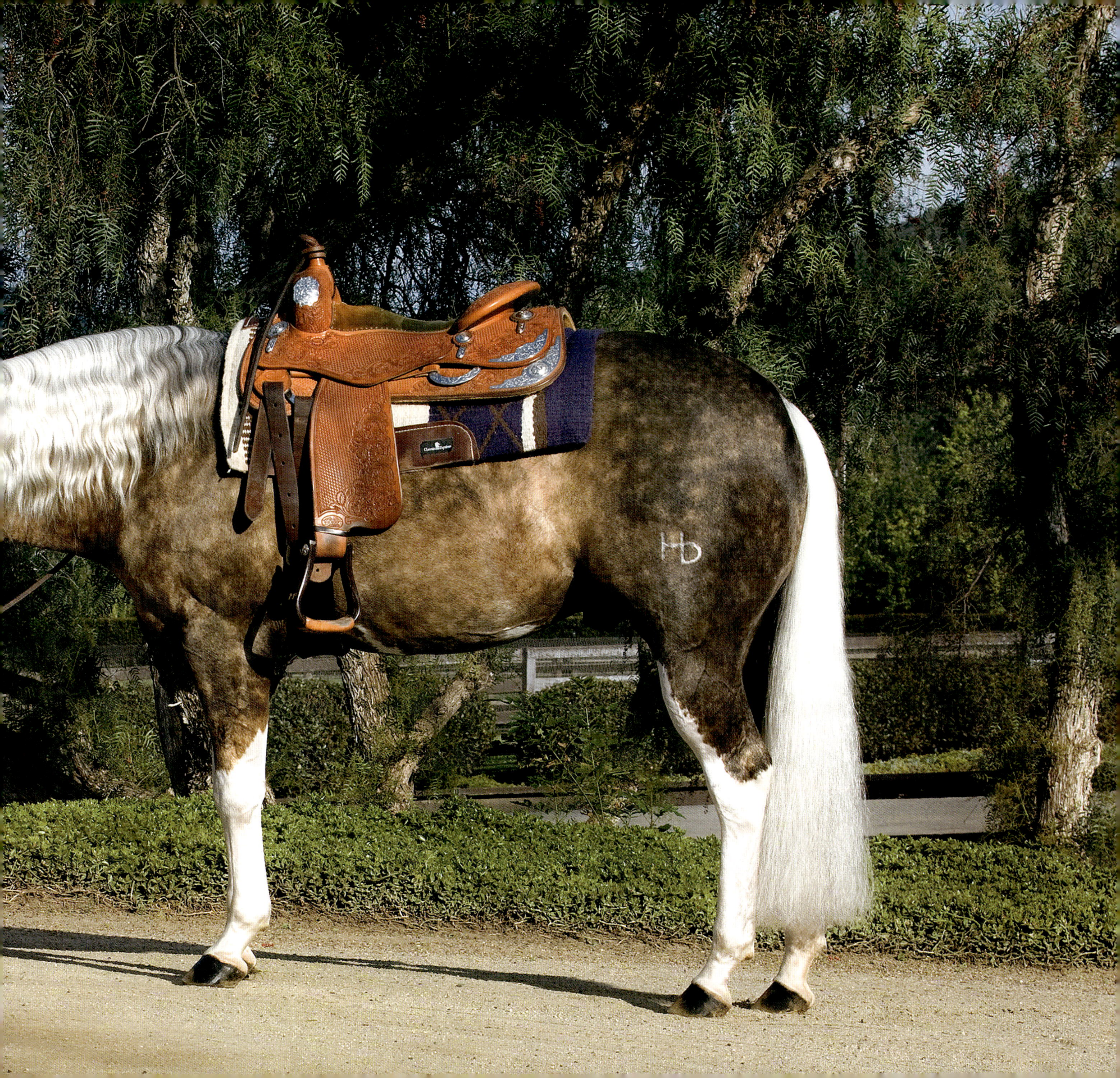

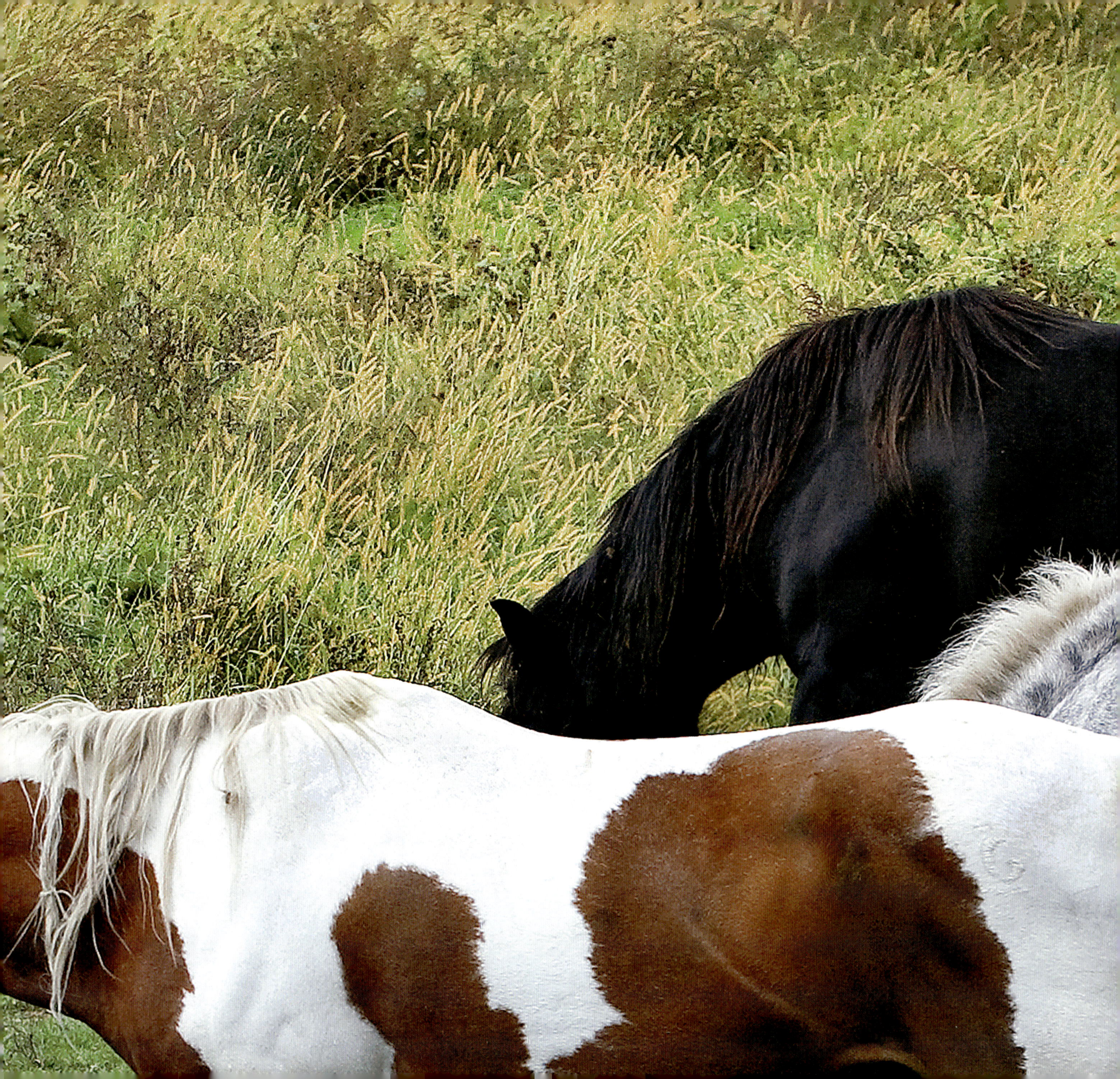

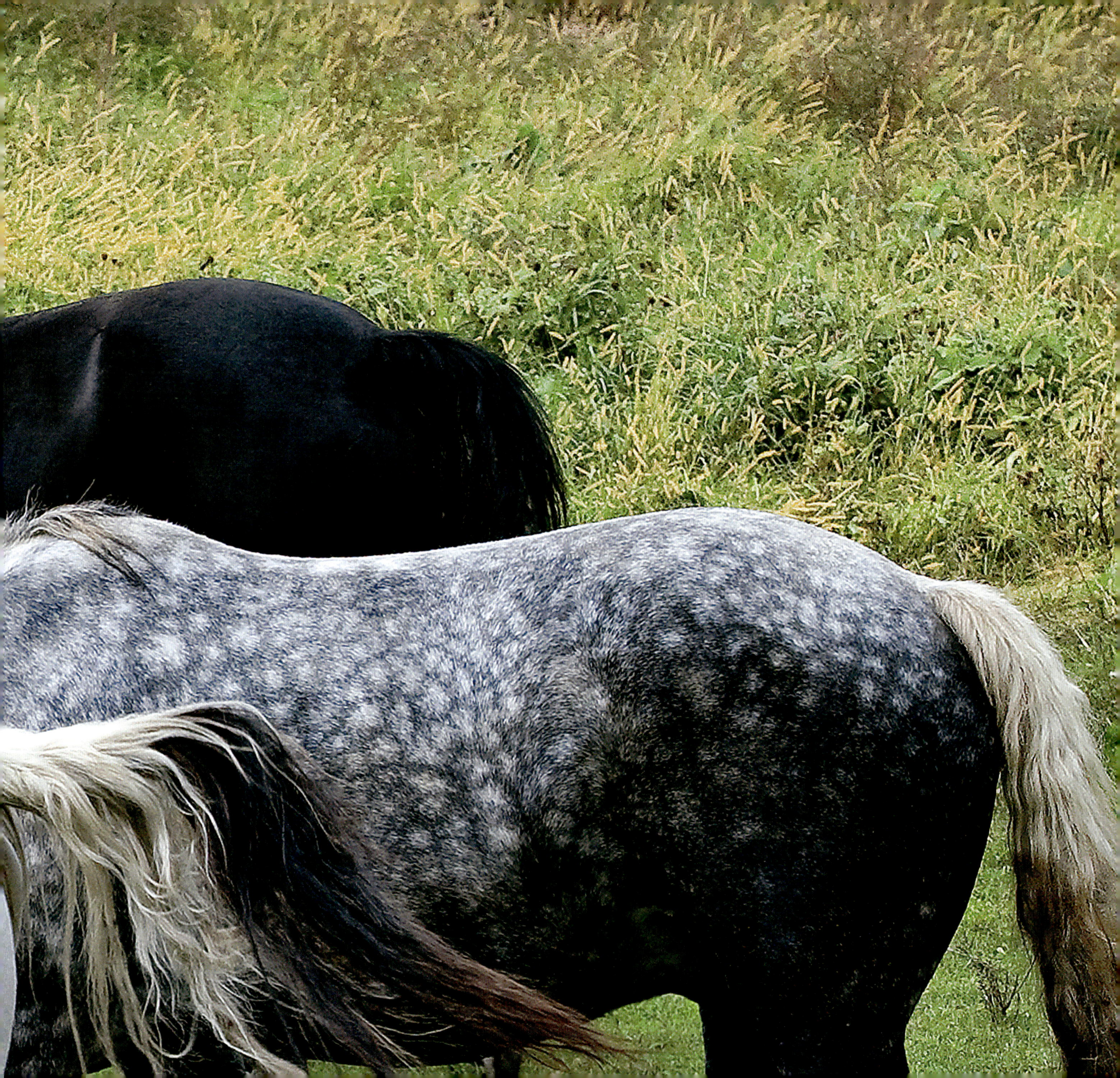

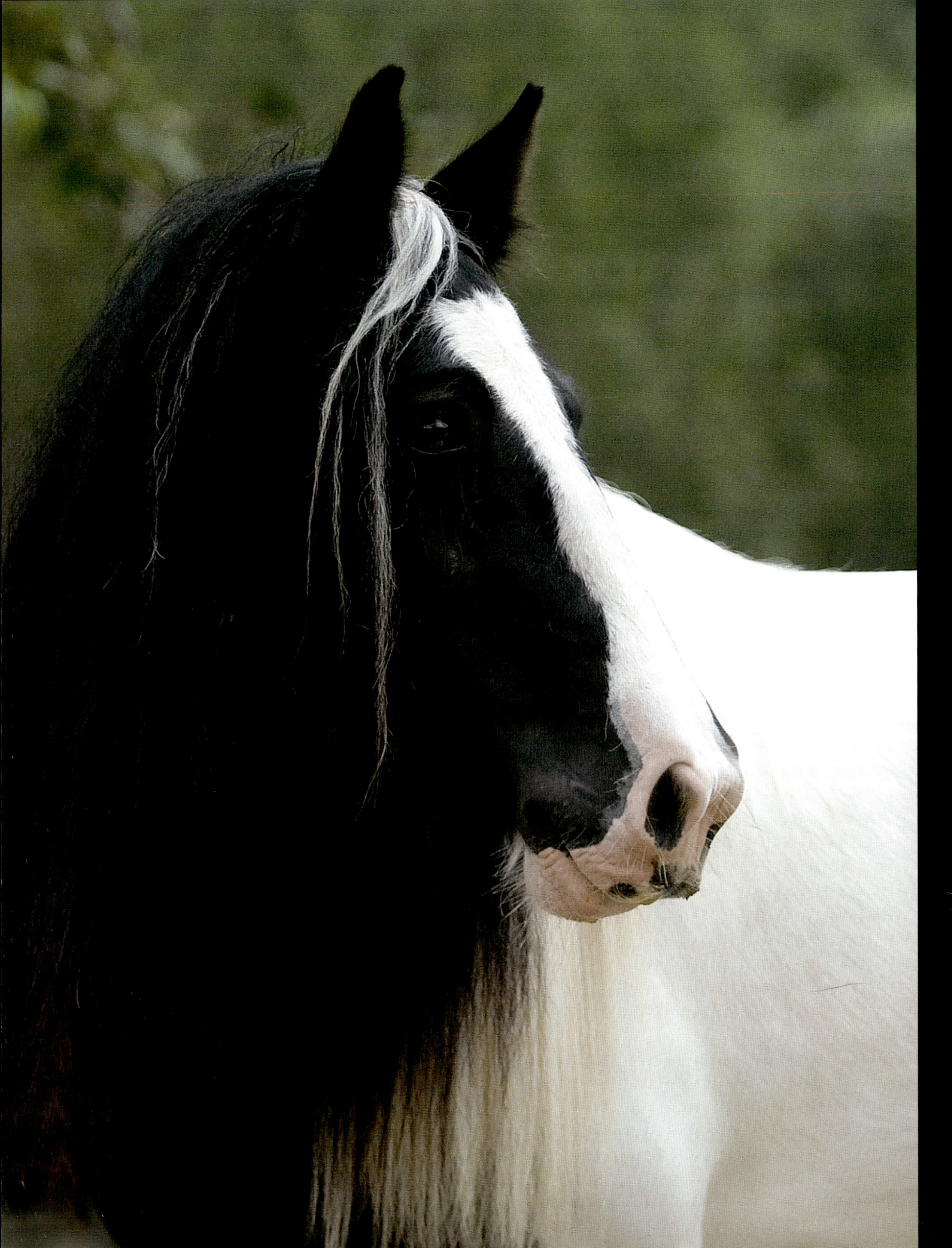

Long, flowing manes aren't particular to any breed. Left is a well-coiffed Gypsy Cob mare and, right, a feral Assateague stallion.

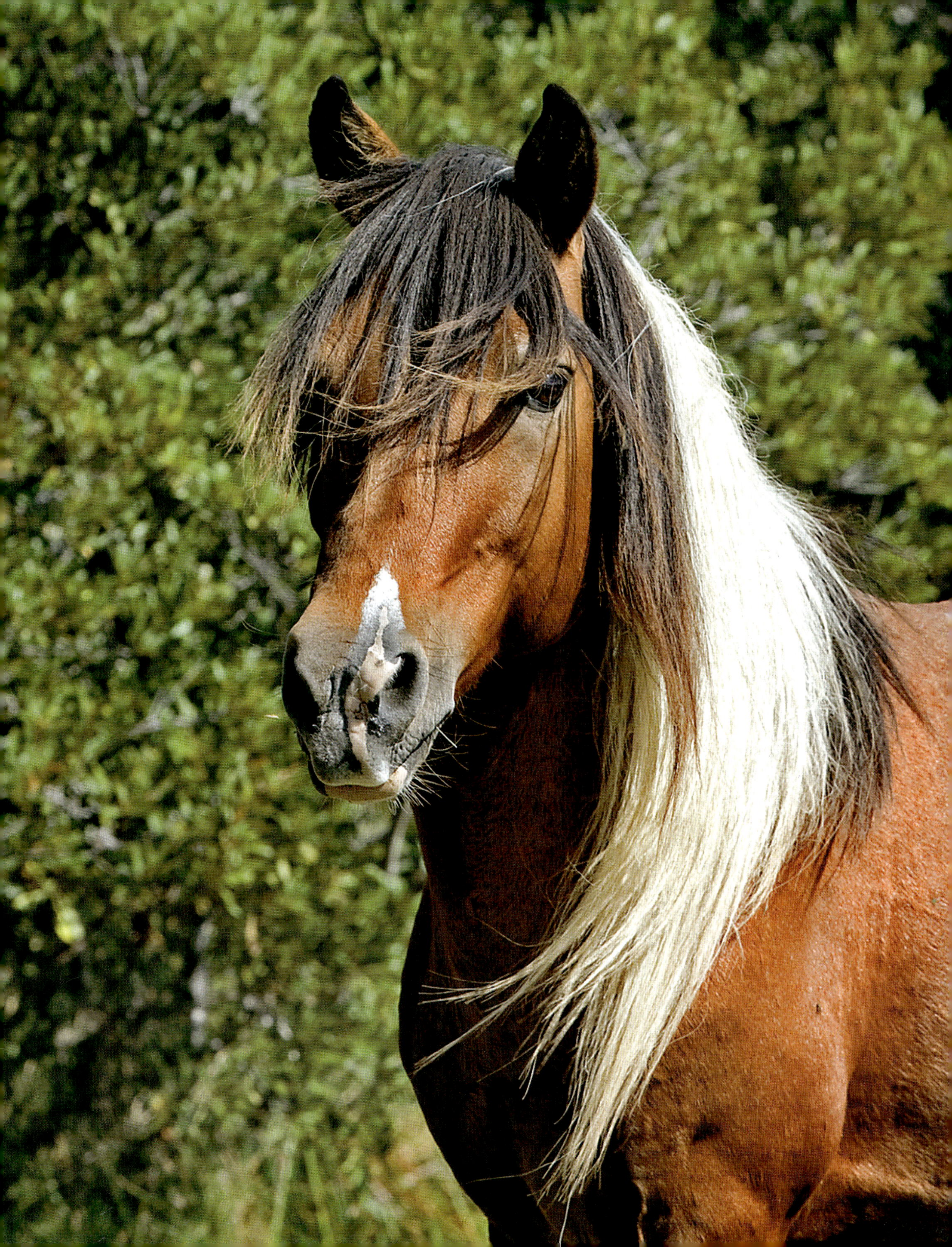

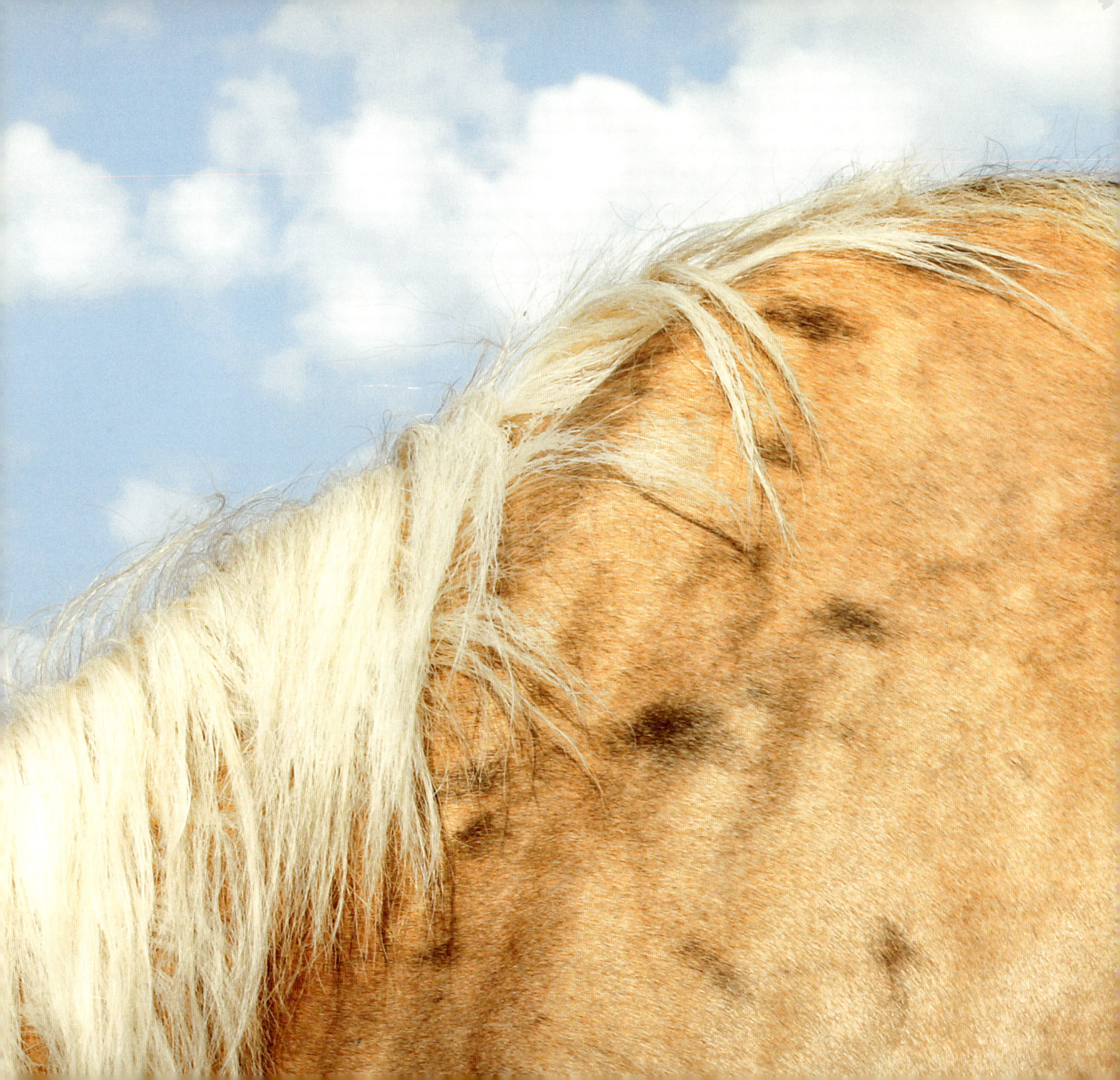

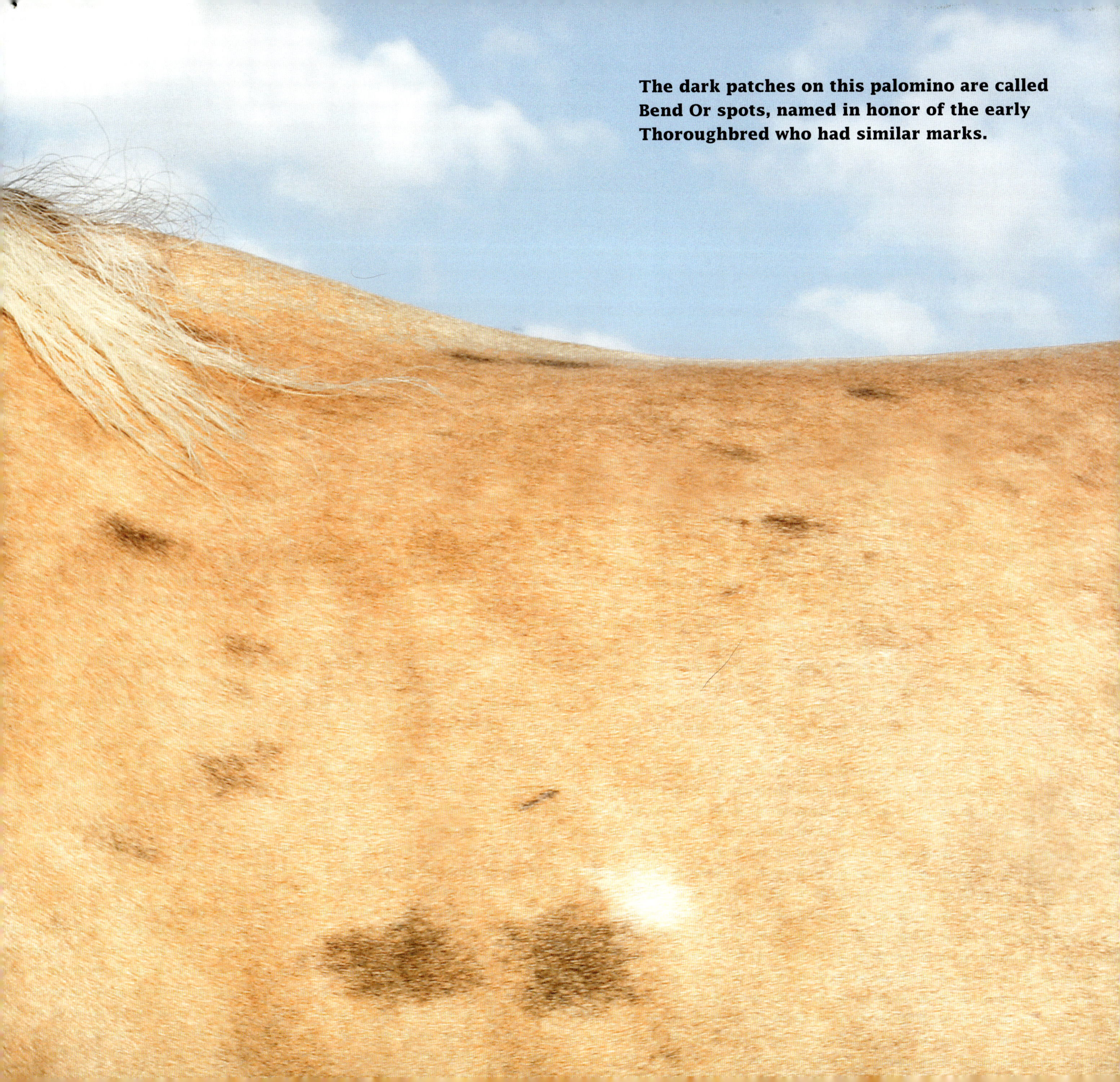

The dark patches on this palomino are called Bend Or spots, named in honor of the early Thoroughbred who had similar marks.

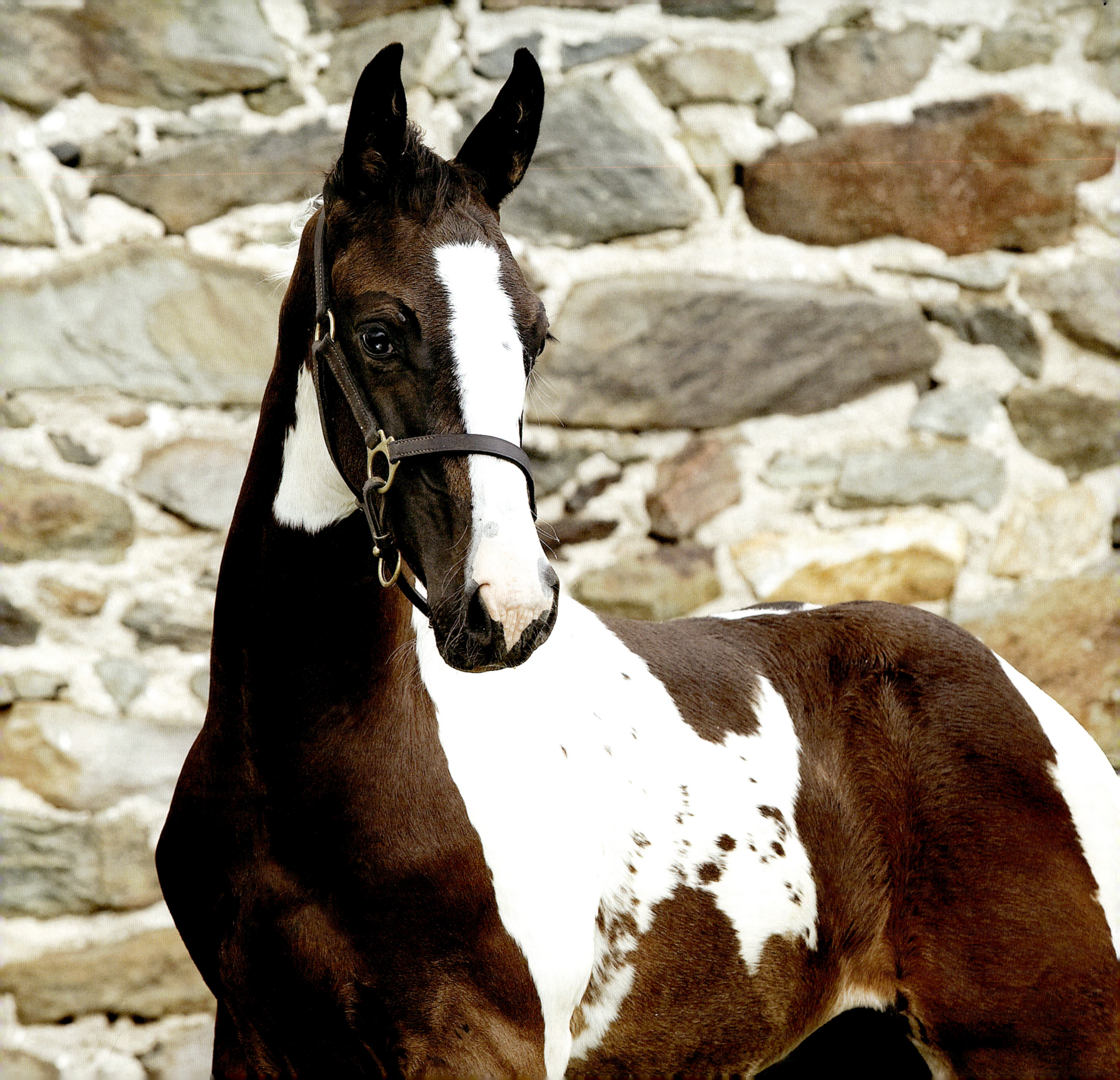

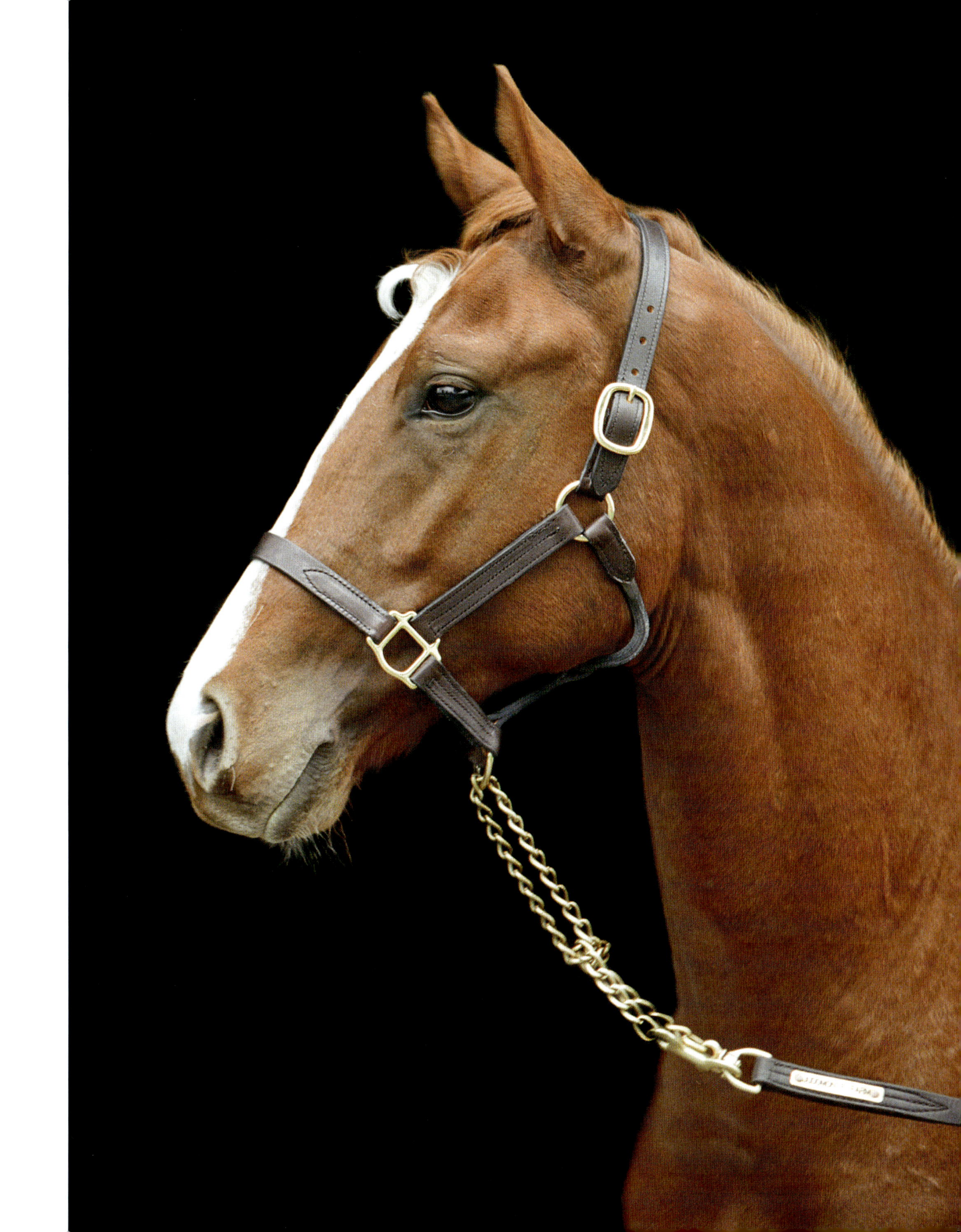

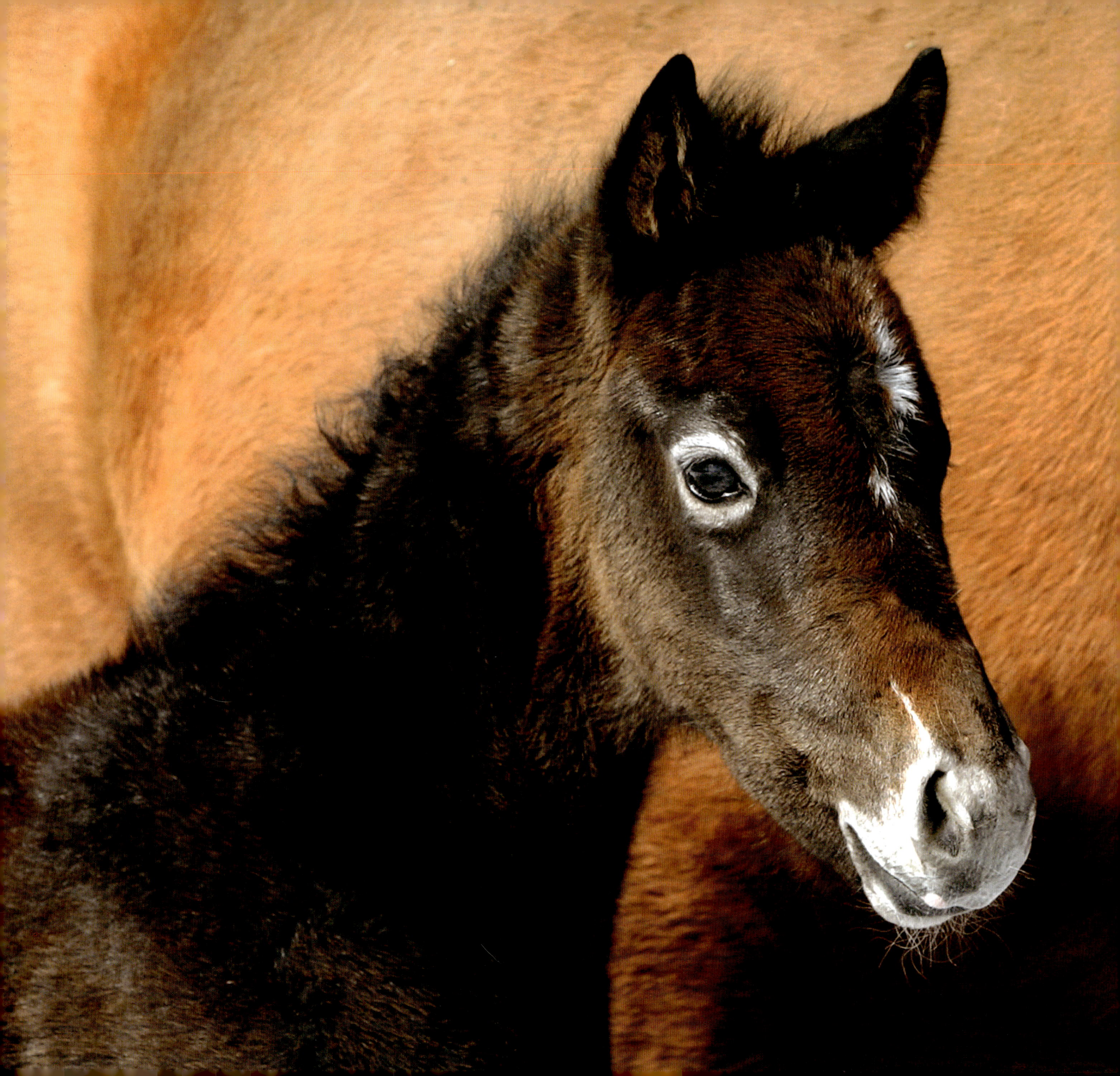

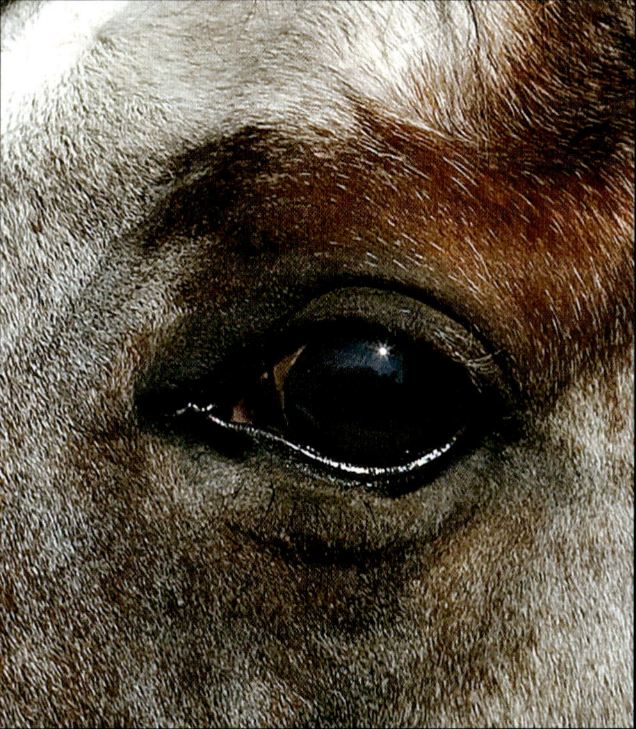

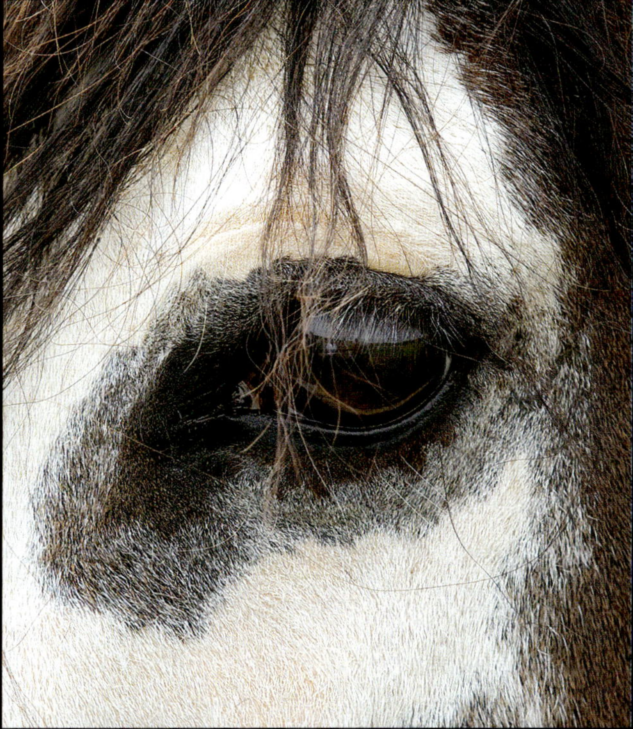

Left, as this precious foal matures, his brown coat will eventually shed out to grey, and the ring around his eye will disappear. Above, these mature horses show just how exotic eyes can be.

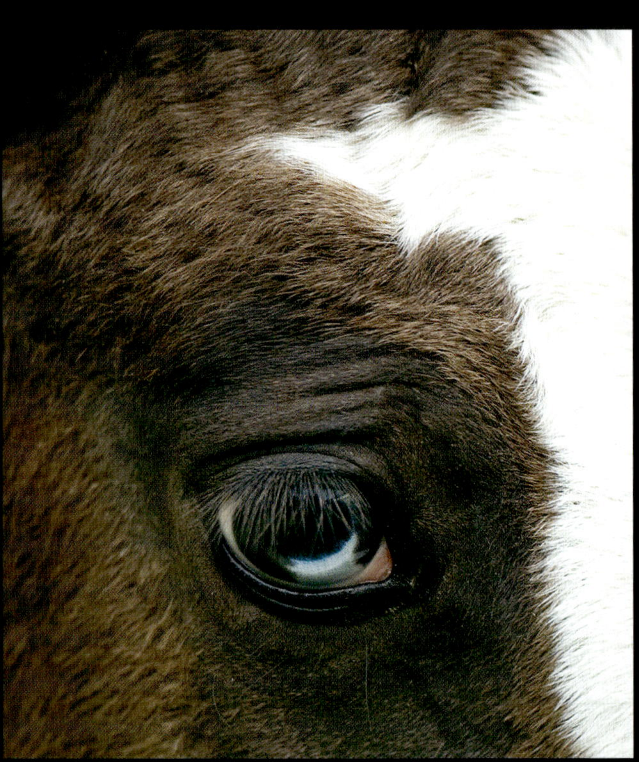

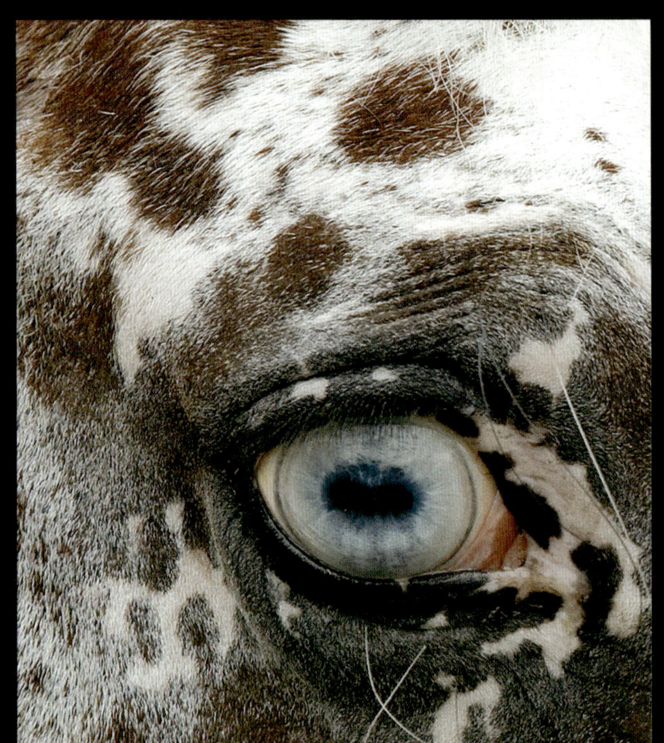

Above, equine eyes come in a variety of colors, including partial blue, such as the Appaloosa foal at left.

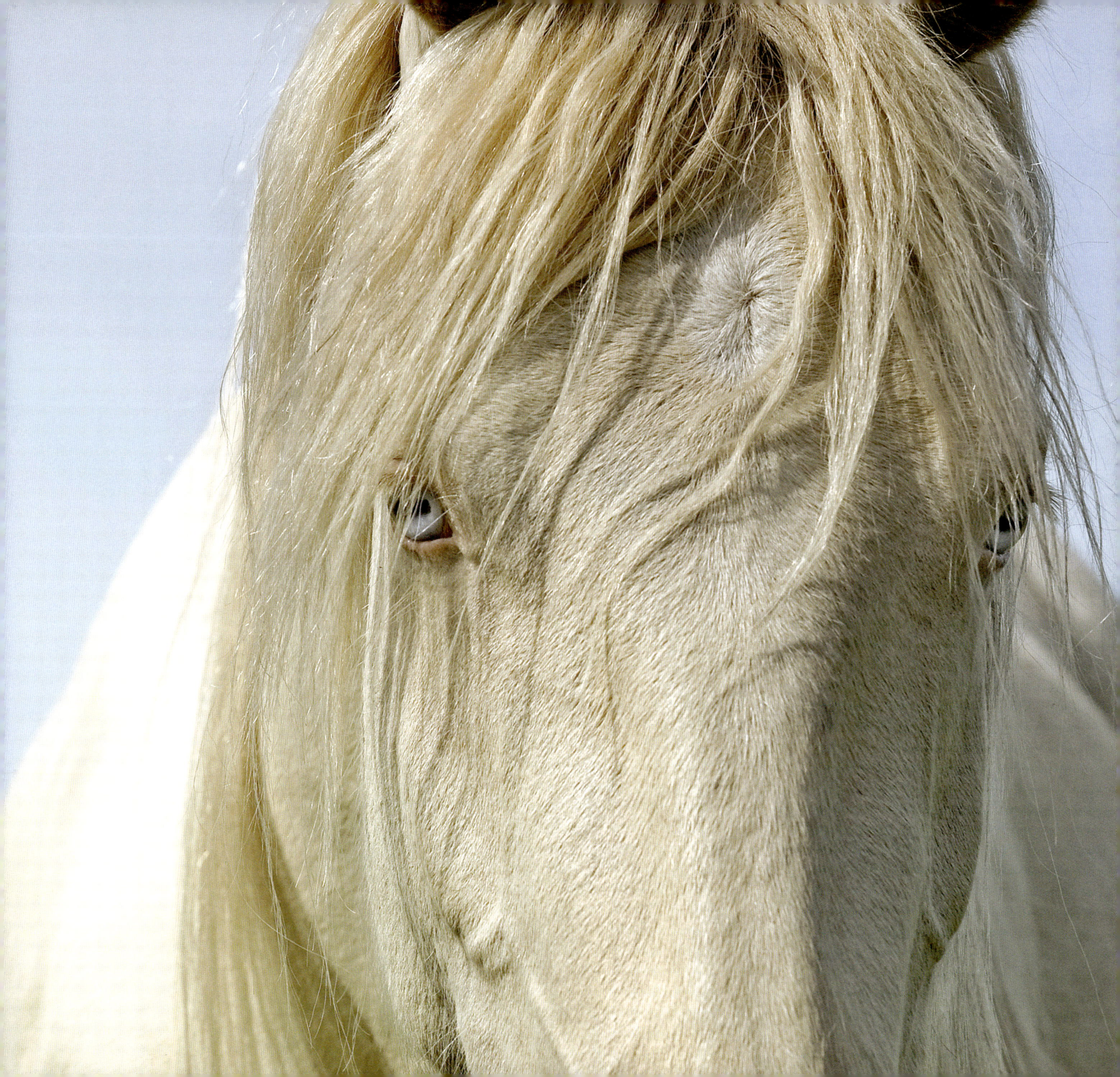

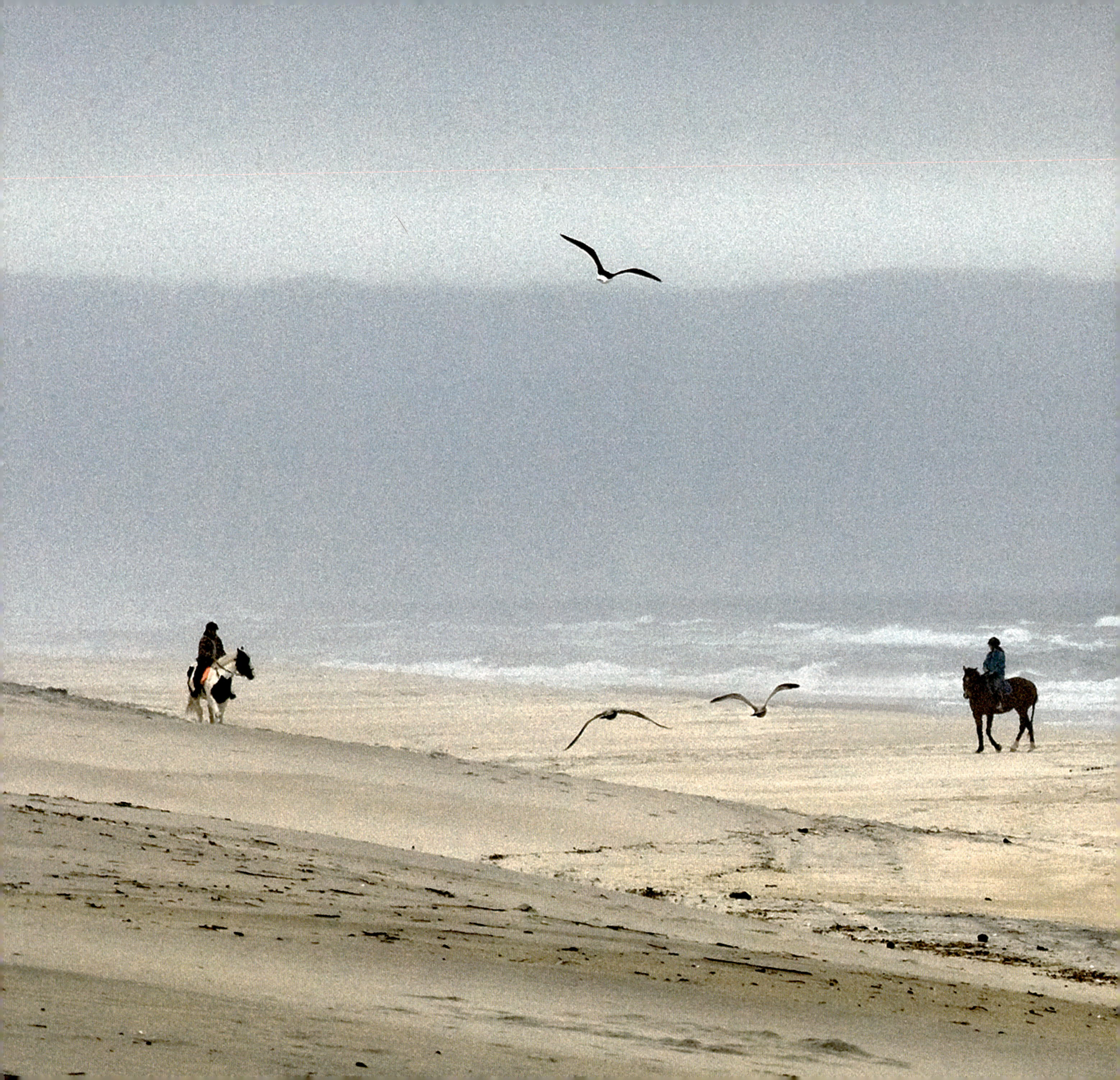

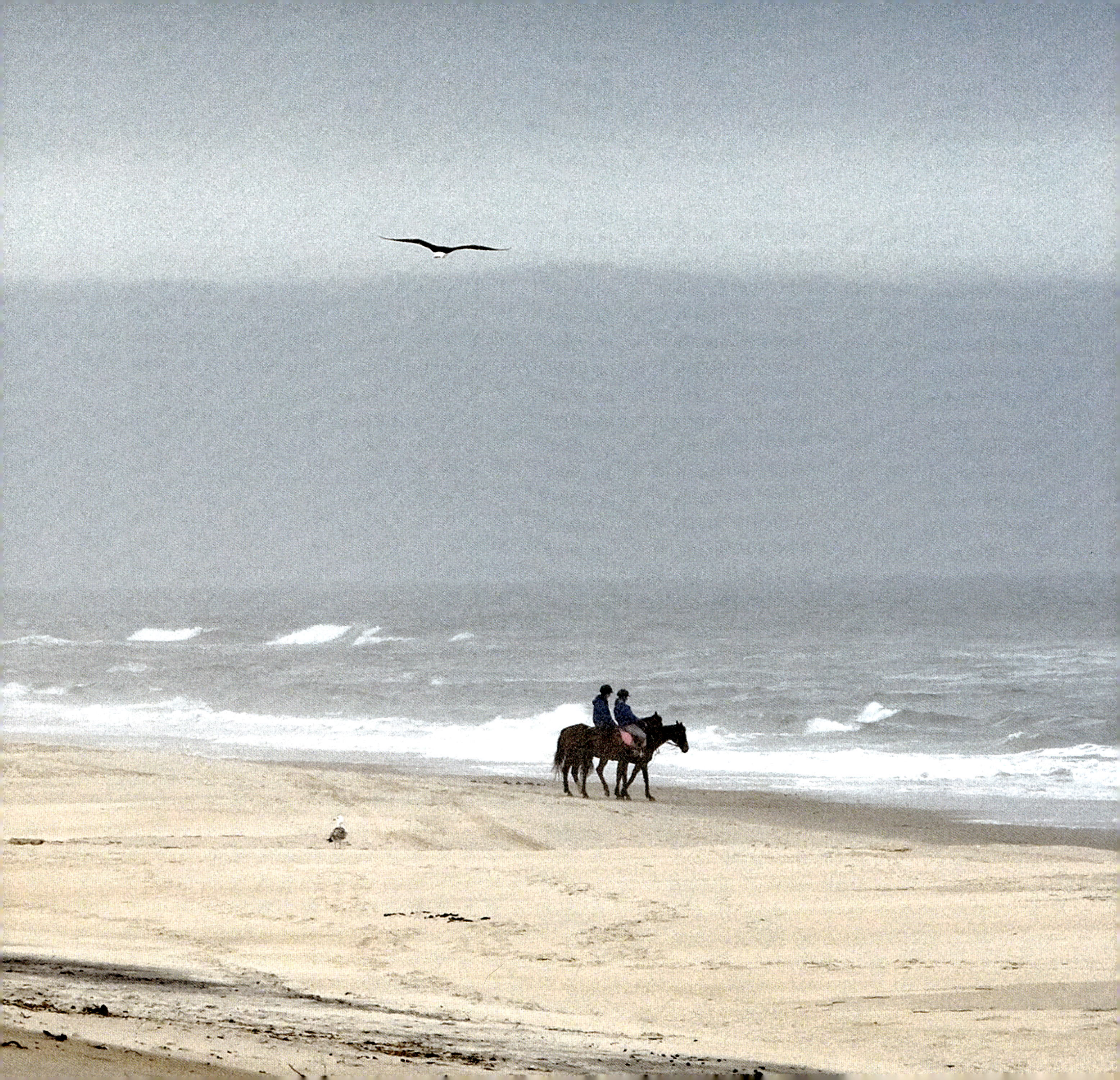

This grey Thoroughbred at Aqueduct displays a dark patch that, like many other traits of color, is not readily understood.

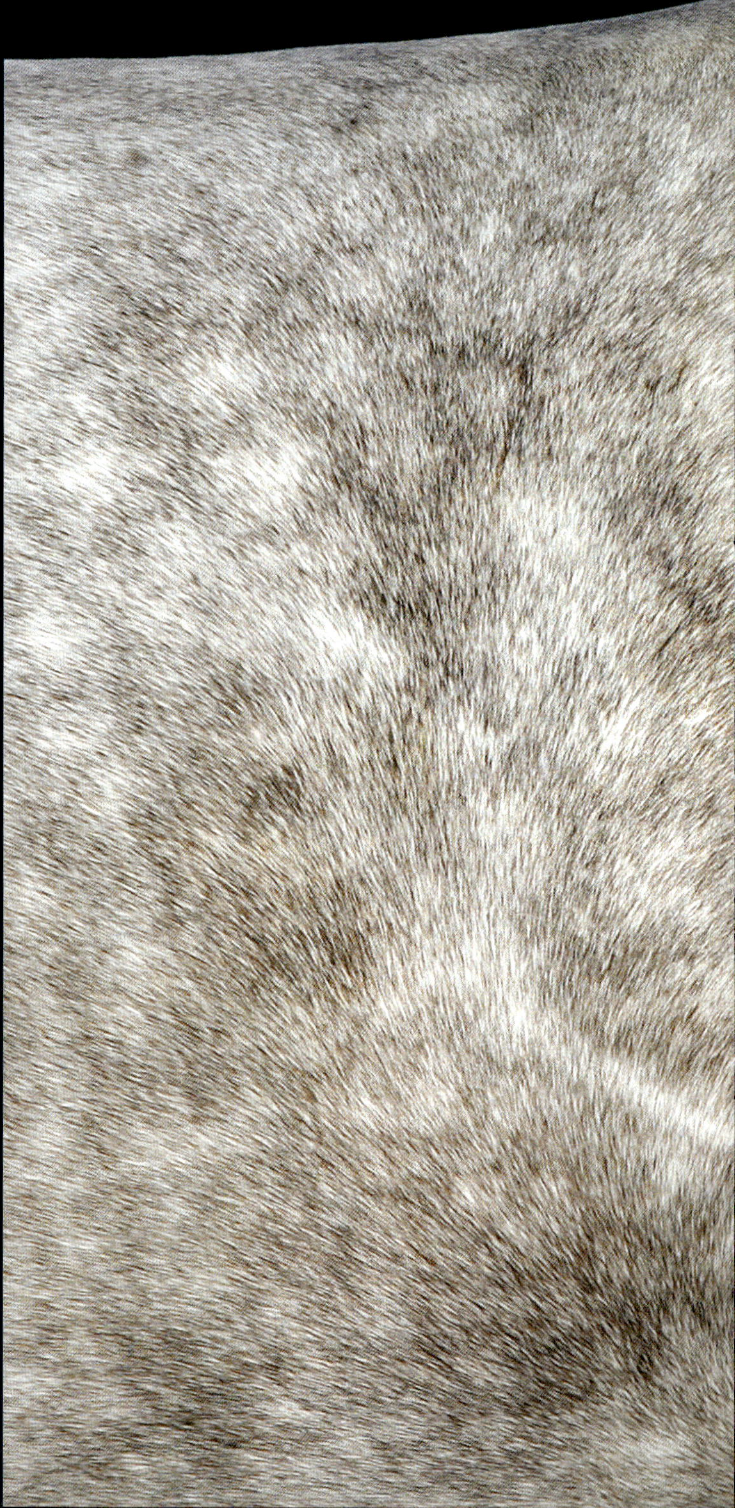

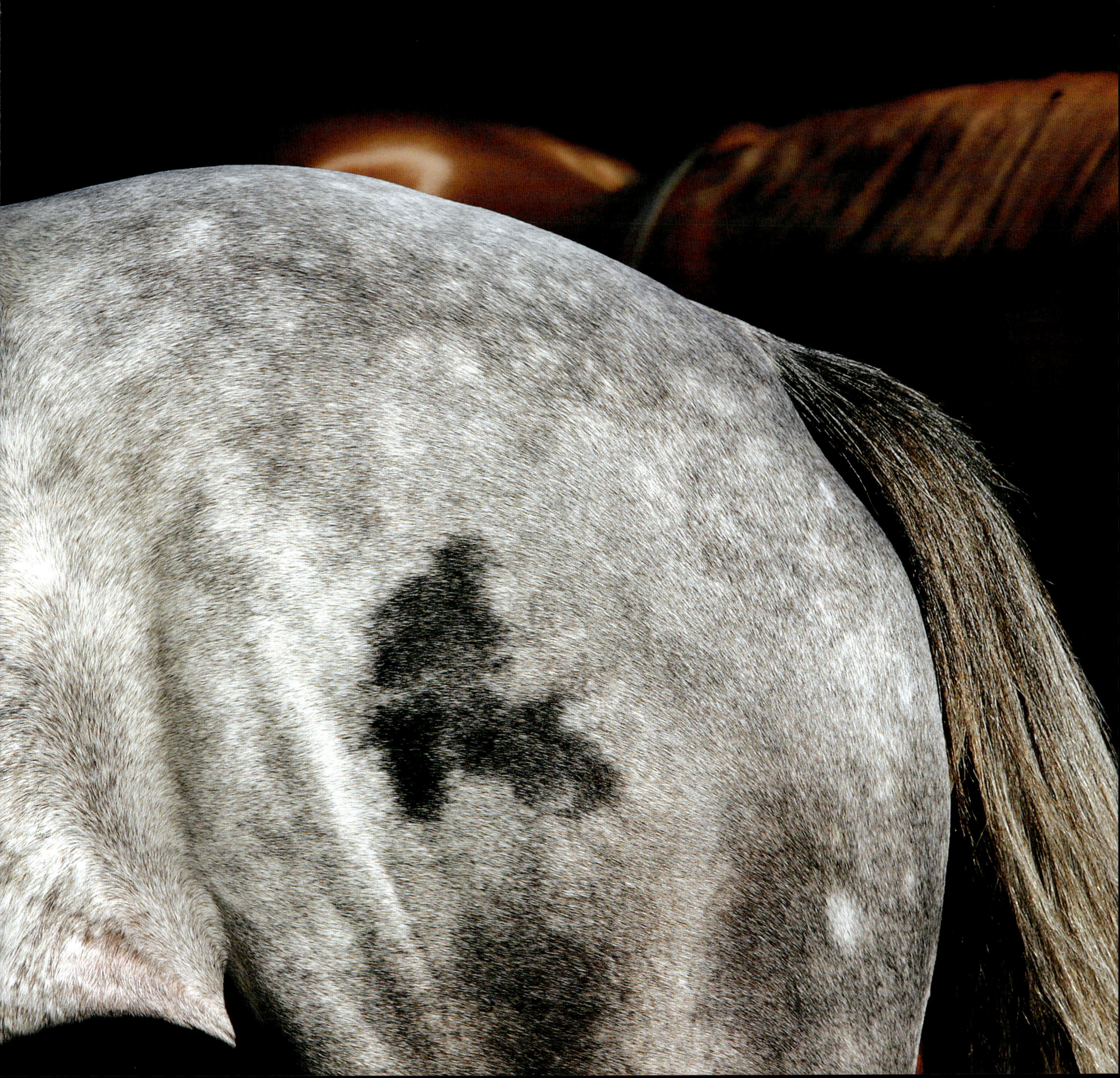

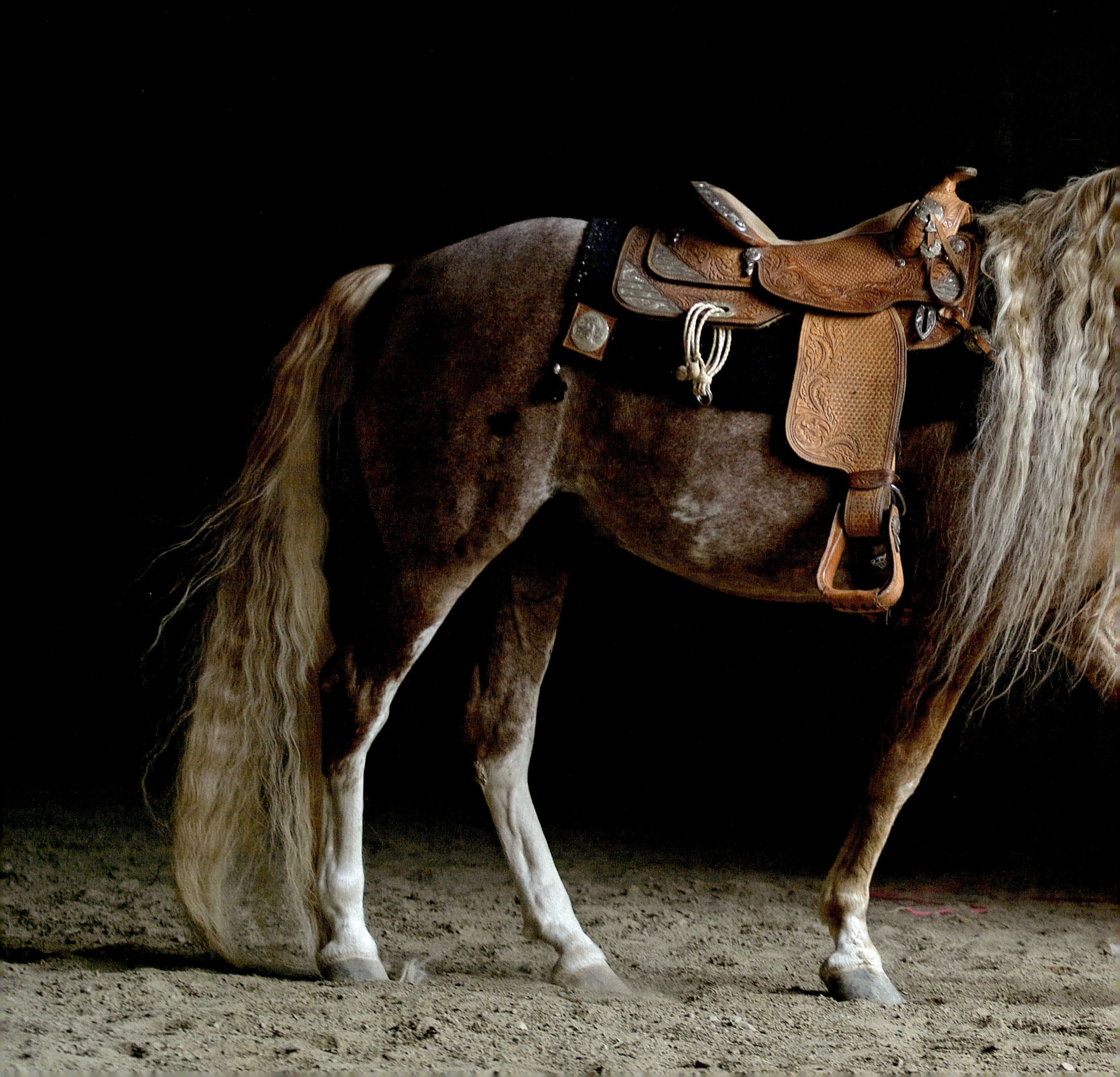

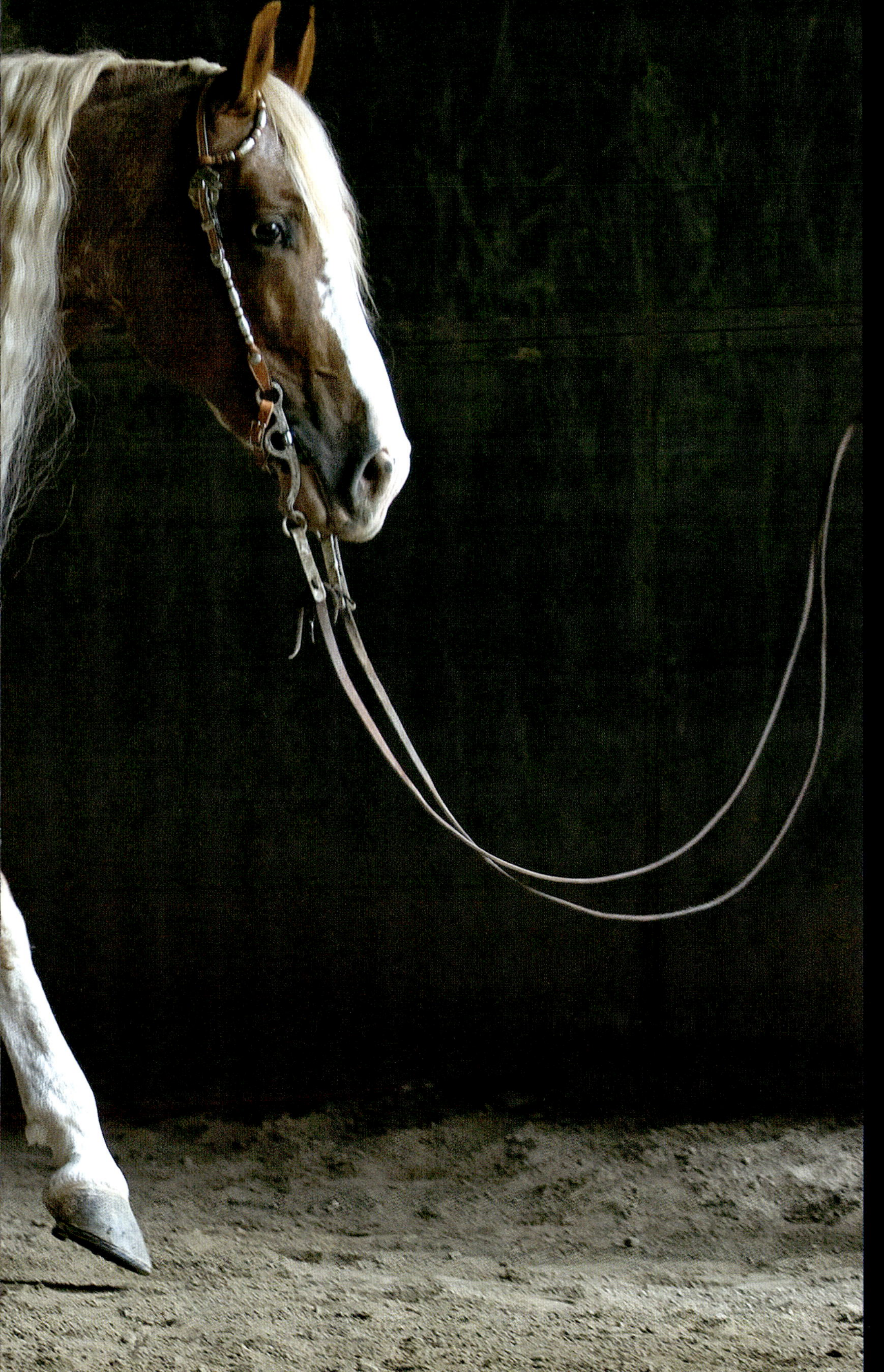

This double-registered Tennessee Walker and Spotted Saddle Horse is a chestnut sabino, the product of a black sire and a dark brown dam.

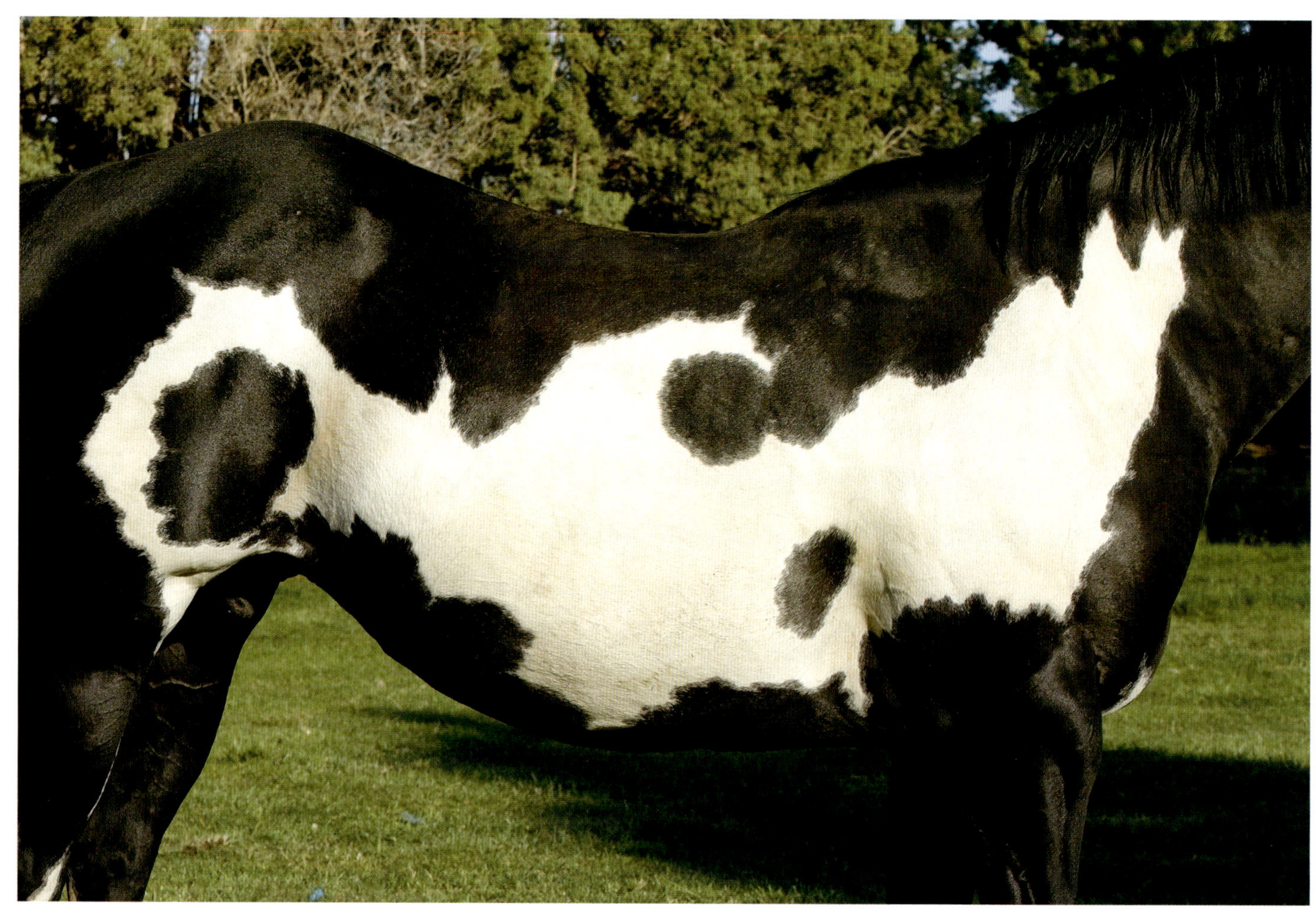

Combinations of black and white grace many breeds, including the Paint mare above (the seahorse shape on her side led to her name Seahorse Dance) and the Miniature stallion, right.

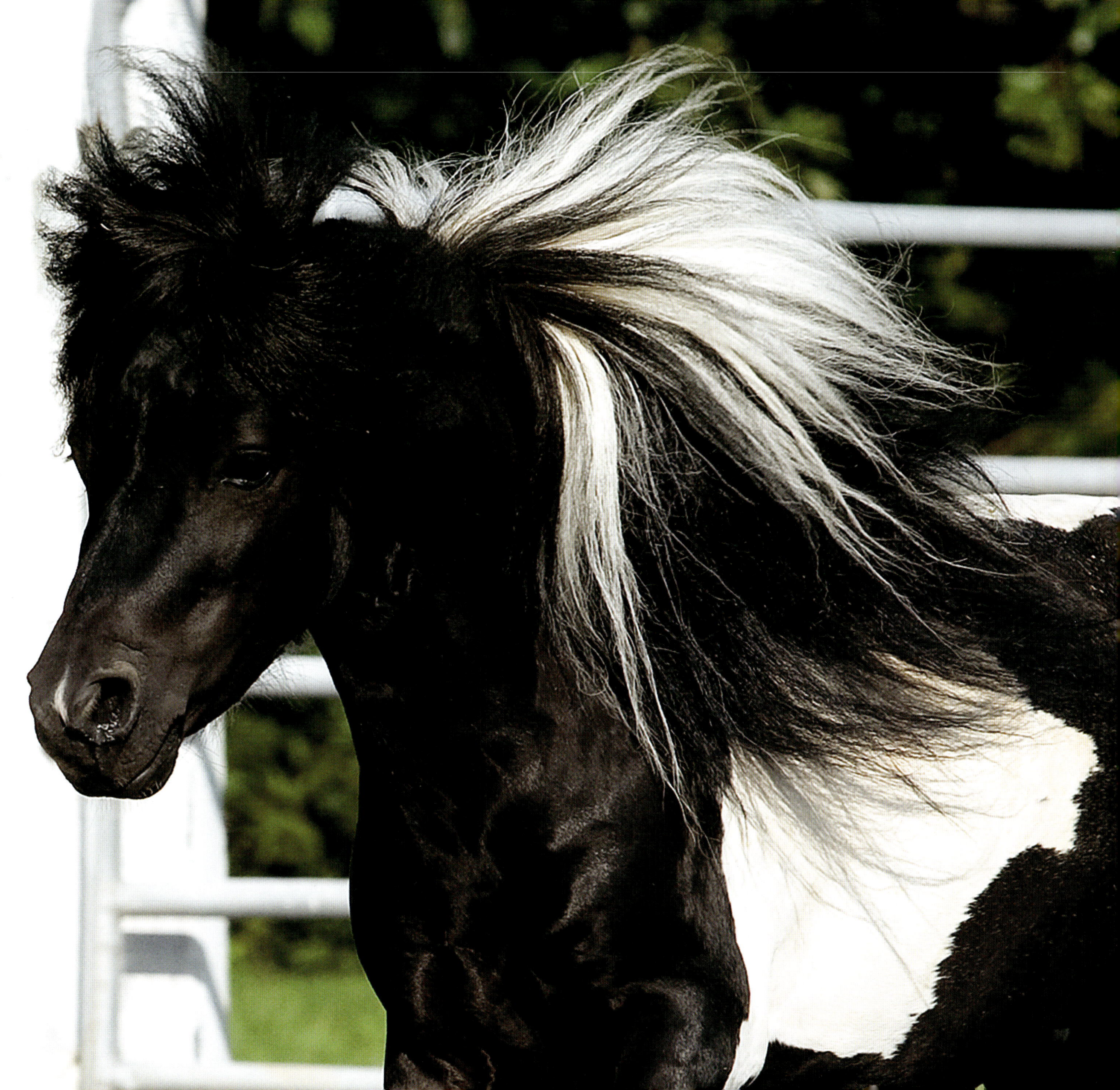

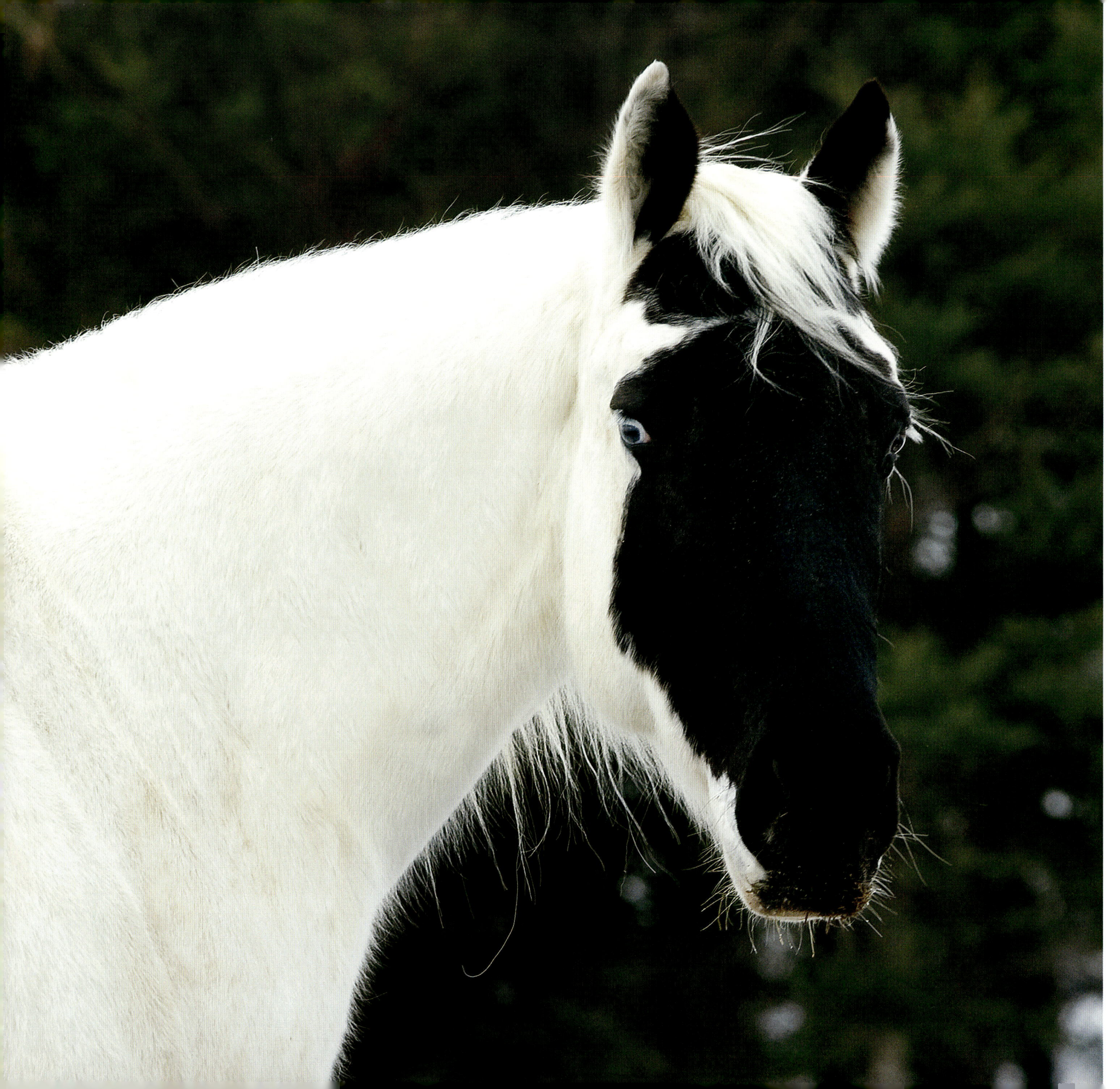

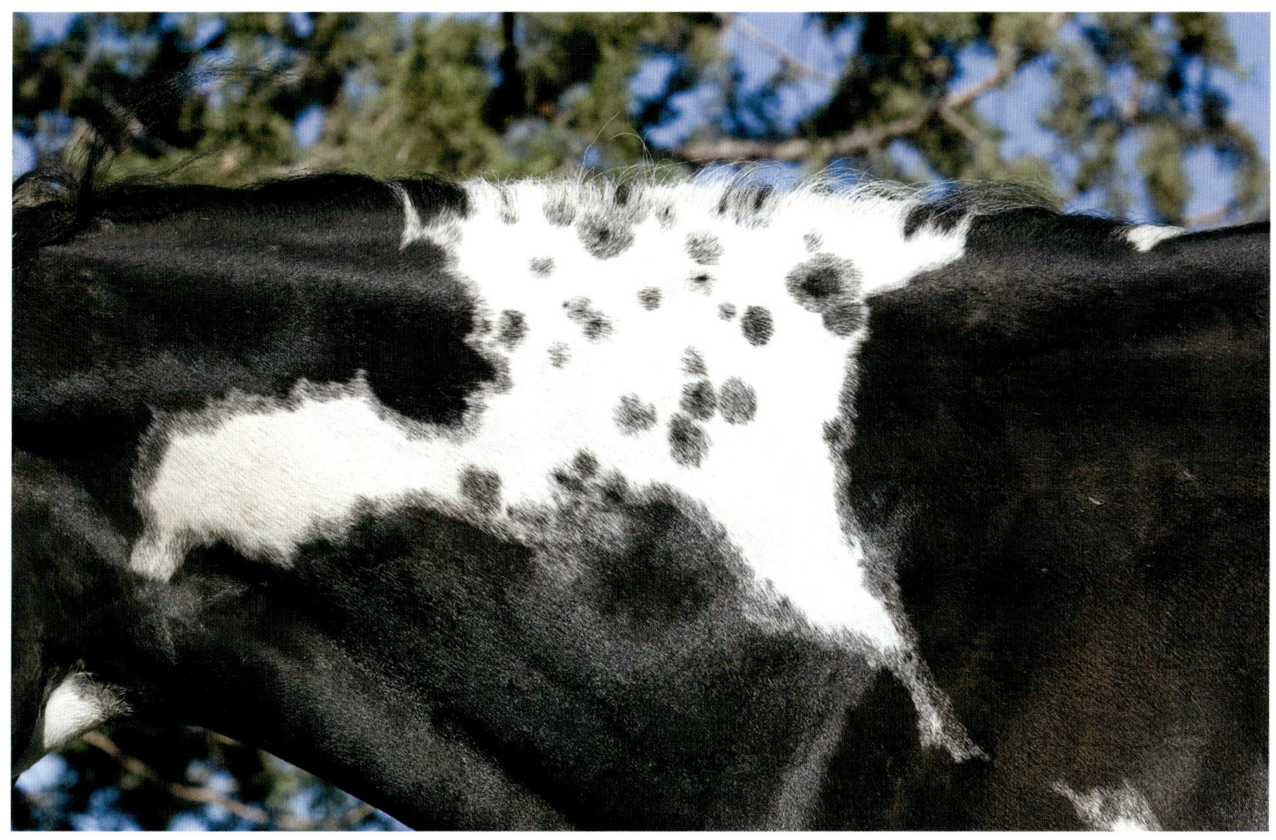

Horses with badger faces, such as this mare at left, are eye-catching and rare. Above, the random black spots within this white marking are sometimes called ink spots, and the rough edges between white and black are generally referred to as shadows or halos.

This young colt with the beautiful spotted blanket exhibits Appaloosa markings, which can change dramatically over the years. This horse might look significantly different later in life.

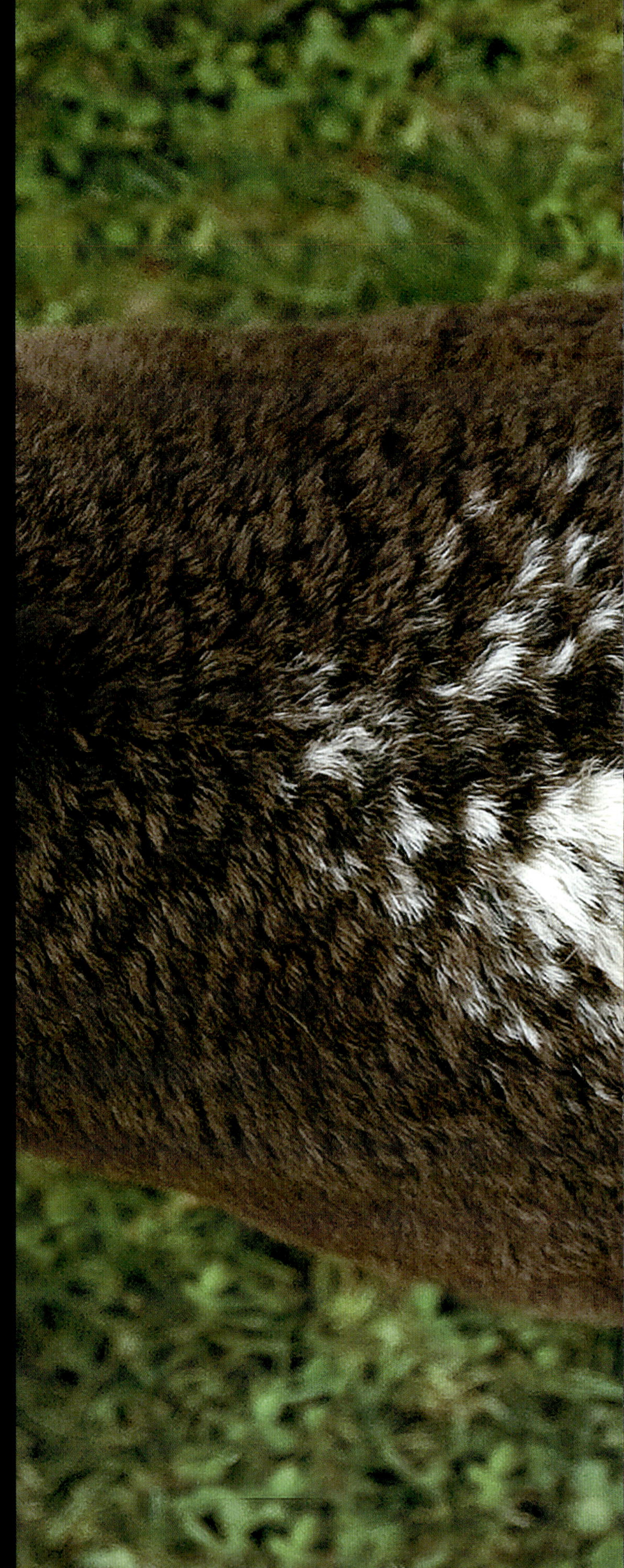

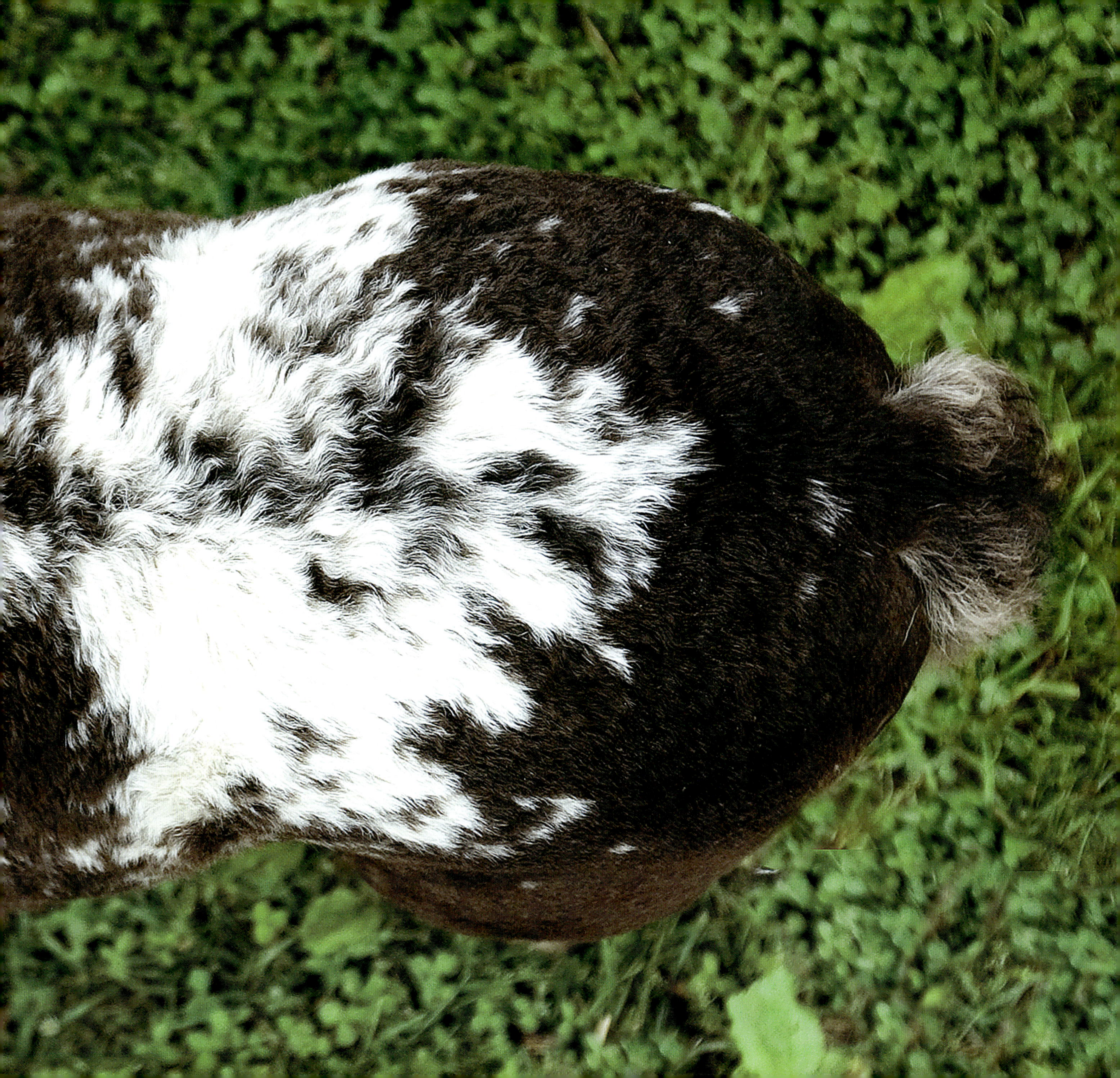

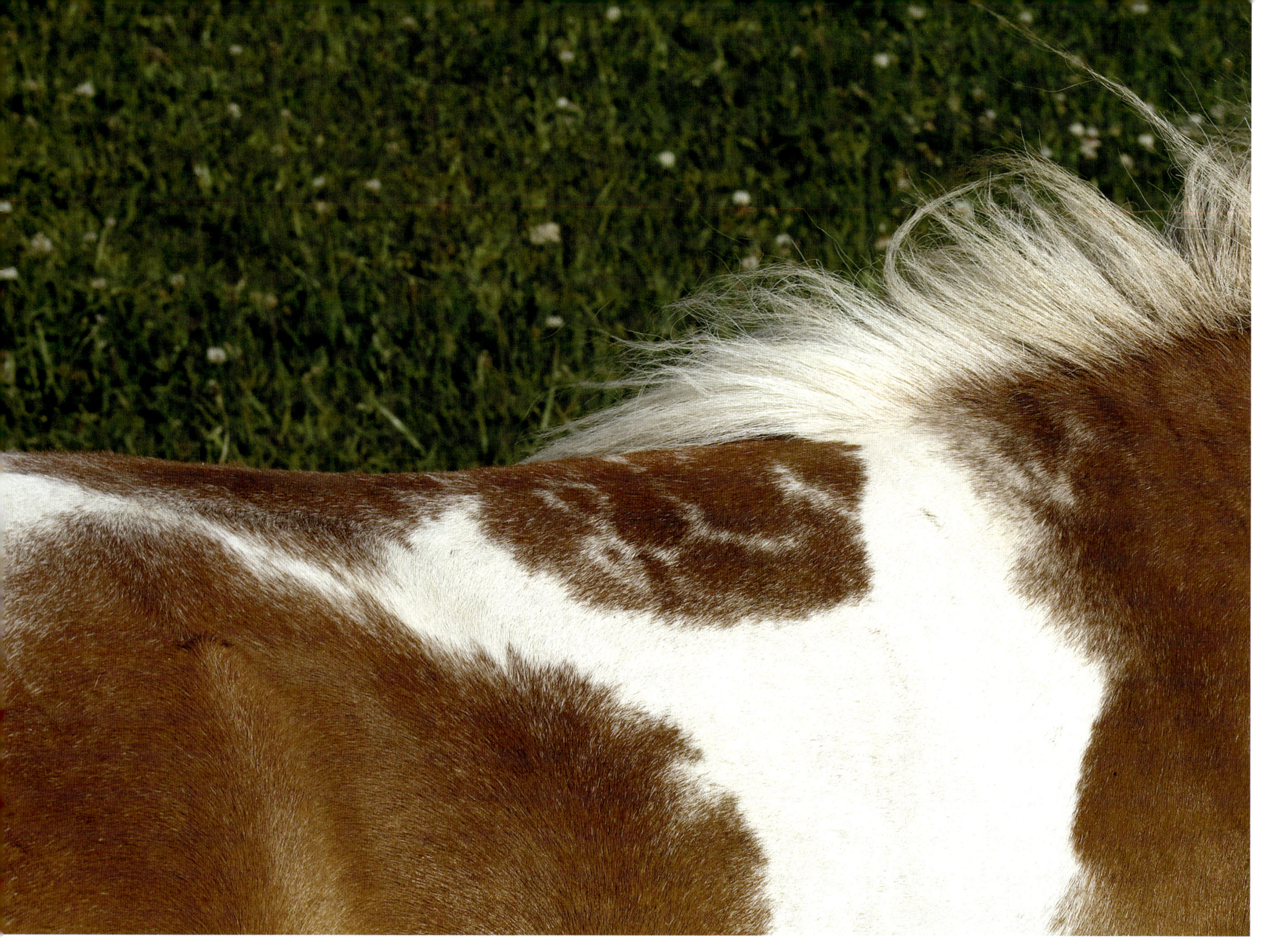

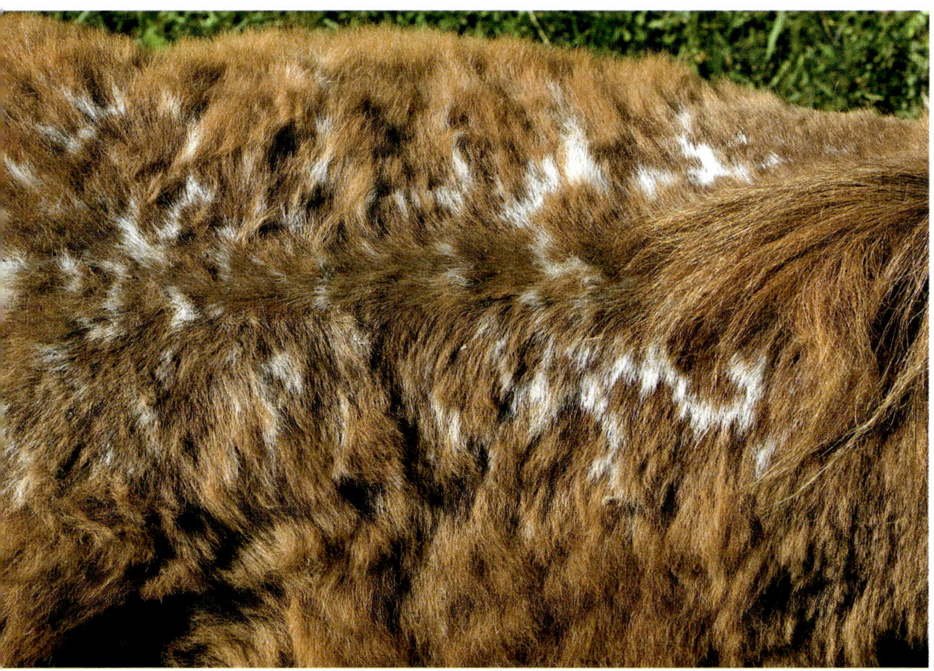

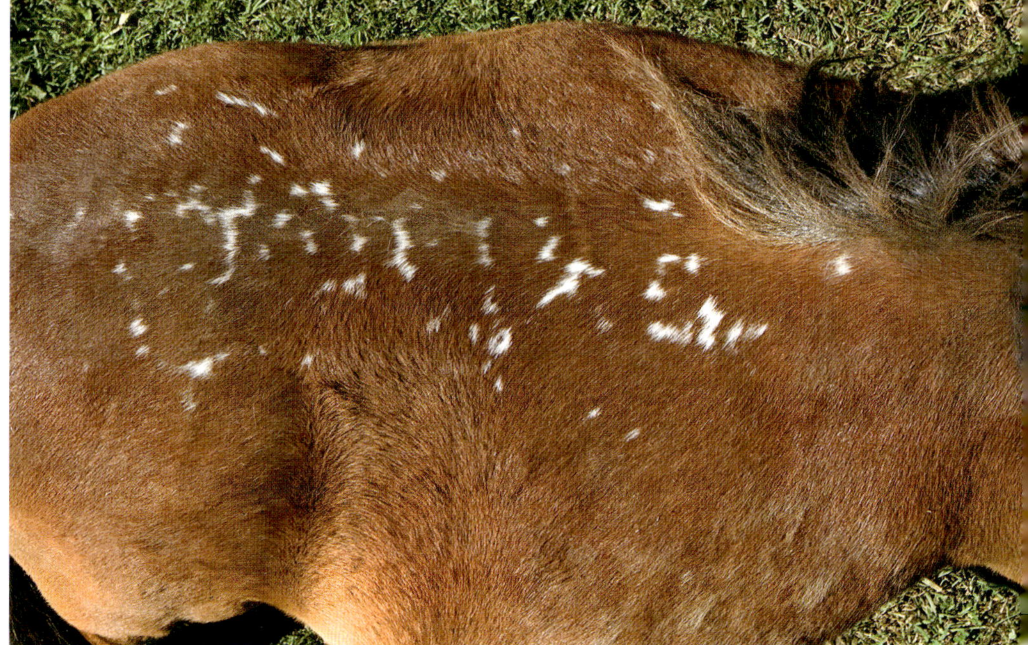

Lacing is a rare pattern, the cause of which is uncertain. It usually appears on yearlings or older horses and spreads across the back in varying degrees. It is more common in Miniature Horses than in most other breeds.

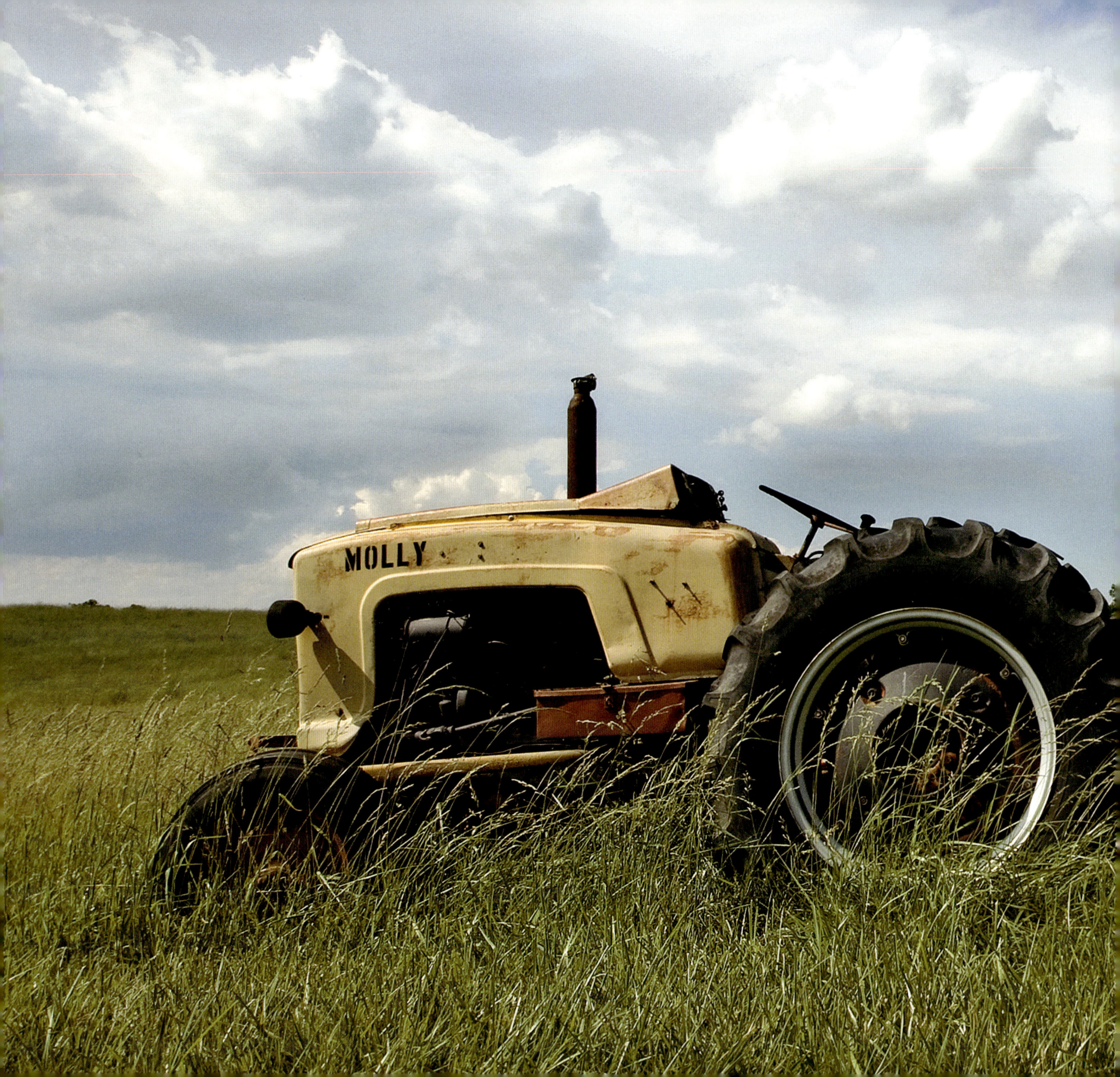
MOLLY

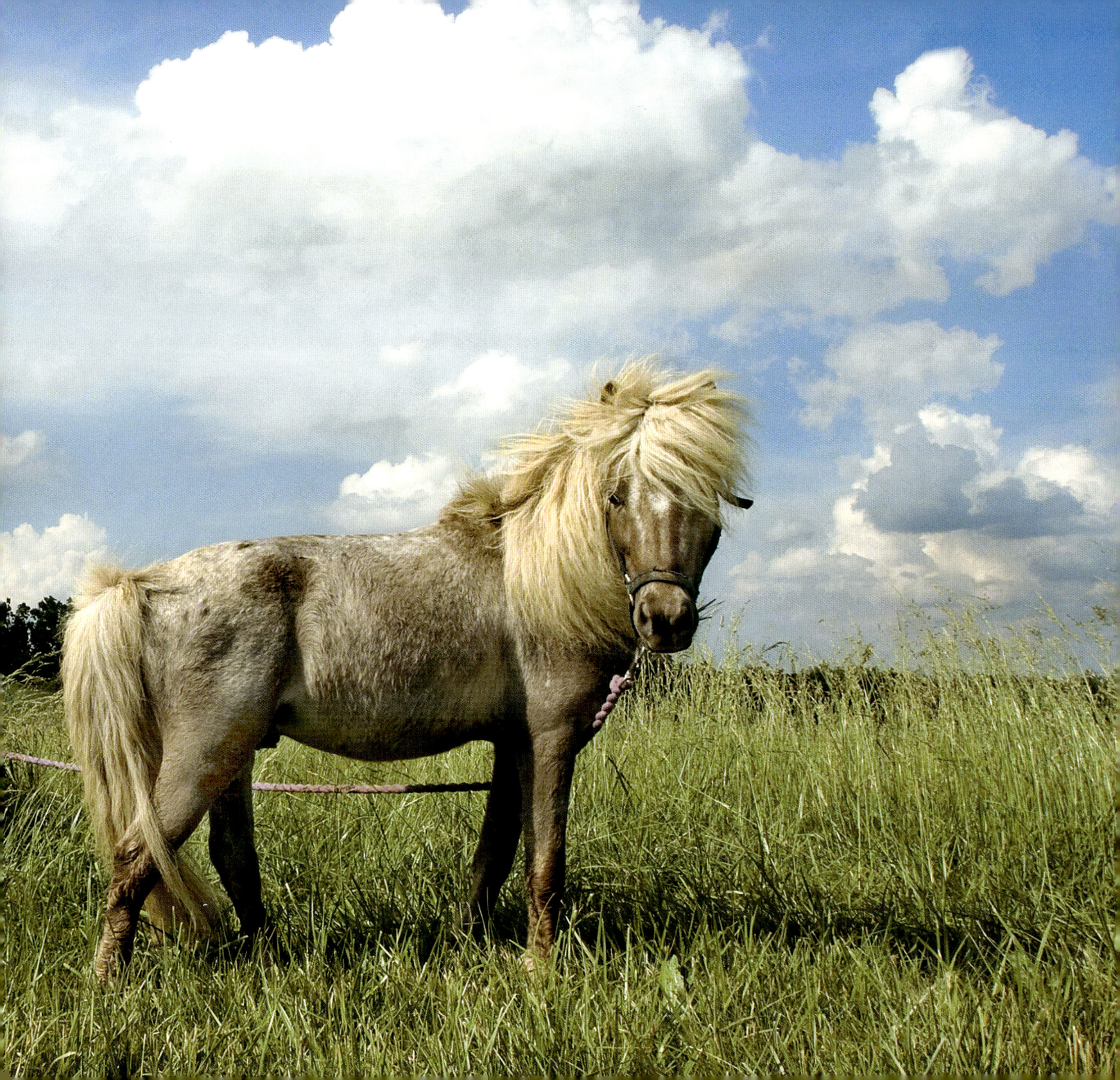

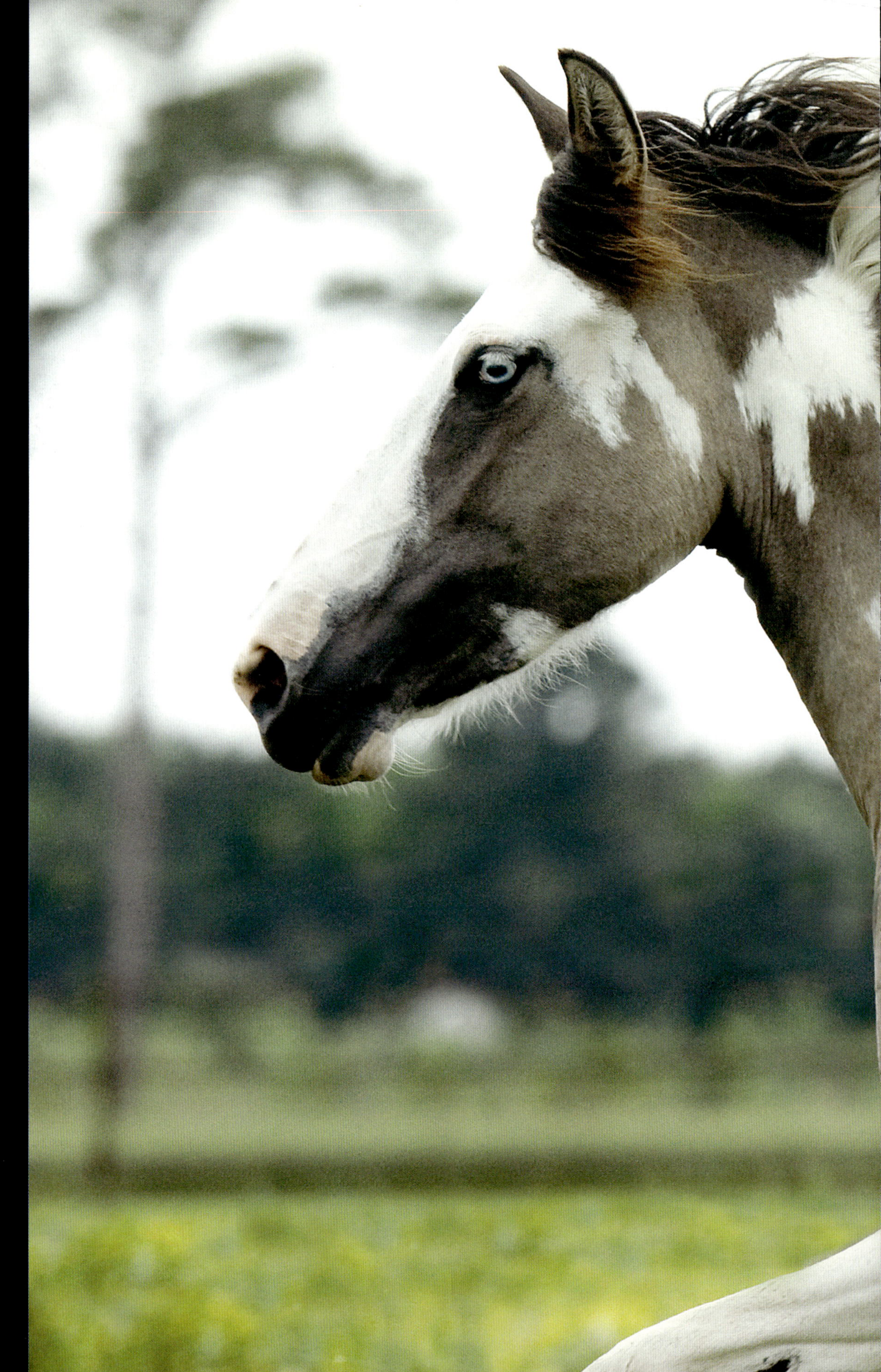

This Colonial Spanish Horse is striking for many reasons, including her pale blue eye, multi-colored mane (see next page), a wide dorsal stripe, and withers stripes.

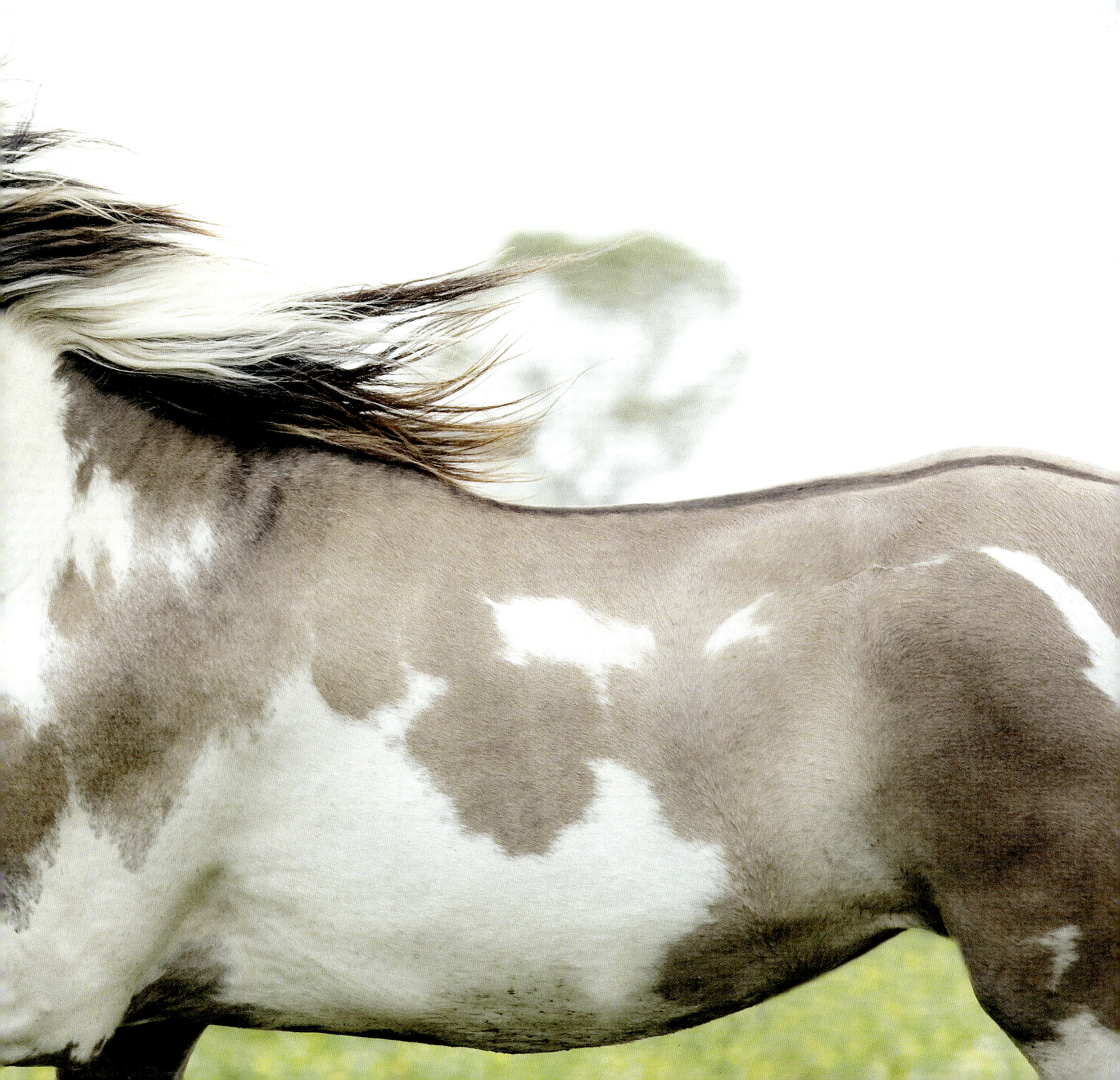

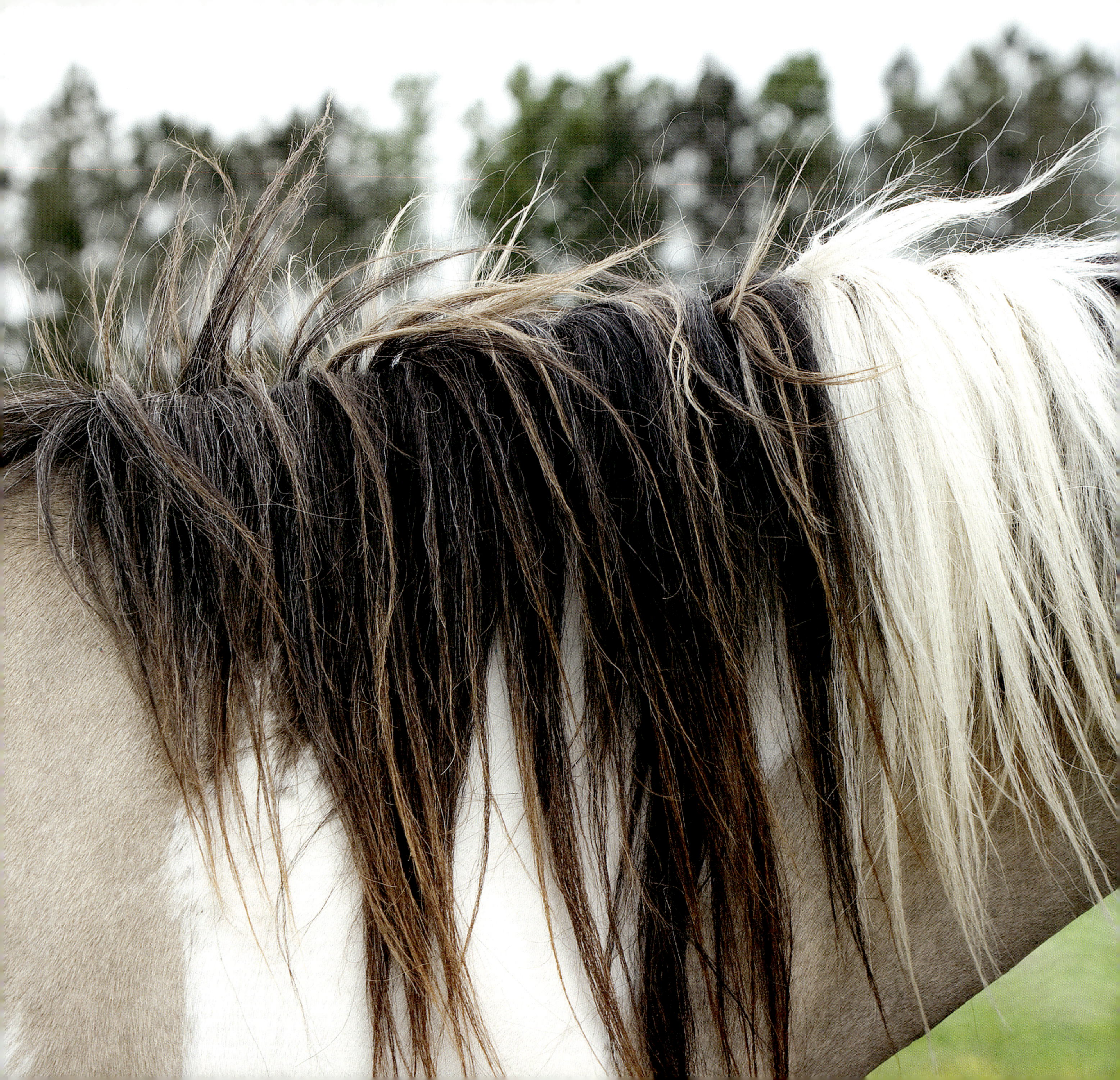

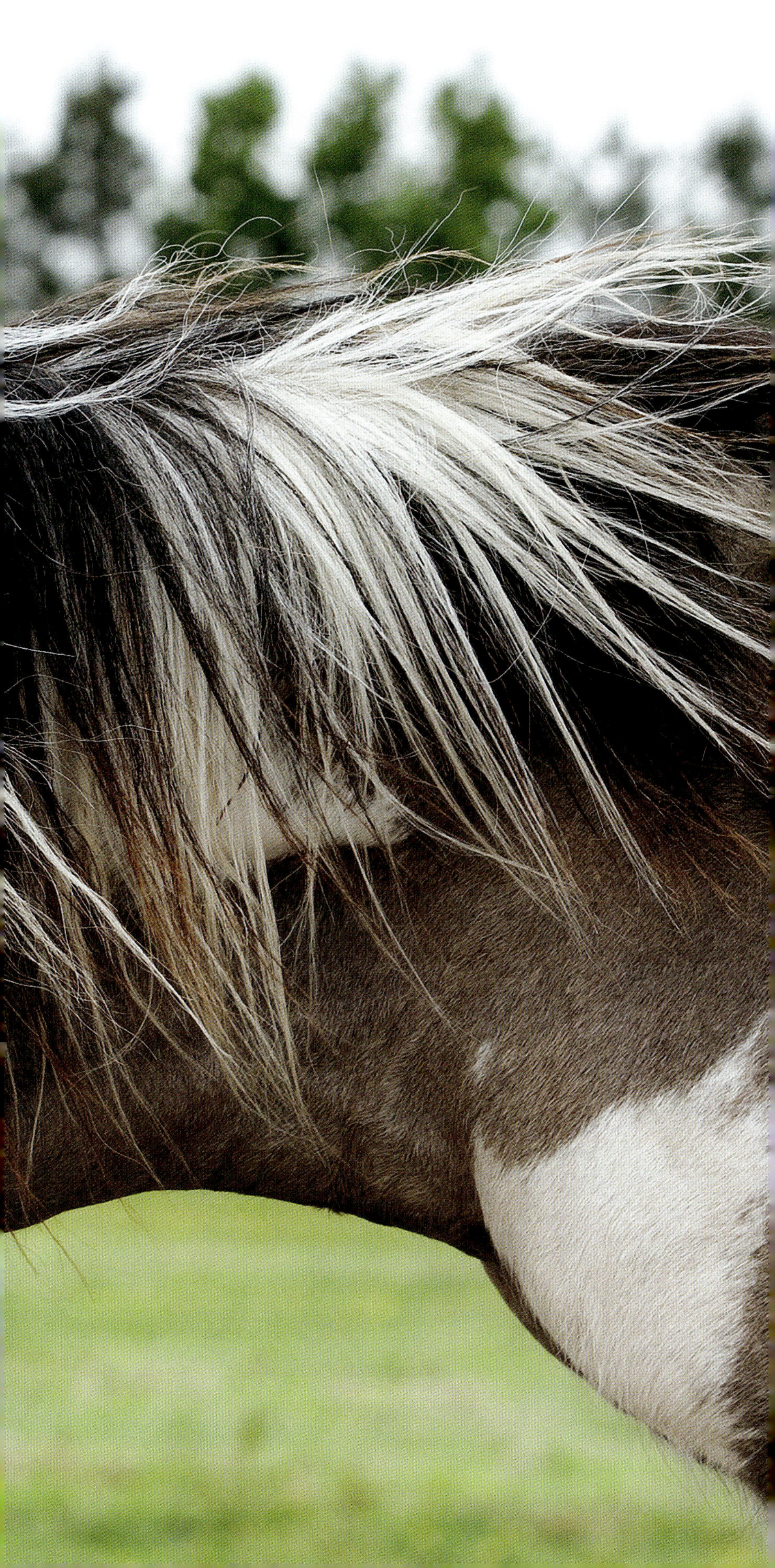

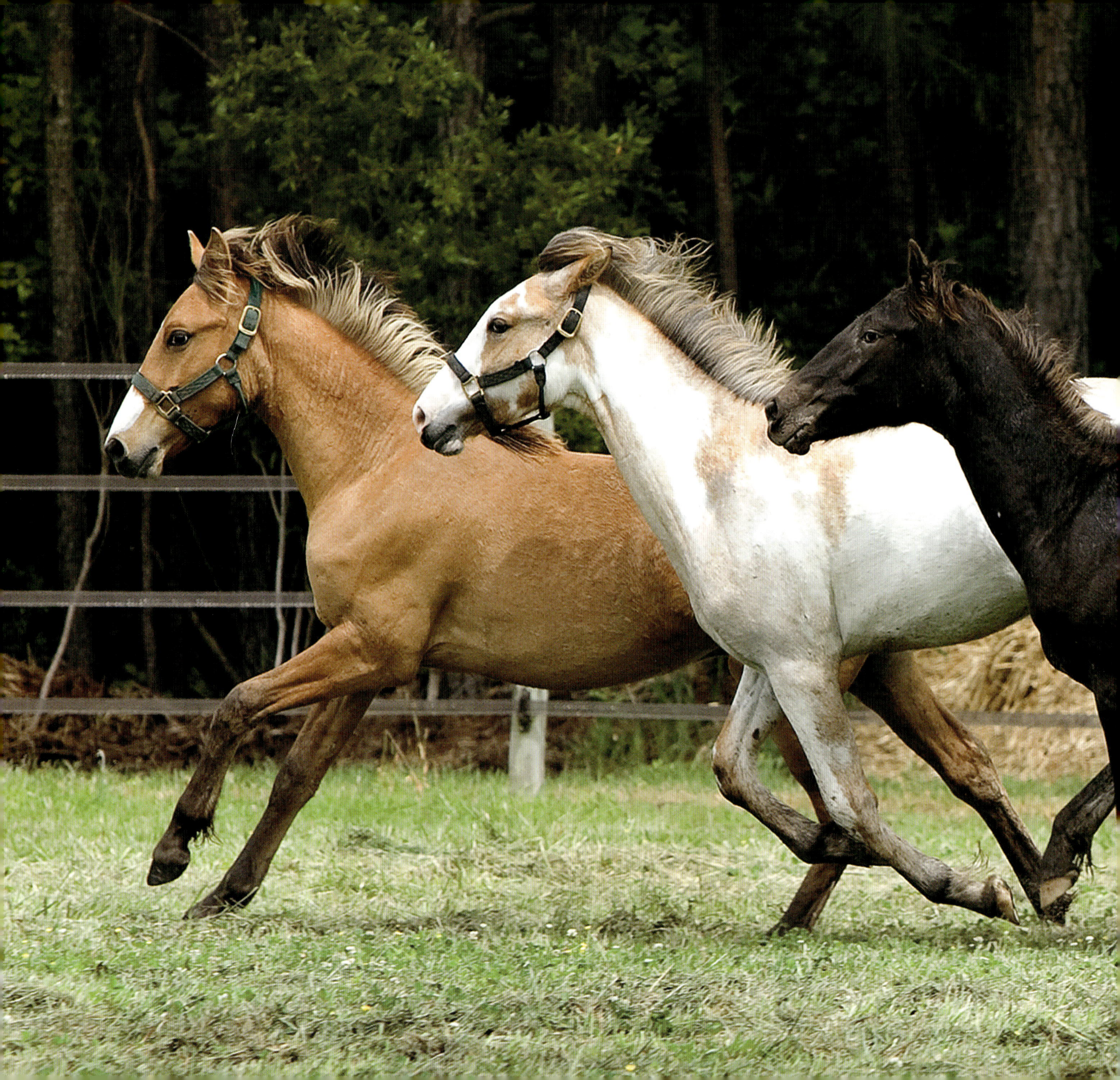

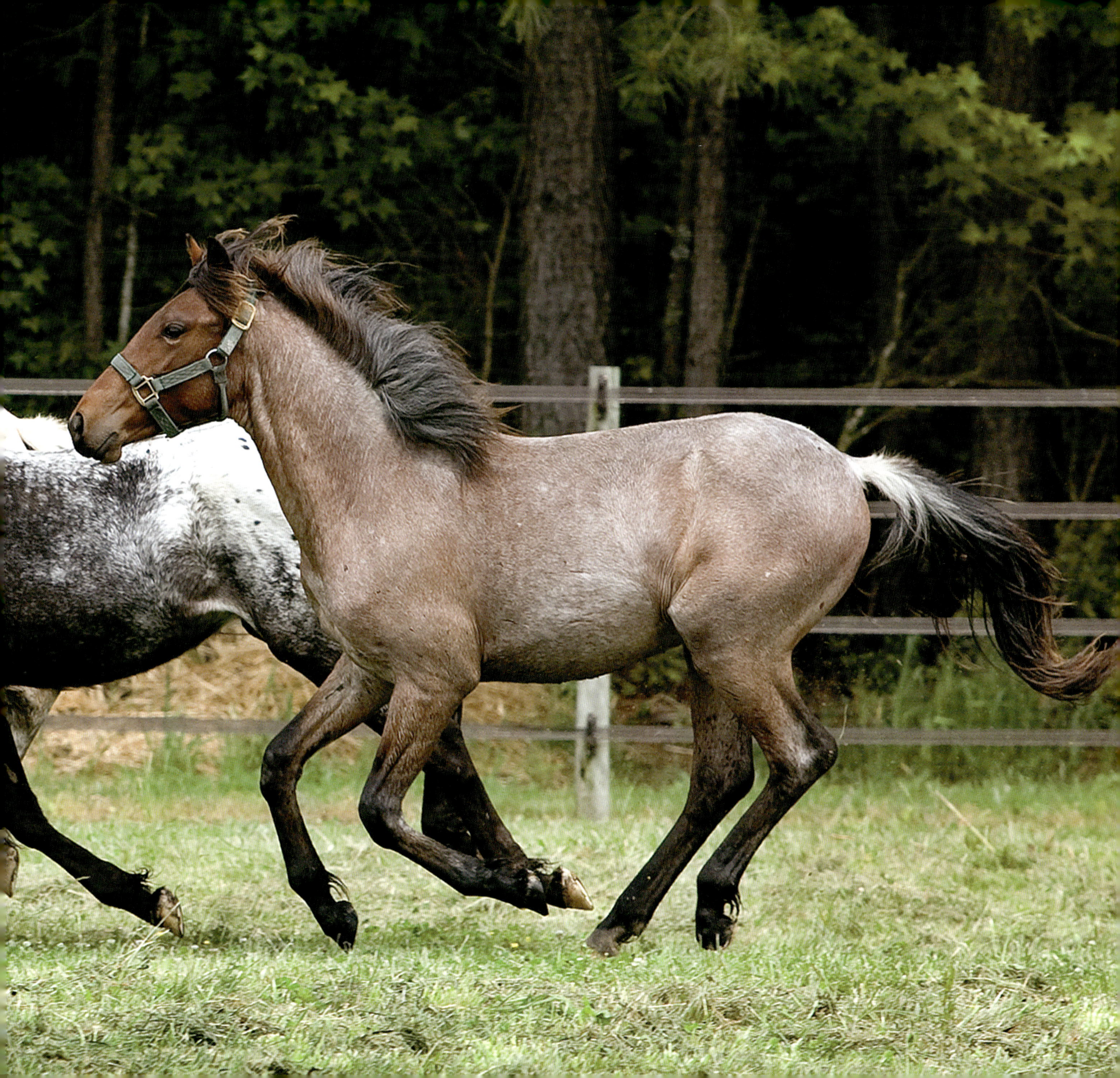

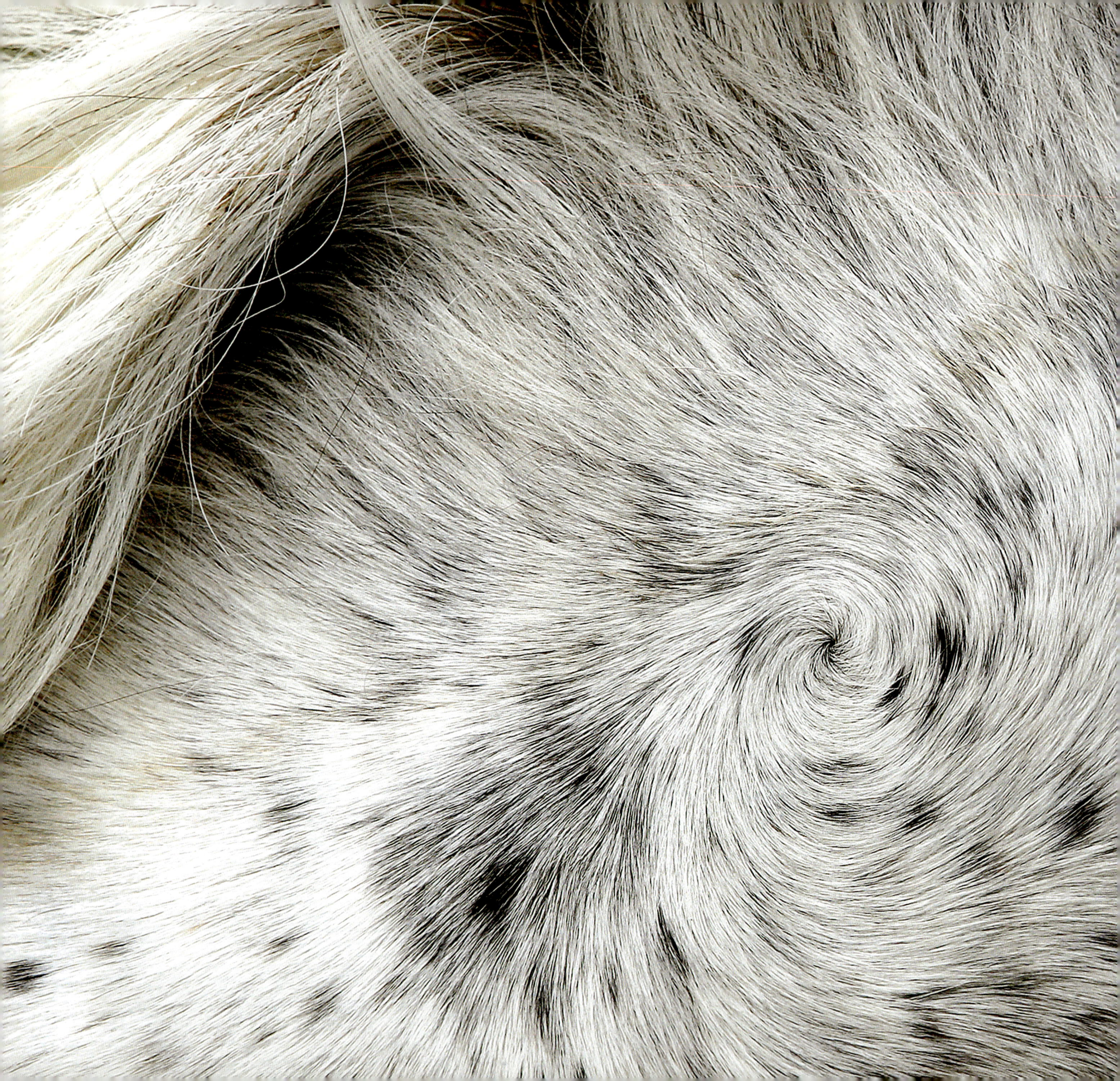

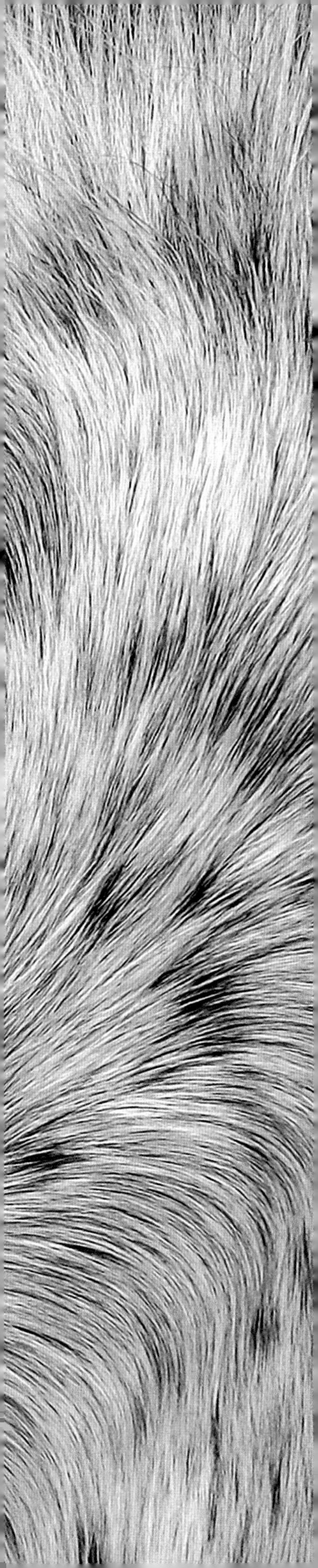

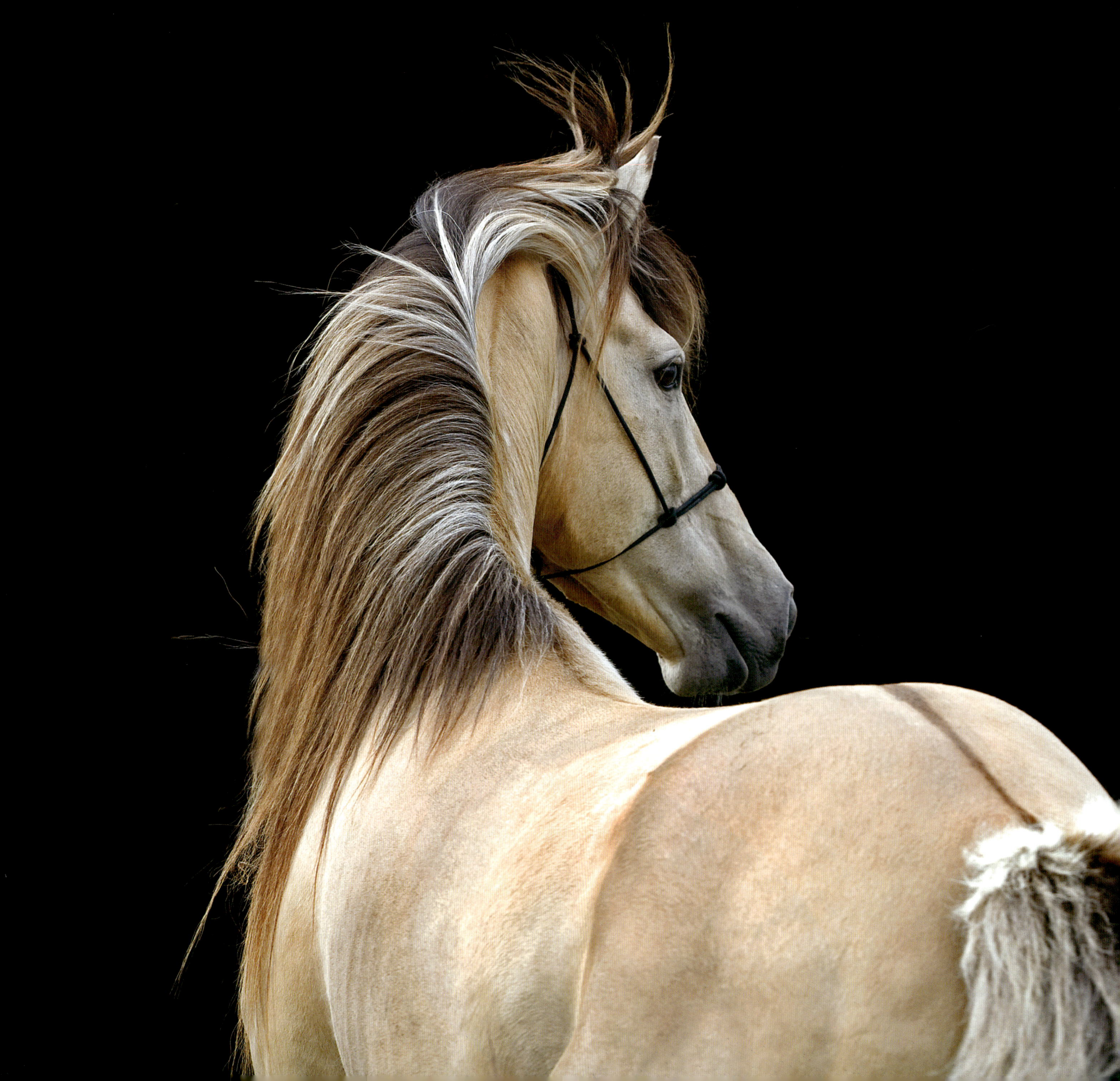

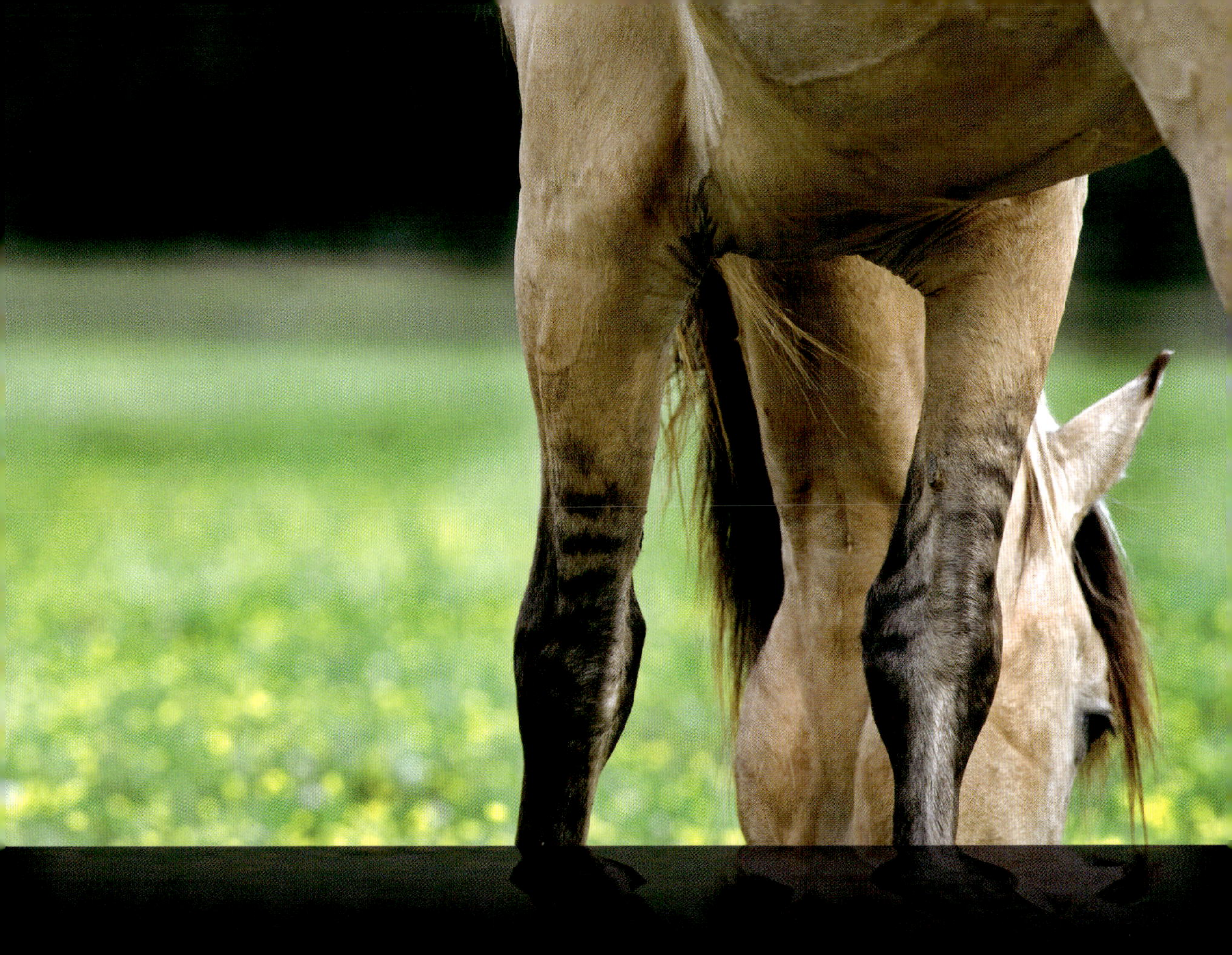

Among the unusual features of this Colonial Spanish Horse stallion (this and following spread) are his prominent dorsal stripe, tiger stripes on his legs, a withers stripe, and a multi-colored mane and tail. The striped markings are called primitive marks.

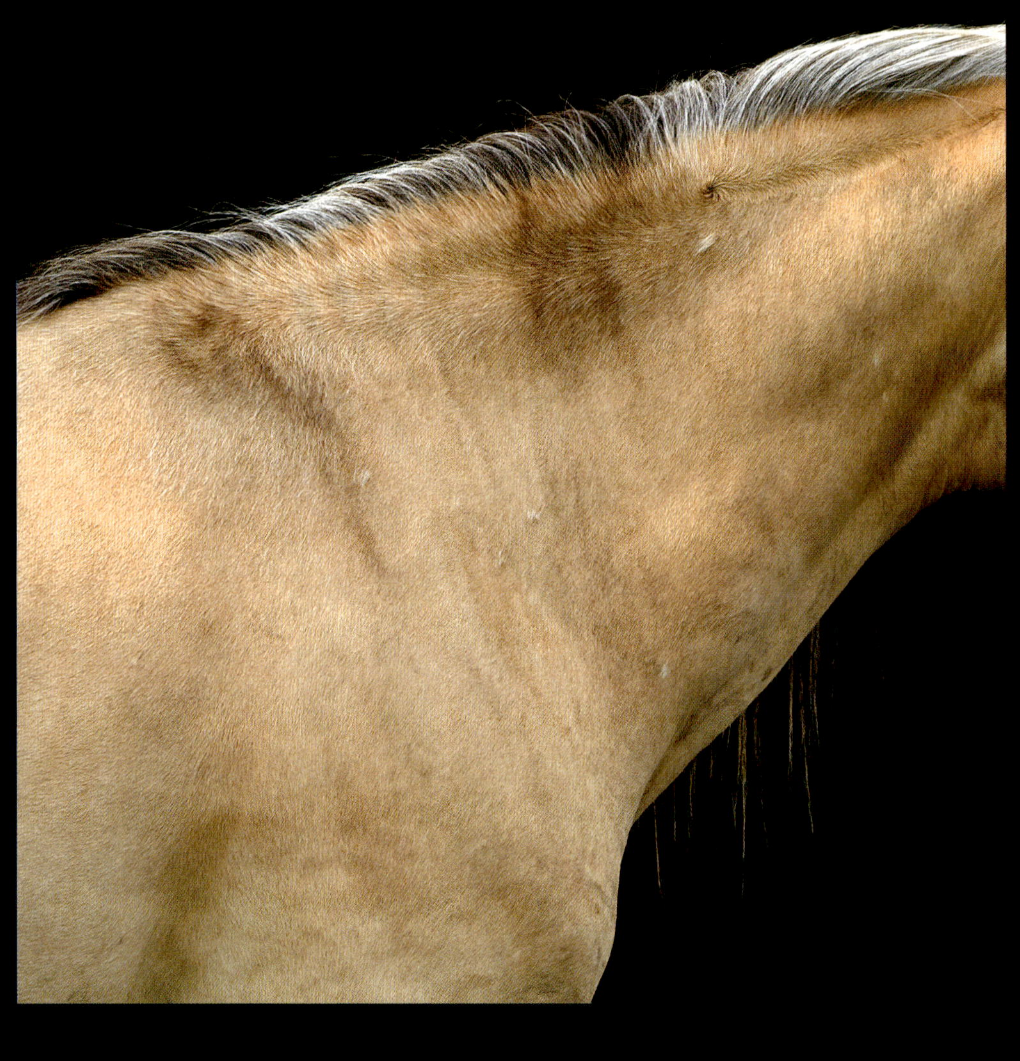

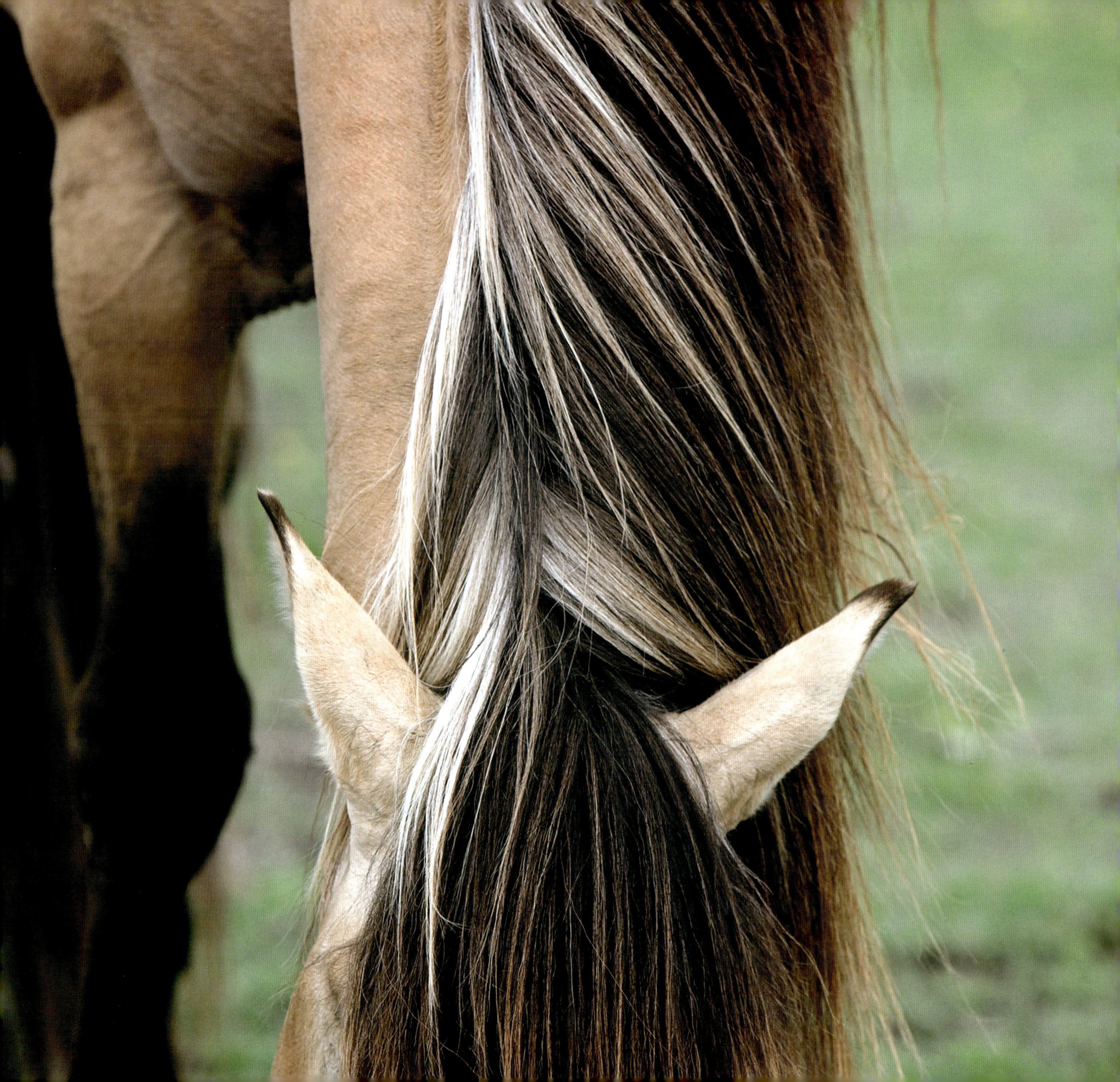

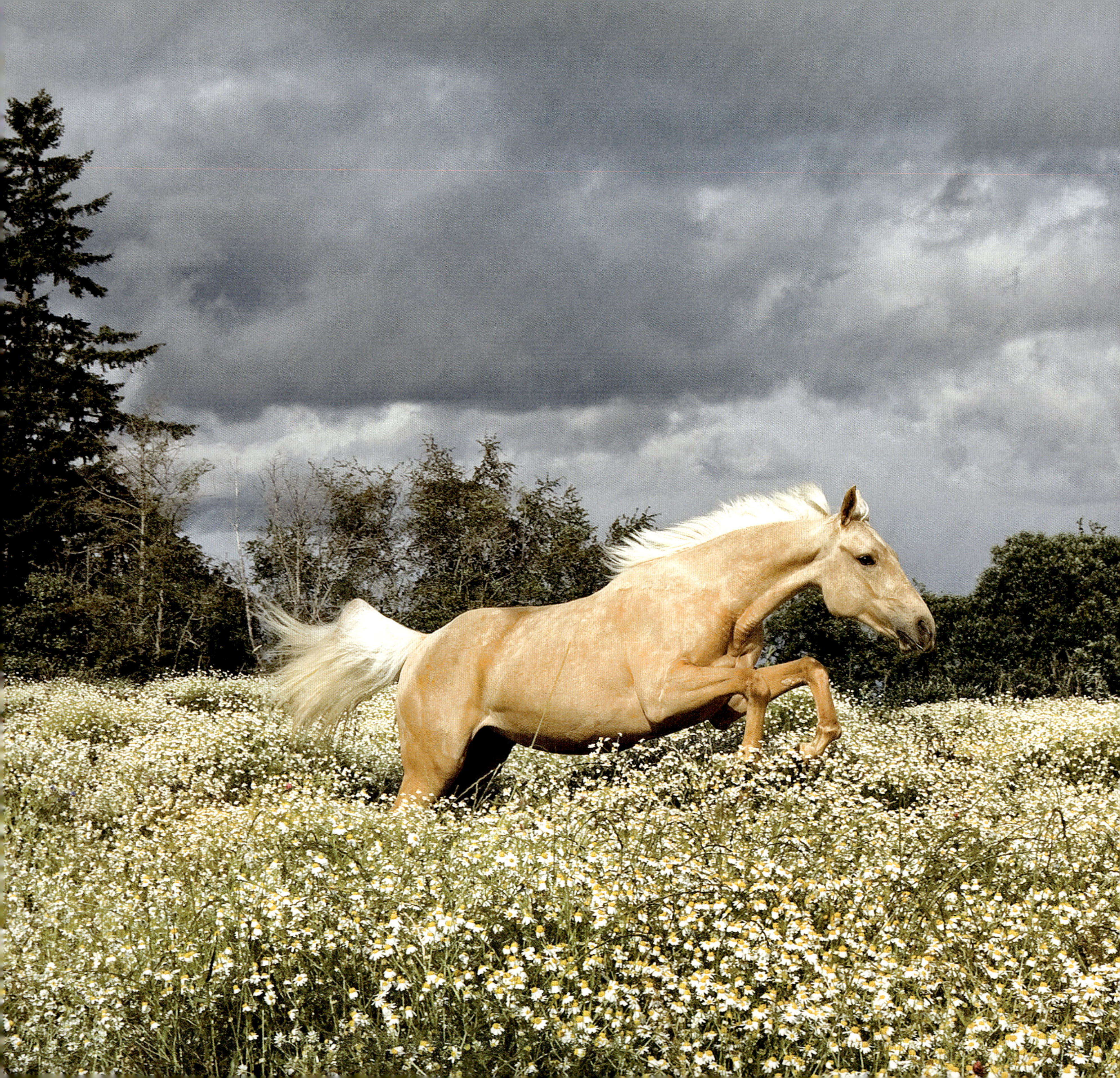

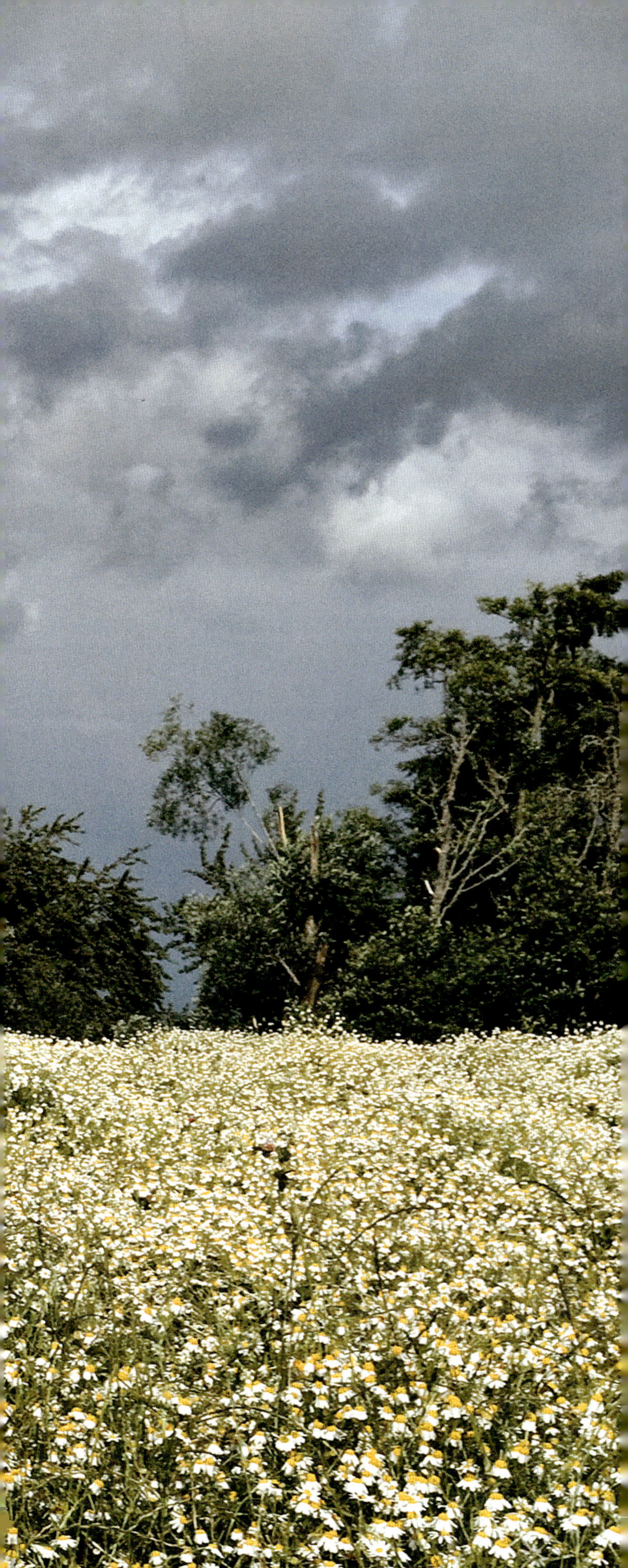

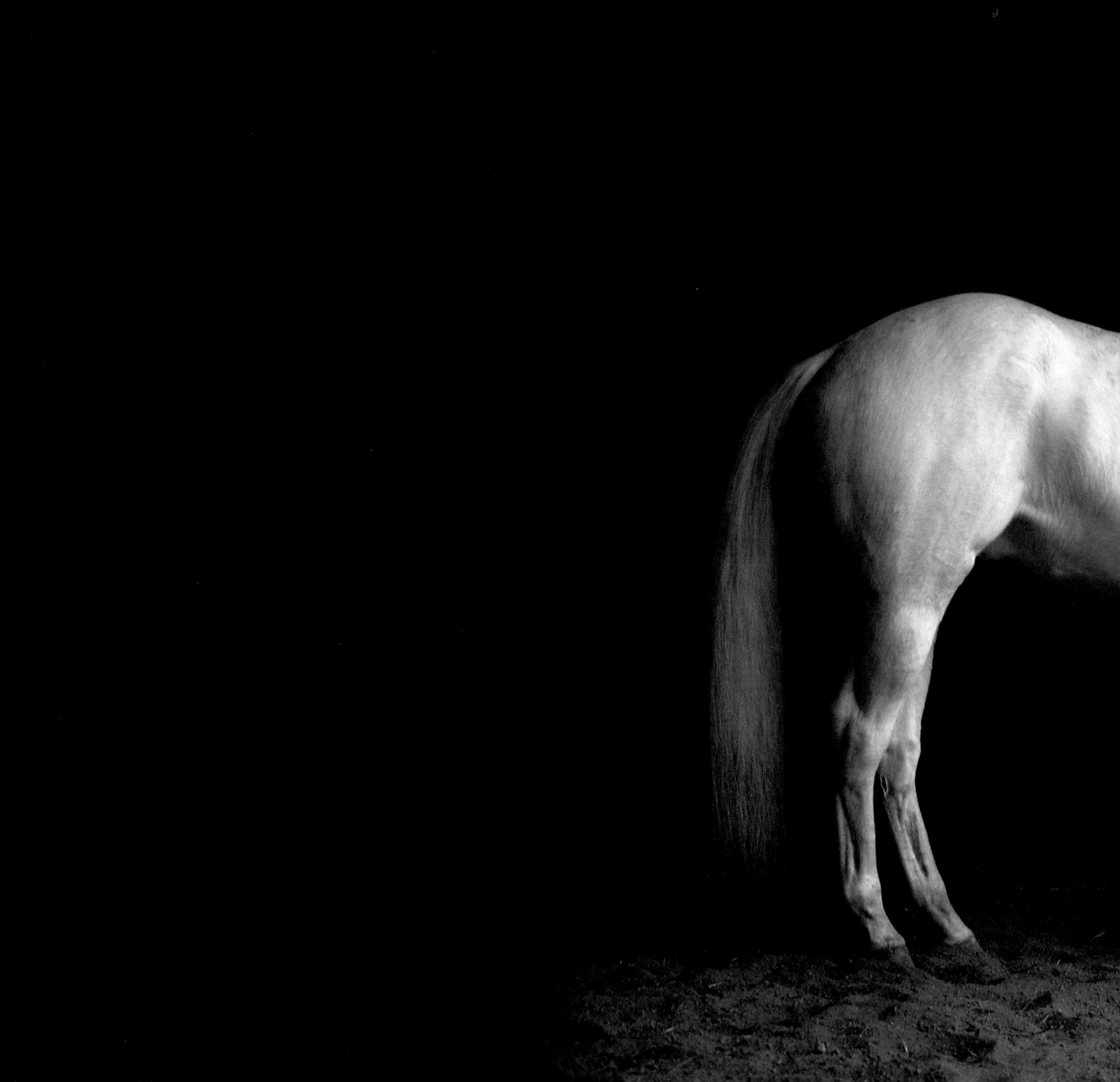

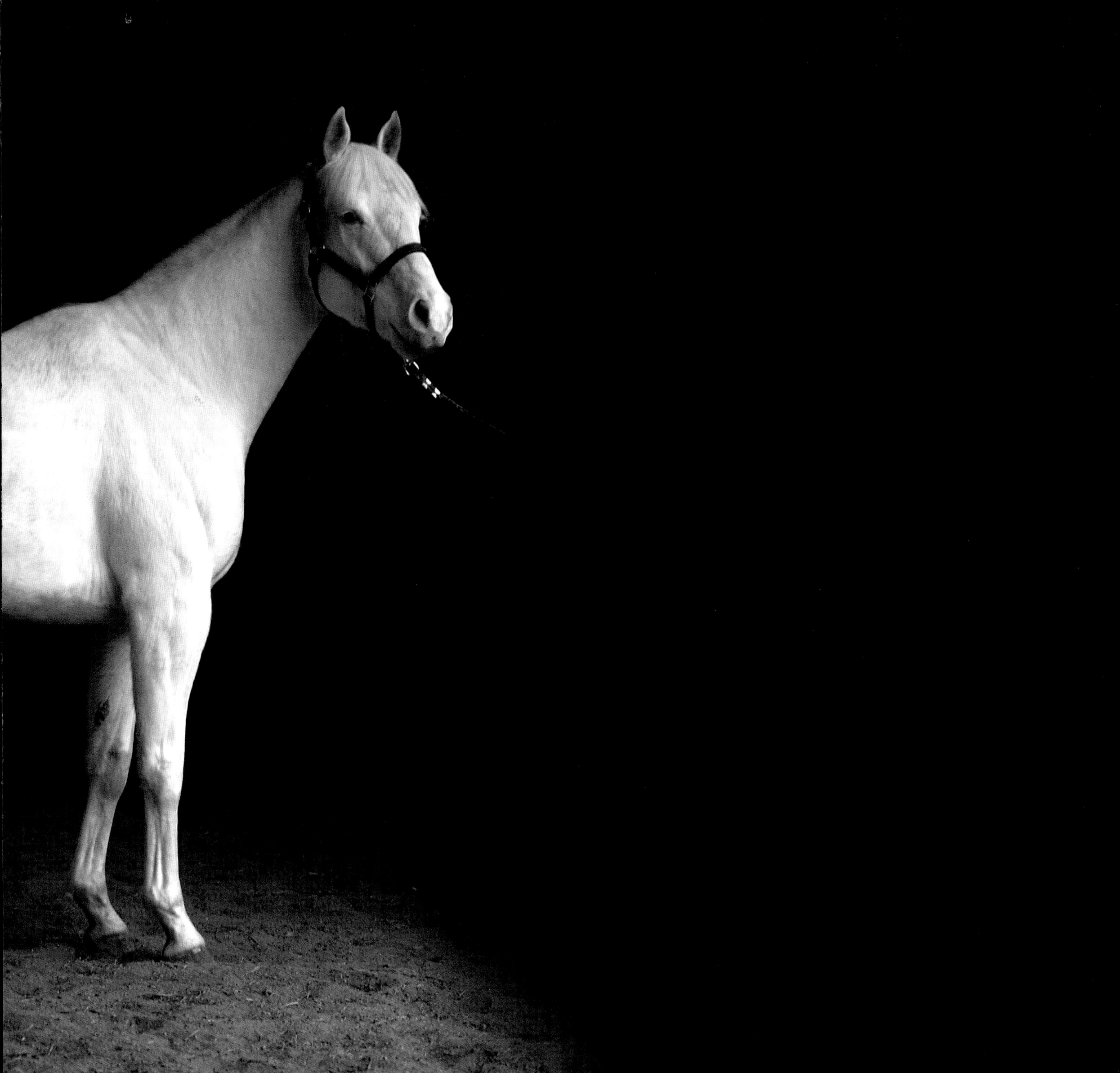

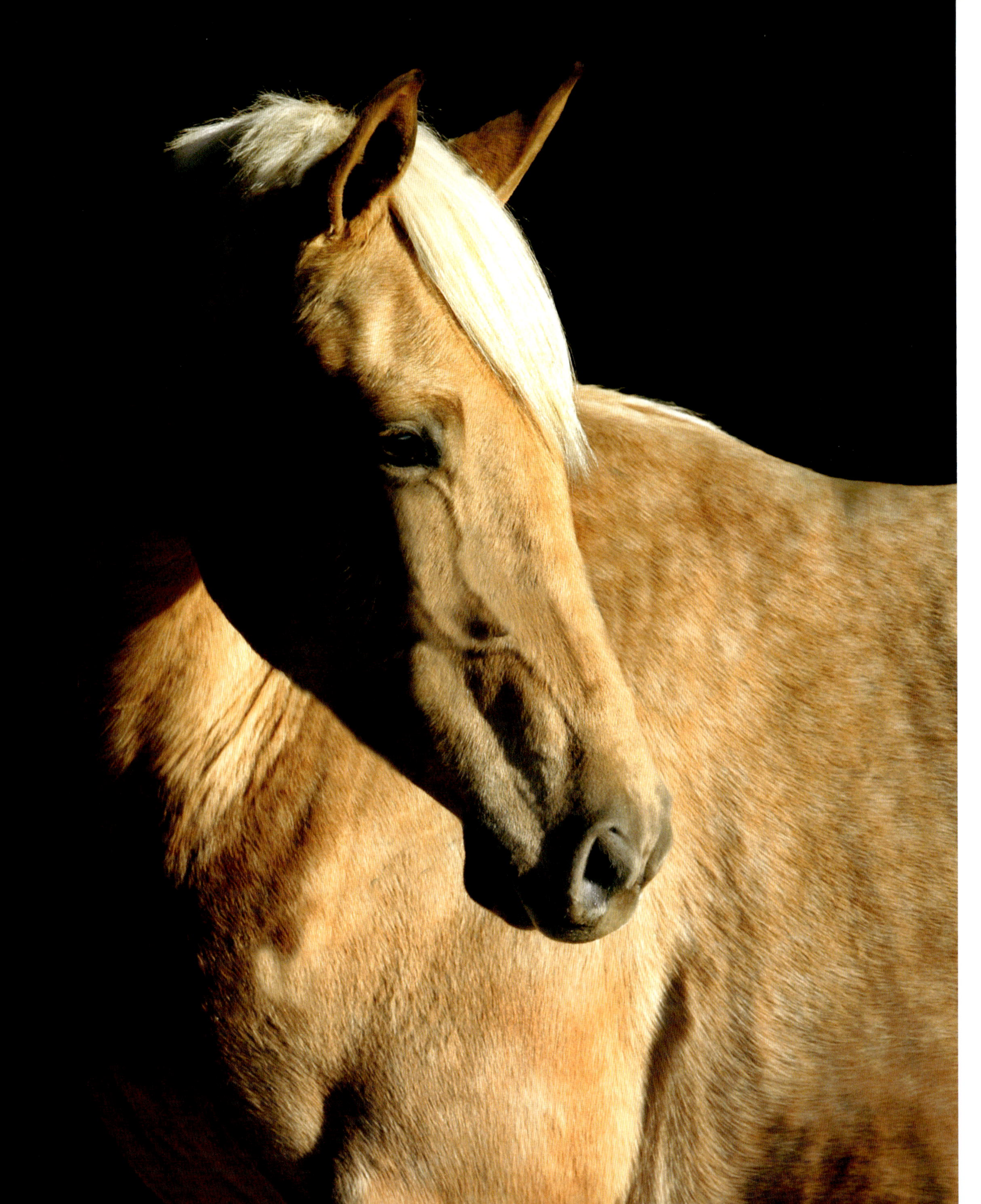

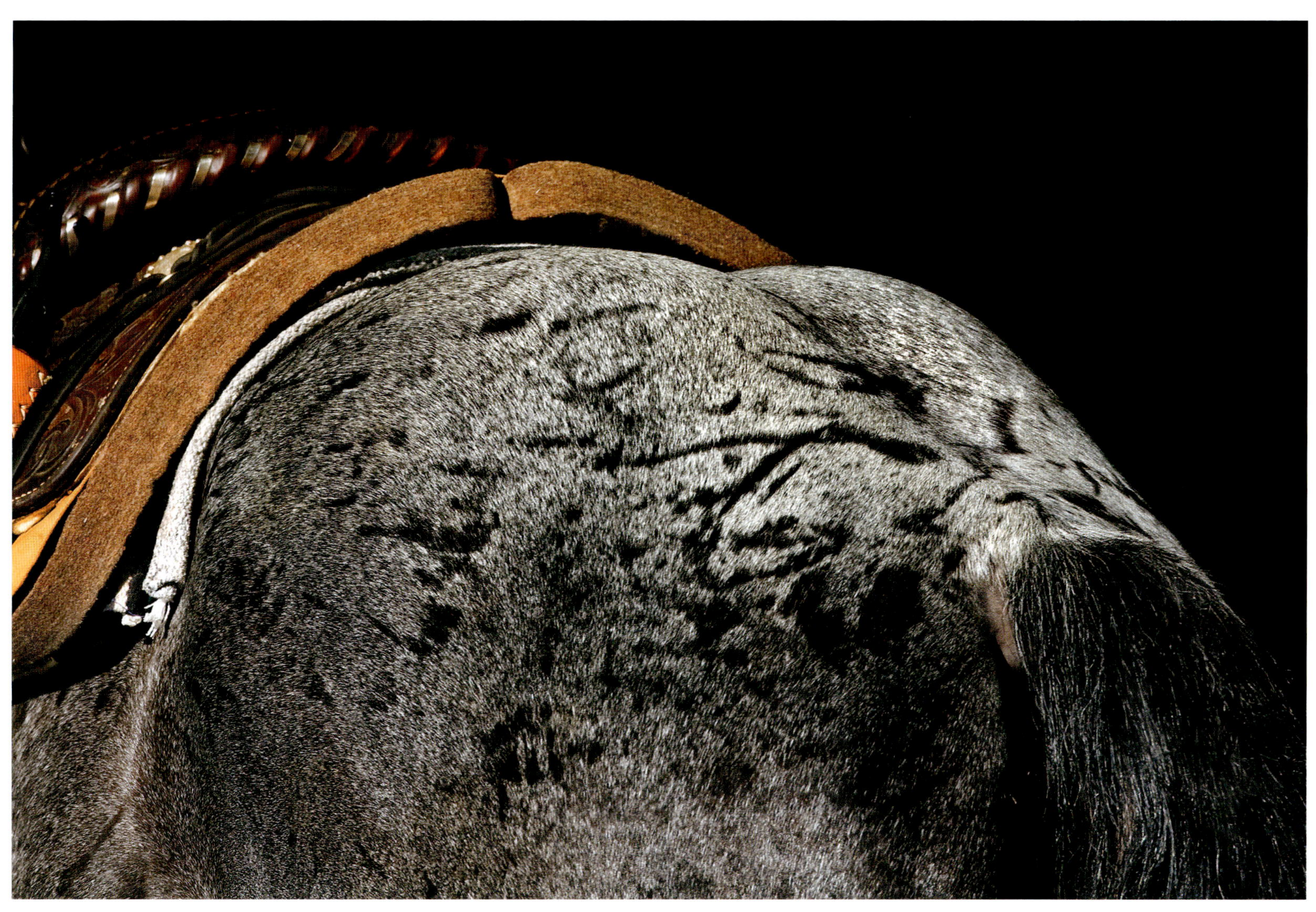

Dark spots occurring on roan horses — whether genetically based or due to scarring — are called corn spots.

The Thoroughbred stallion at right, registered as dark bay or brown, is genetically unable to produce chestnut offspring. Nearly all of his foals, such as the two pictured, are registered as bay or dark bay/brown. Occasionally, when mated to grey mares, he will also sire a grey foal.

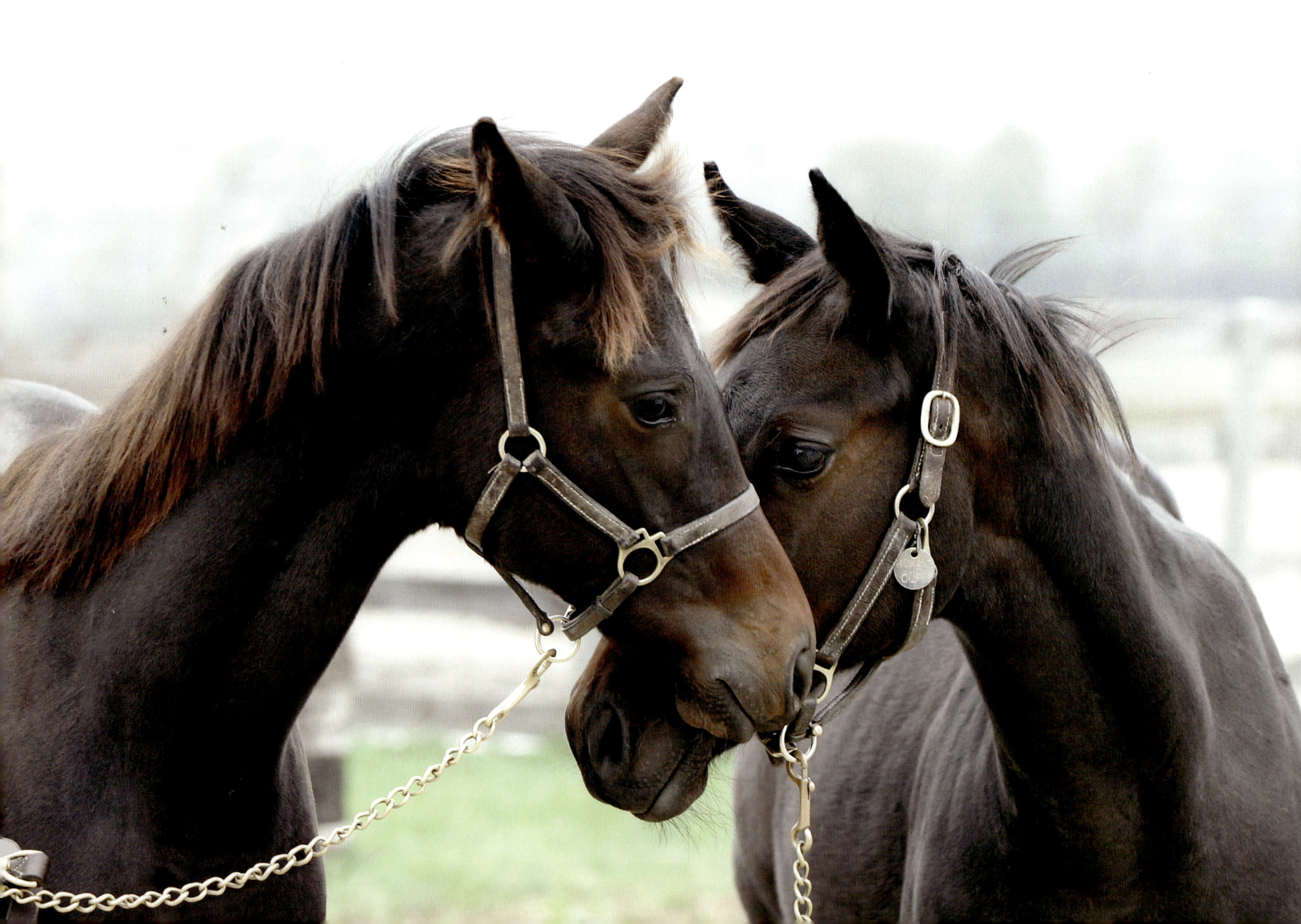

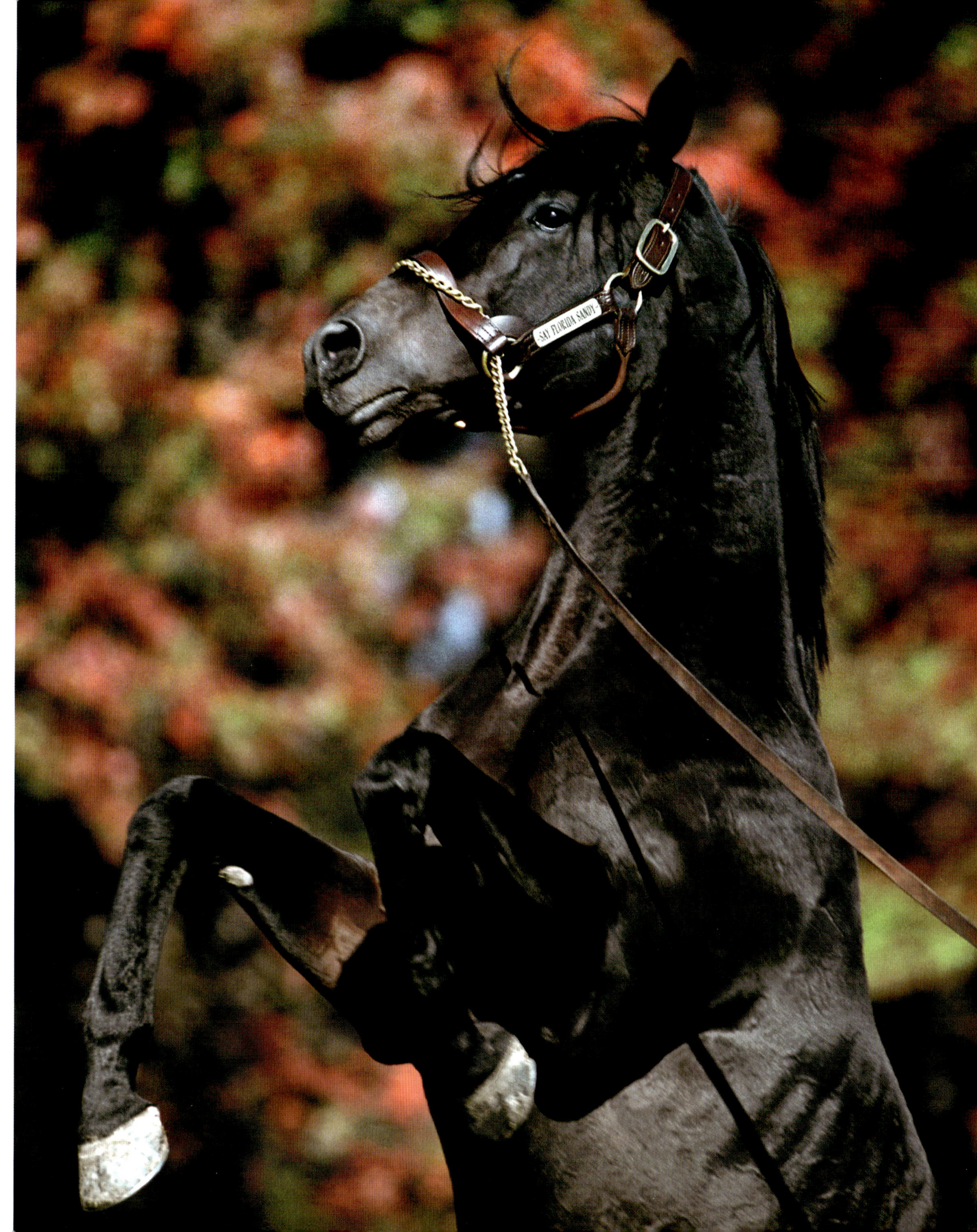
SAY FLORIDA SANDY

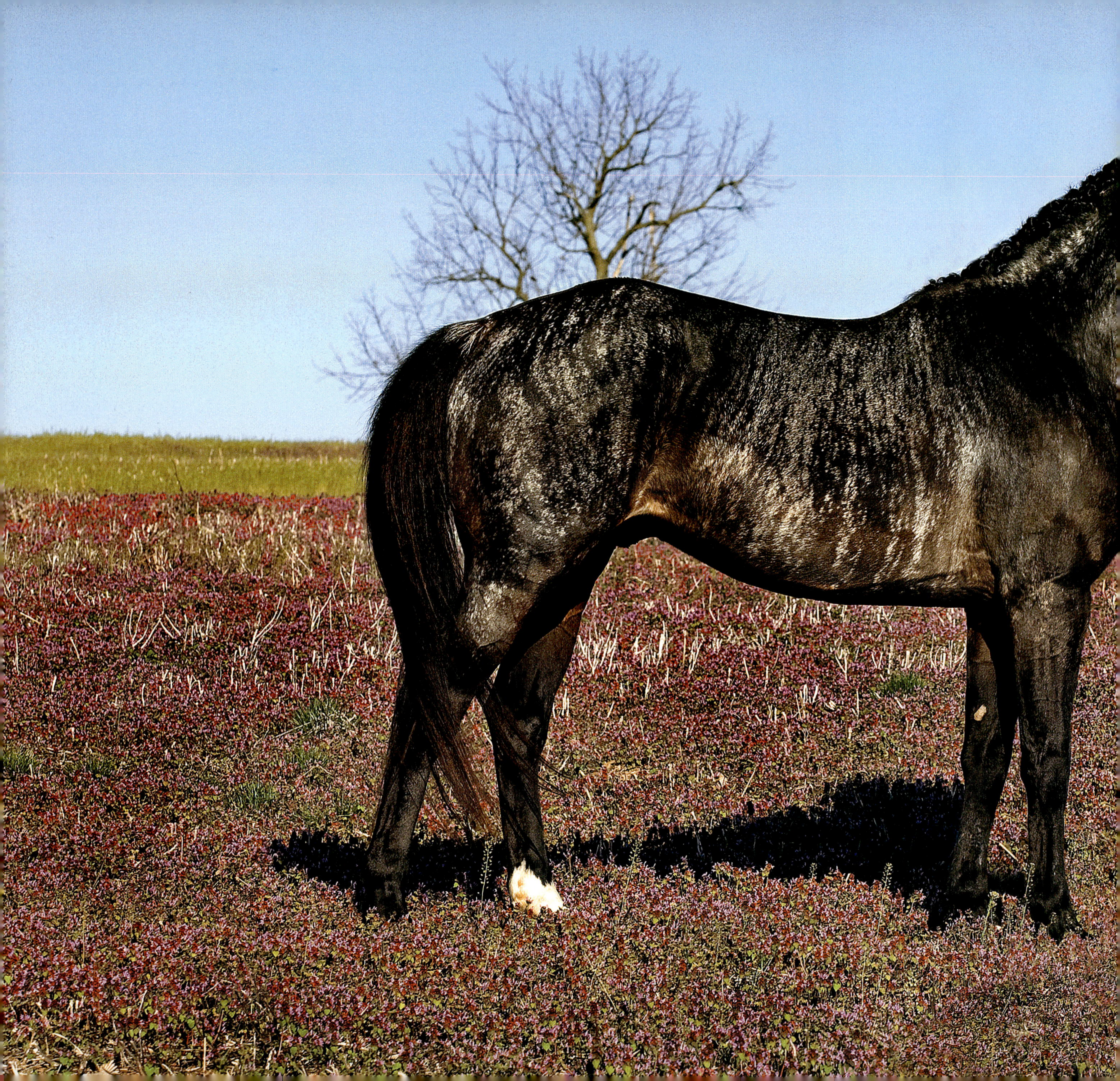

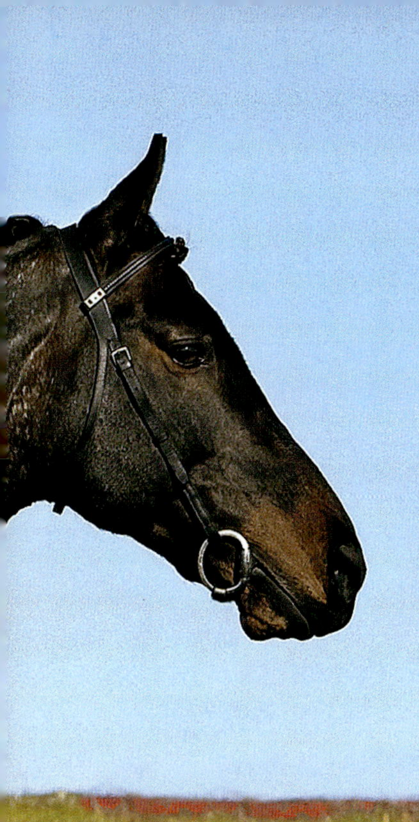

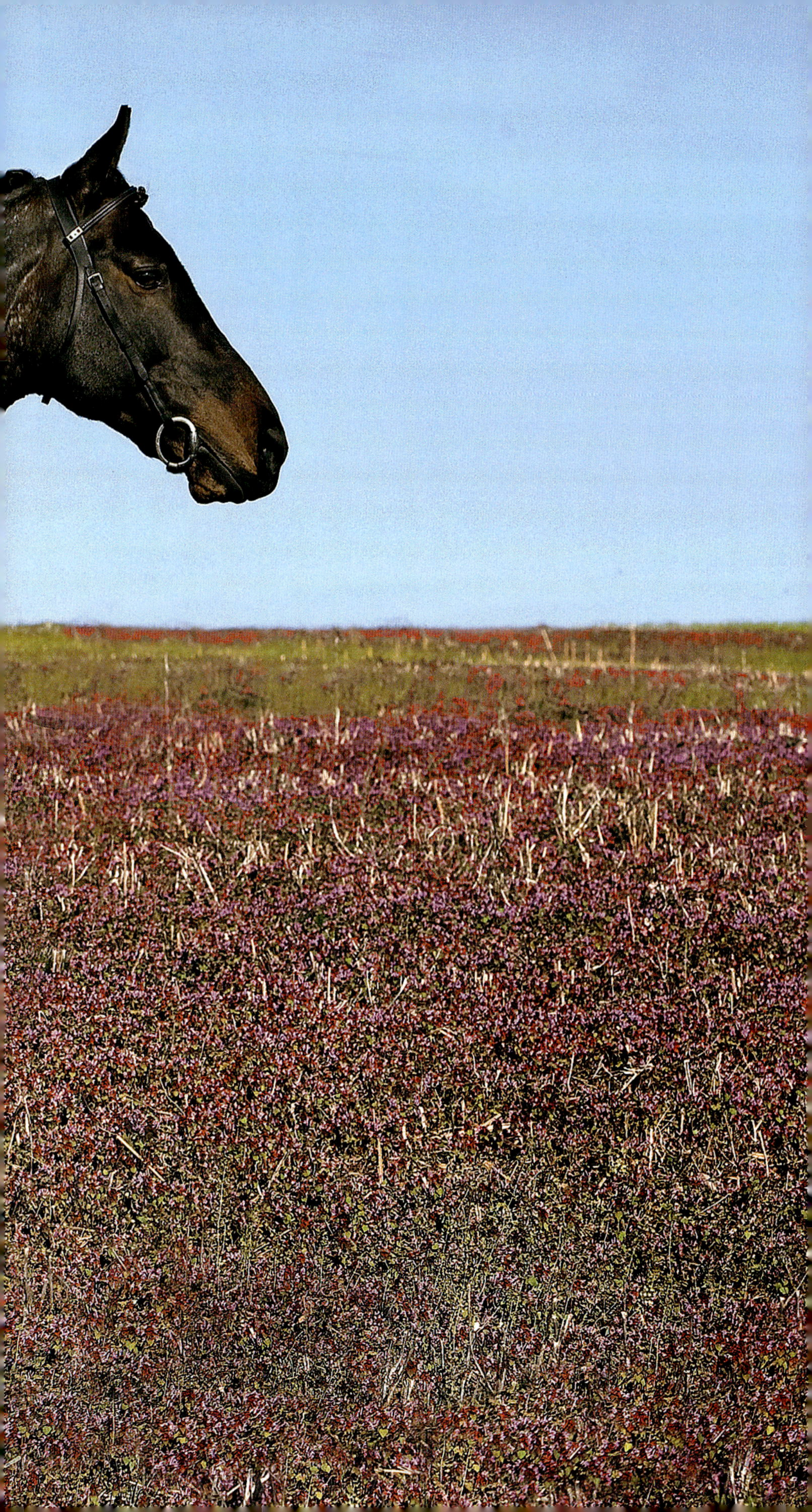

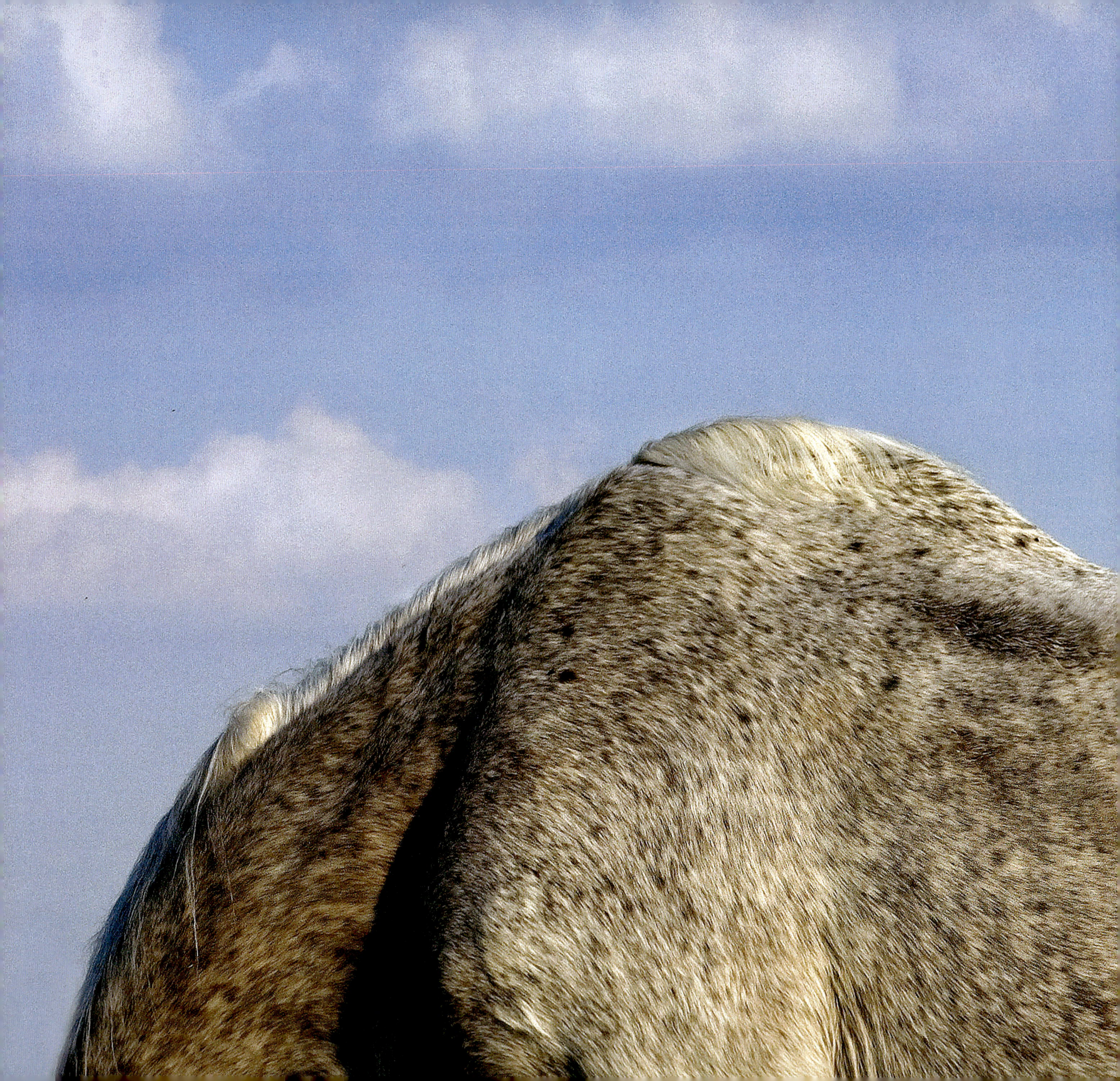

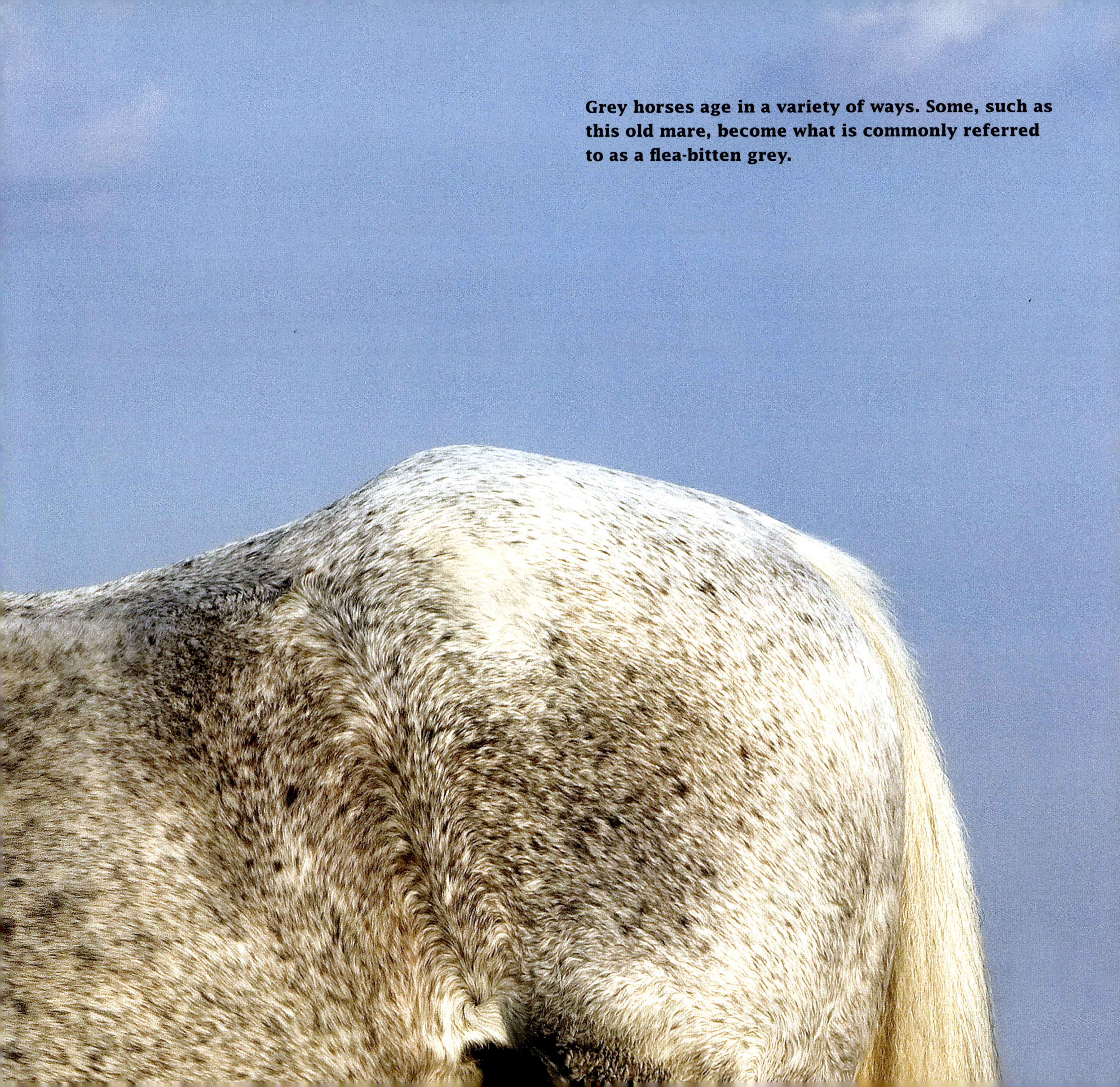

Grey horses age in a variety of ways. Some, such as this old mare, become what is commonly referred to as a flea-bitten grey.

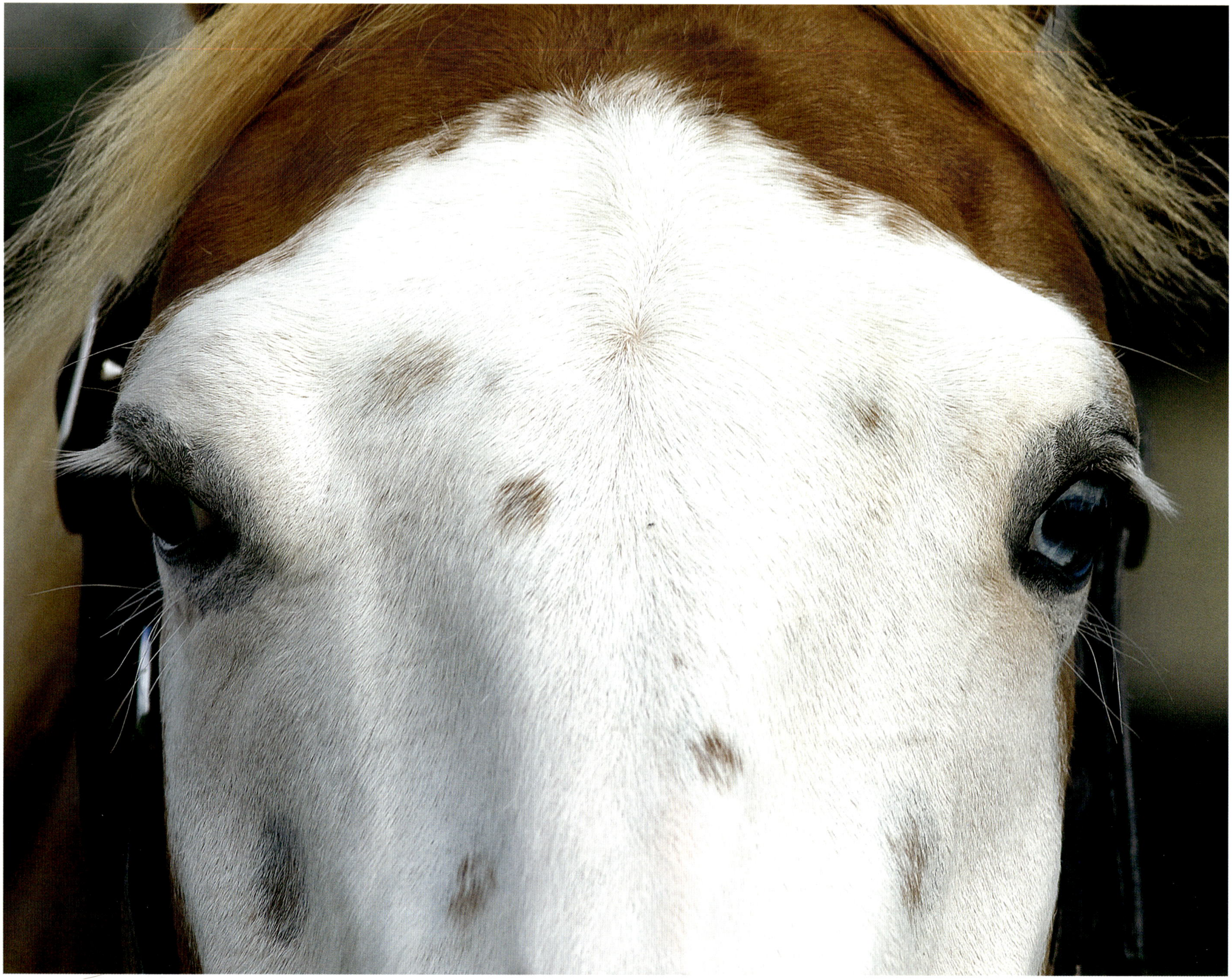

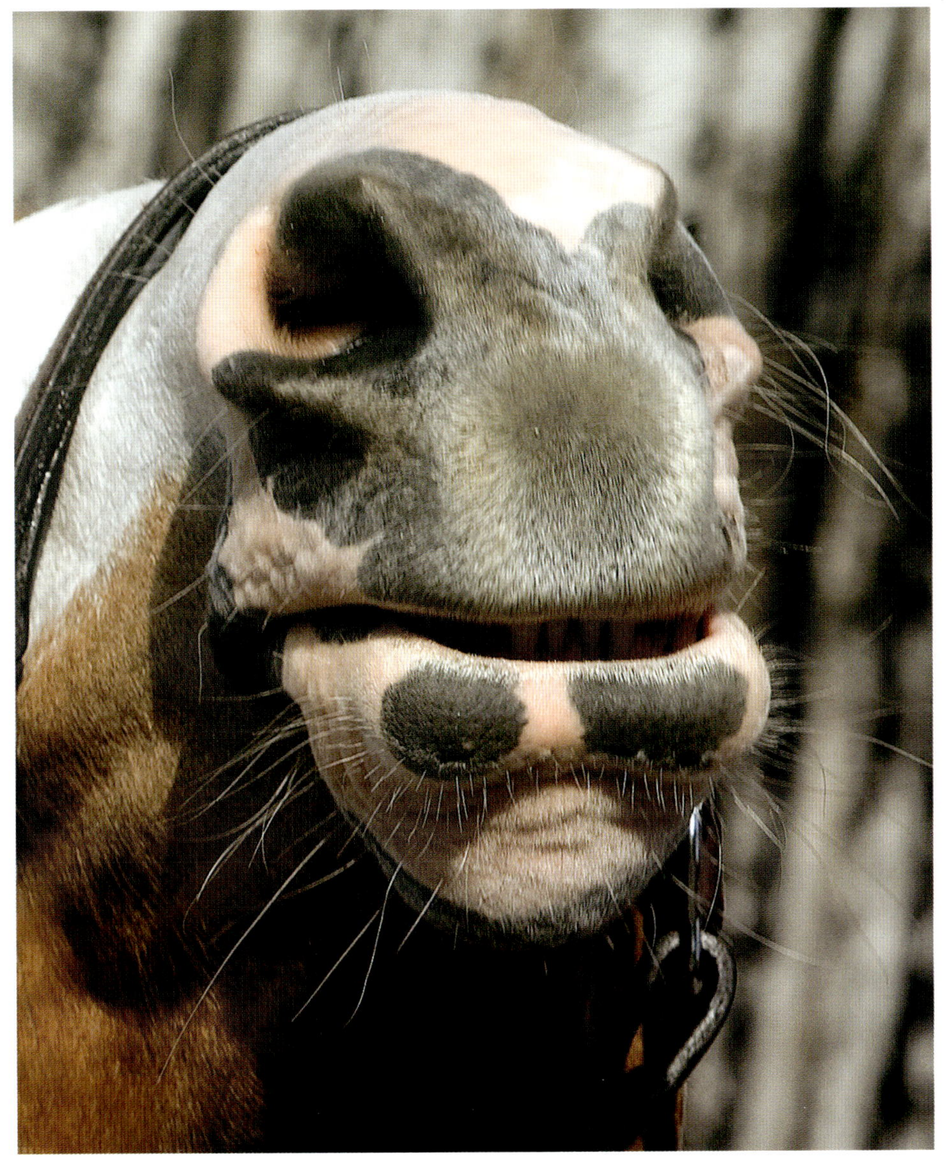

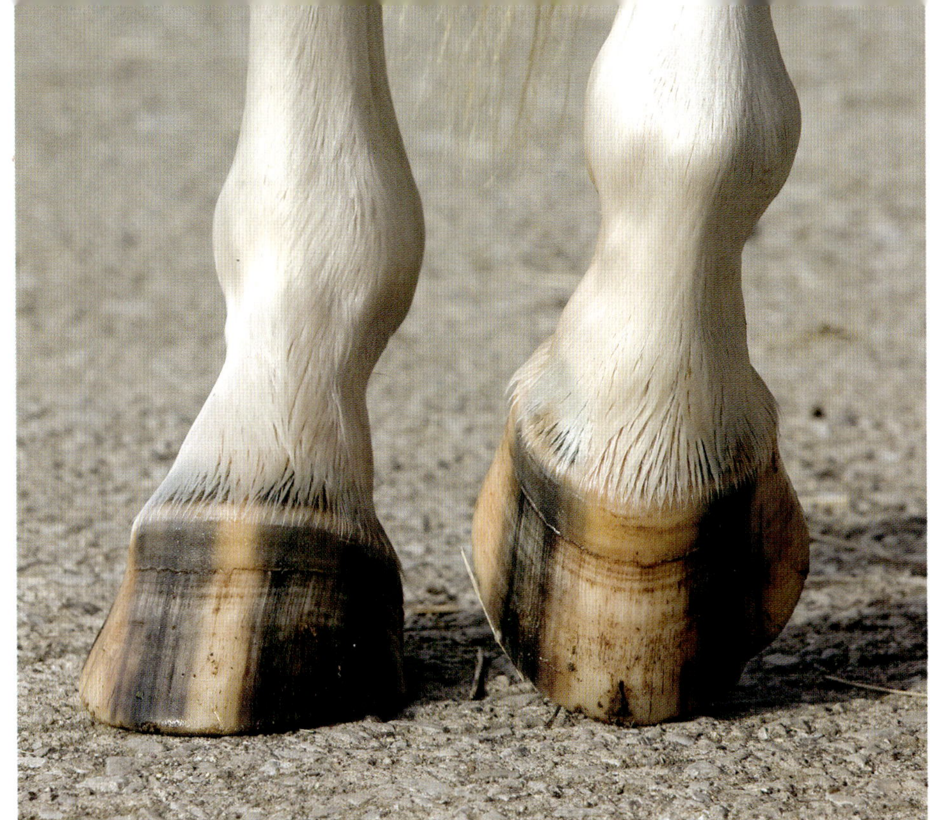

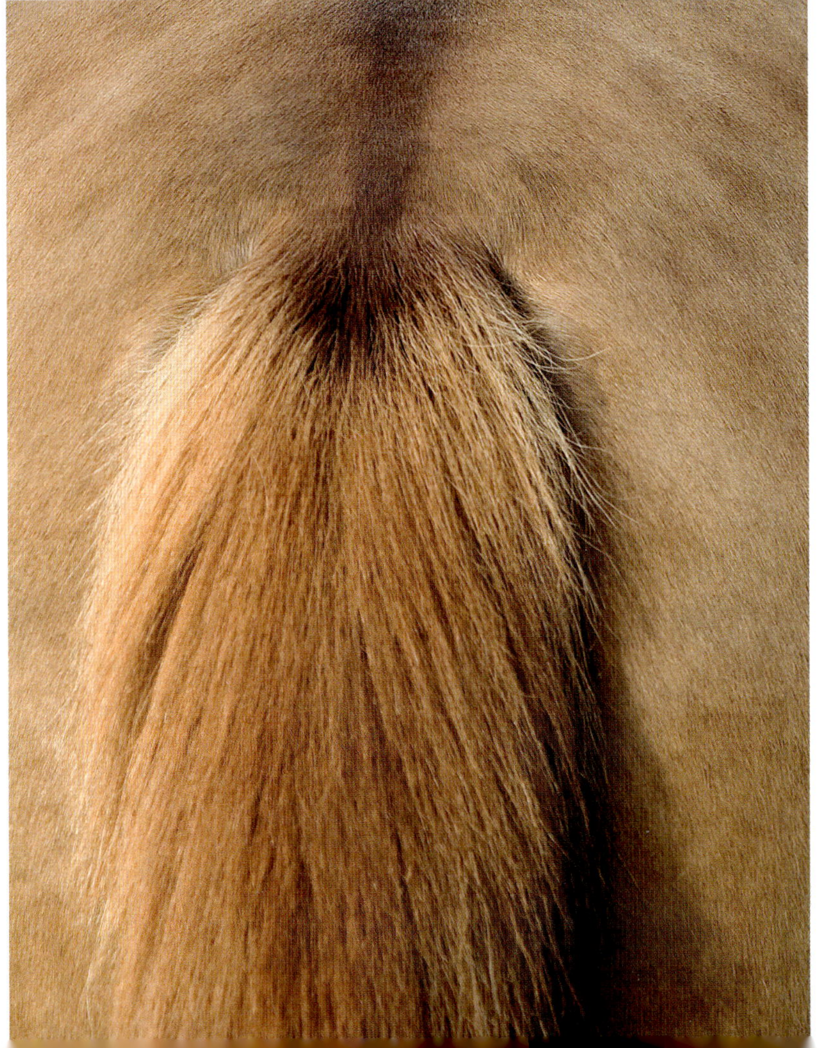

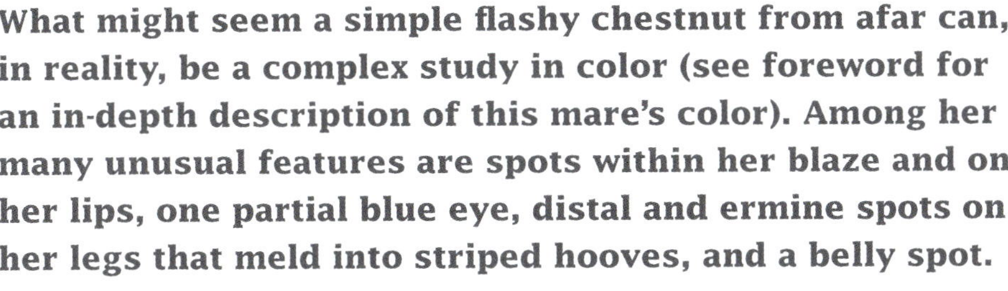

What might seem a simple flashy chestnut from afar can, in reality, be a complex study in color (see foreword for an in-depth description of this mare's color). Among her many unusual features are spots within her blaze and on her lips, one partial blue eye, distal and ermine spots on her legs that meld into striped hooves, and a belly spot.

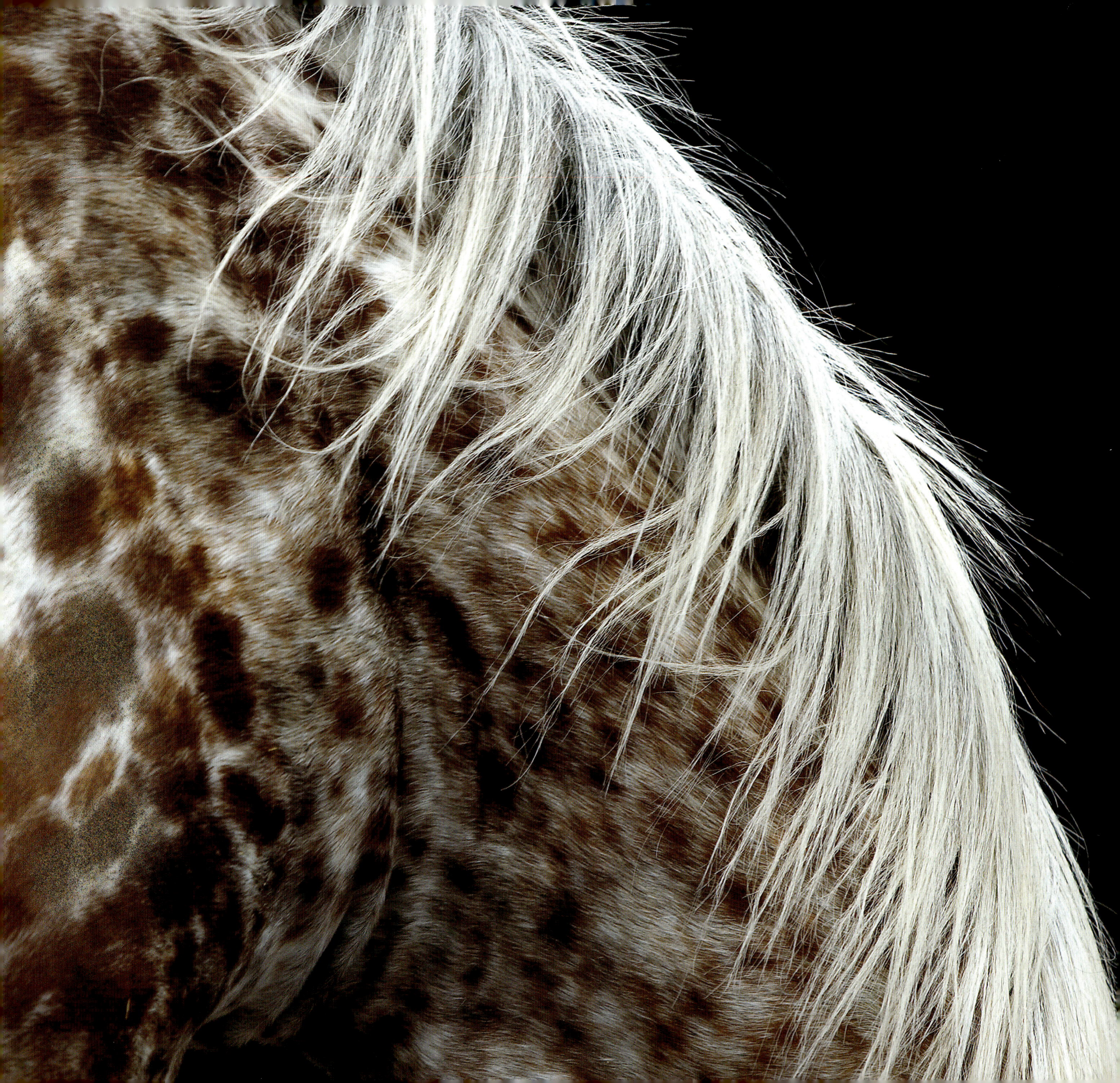

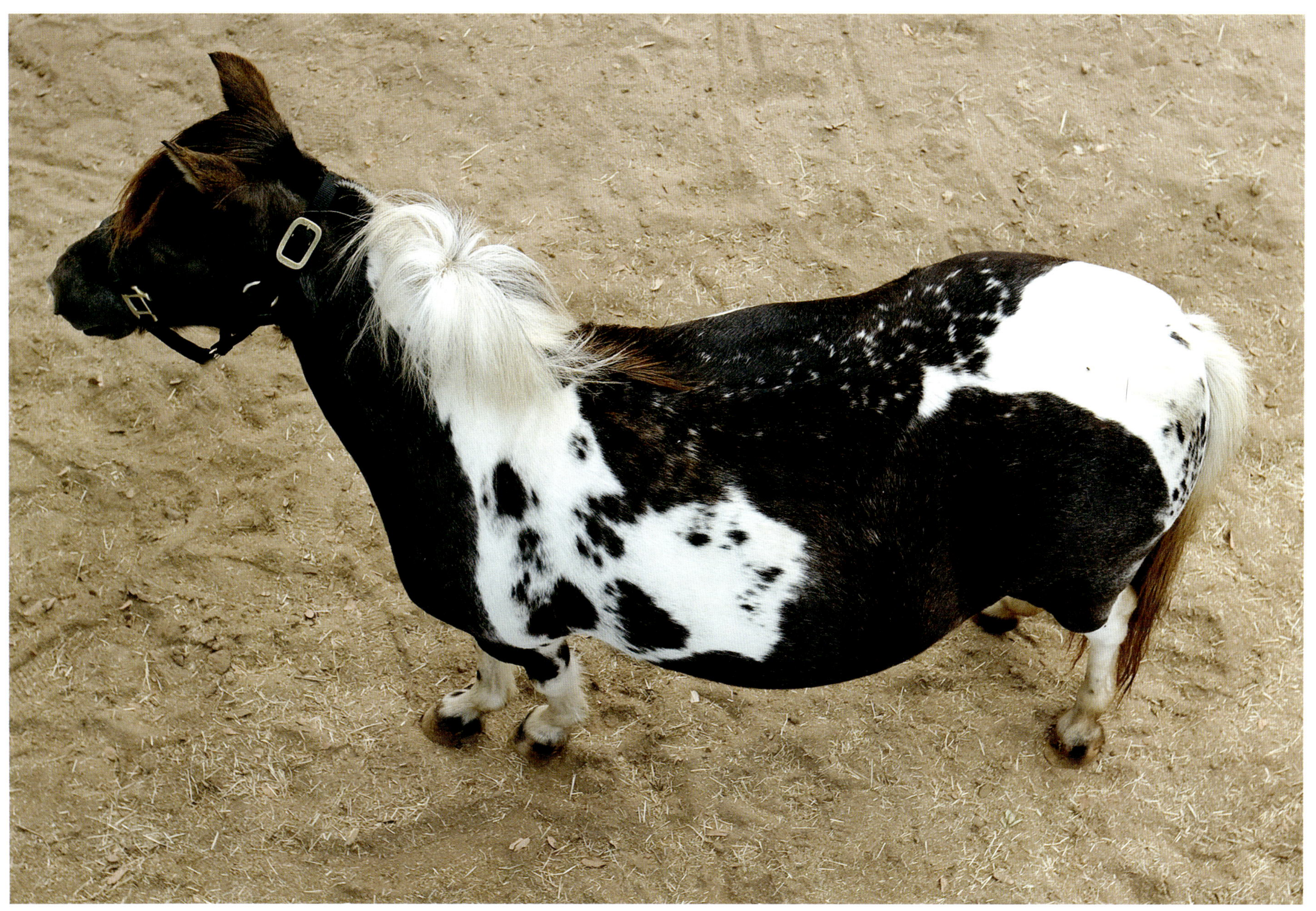

The mare above is a rarity because she exhibits lacing (see pp. 80-81) and is a pintaloosa because her parentage includes both pinto and Appaloosa bloodlines. The mare at left shows that Knabstruppers come in more colors than black and white.

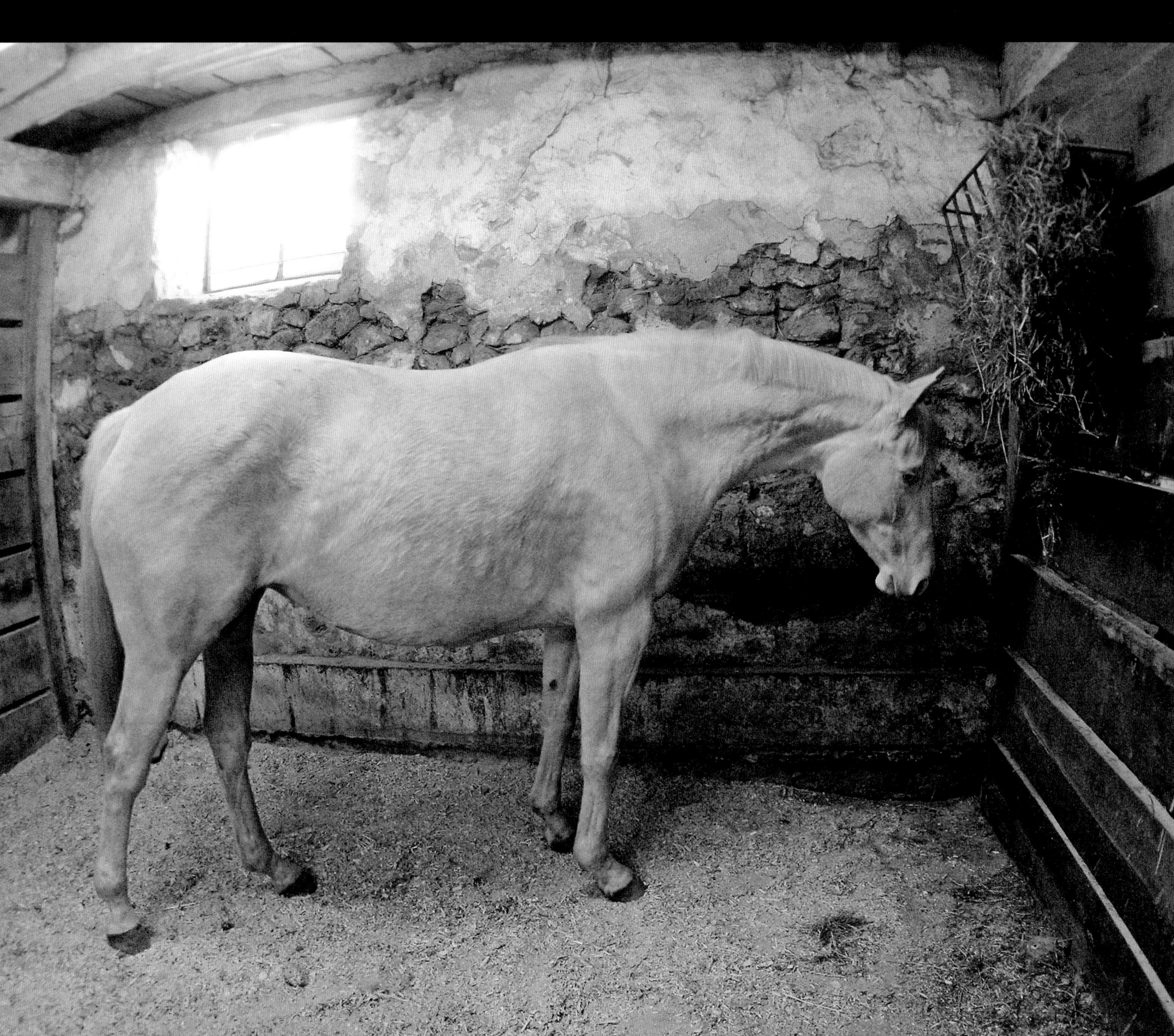

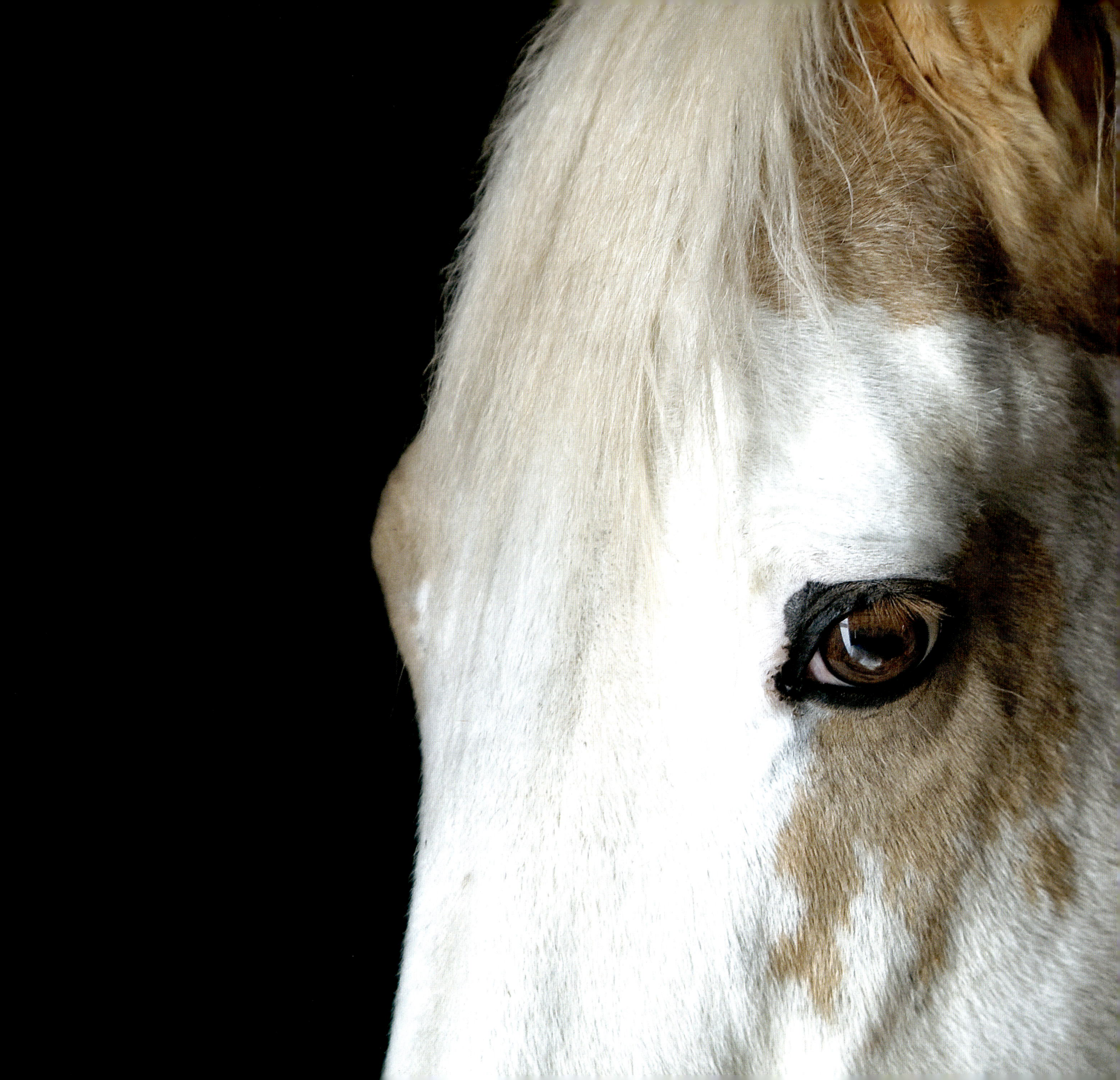

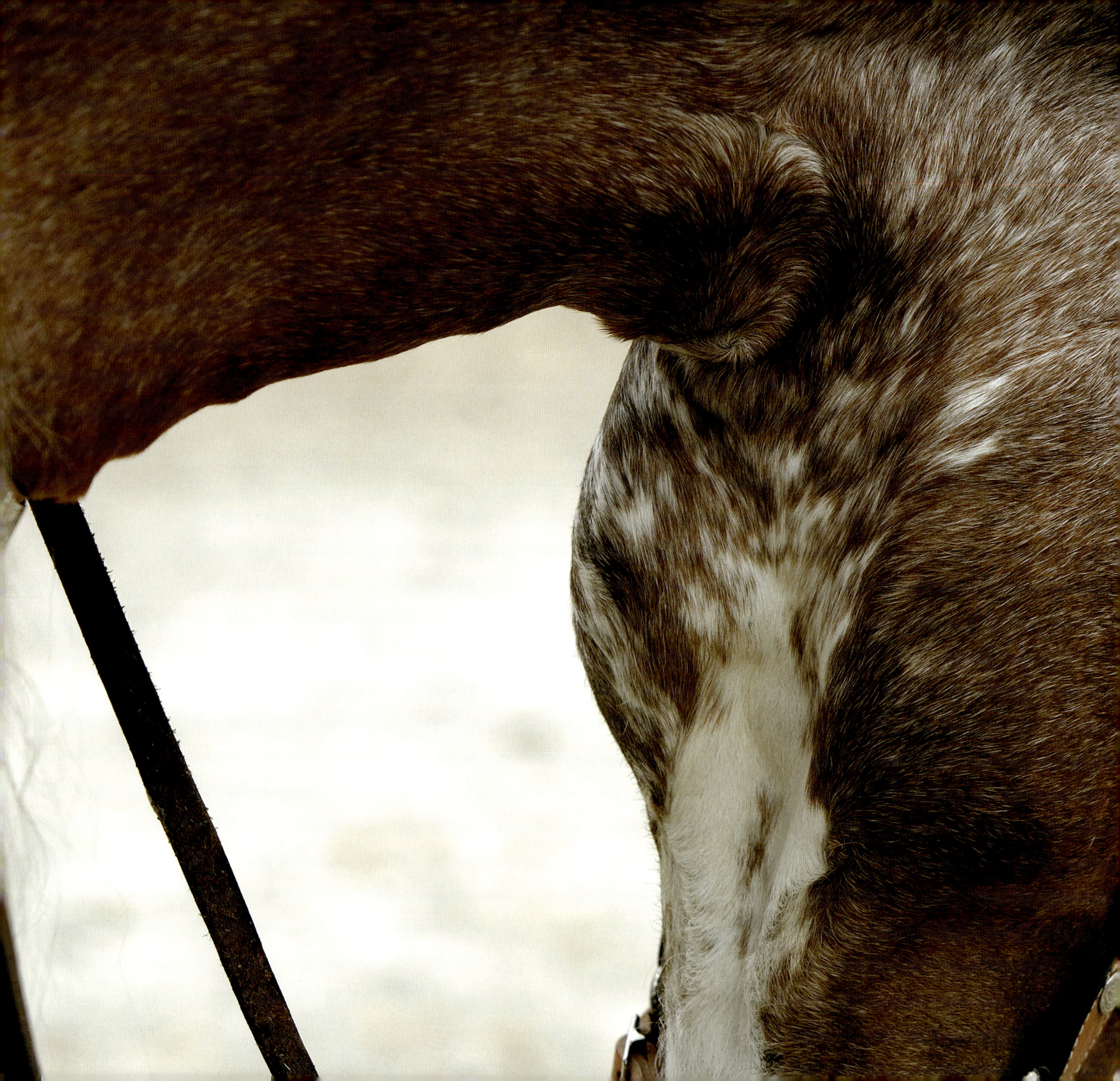

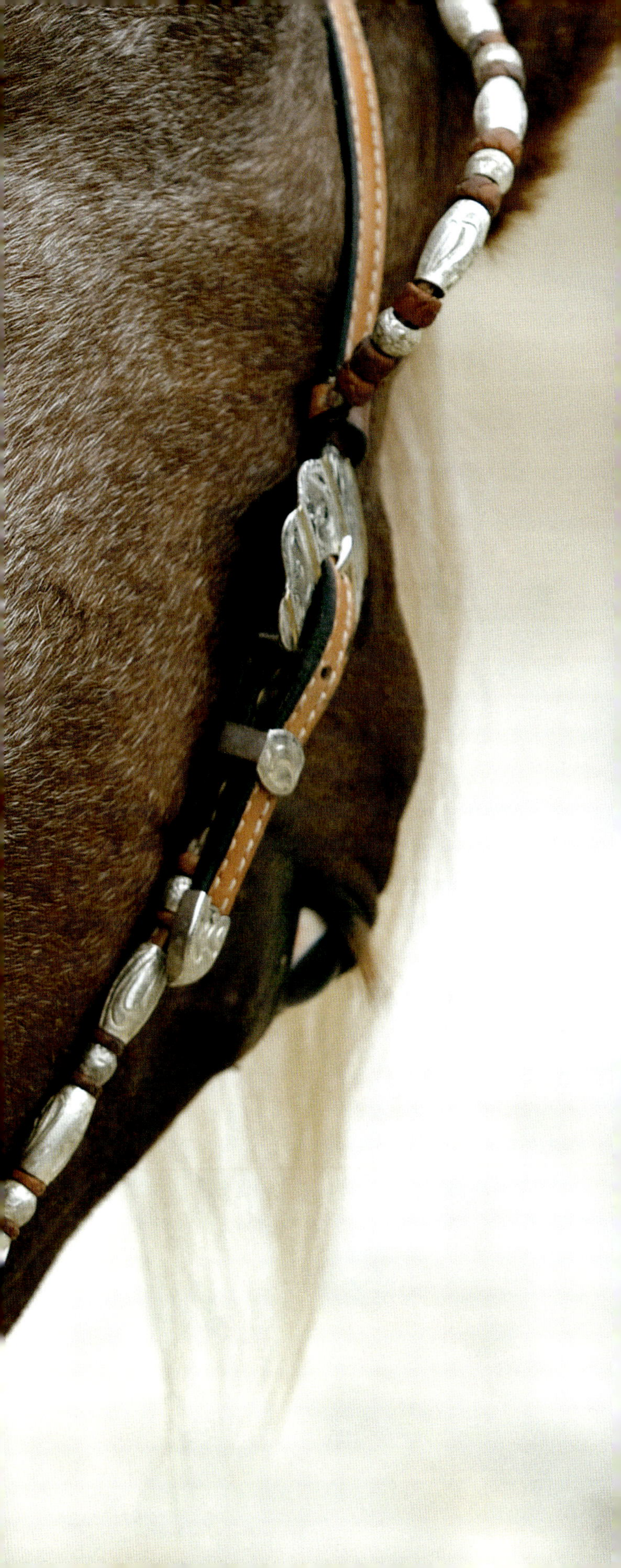

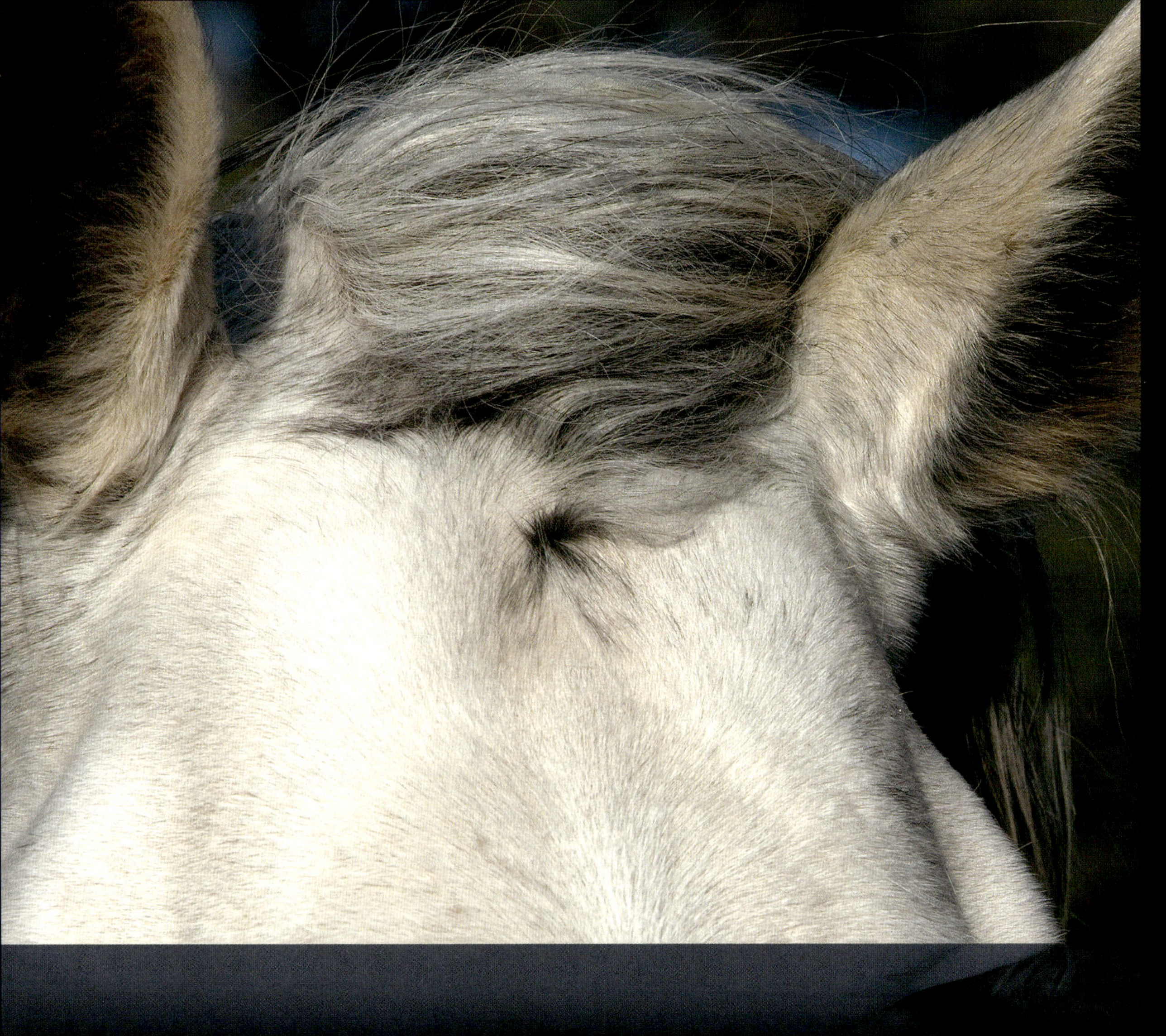

A Thoroughbred doesn't have to be entirely white to be registered as white, as this pair reflects.

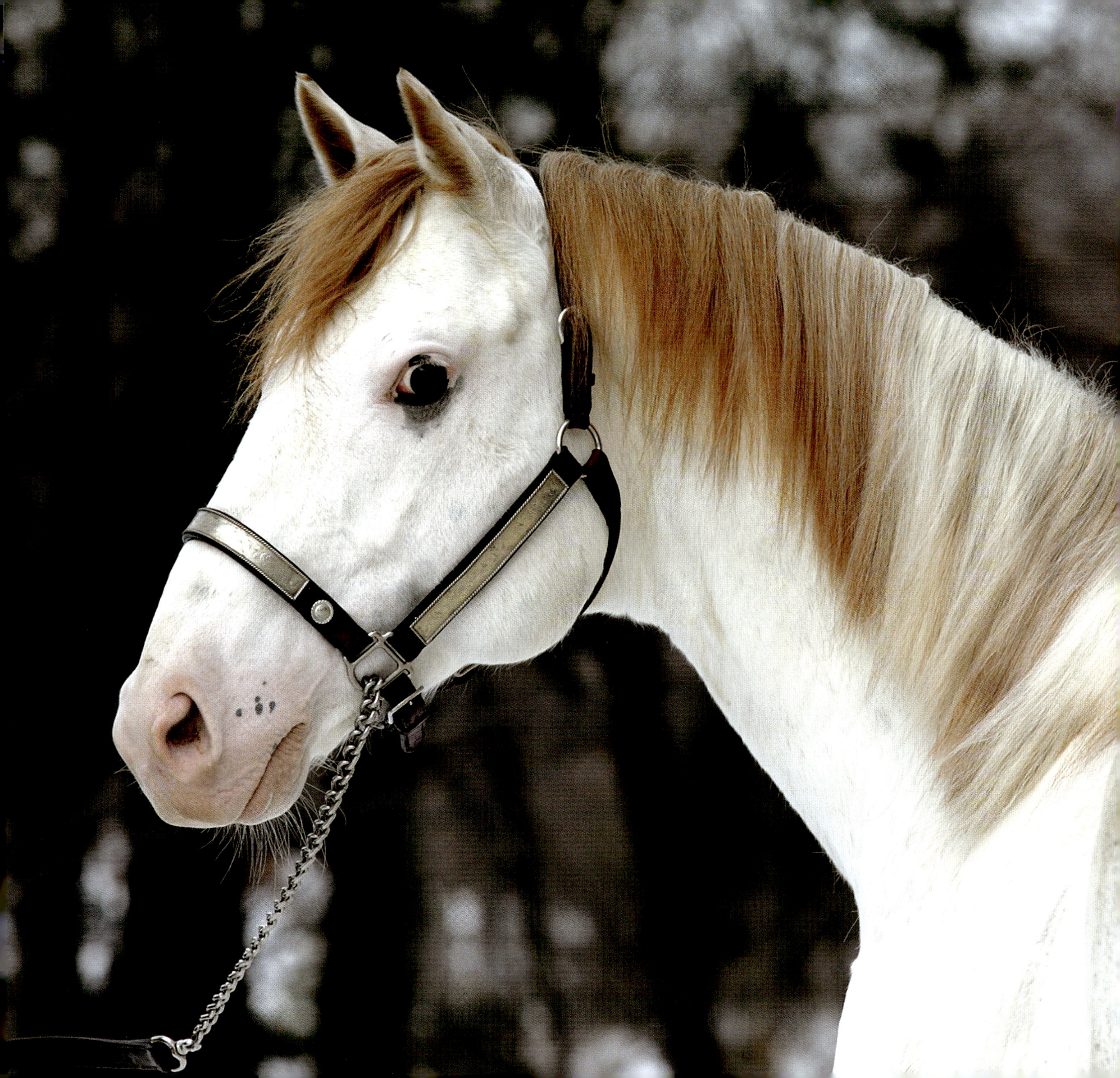

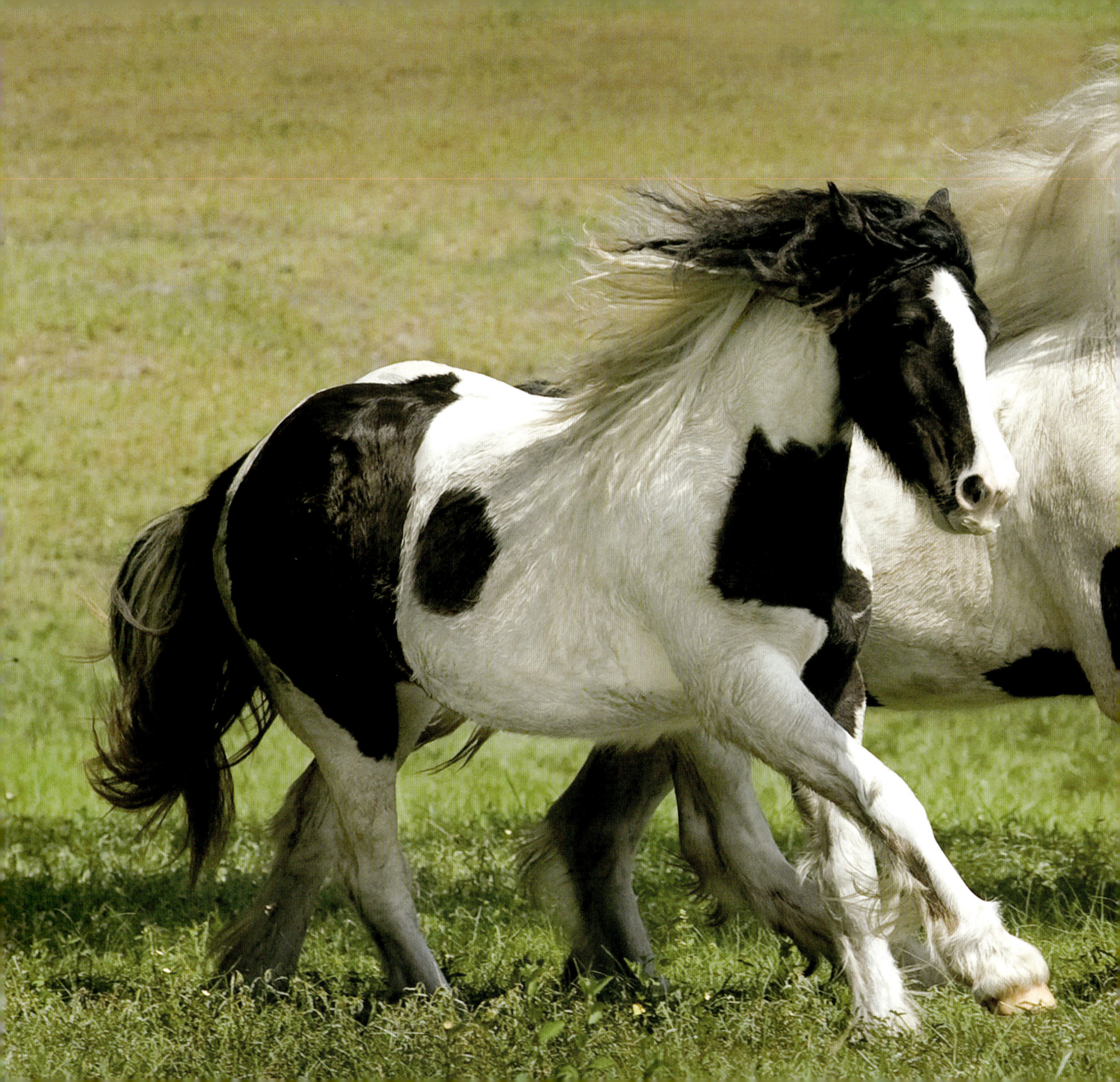

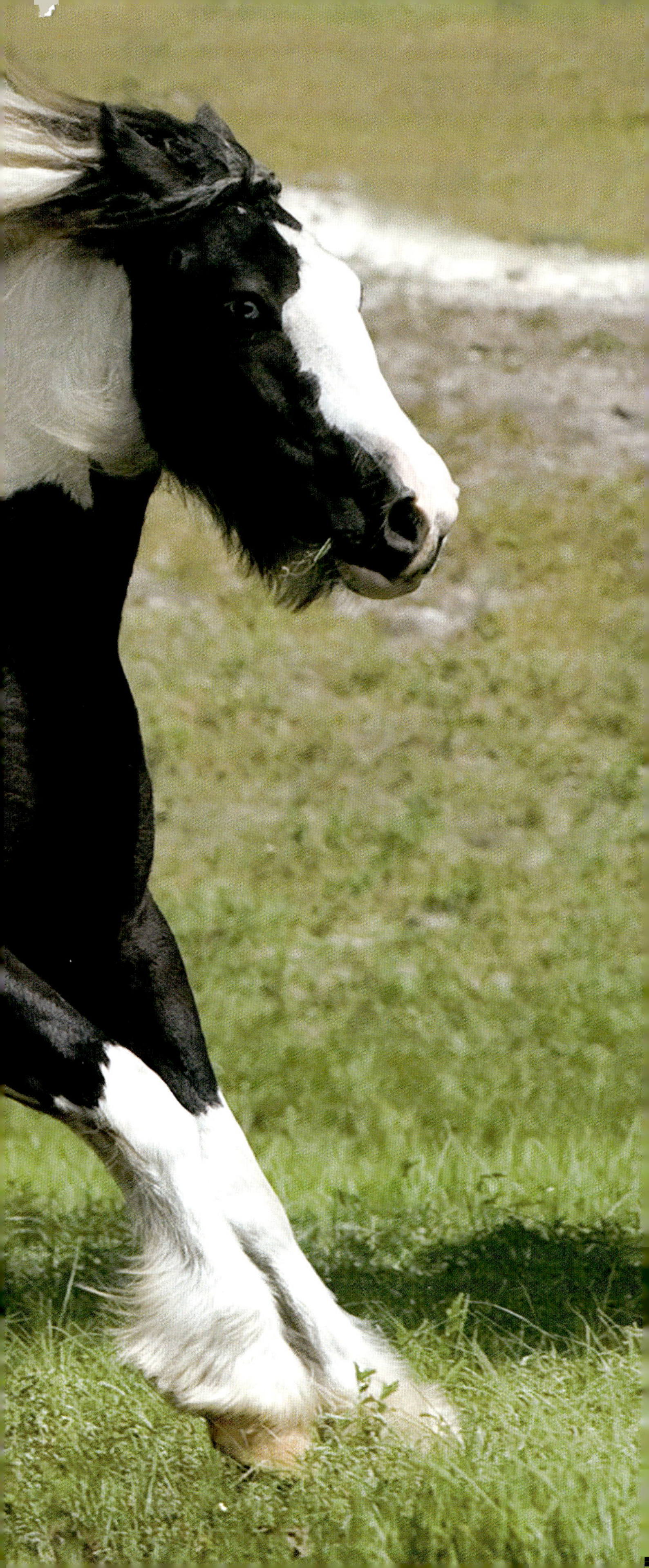

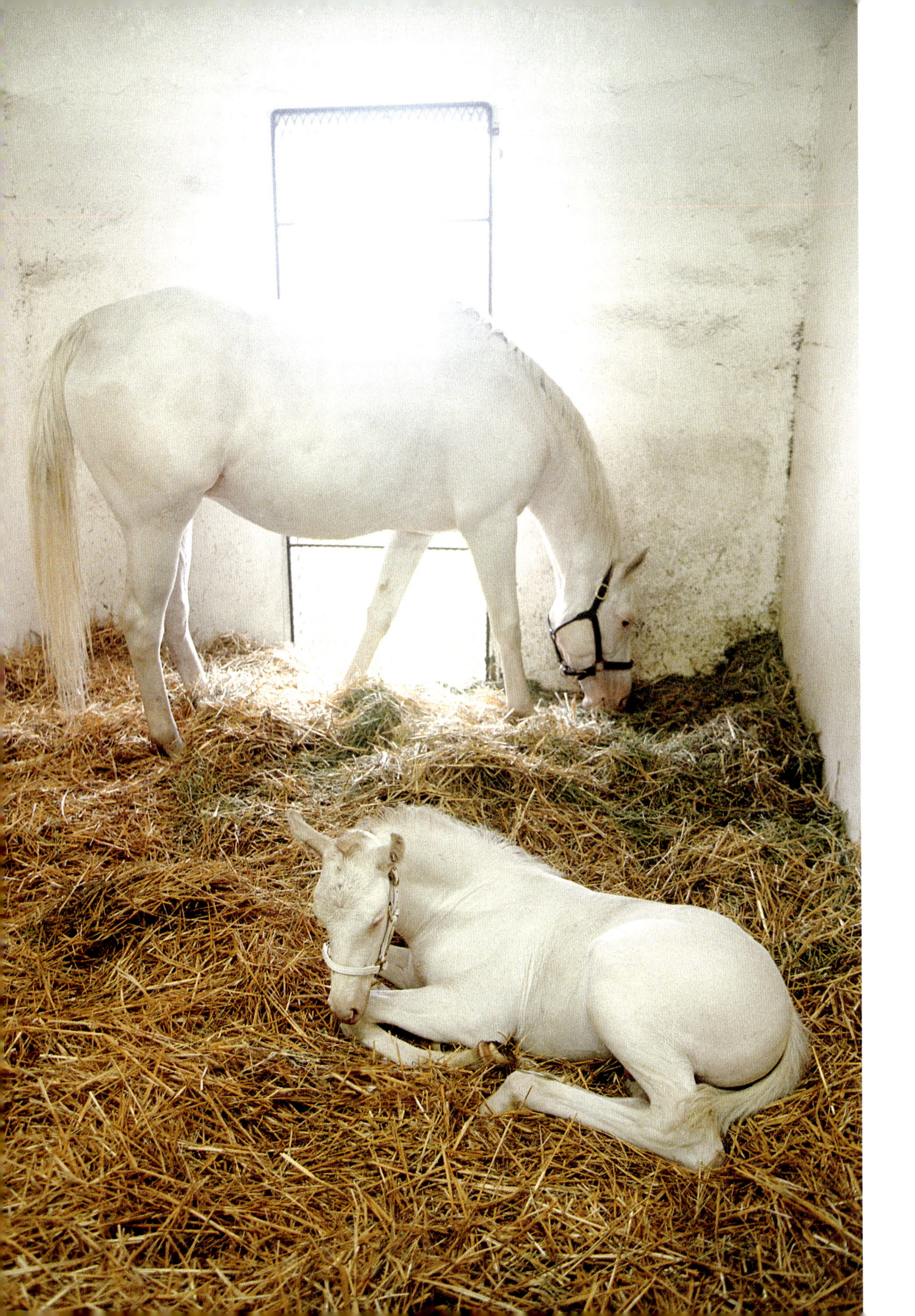

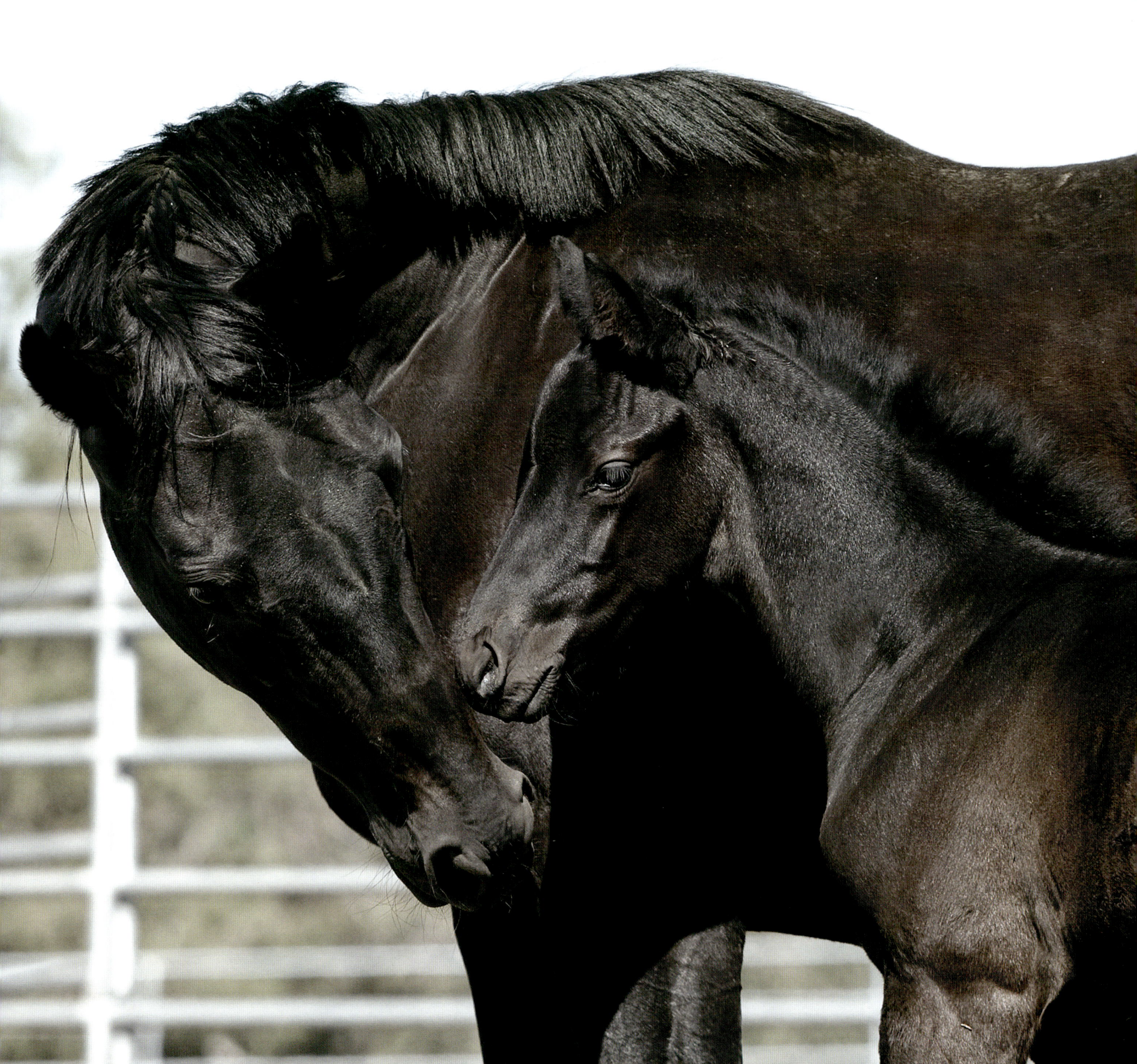

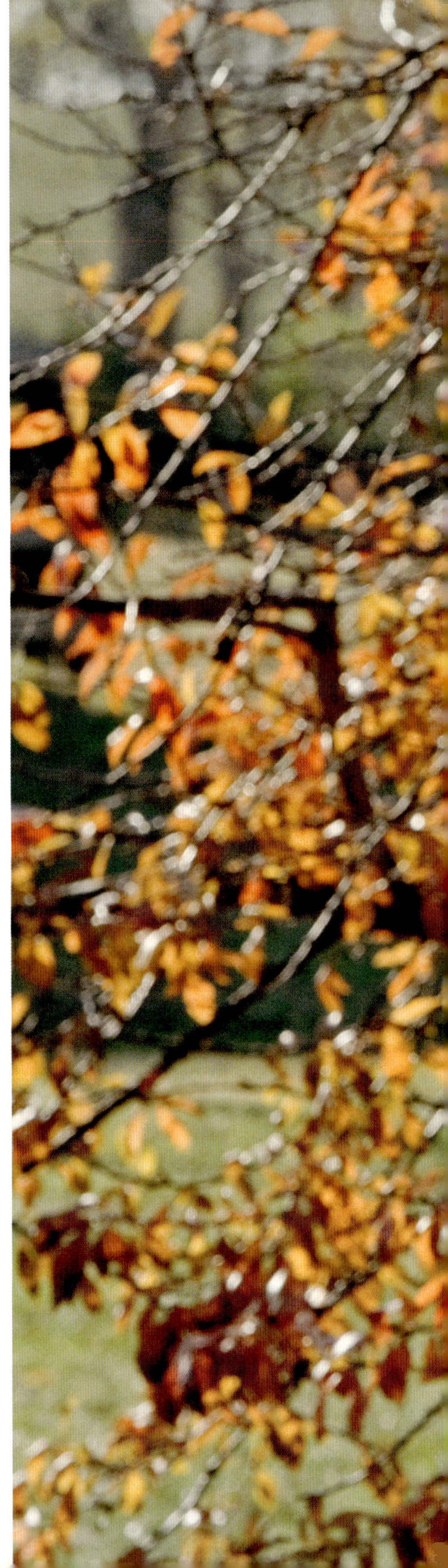

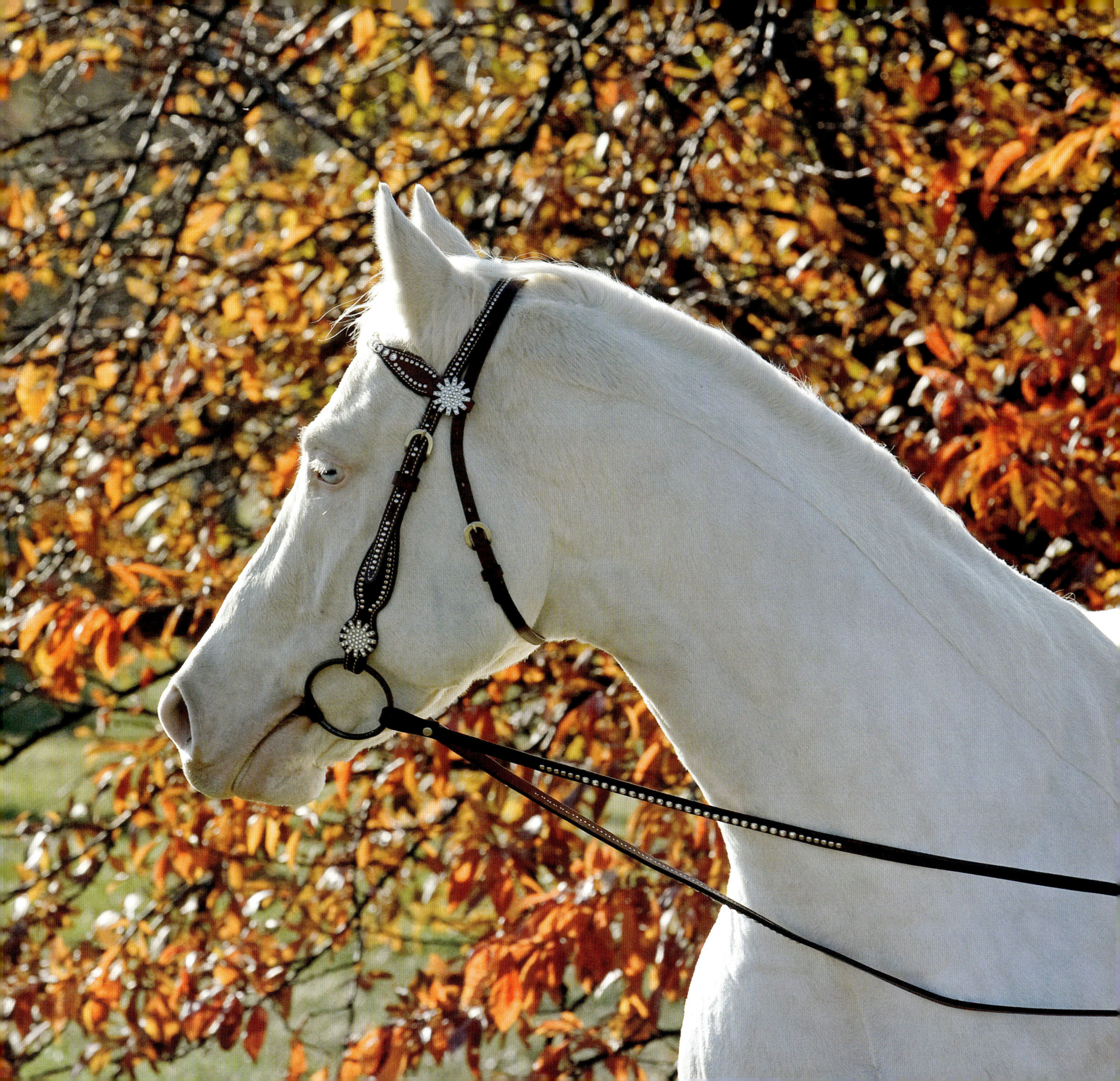

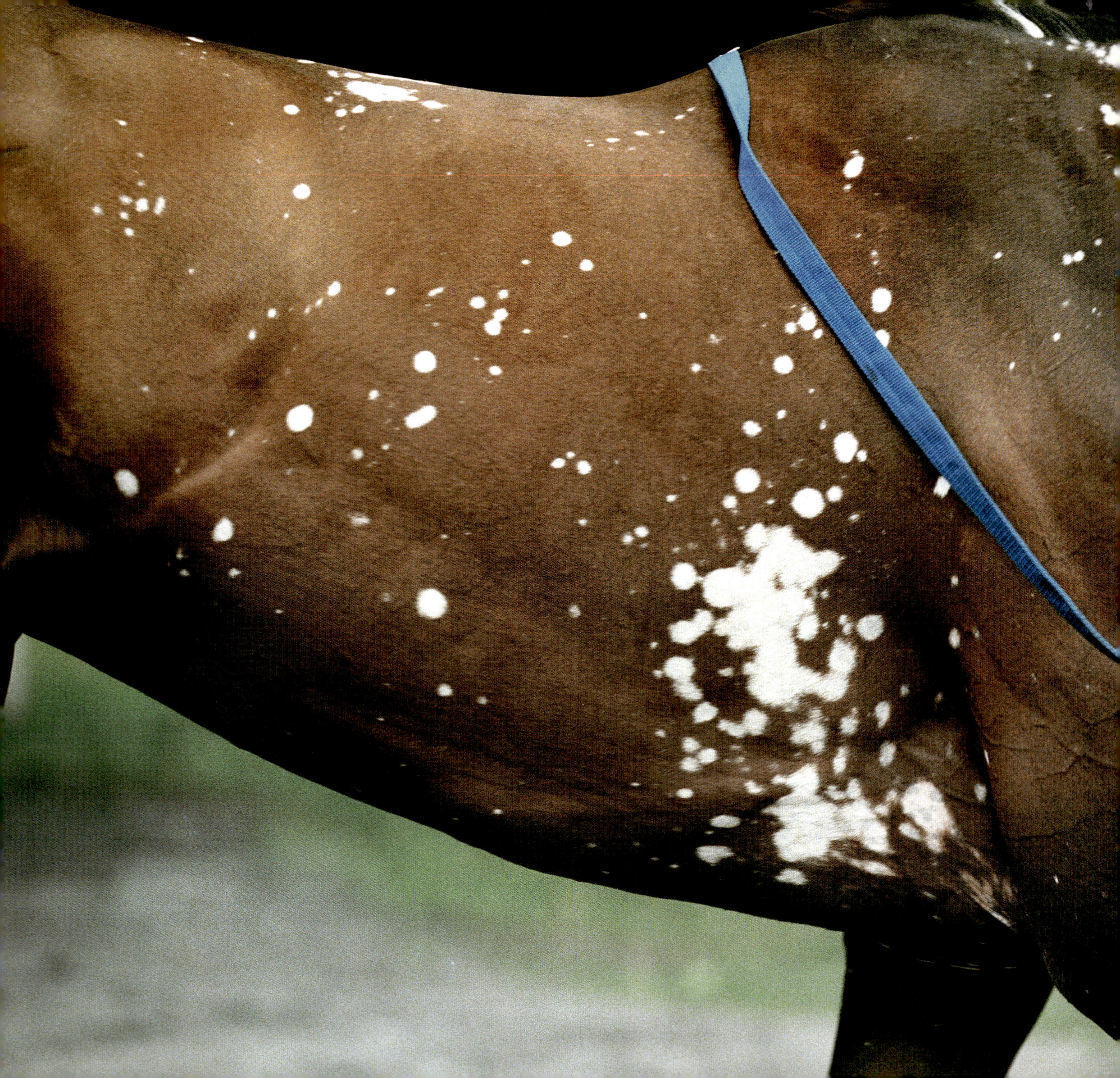

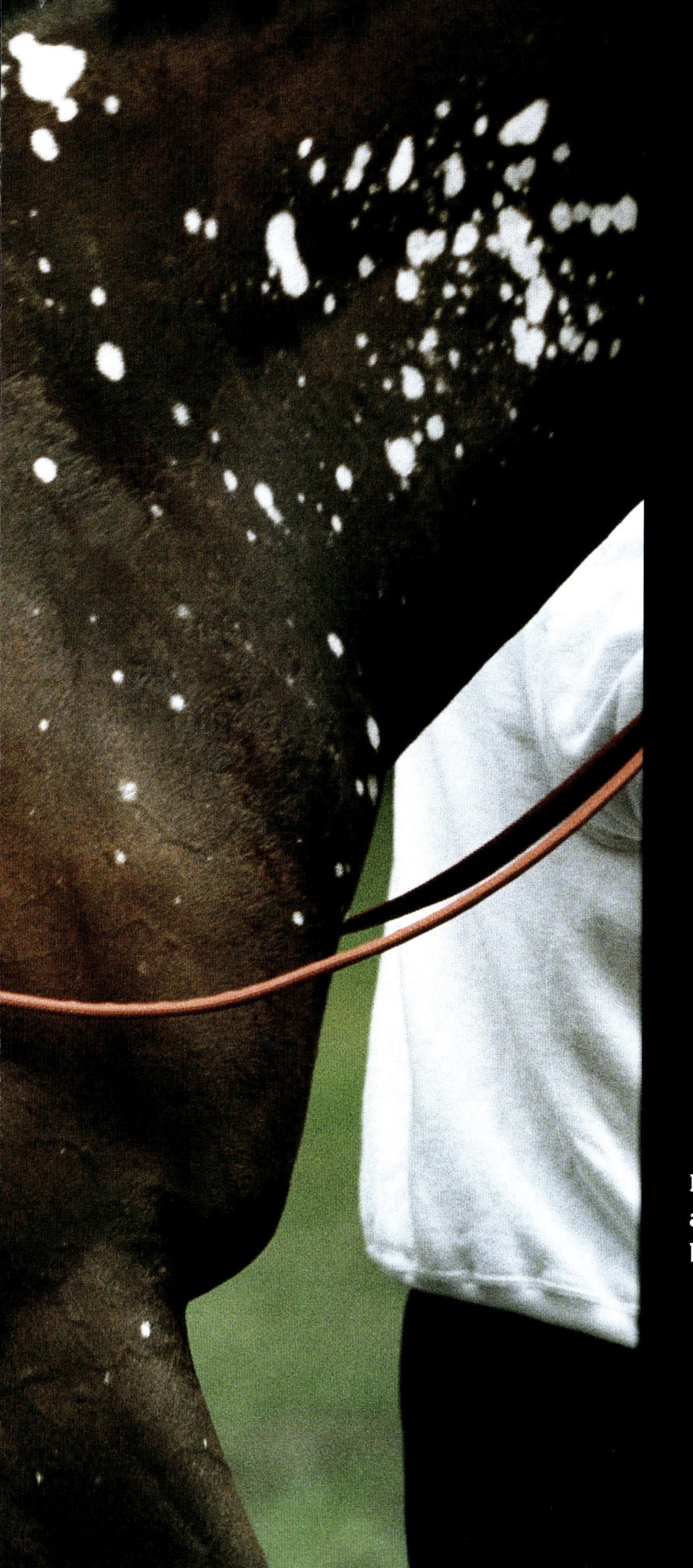

Random white spots such as these, called Birdcatcher spots, are not uncommon. It is very unusual, however, for them to be this abundant.

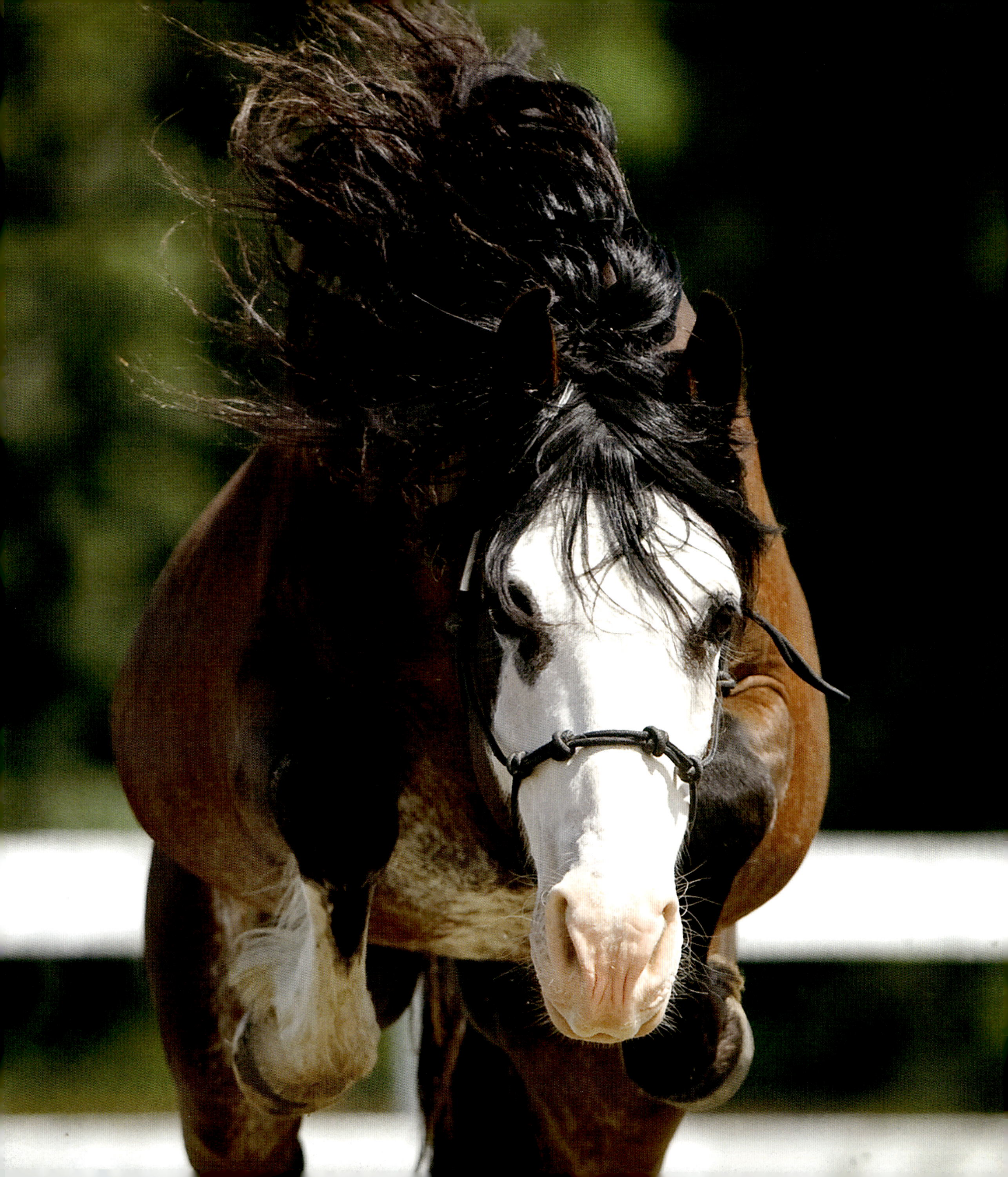

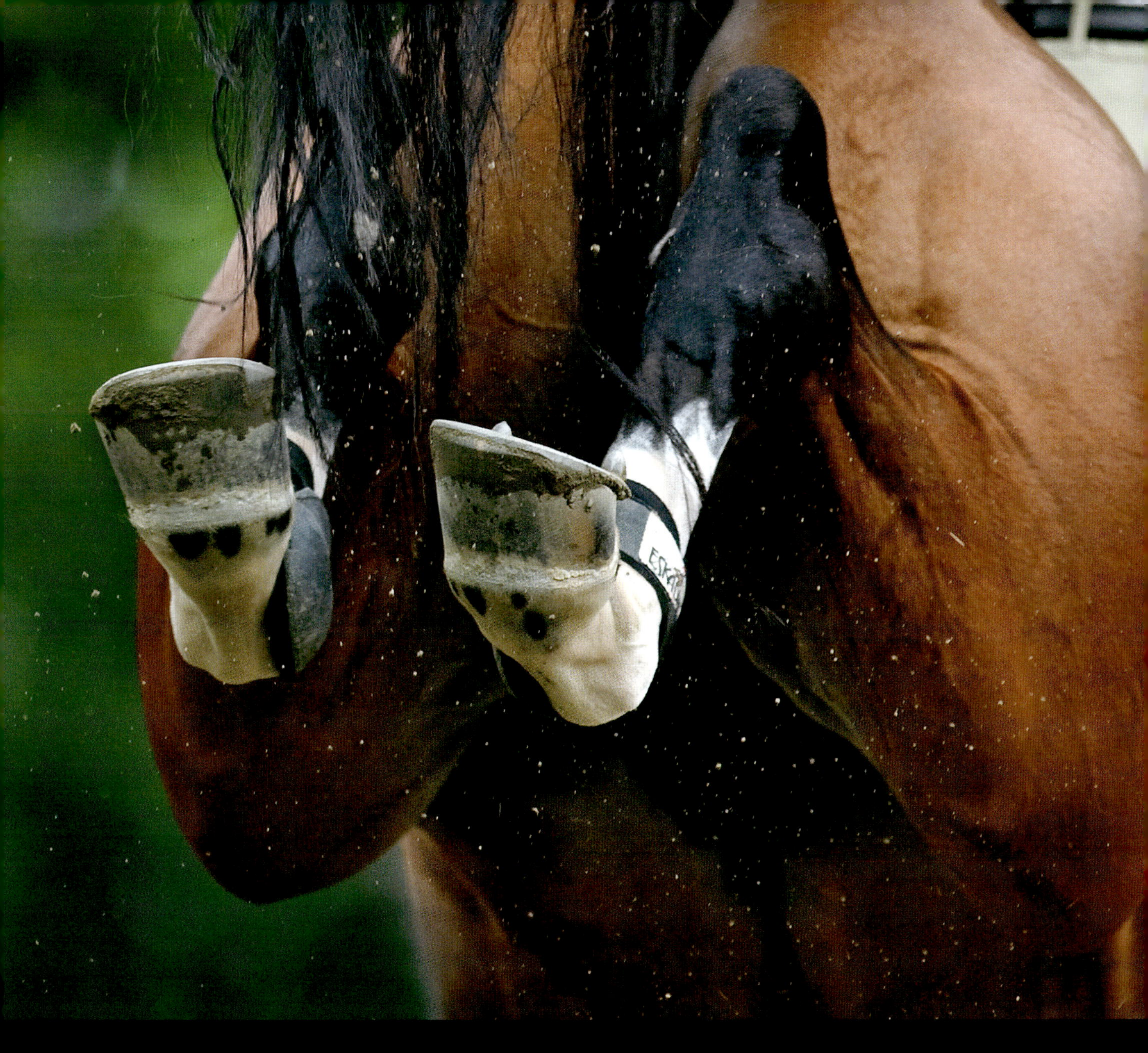

The stallion at left is a sabino, one hint being the white hairs on his belly. The horse above has ermine spots, the black spots touching the coronet band.

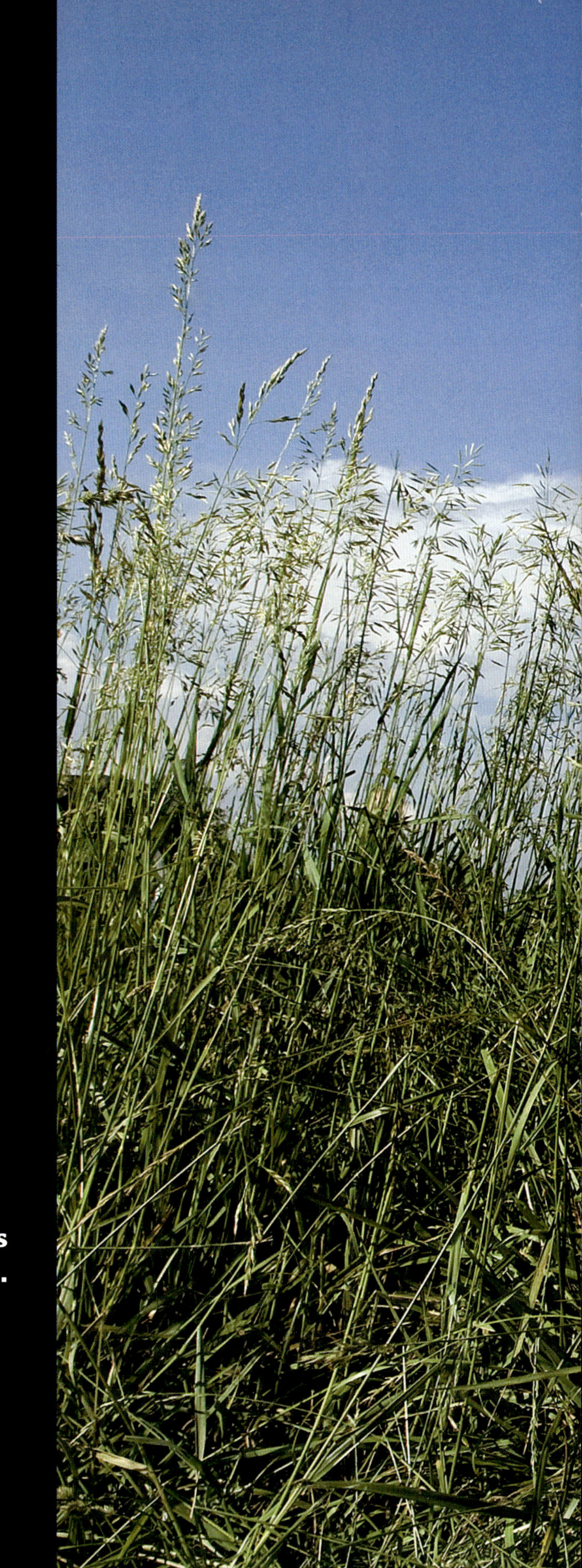

his tobiano Miniature stallion, blind in his left eye, features unusually extensive roaning on his neck and in his mane.

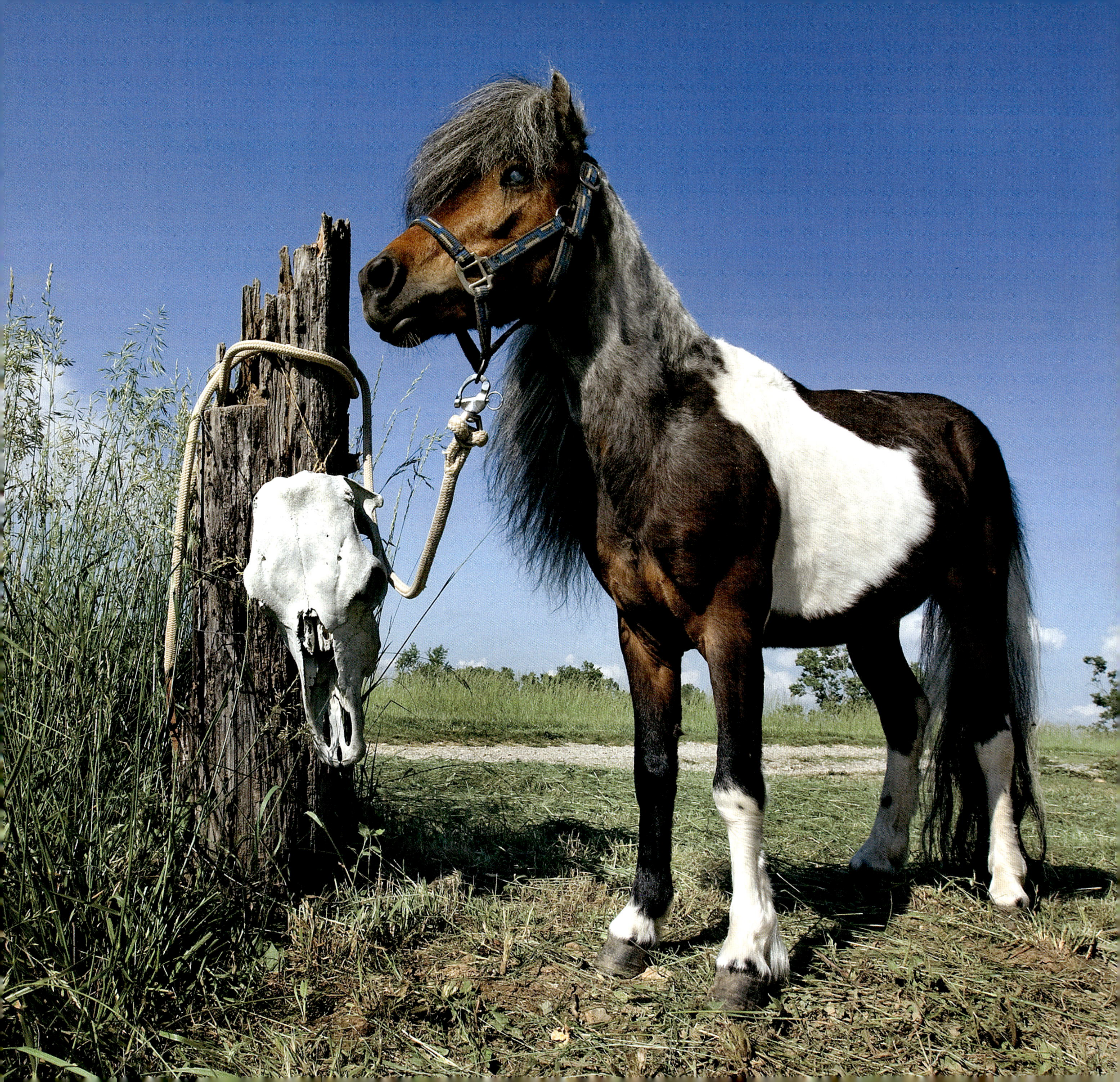

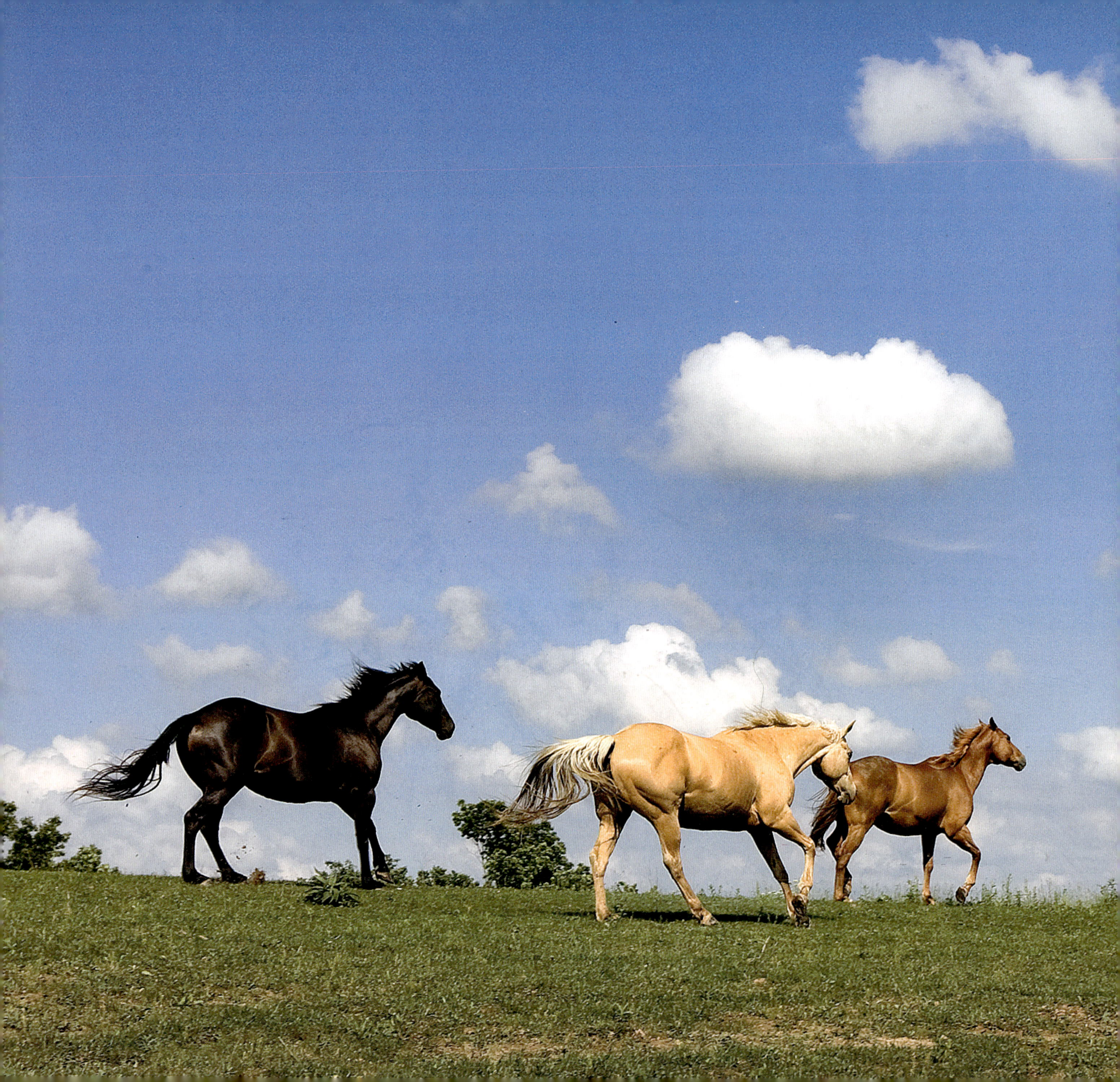

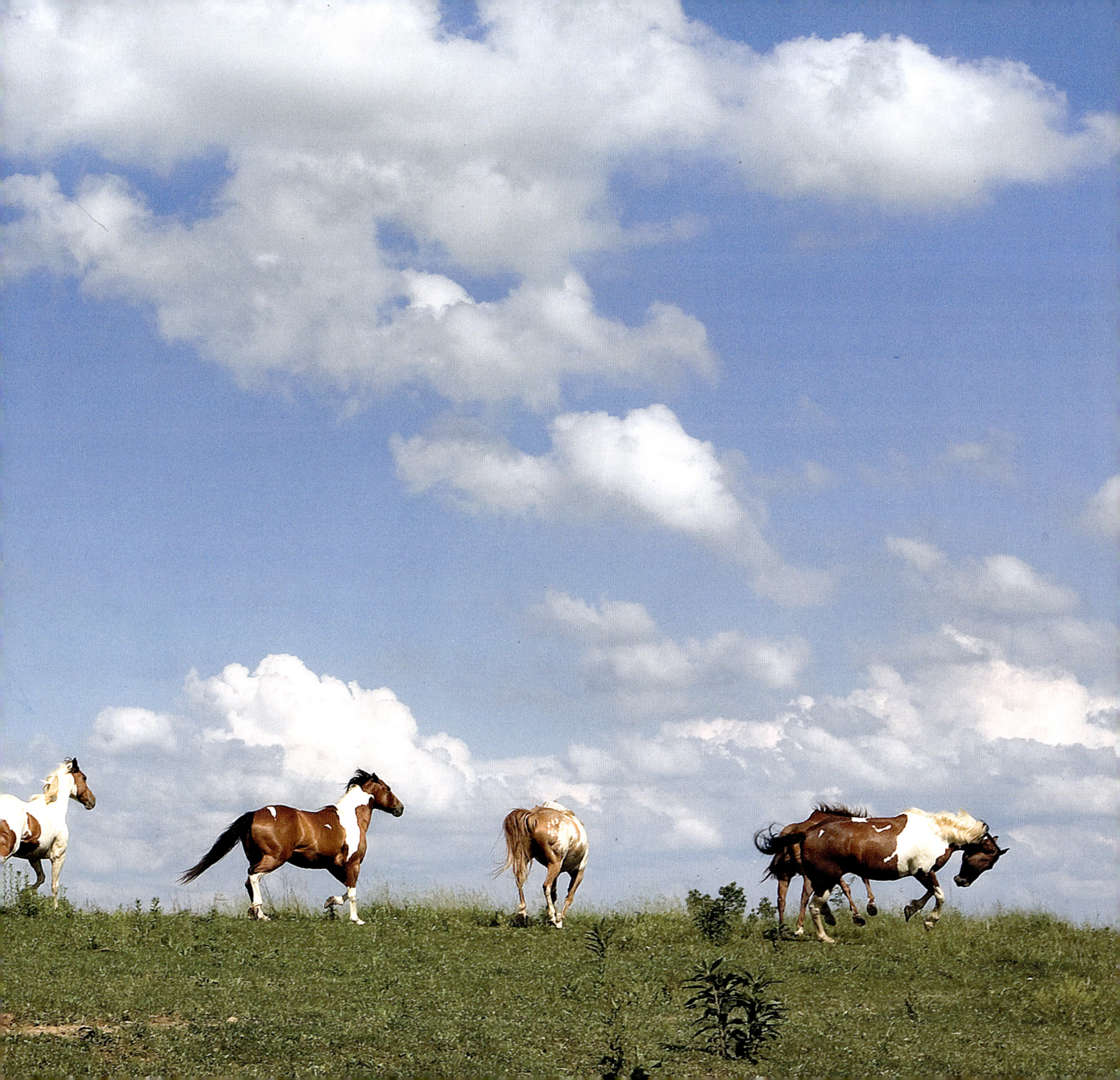

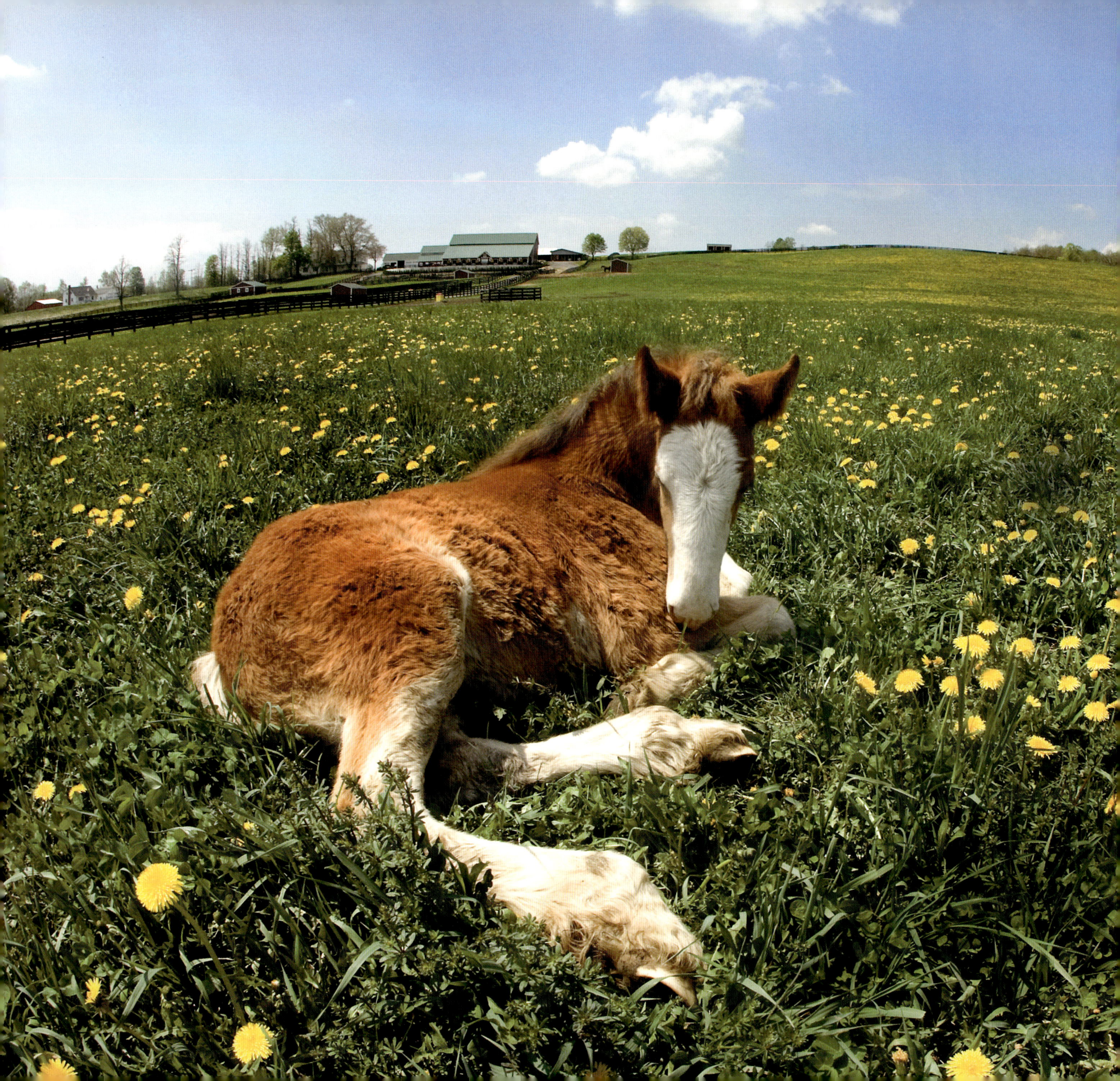

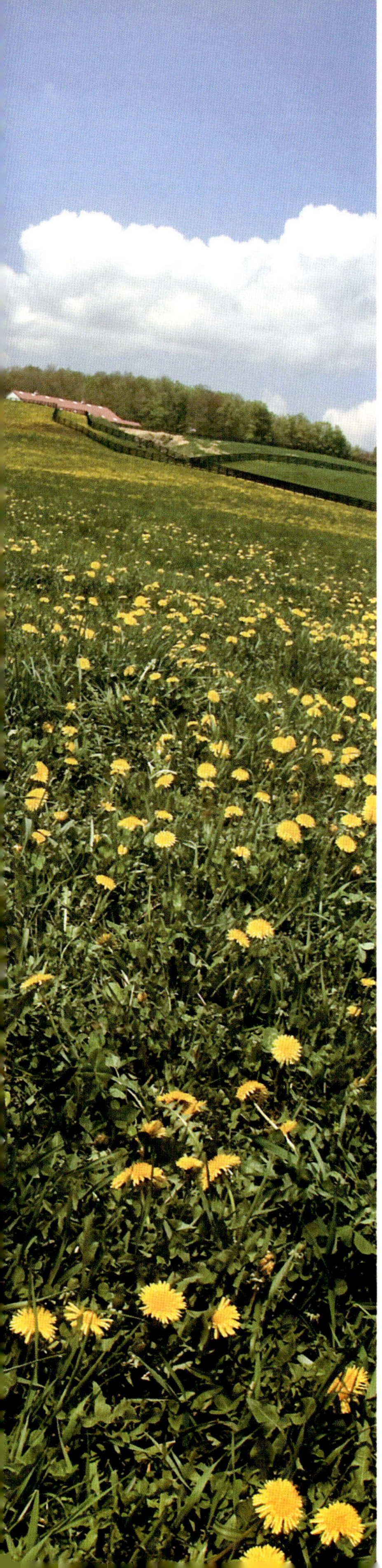

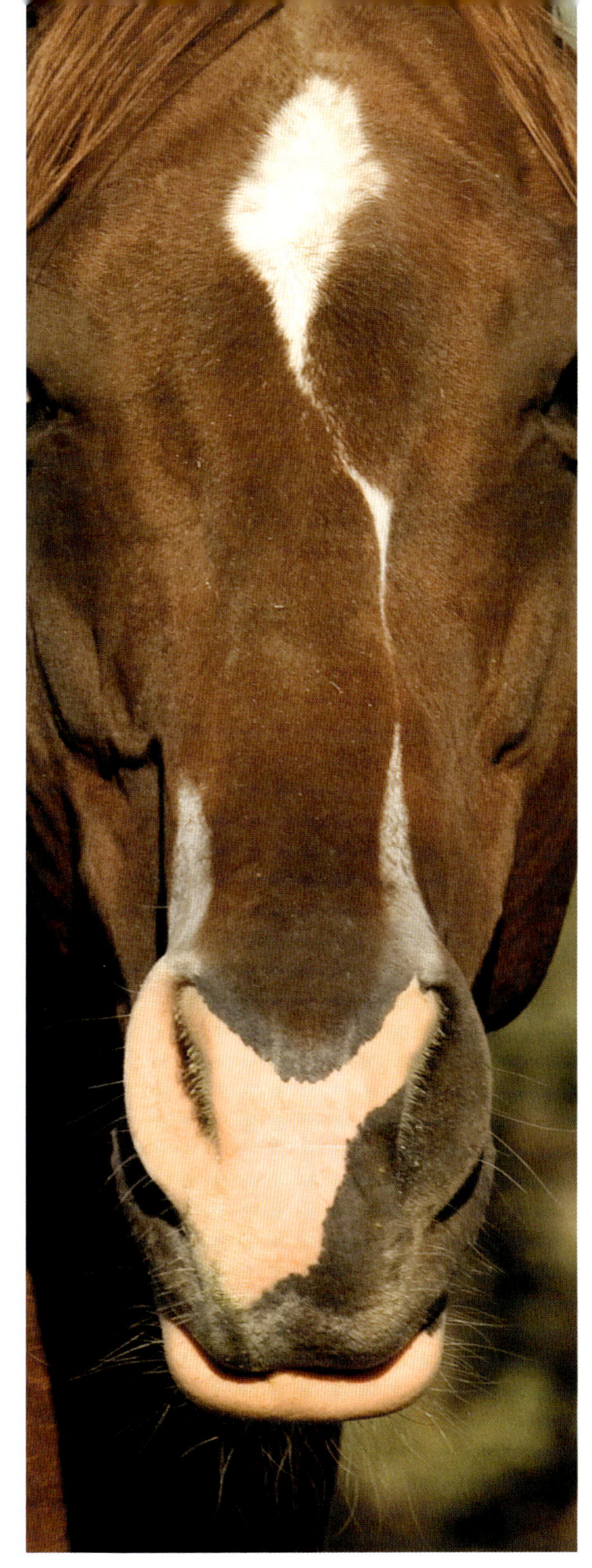

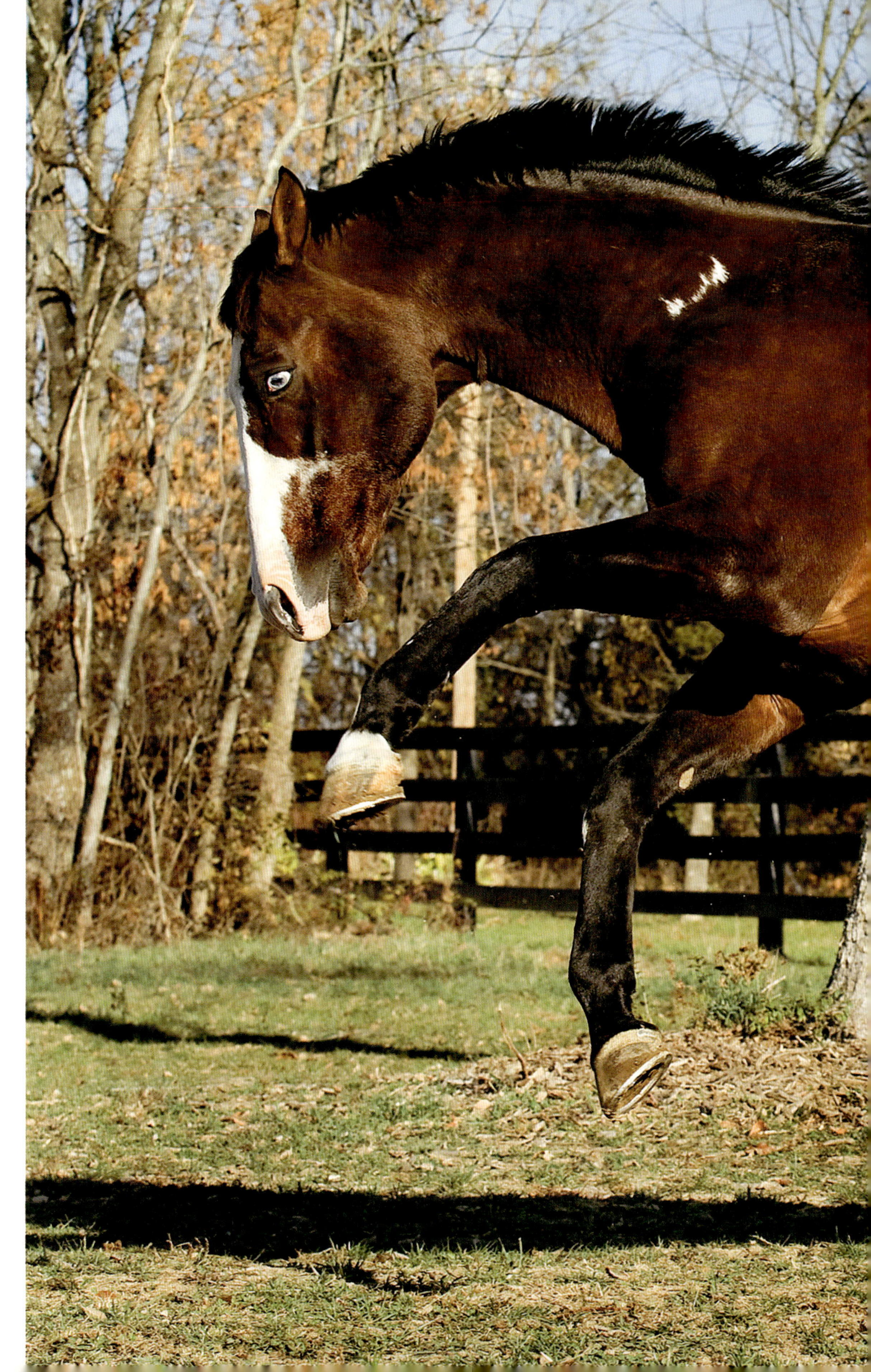

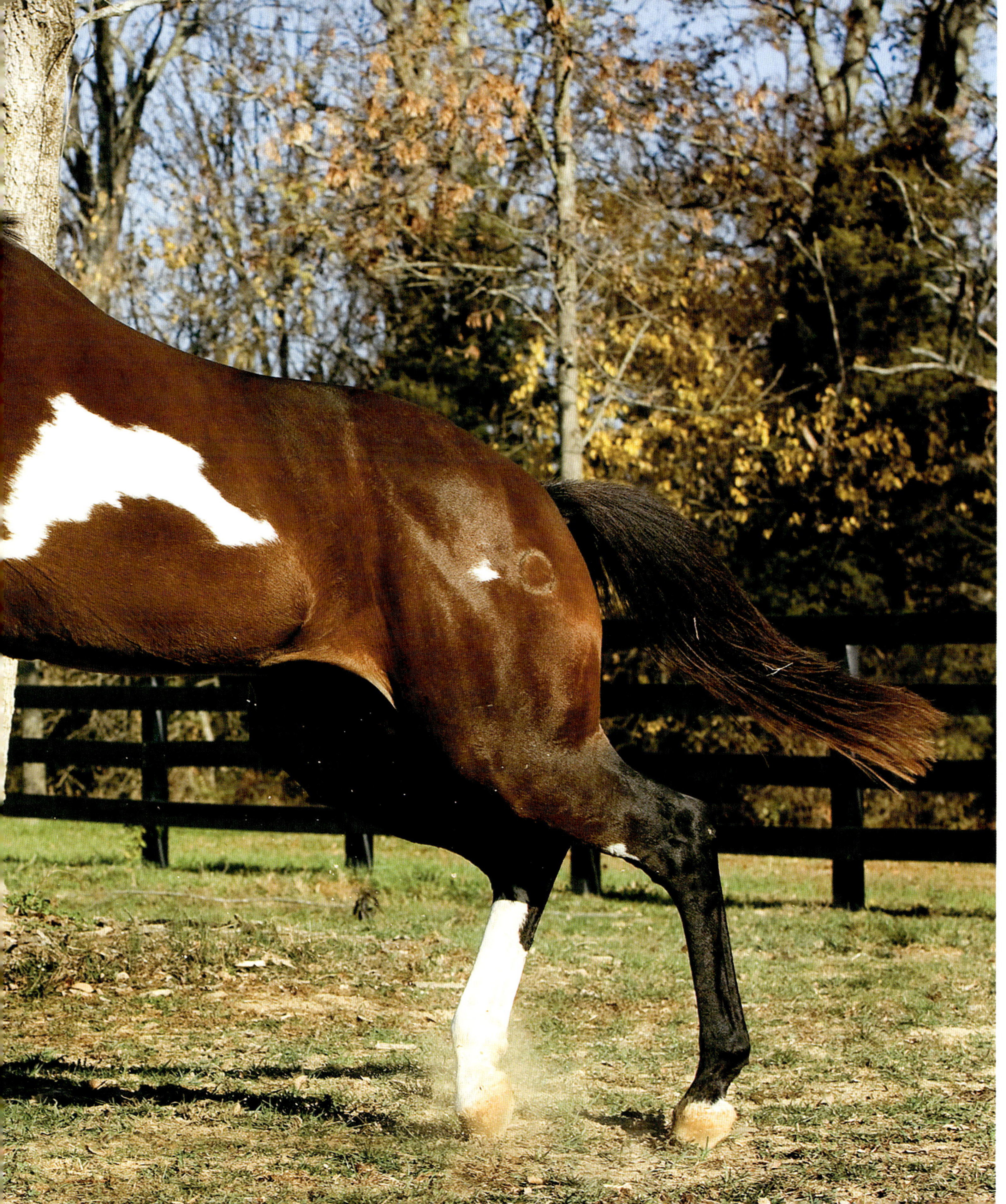

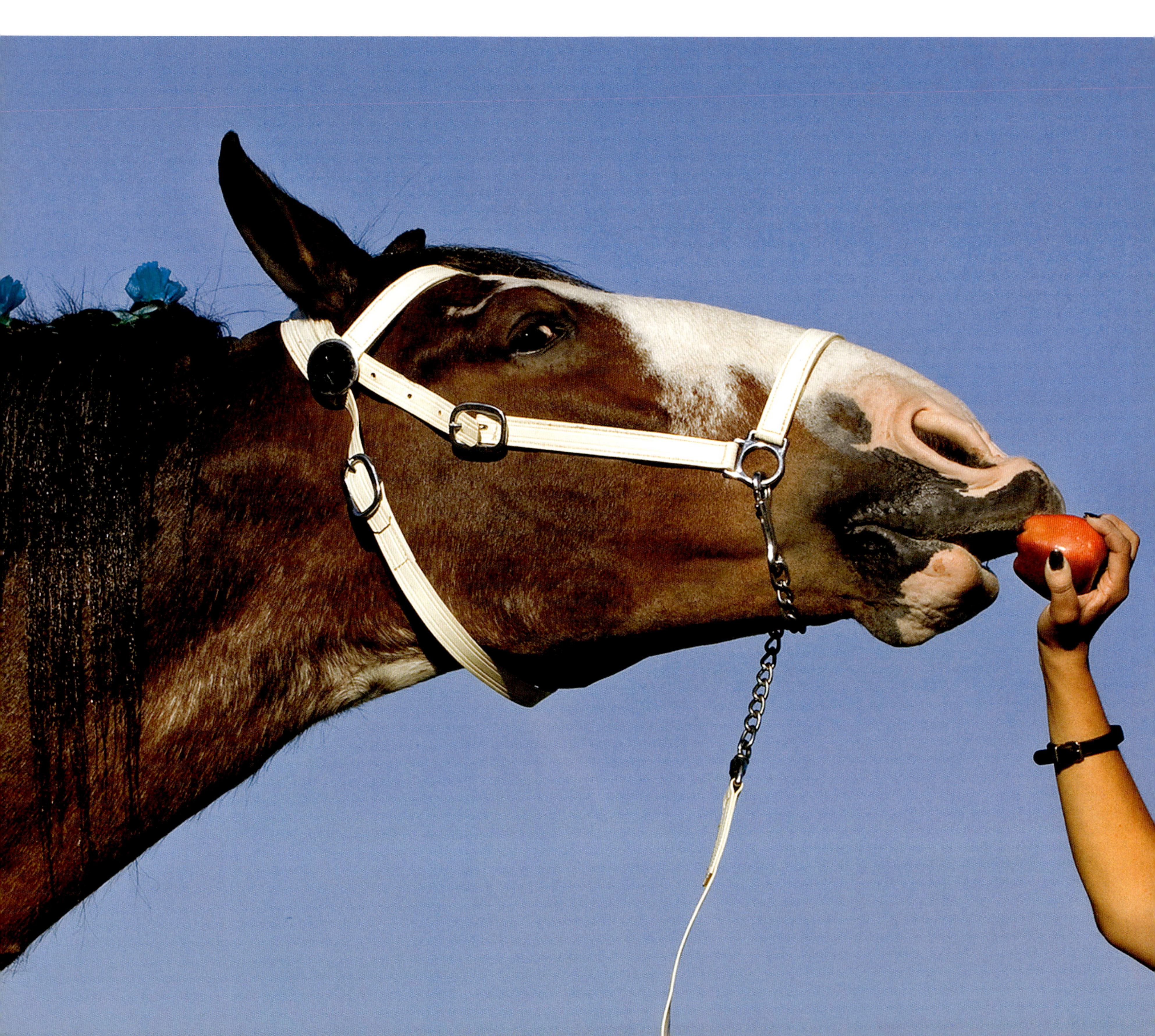

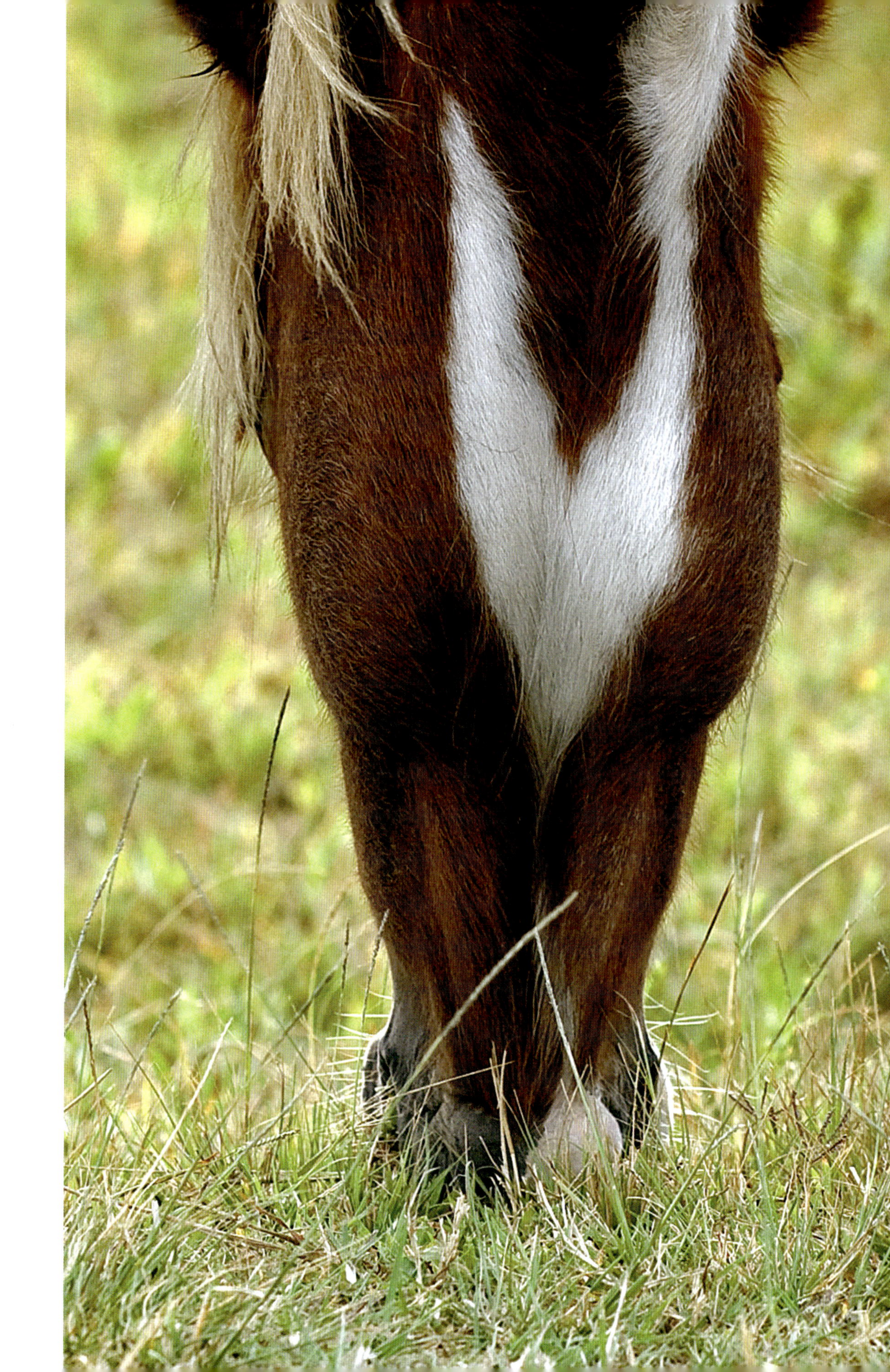

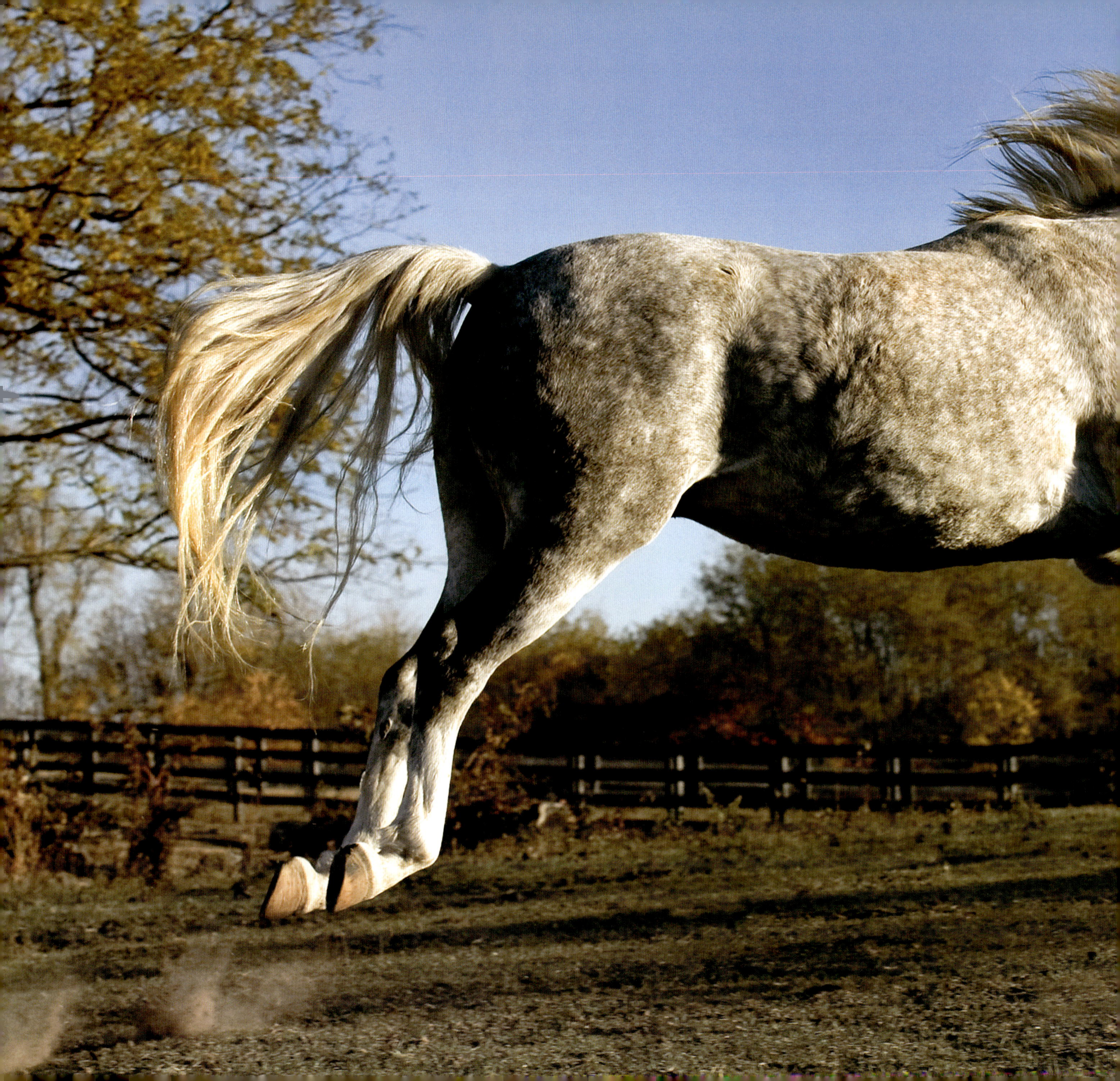

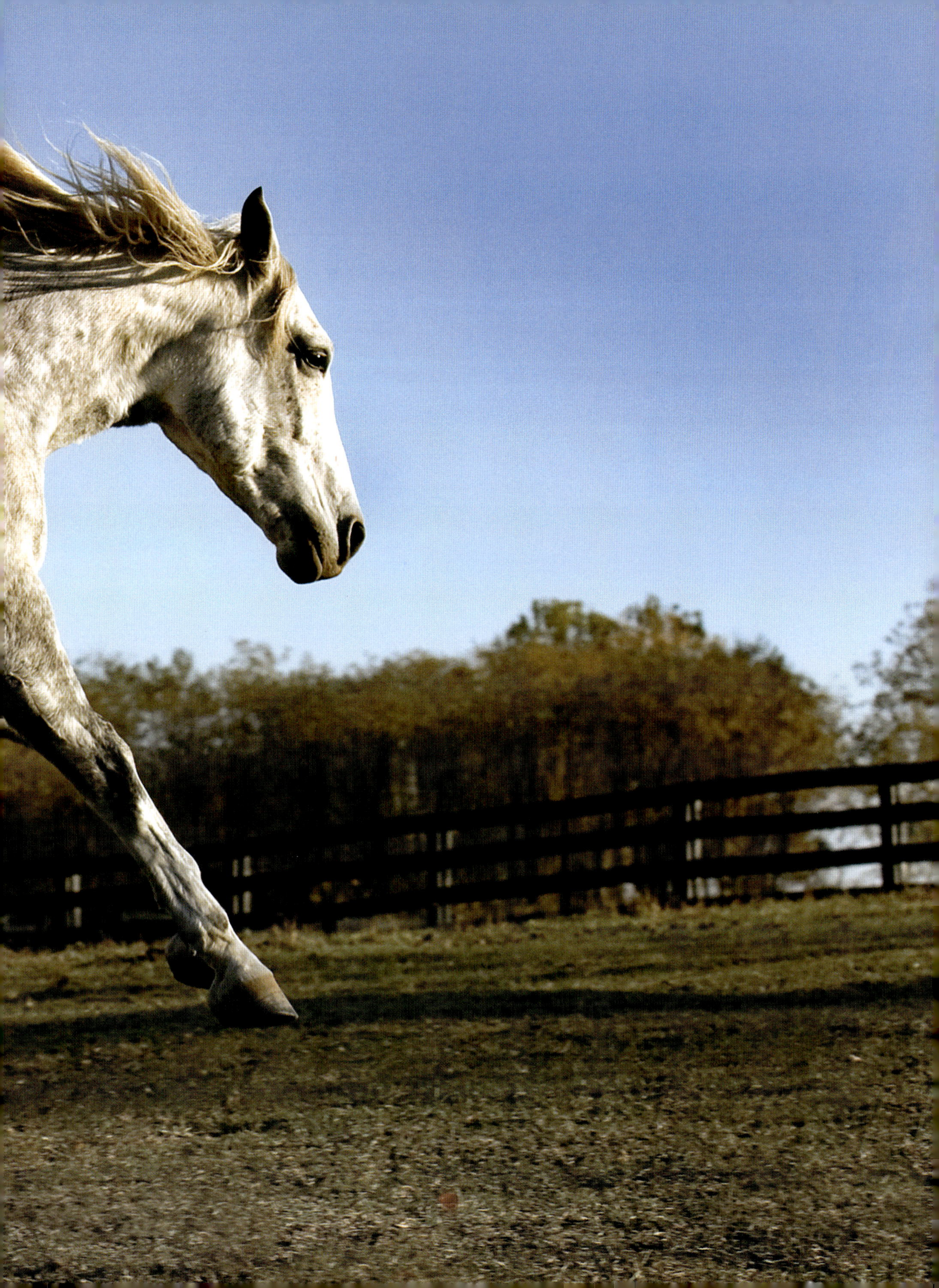

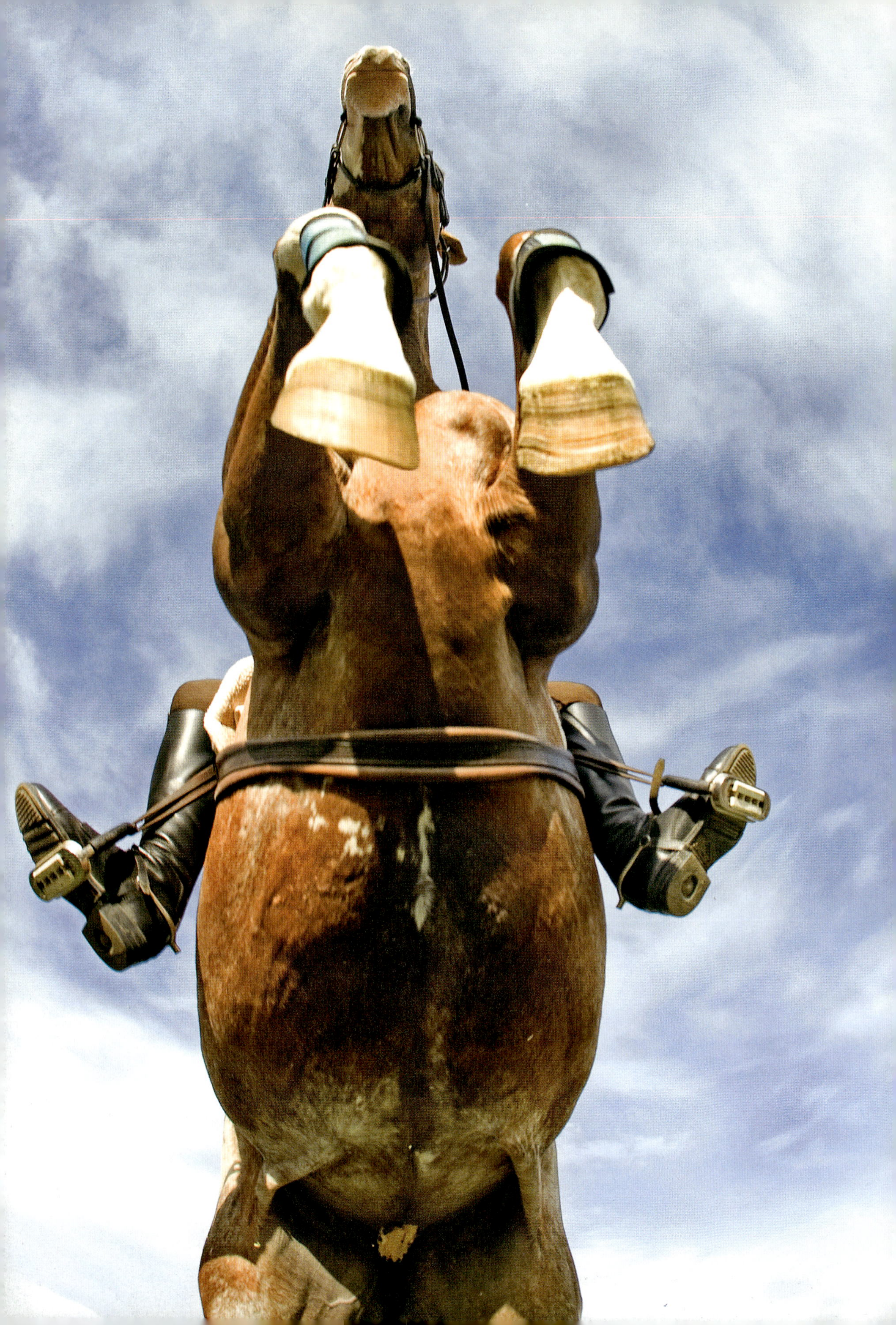

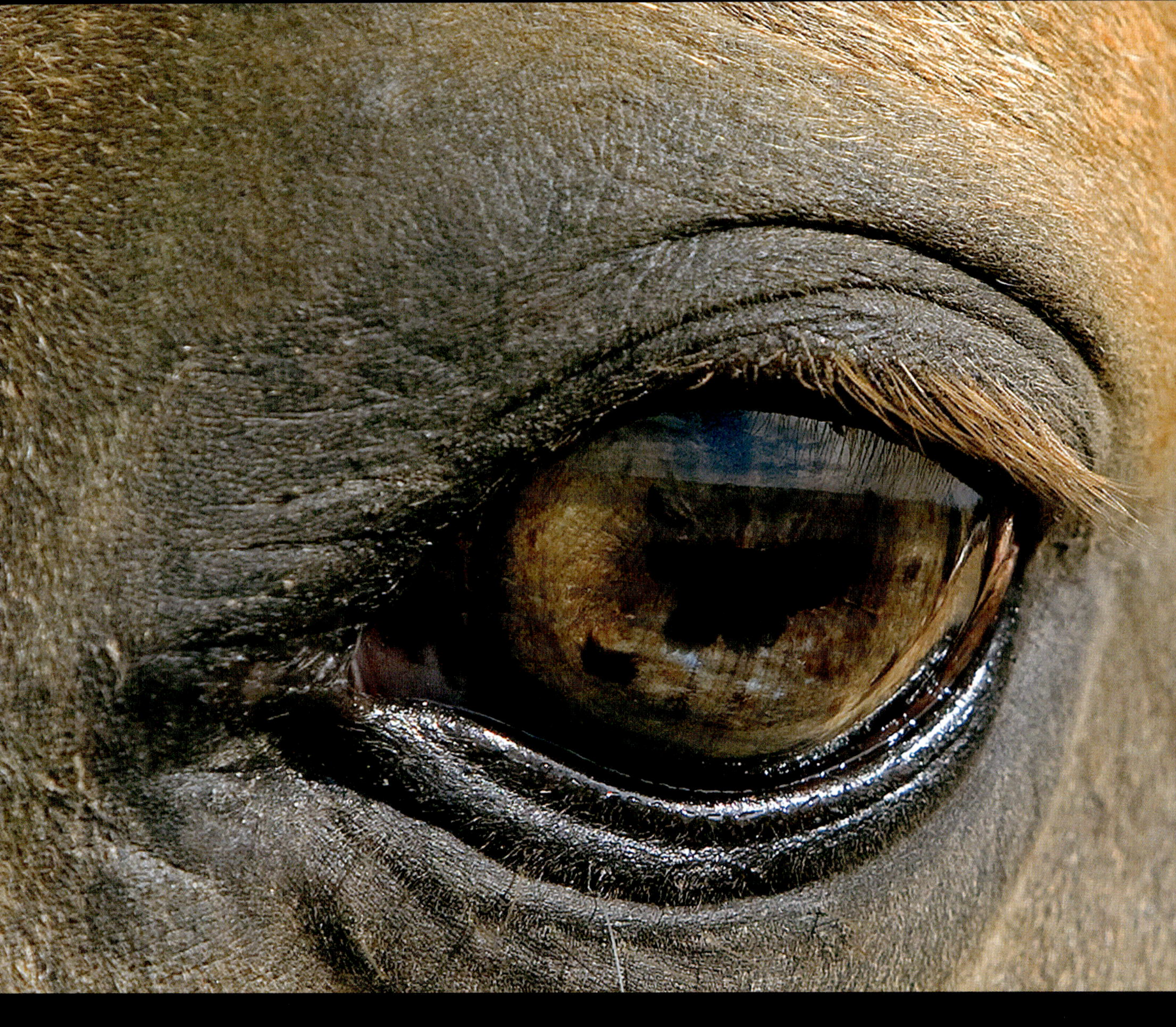

This amber eye reflects a surprising variety of subtle shades and colors, including light blue.

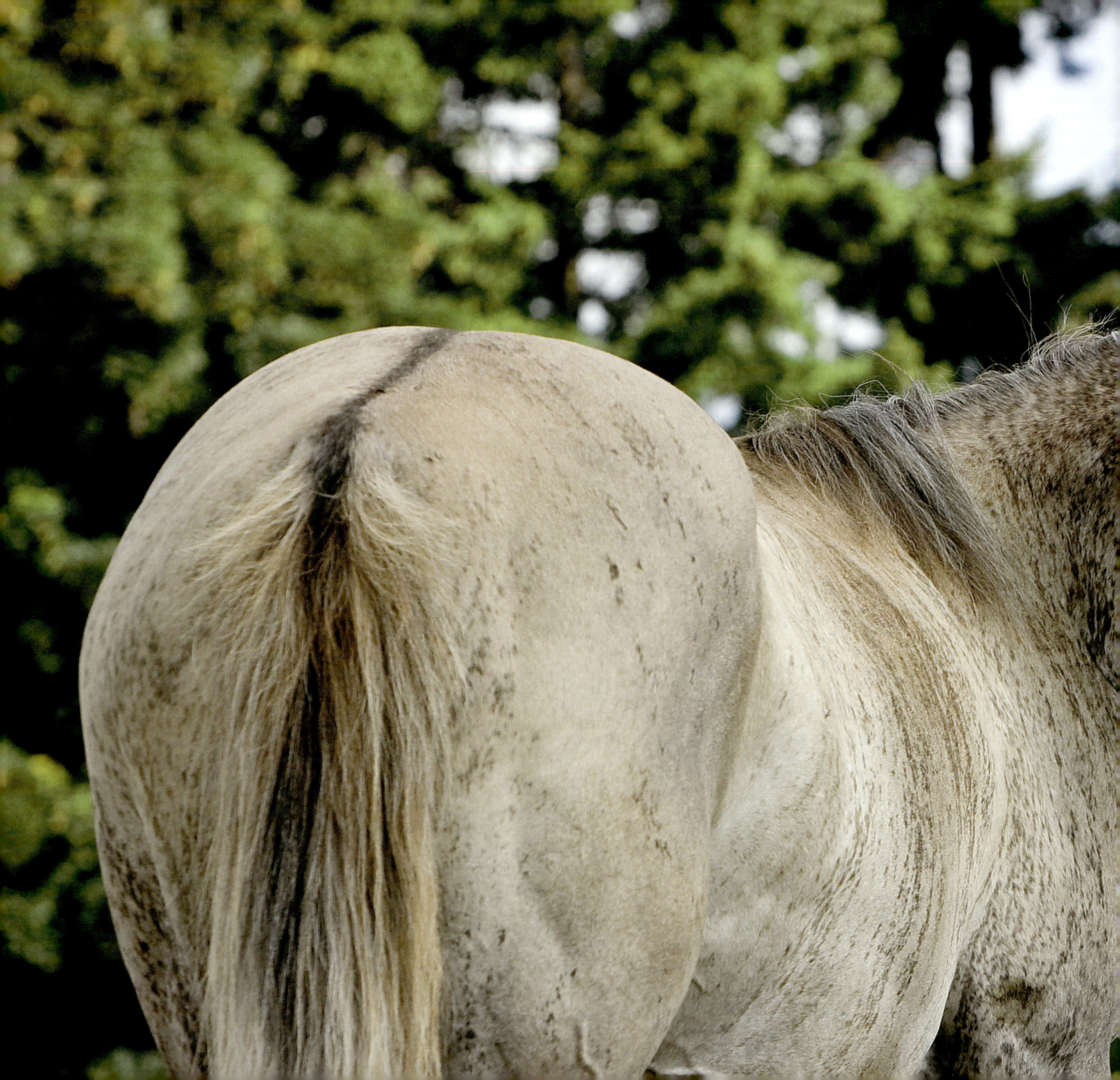

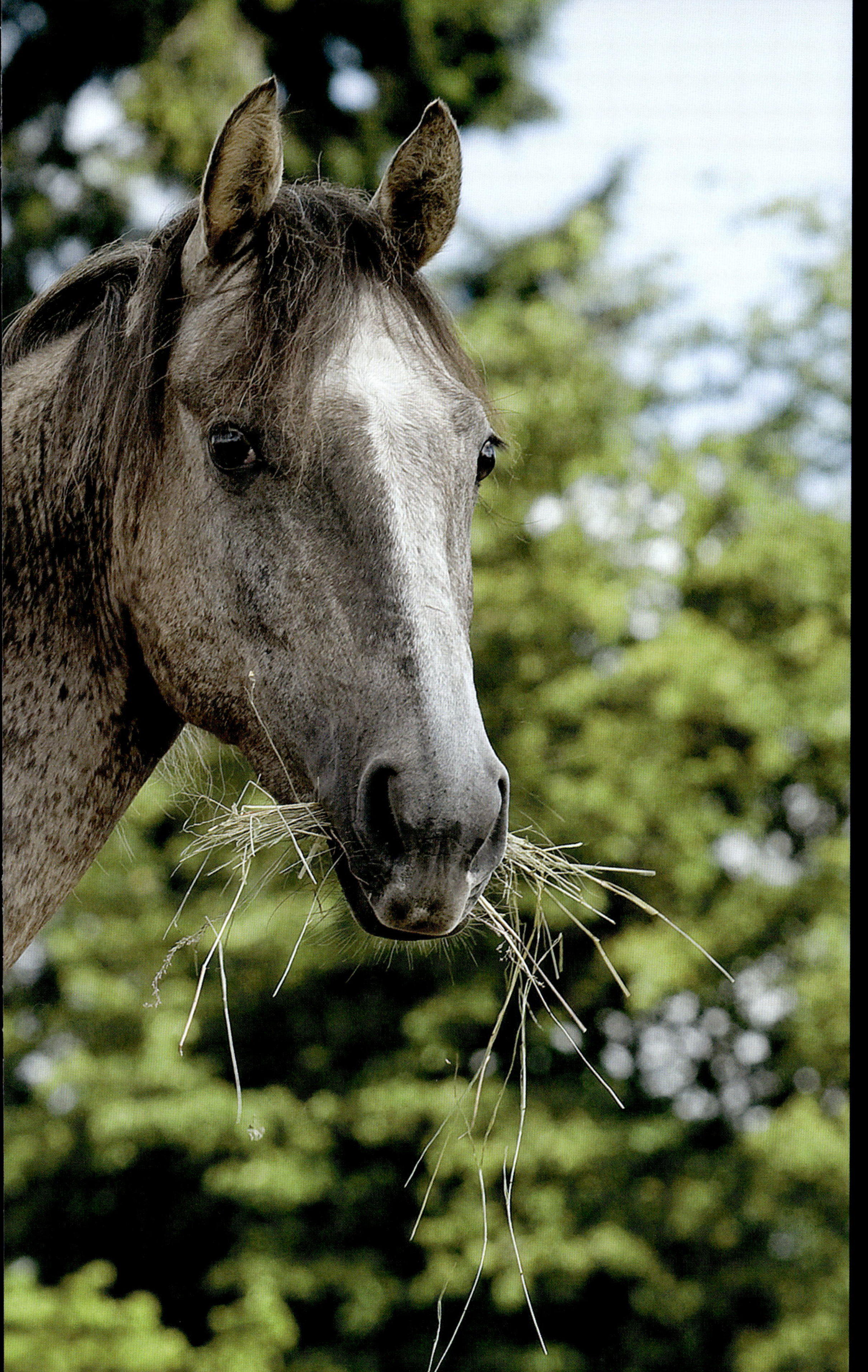

This brindle began life looking like the regular chestnut daughter of a grey mare. As she aged, her brindle pattern emerged, and her coat began to turn grey.

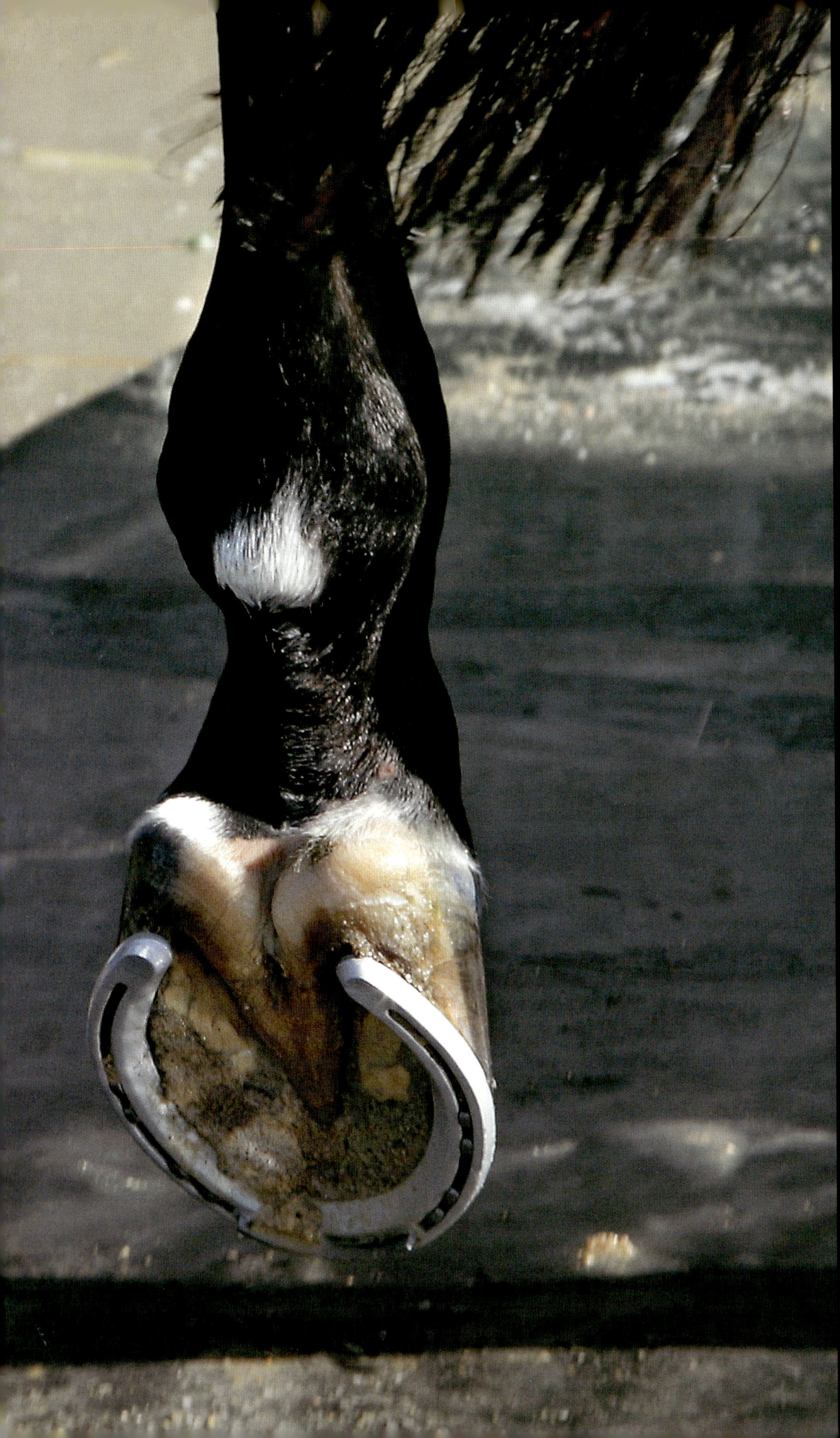

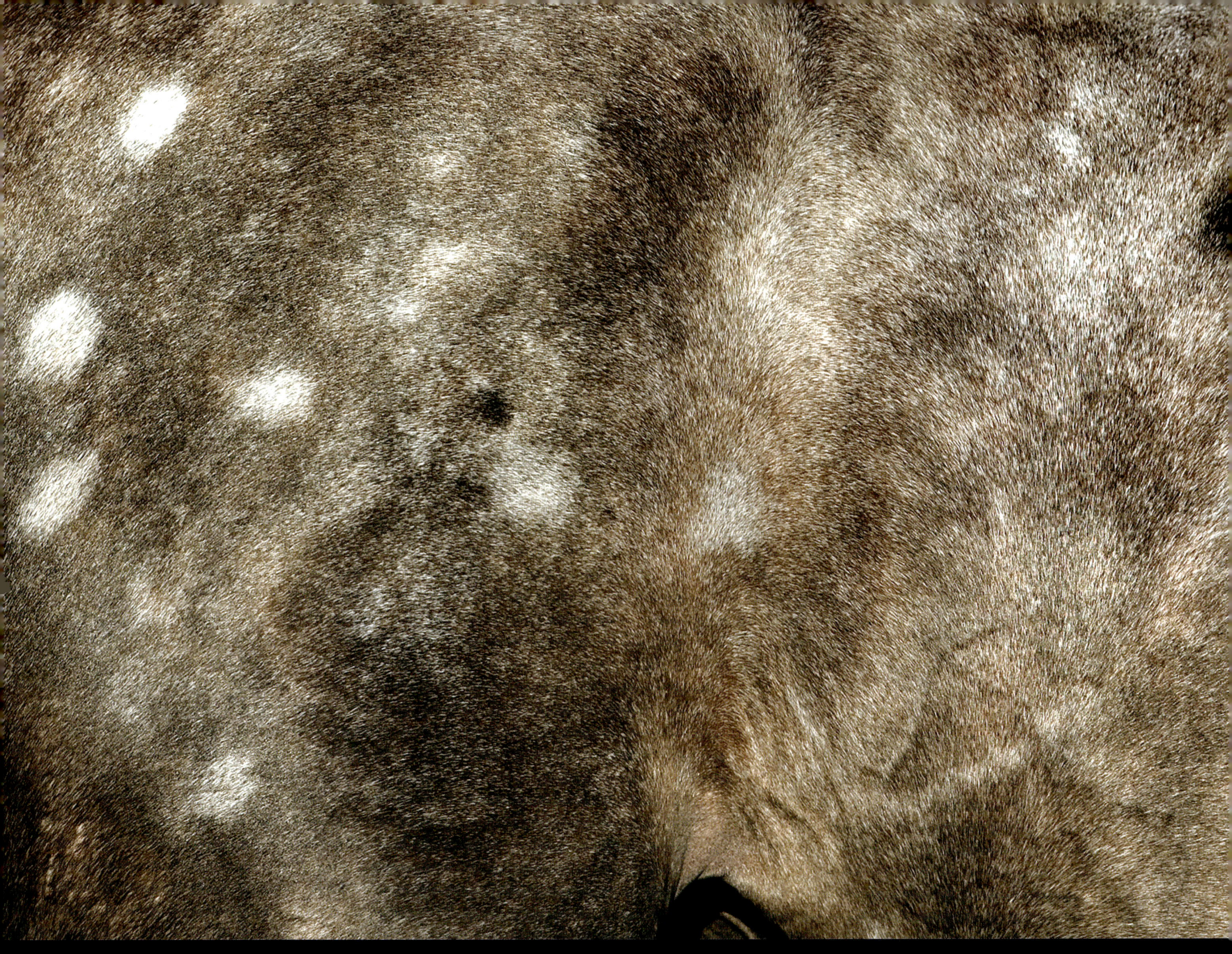

Left, this ankle with the atypical white spot belonged to the beloved Barbaro. Above, it is not yet understood why some dark grey horses have light splotches. They are often referred to as Tetrarch spots, in honor of the famous Thoroughbred stallion, The Tetrarch, who was similarly spotted. In time, as the dark areas lighten, the spots will eventually blend in.

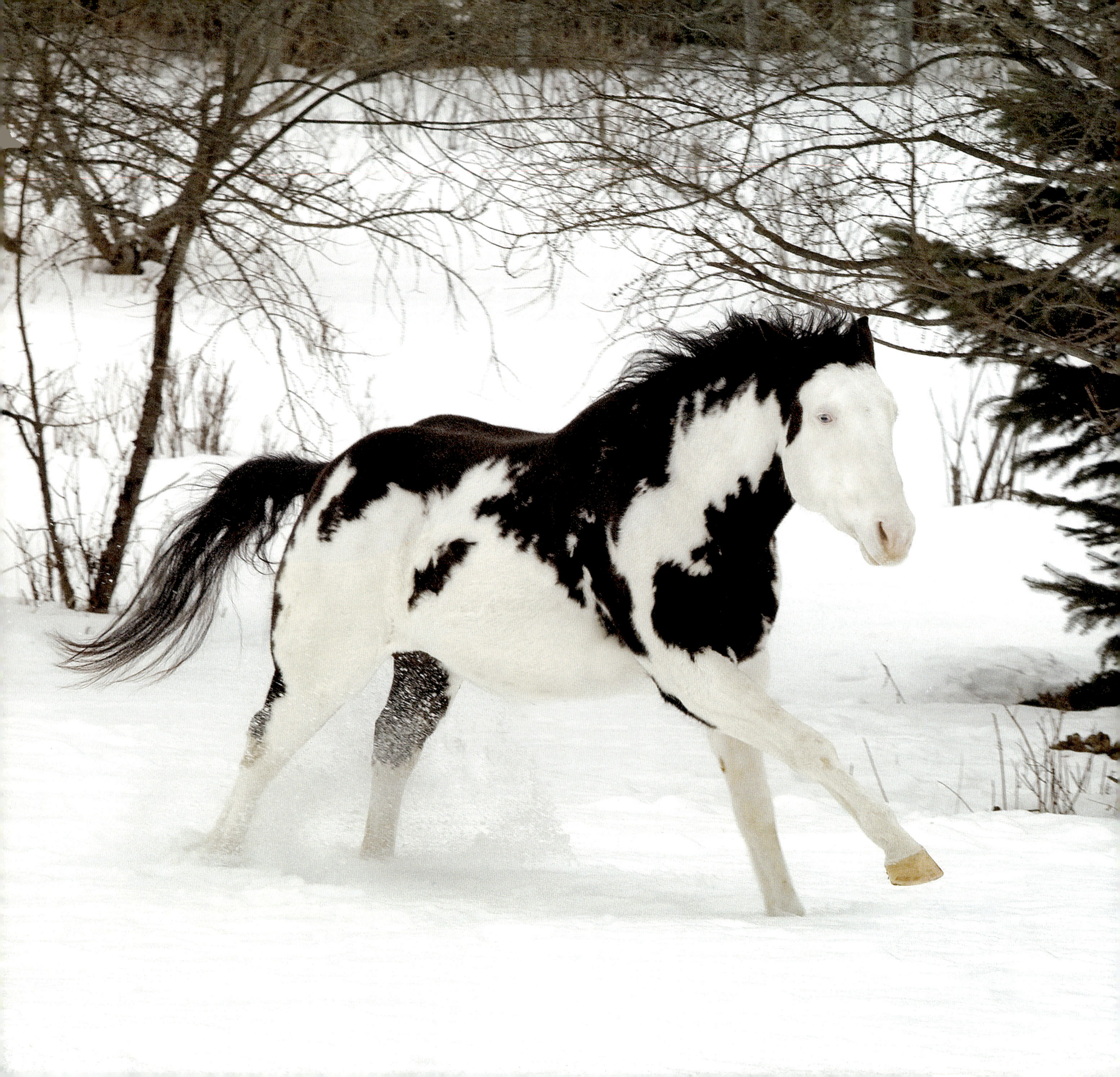

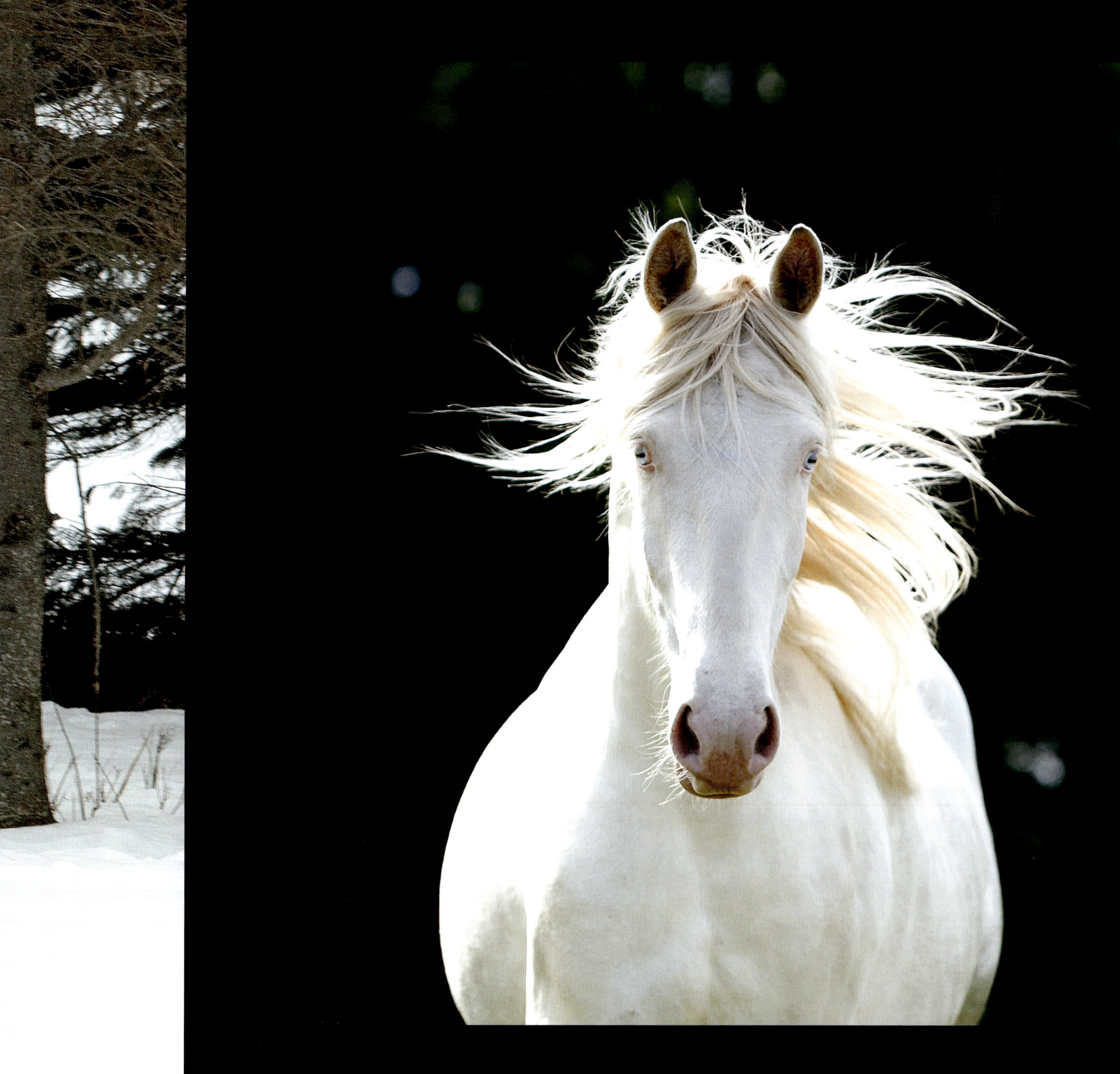

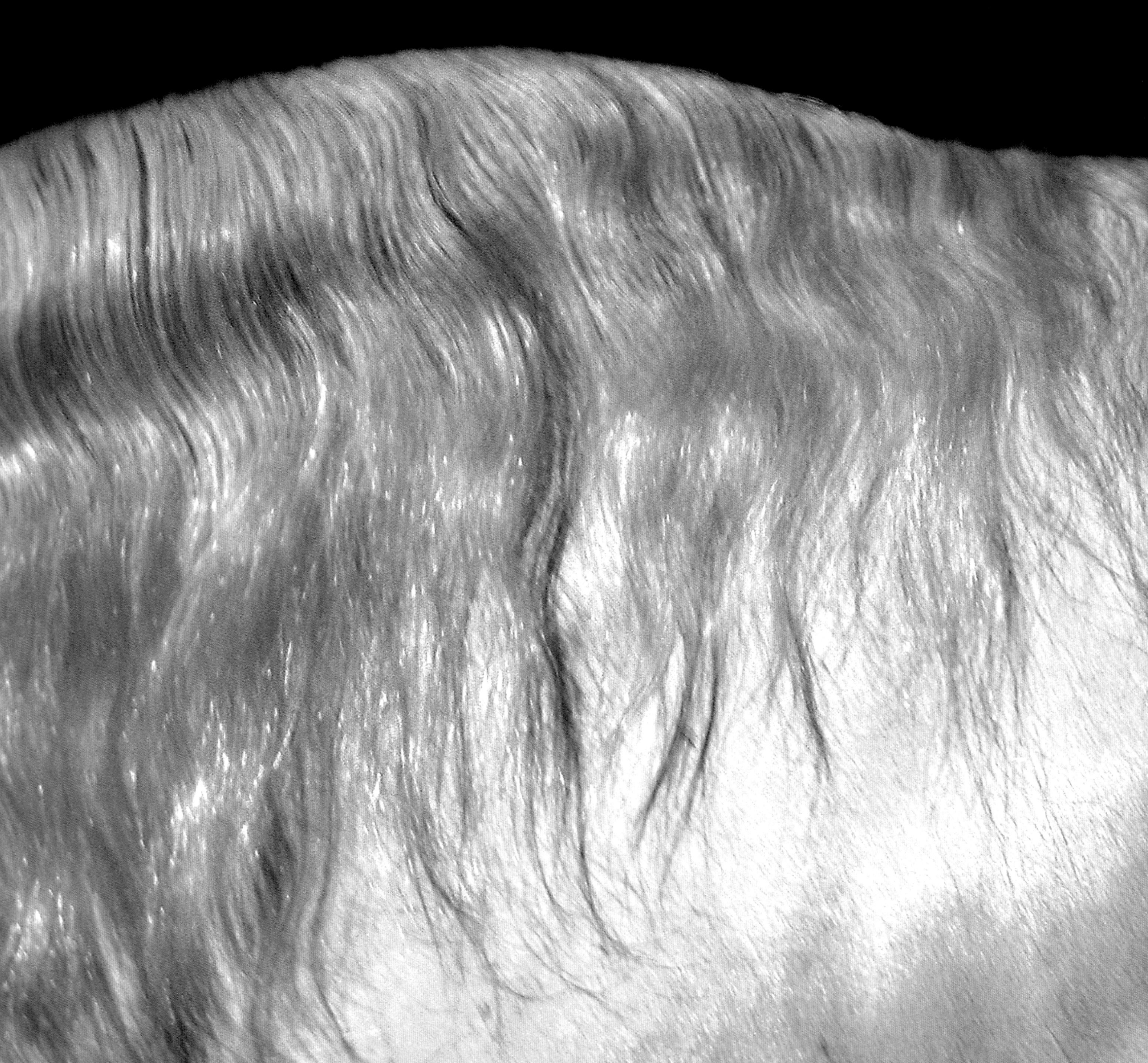

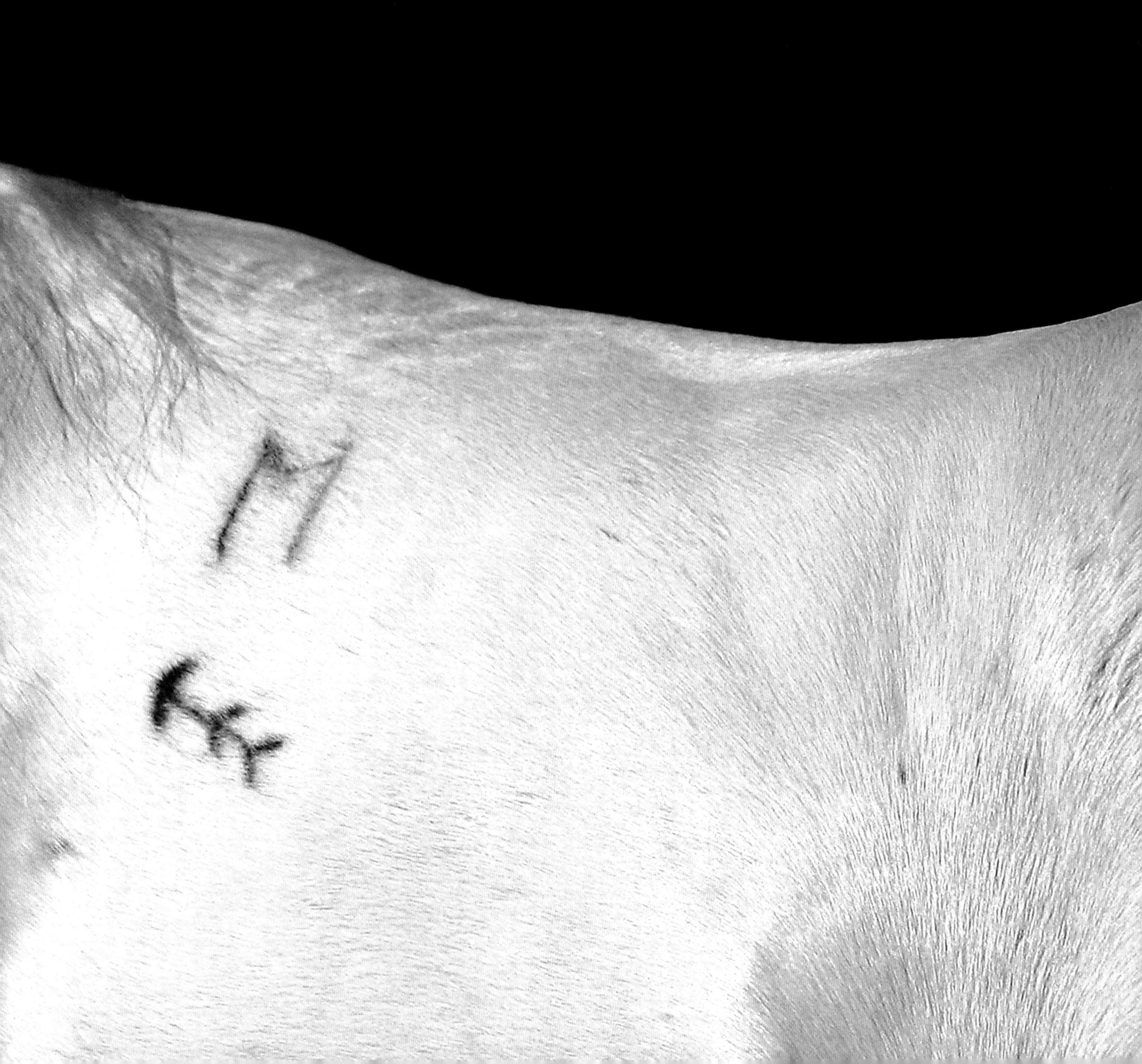

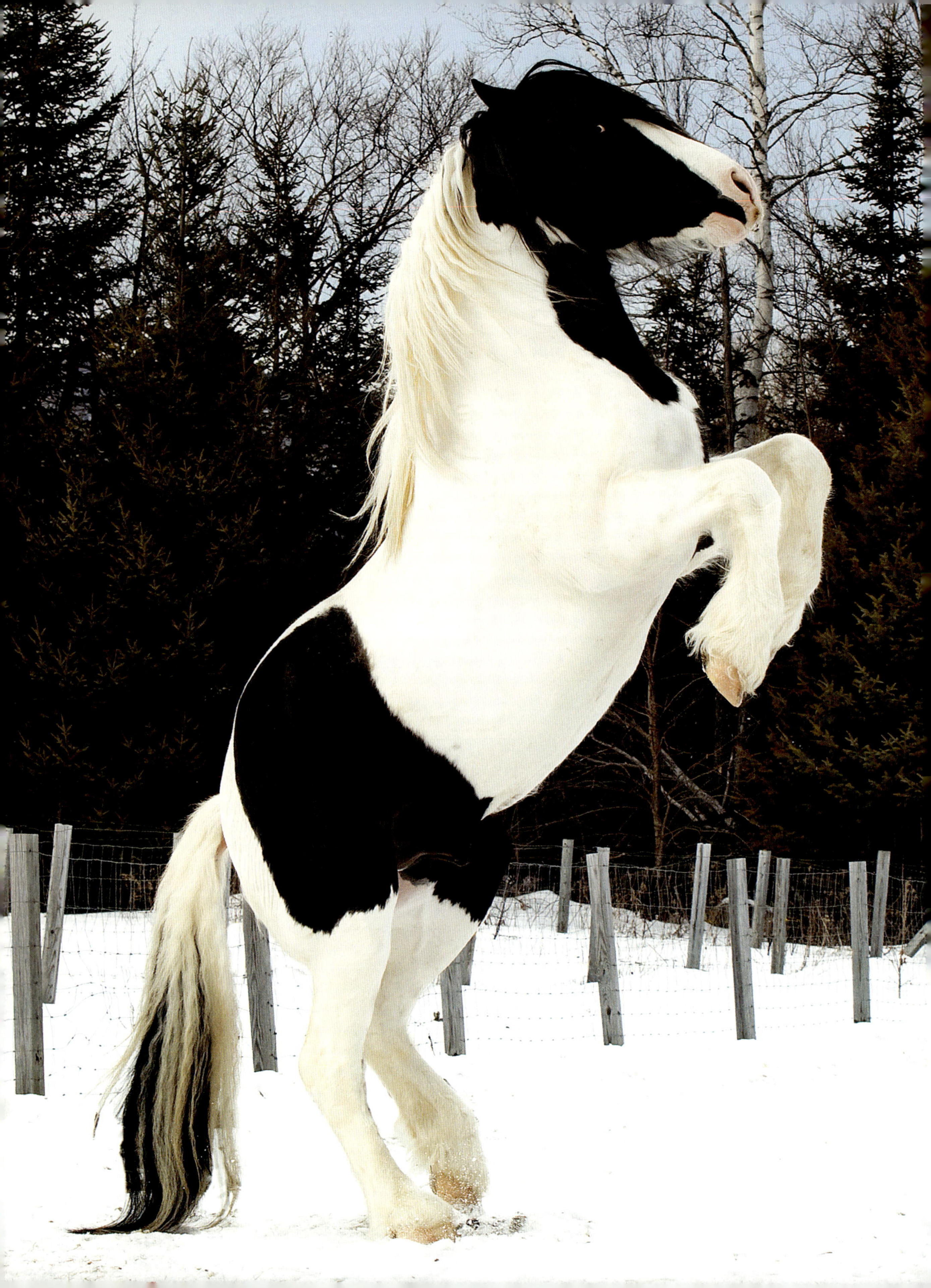

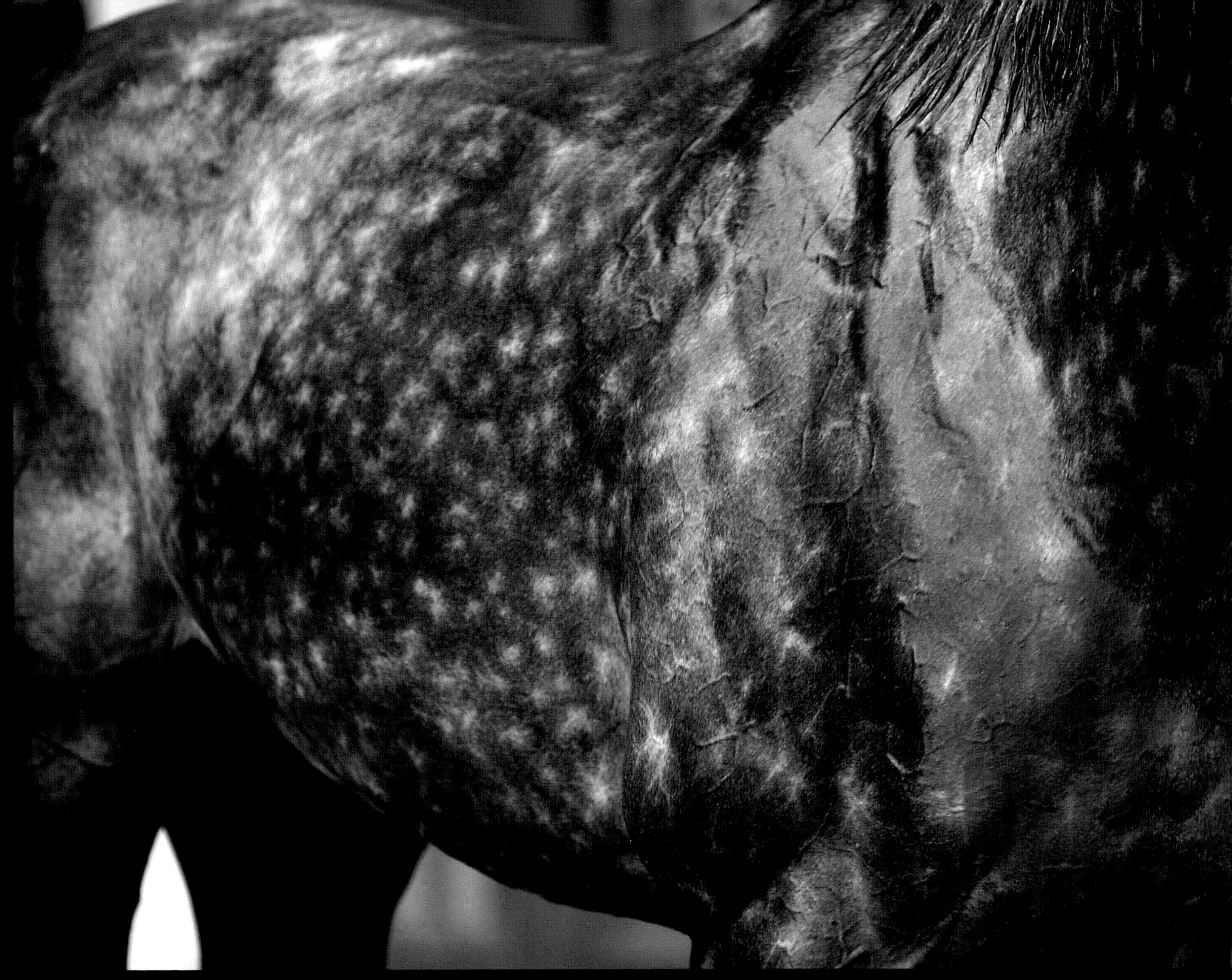

Dapples sometimes indicate a horse in top condition — healthy and well fed. Still, it is not fully understood why dapples appear and what their purpose is.

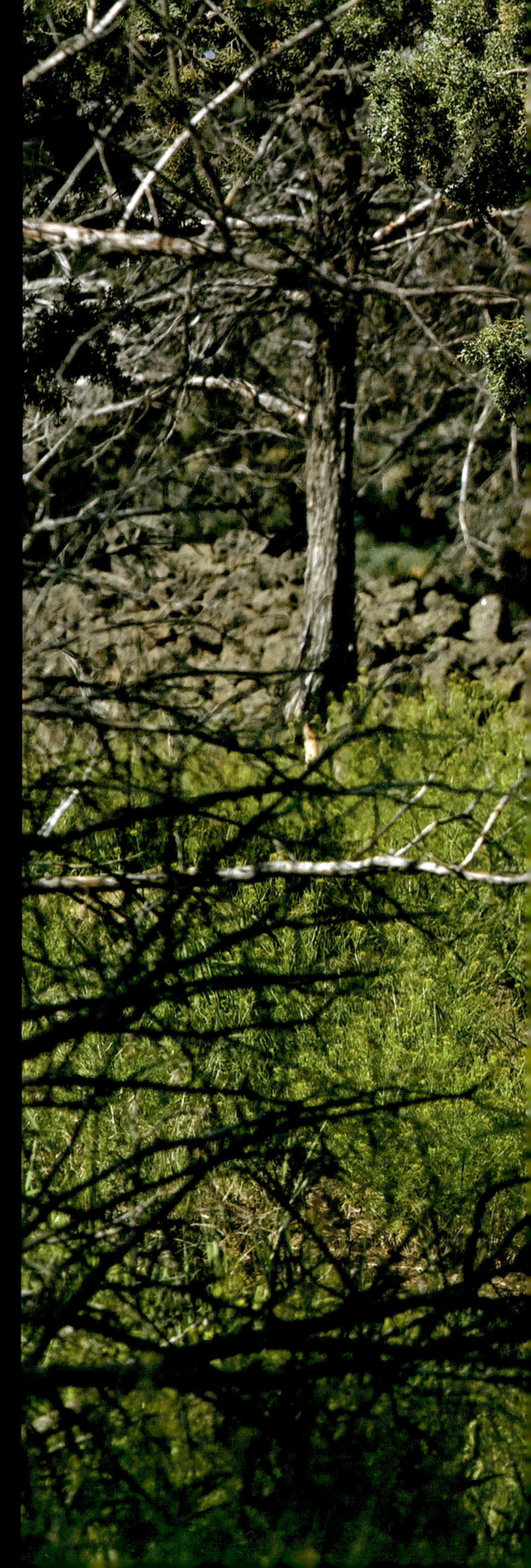

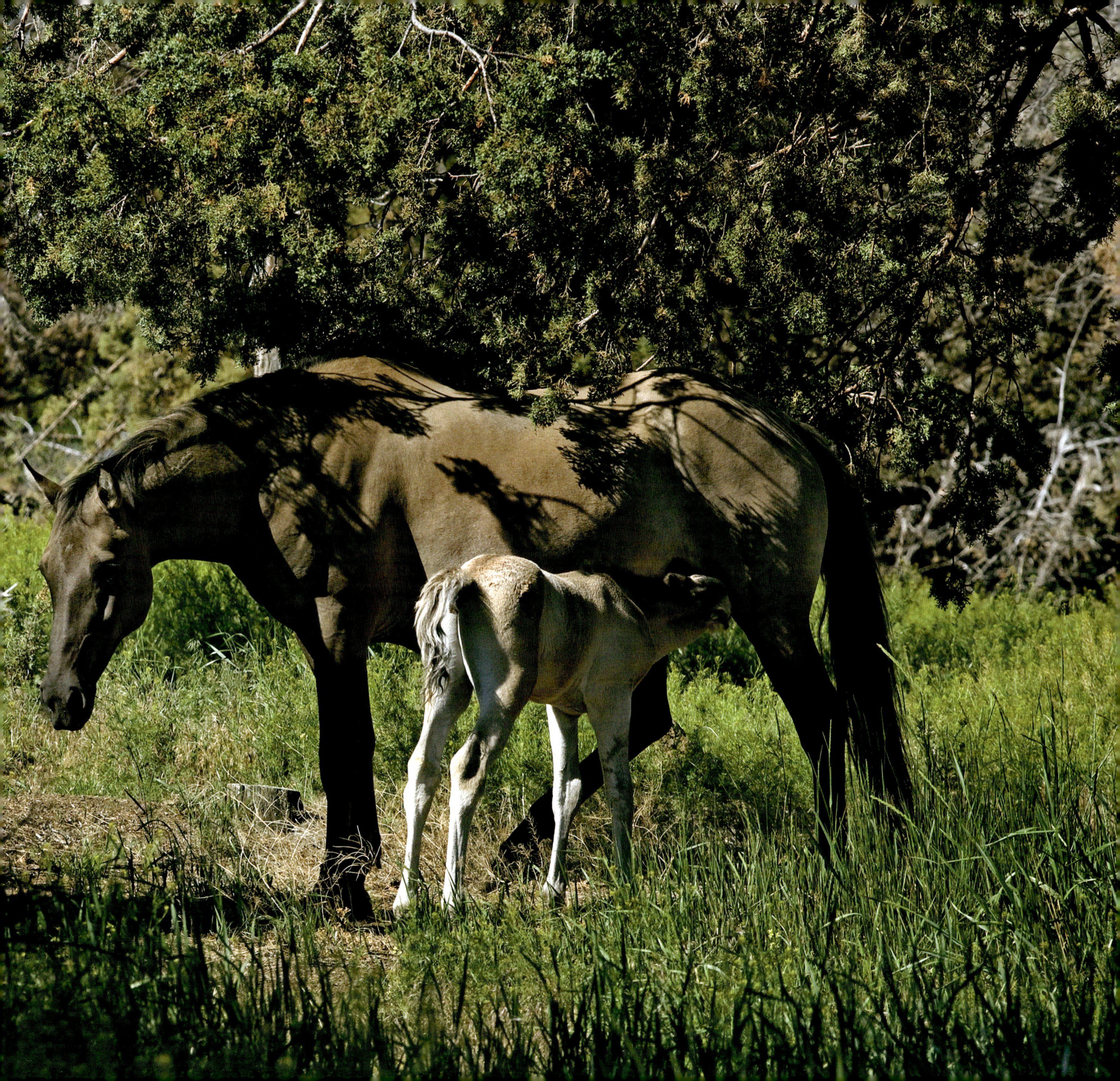

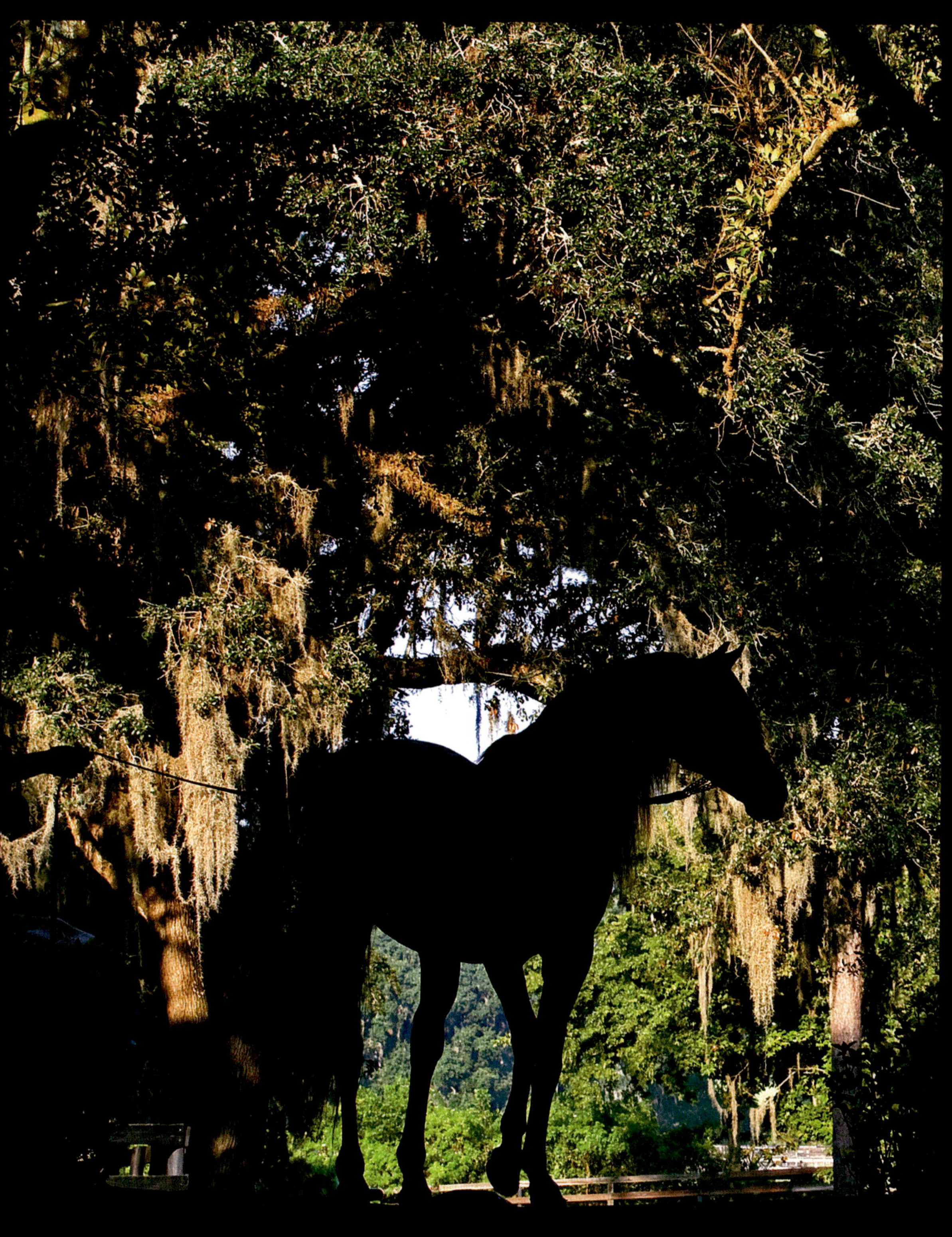

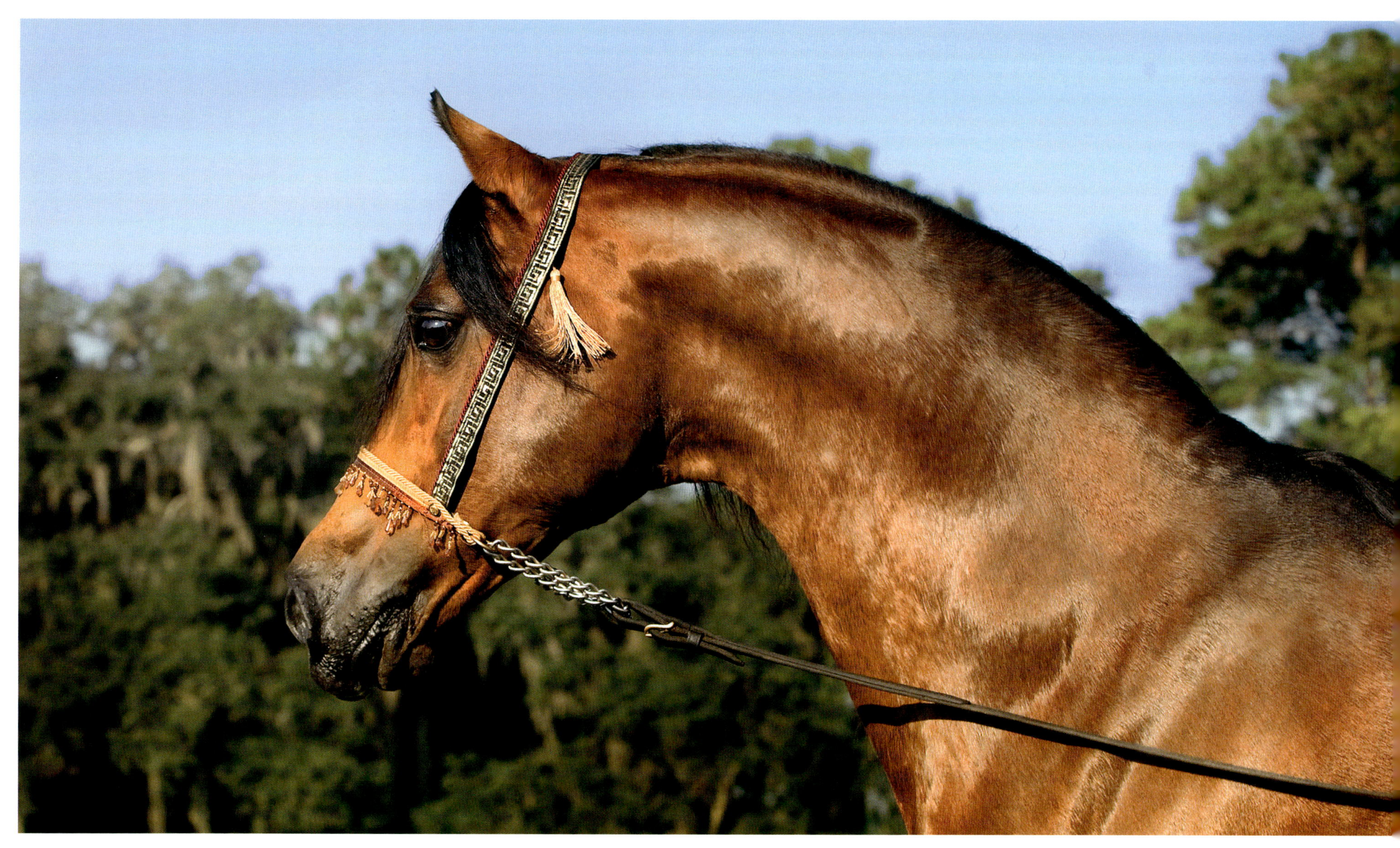

Good Thunder, left and above, the all-time winningest Arabian stallion, was a magnificent example of the bay color.

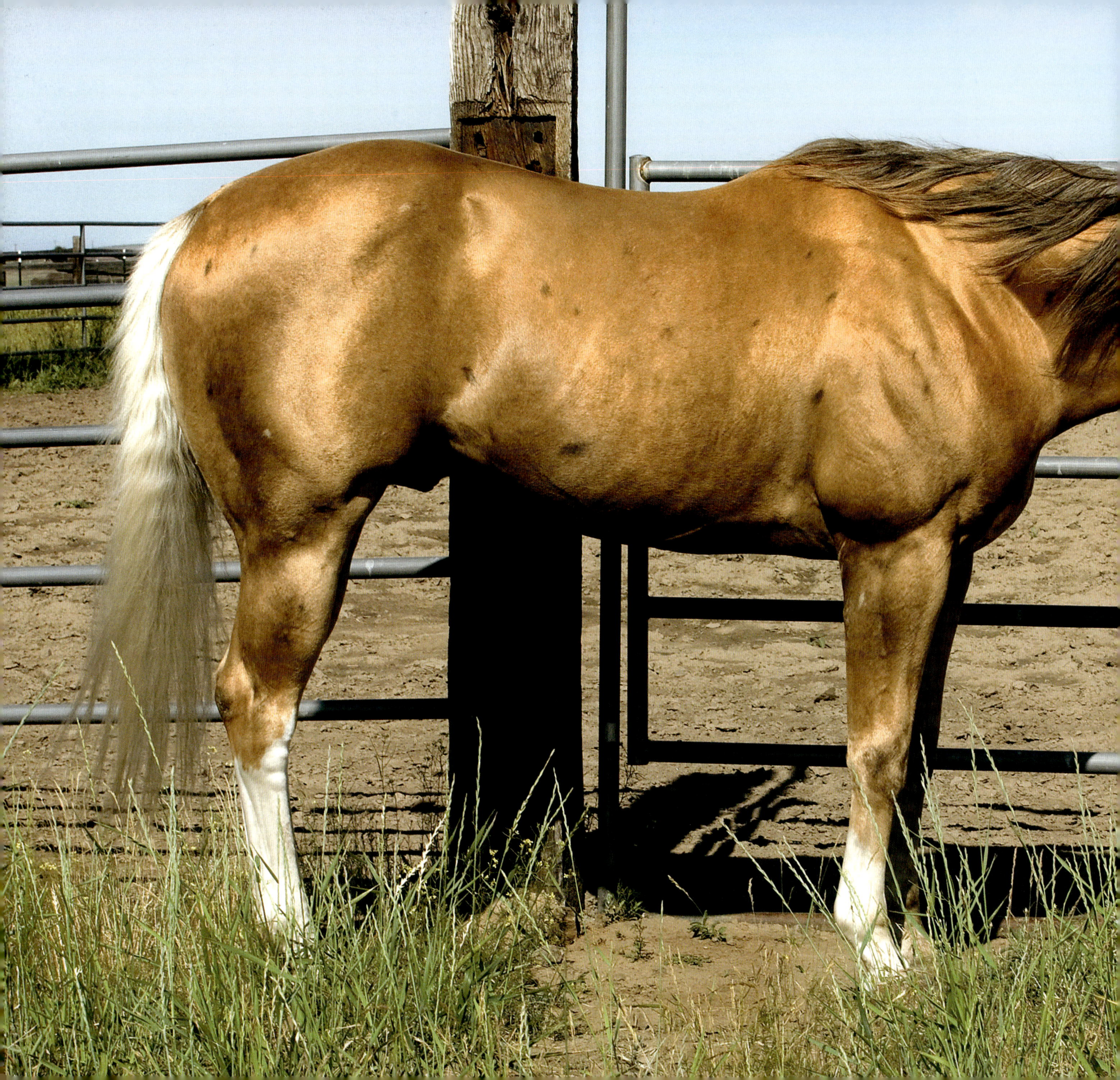

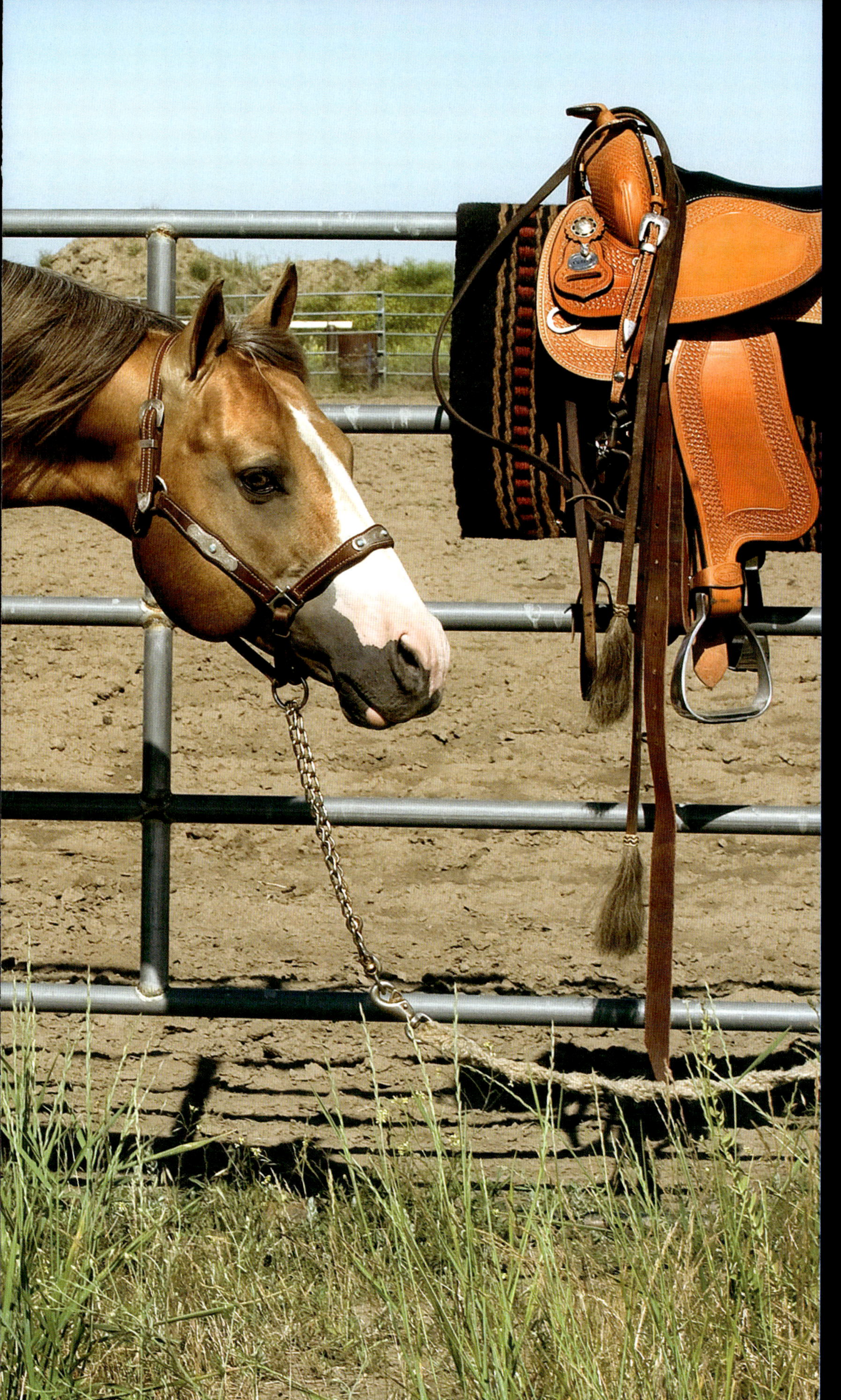

Sooty palominos have areas of black hairs in addition to the golden color associated with palominos. This flashy Quarter Horse stallion has the unusual combination of a dark mane and light tail, as well as Bend Or spots.

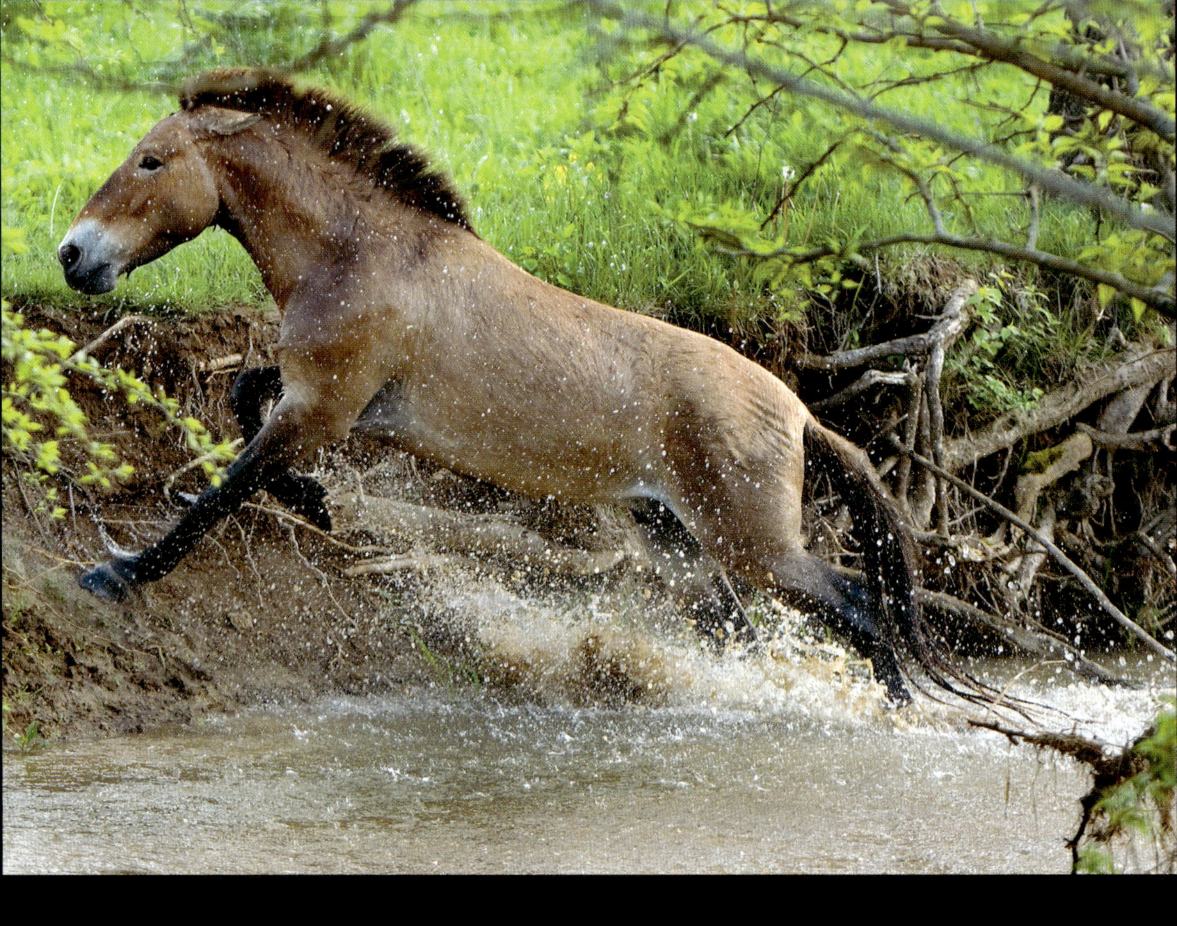

The Przewalski's Horse is considered, genetically, the only remaining truly wild horse in the world. (Other breeds, such as Chincoteague ponies, were once domesticated before adapting to life on their own.) This stallion is one of only about 1,500 known Przewalski's Horses, according to a 2005 census.

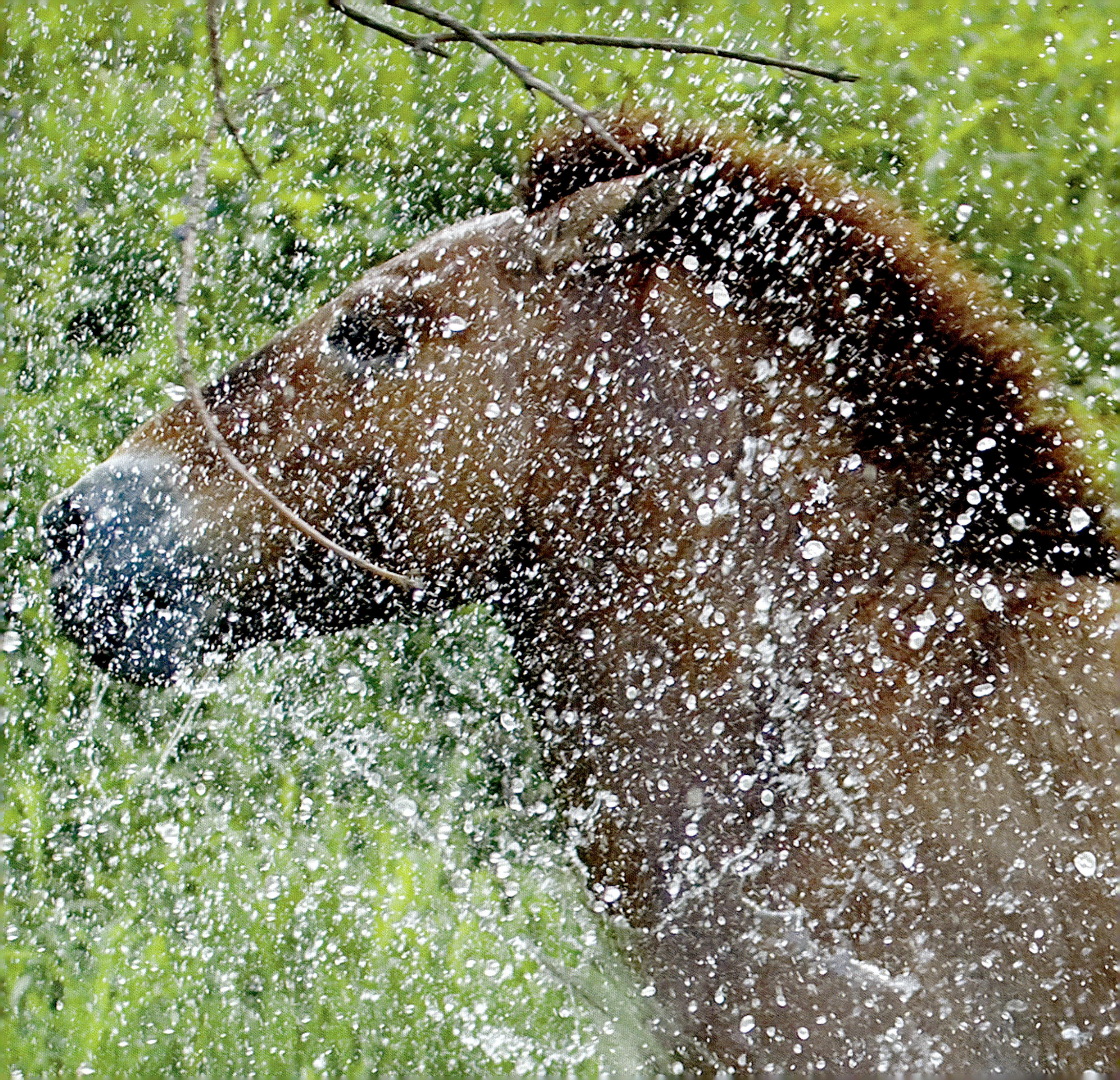

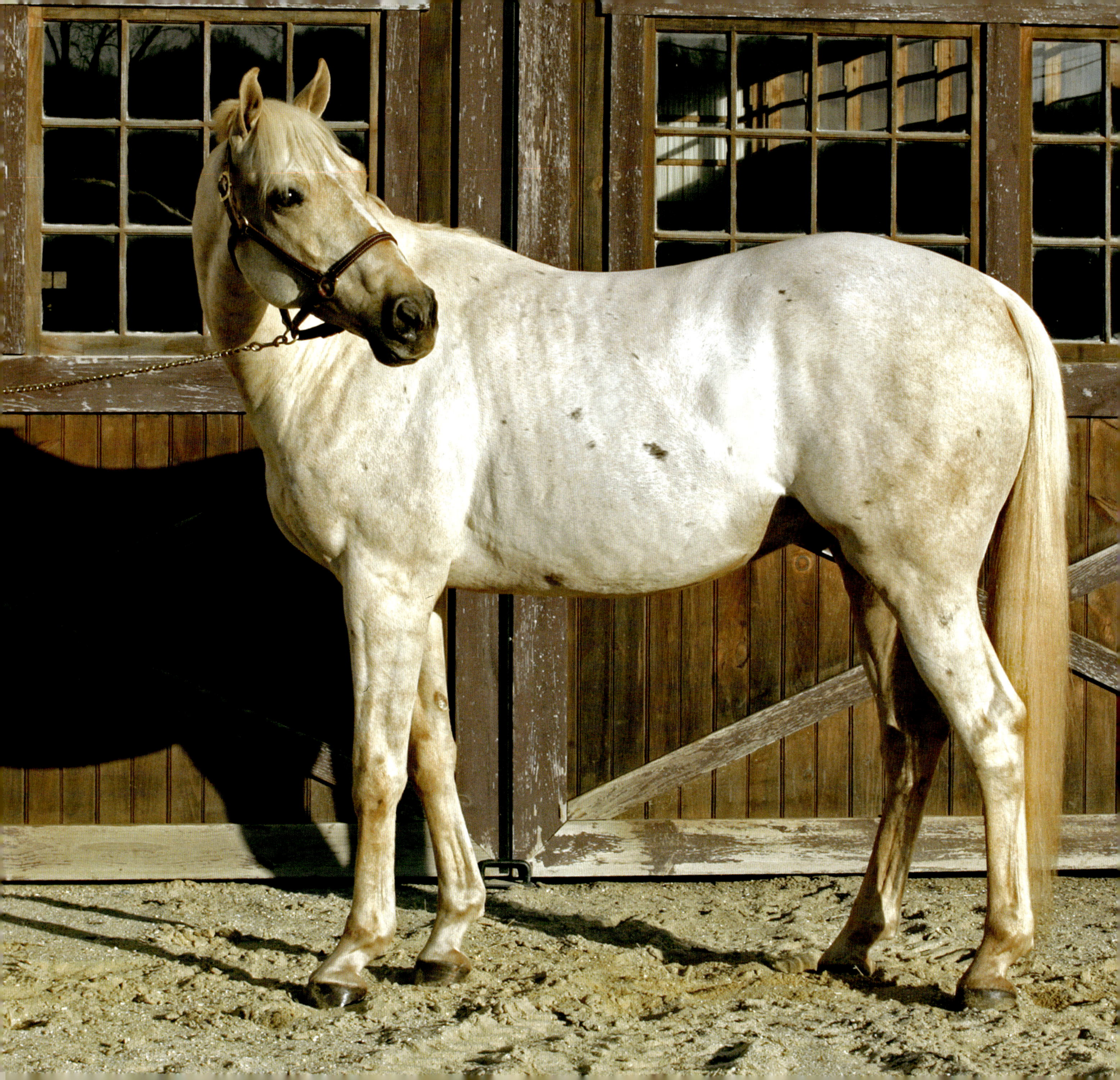

Some horses' coats change seasonally, such as this handsome blue roan Brabant gelding, shown at right in his winter coat. In early spring, he sprouts a soft, white layer of hair and by summer, his slick body has a light grey-roan coloration that, in certain light, appears to have a blue cast.

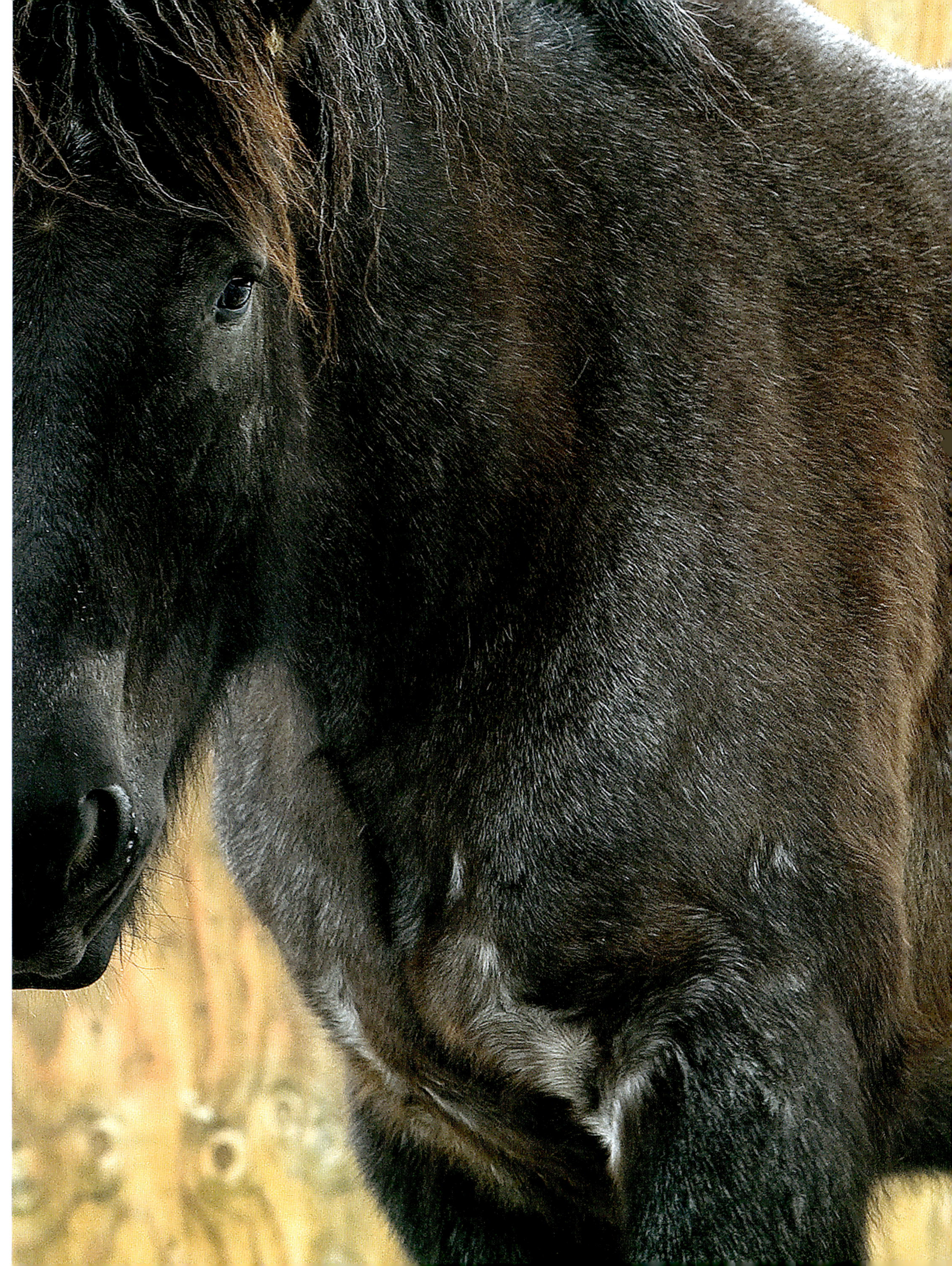

This patterned brindle mare is a chimera, a result of two nonidentical twin embryos fusing early in pregnancy. Amazingly, her blood reflects two different DNA types.

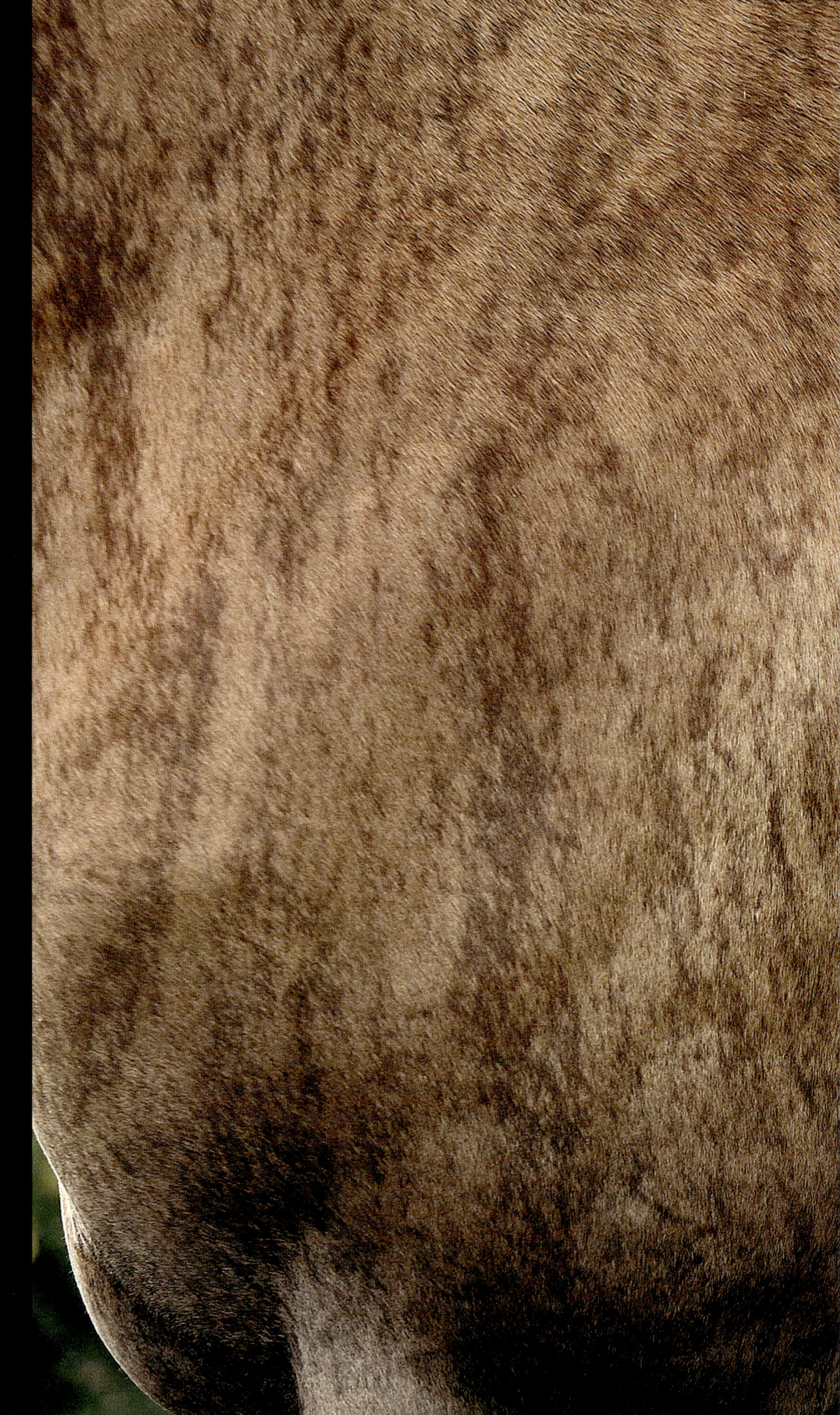

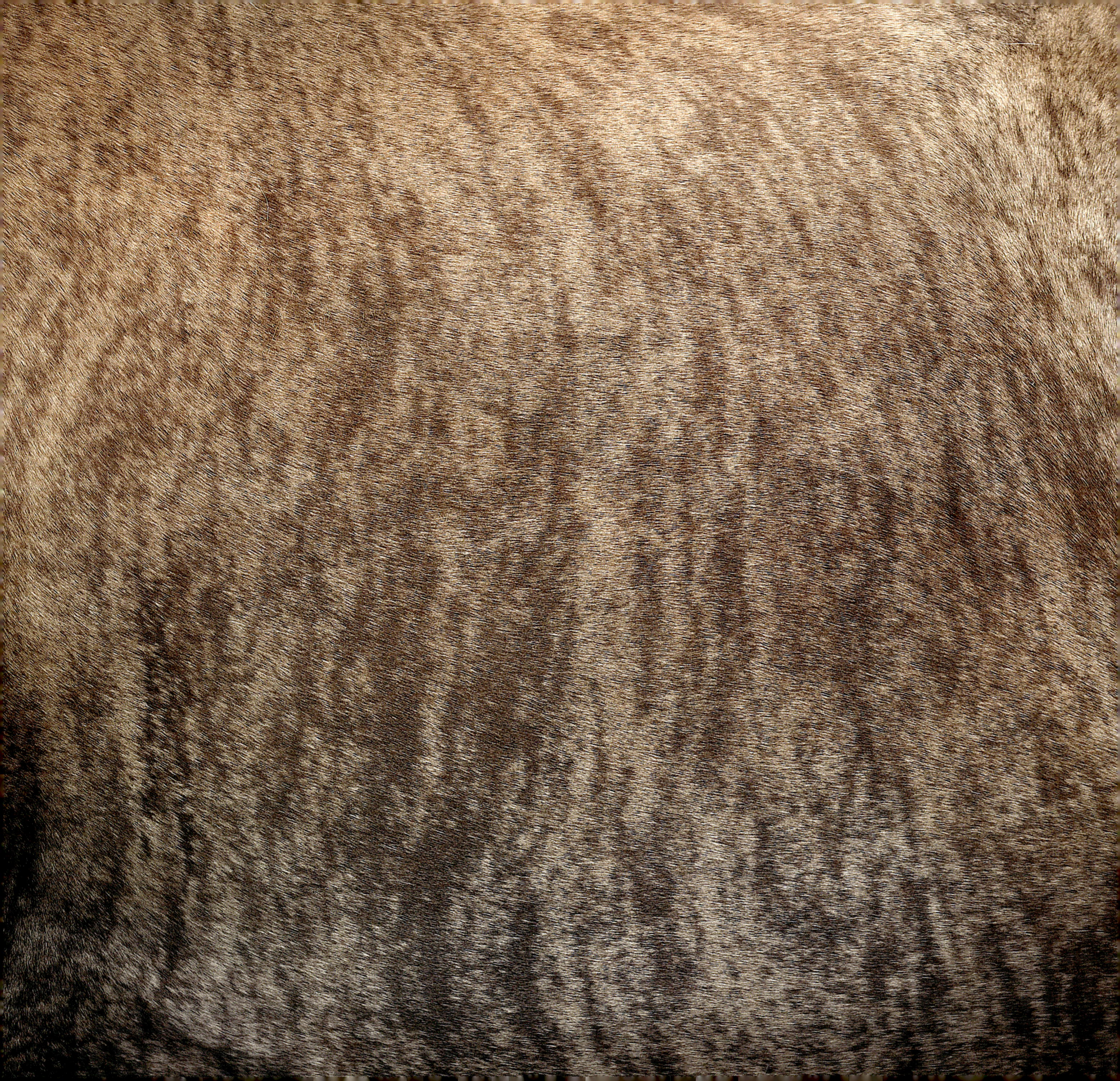

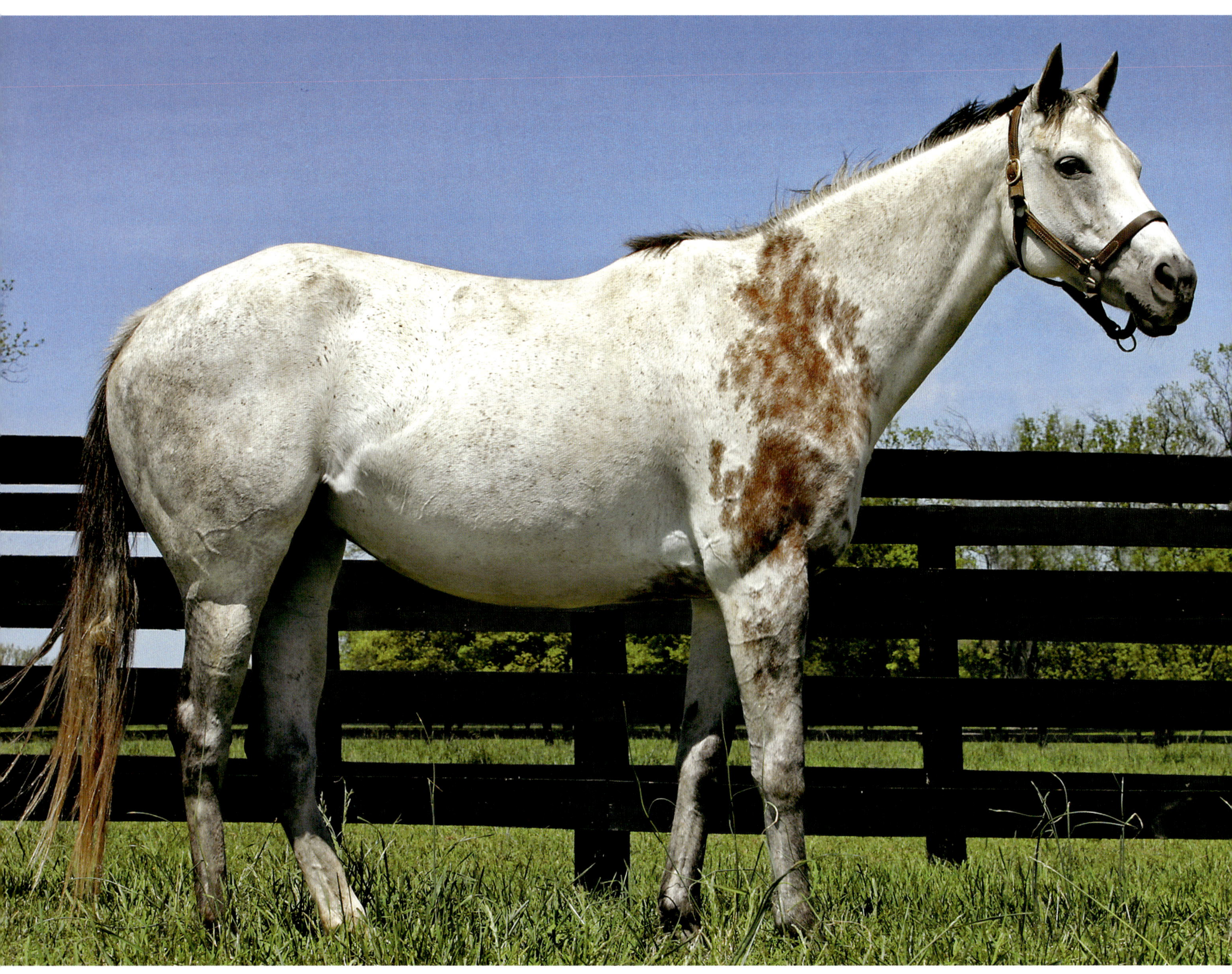

Left, this mare features an extensive red marking called a "bloody shoulder mark" on her otherwise unremarkable grey coat.

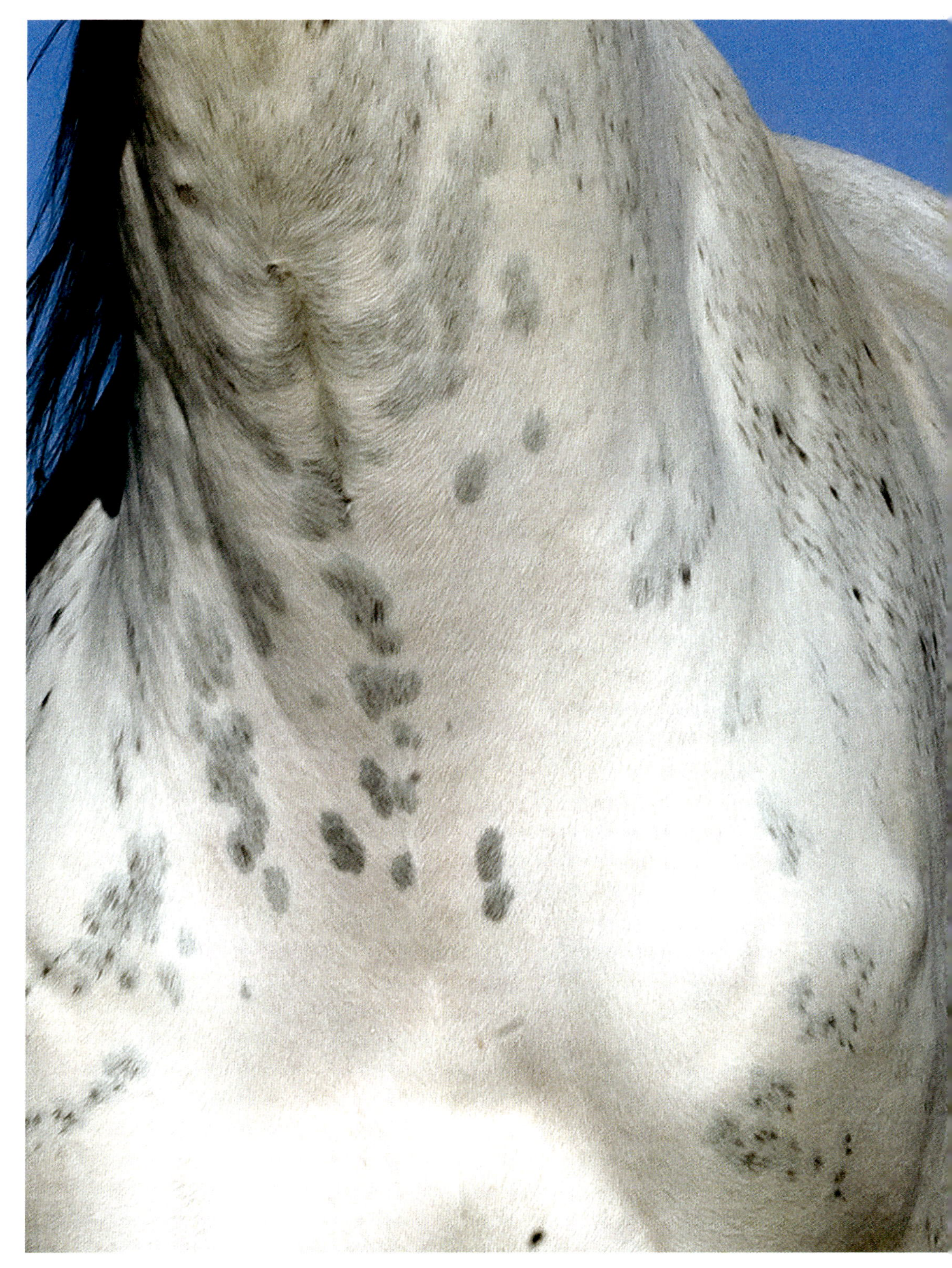

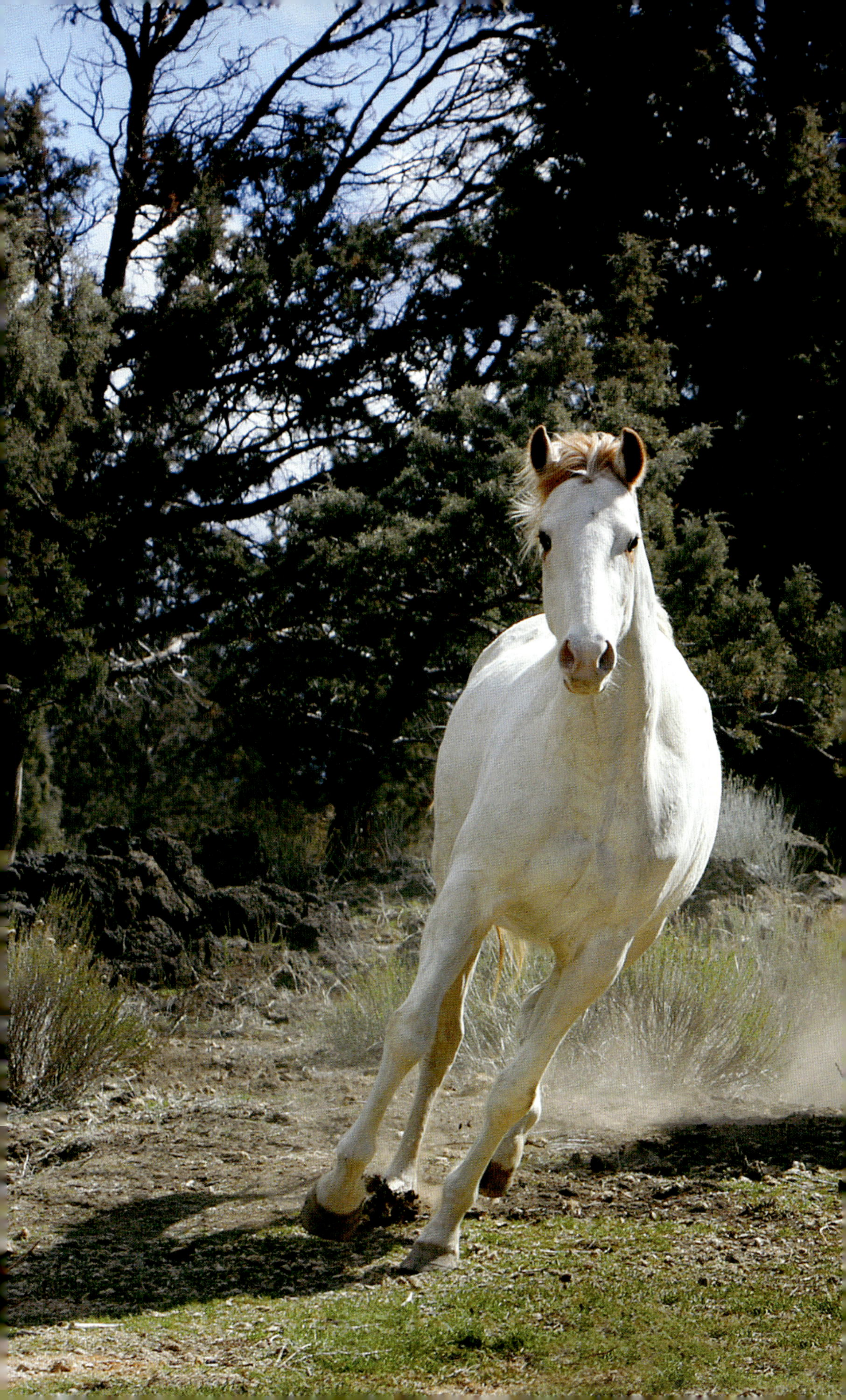

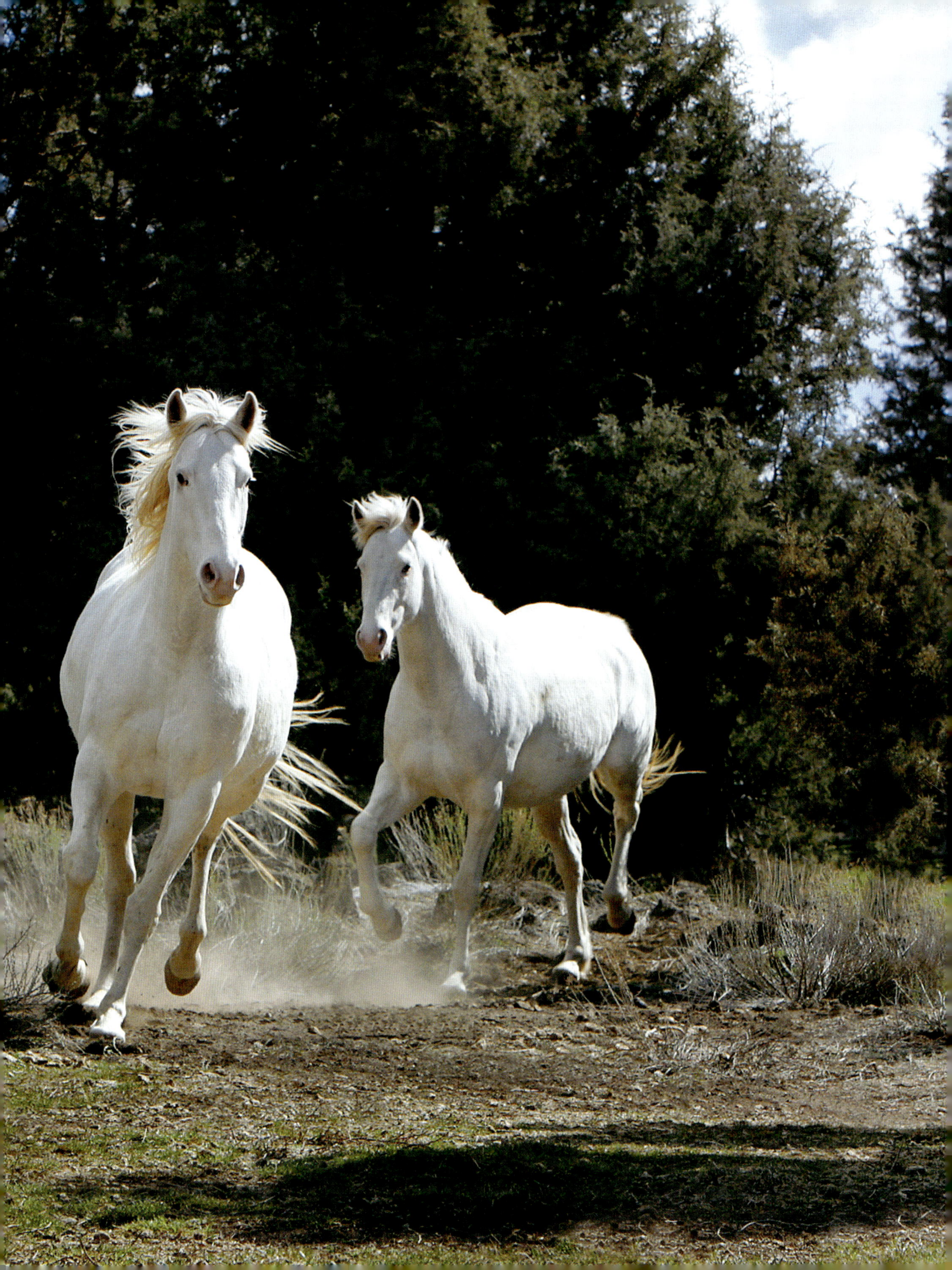

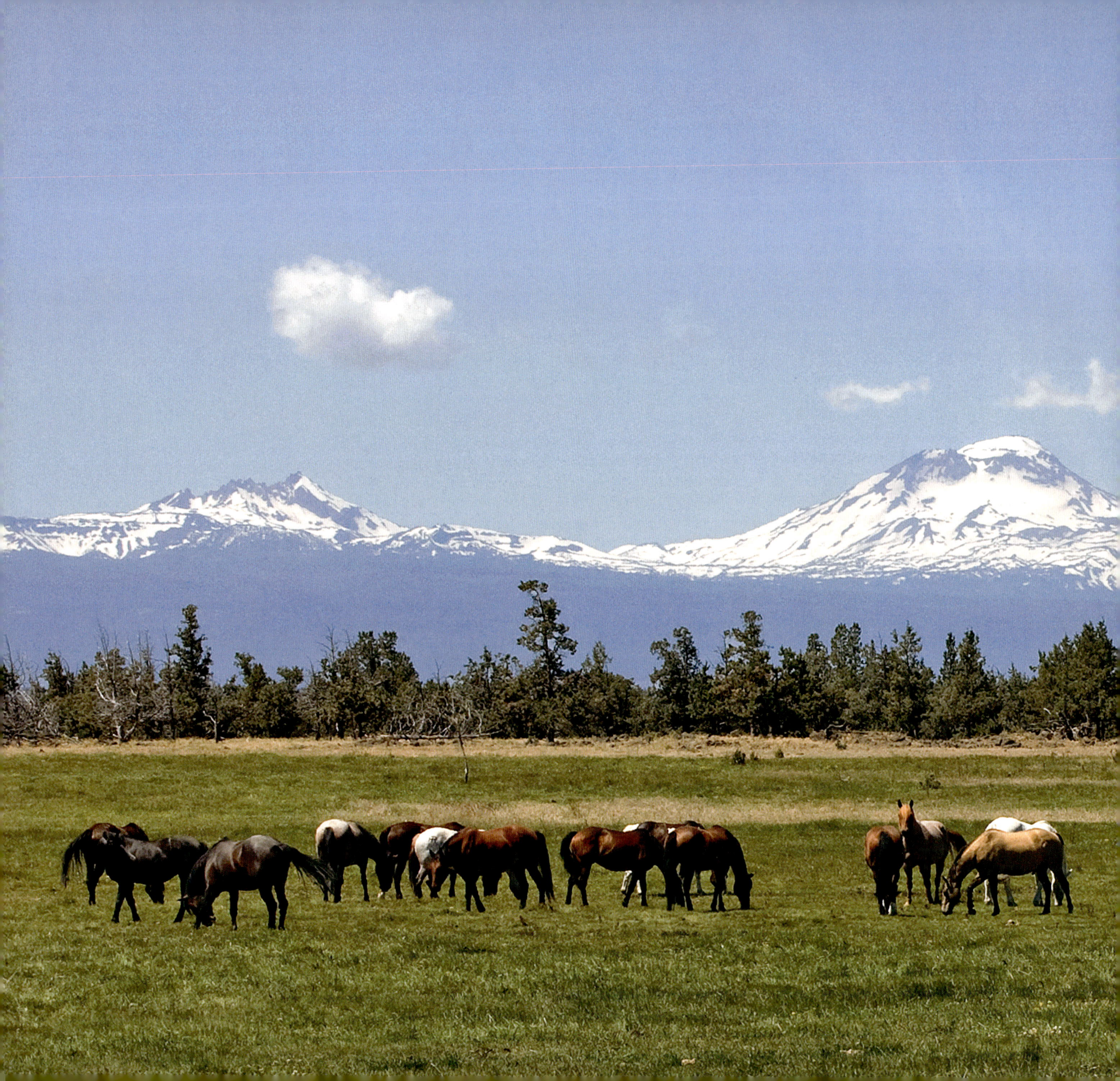

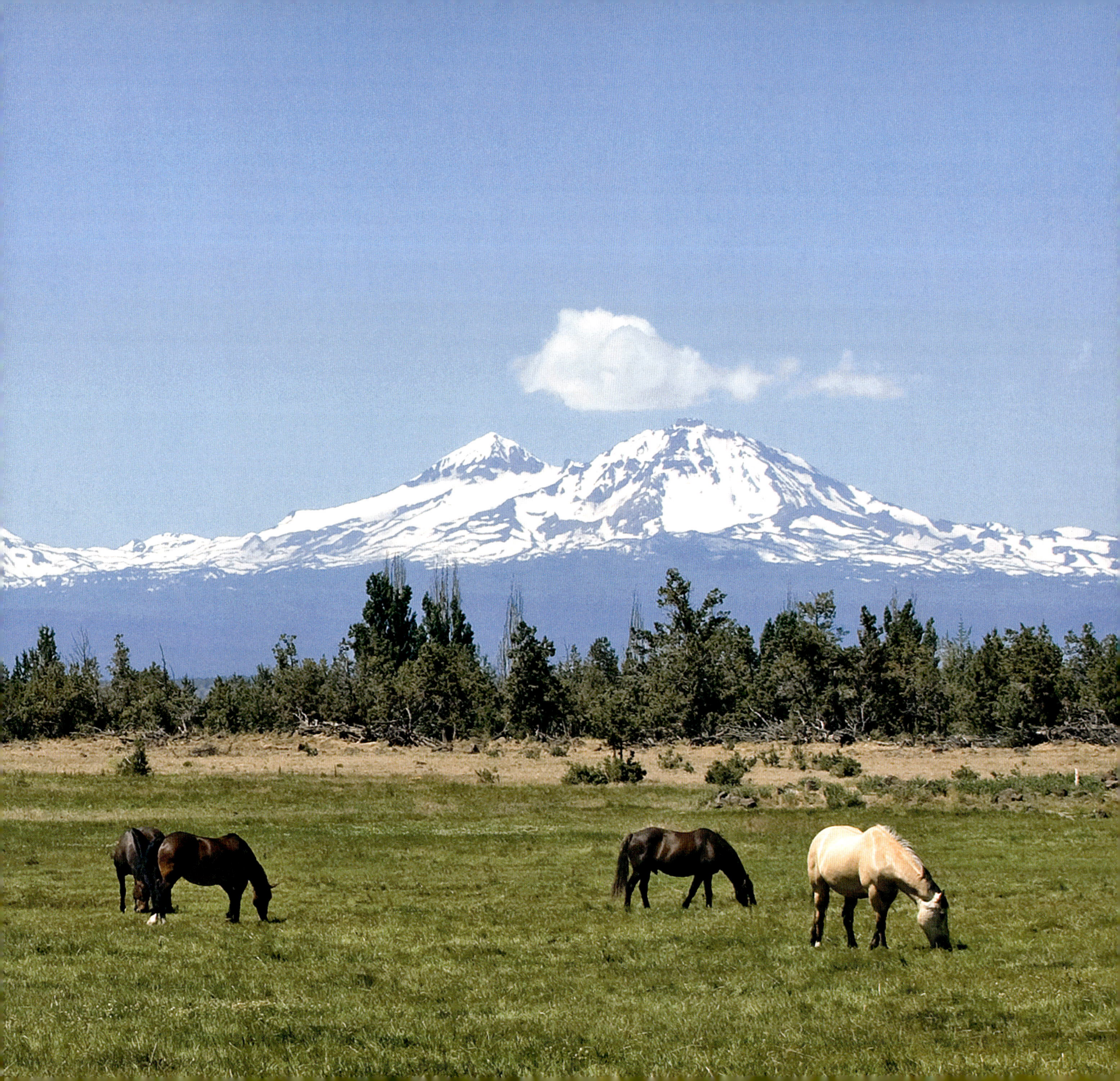

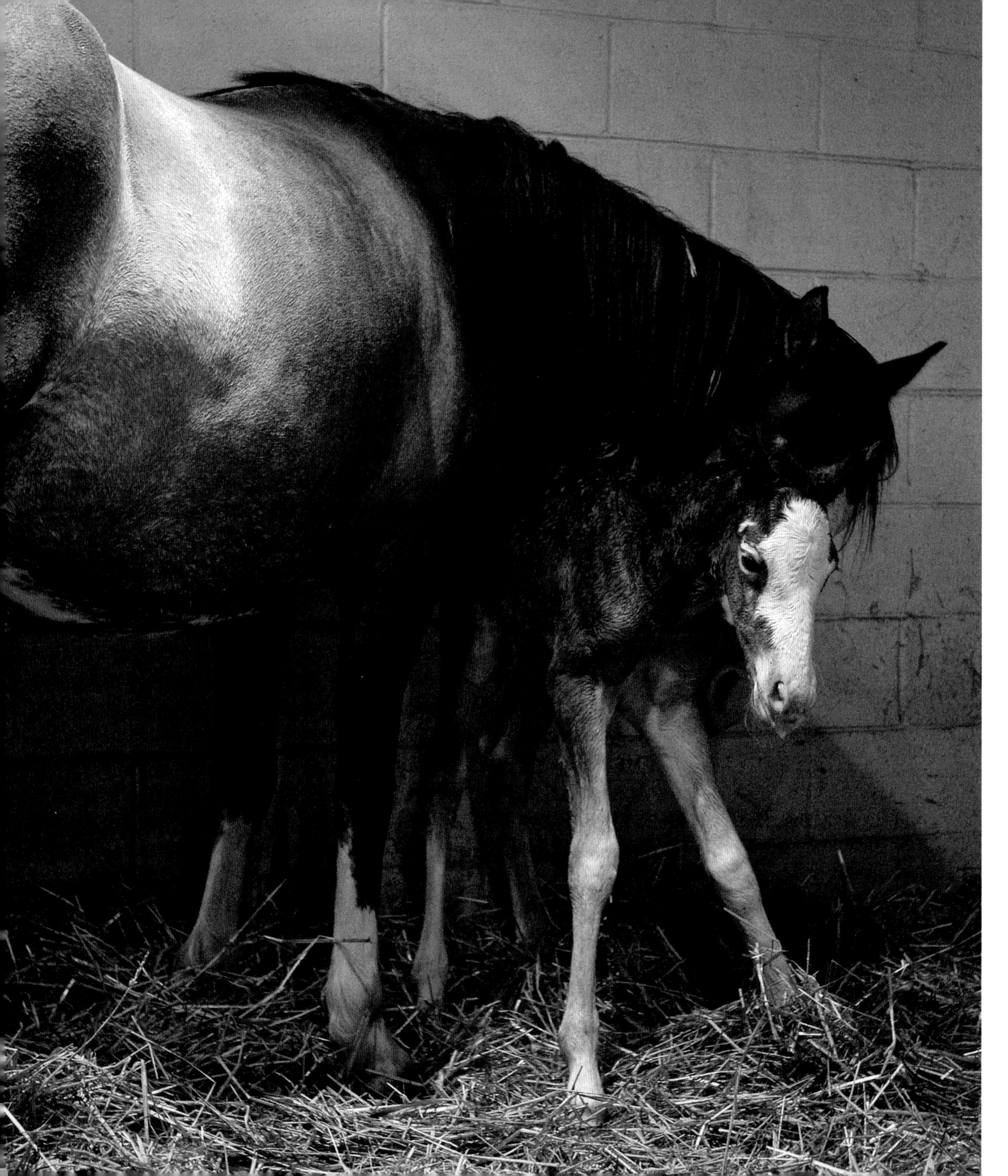

A Colonial Spanish Horse mare watches her young filly, soon after the foaling and eight hours later. The visual appearance of this foal's coat is likely to change when her baby hair sheds out.

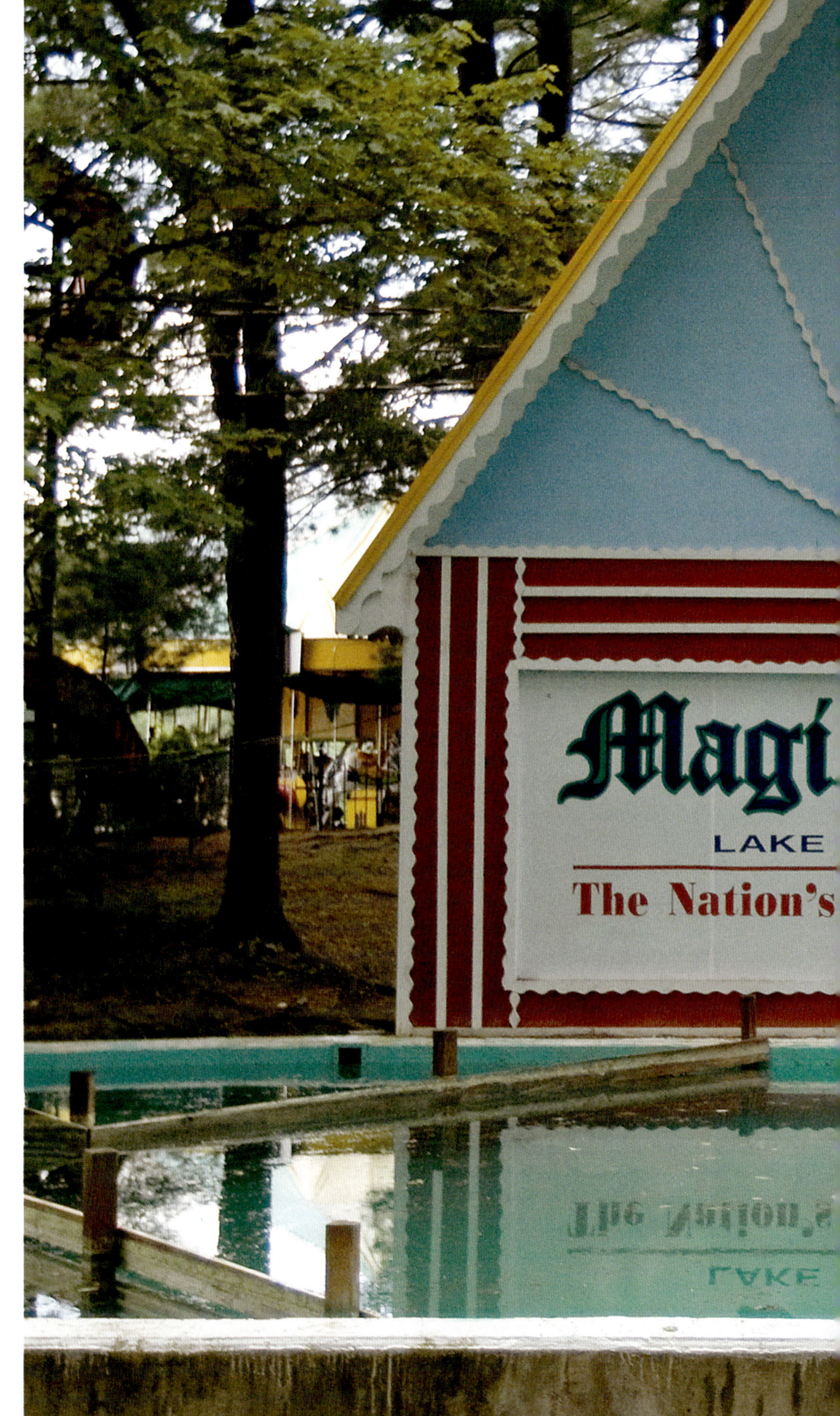

Lightning, billed as the country's only diving horse, takes the plunge to entertain summer crowds in upstate New York.

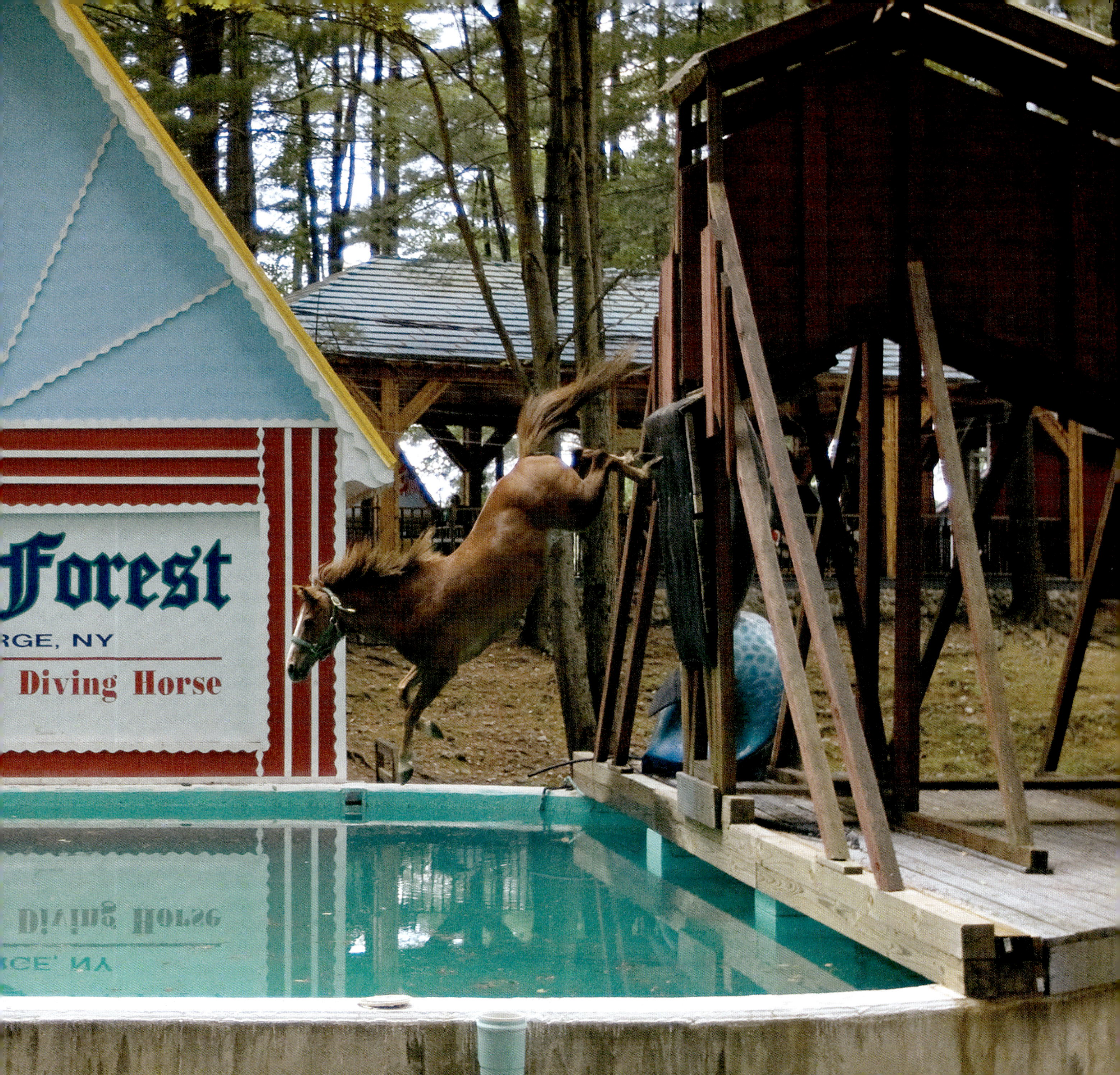
Forest
RGE, NY
Diving Horse

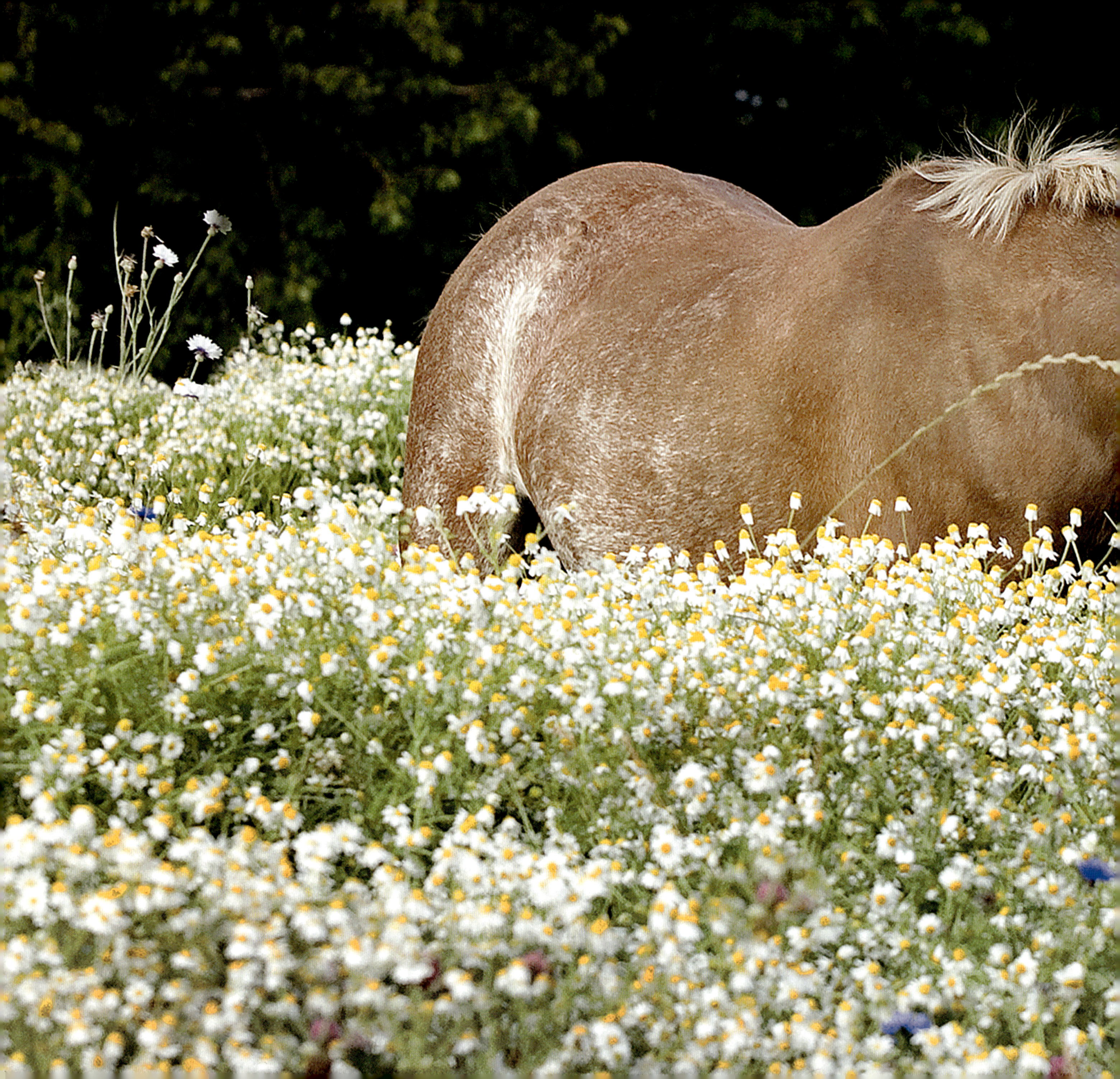

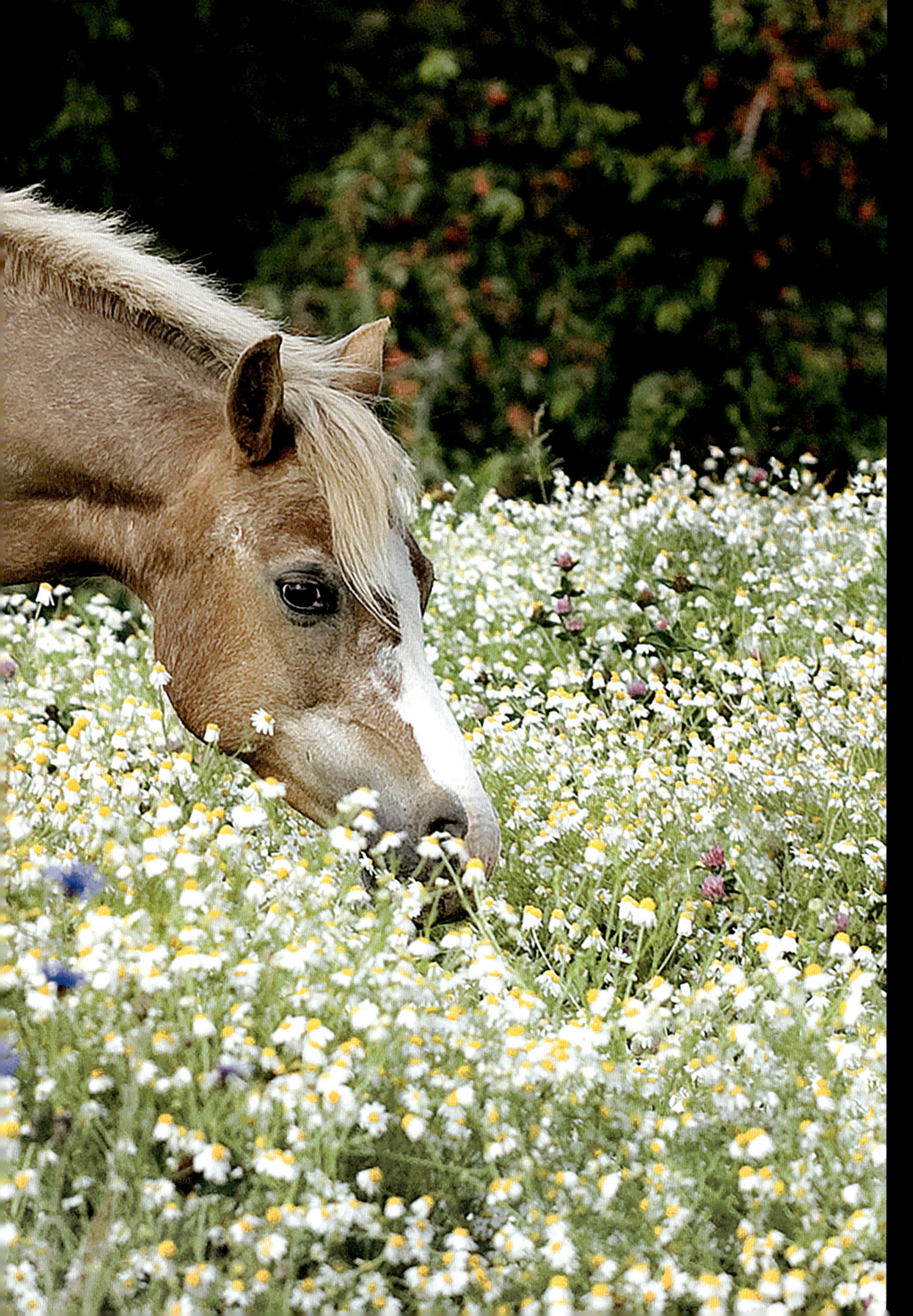

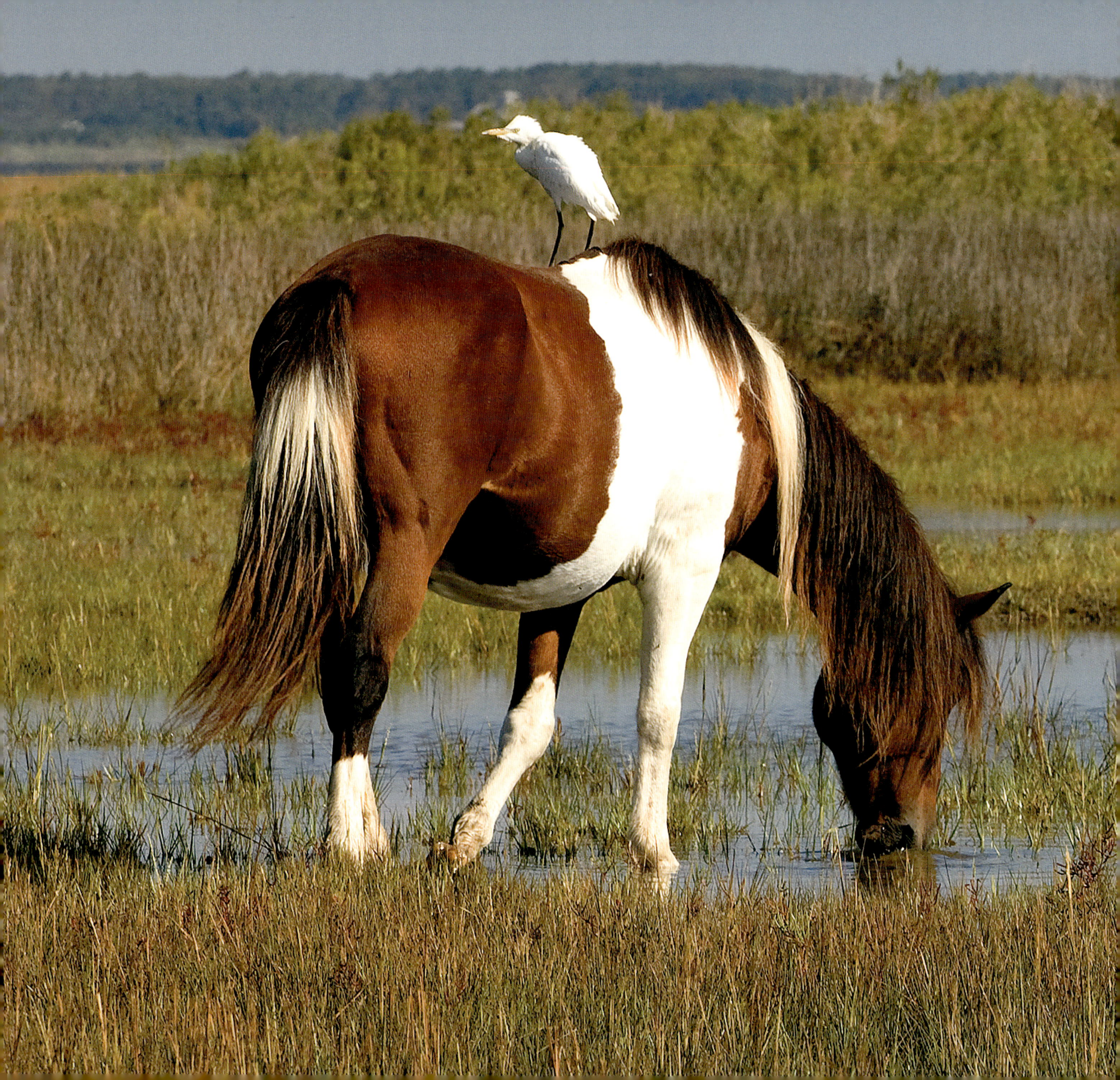

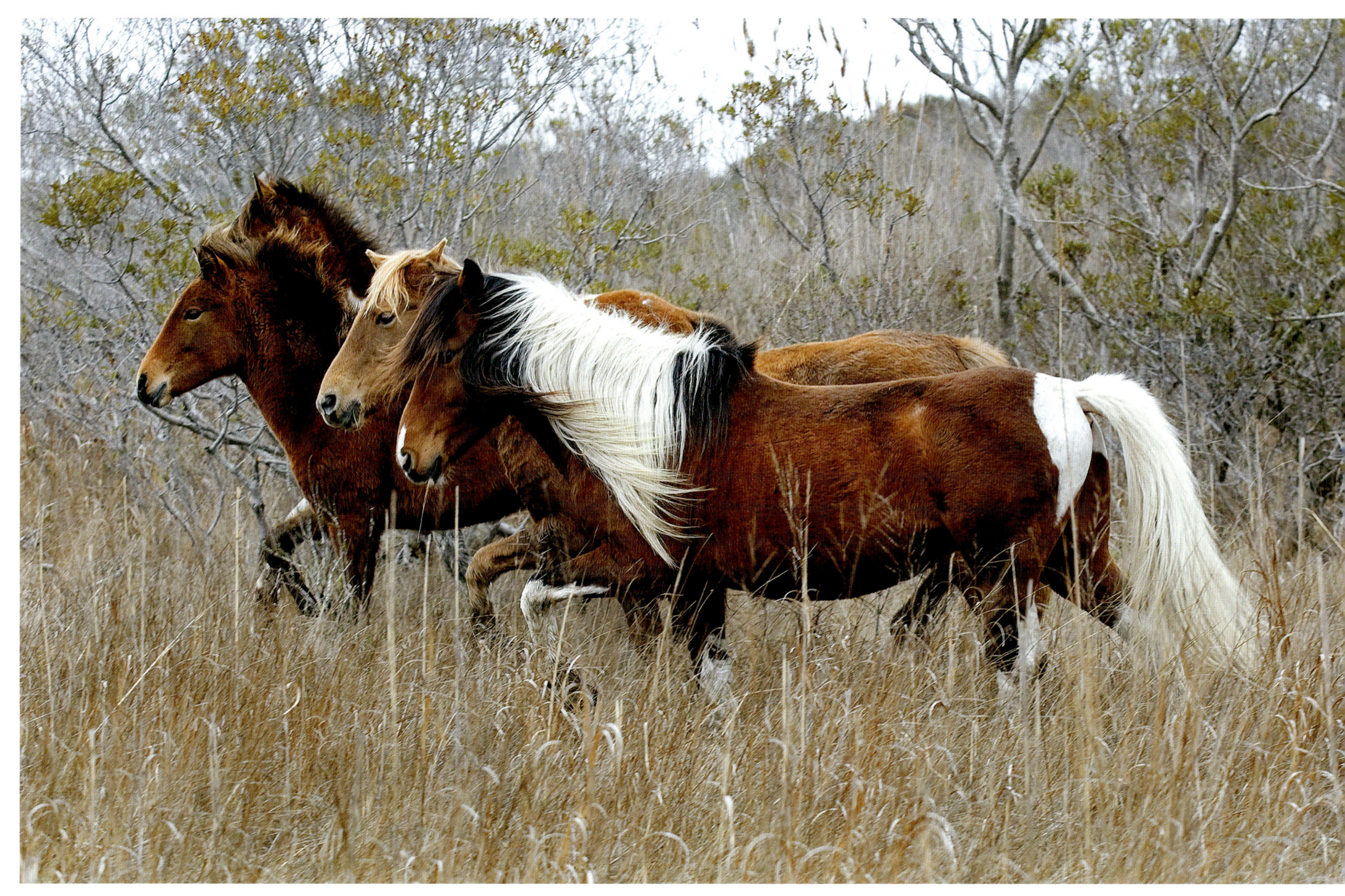

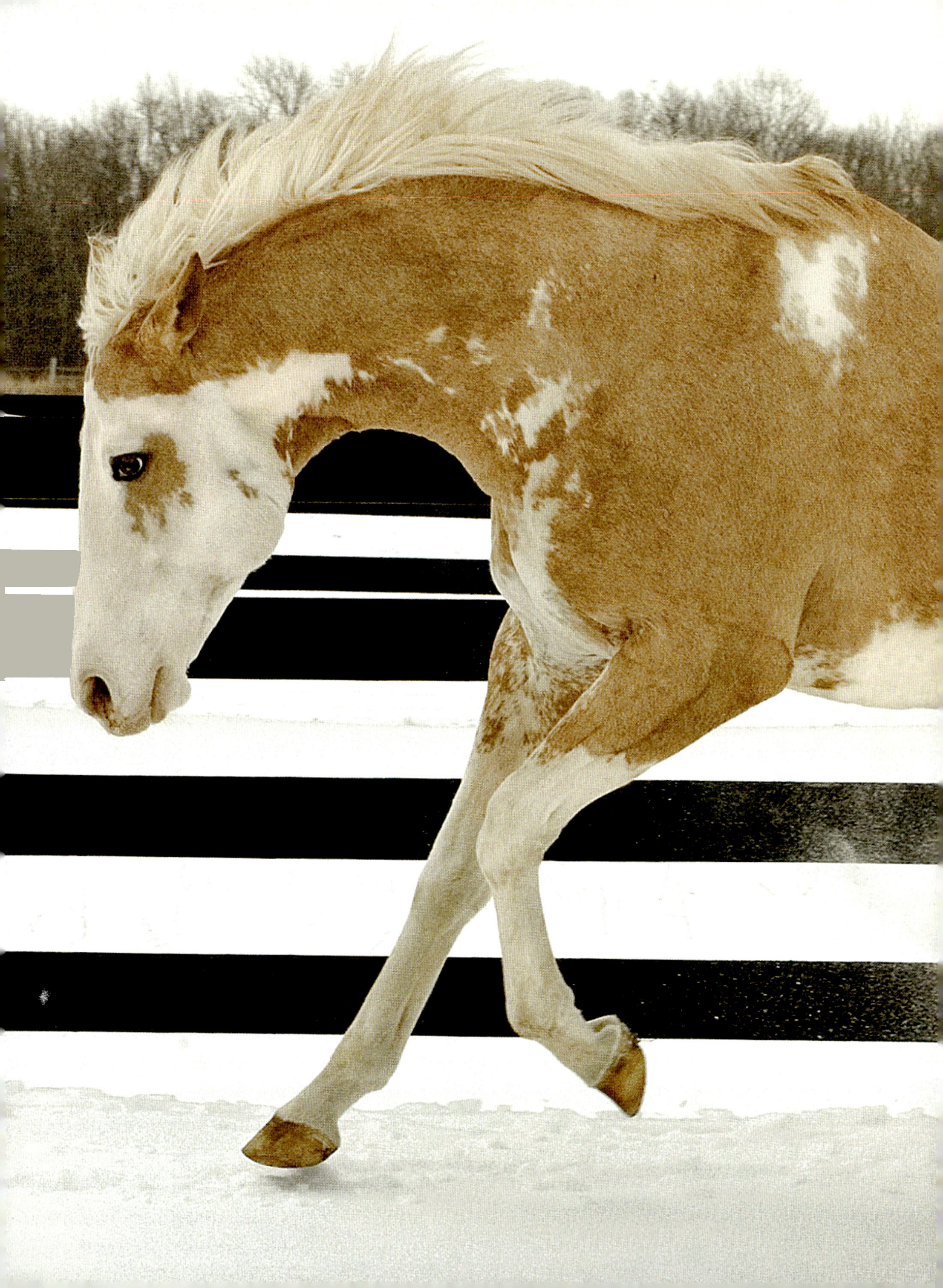

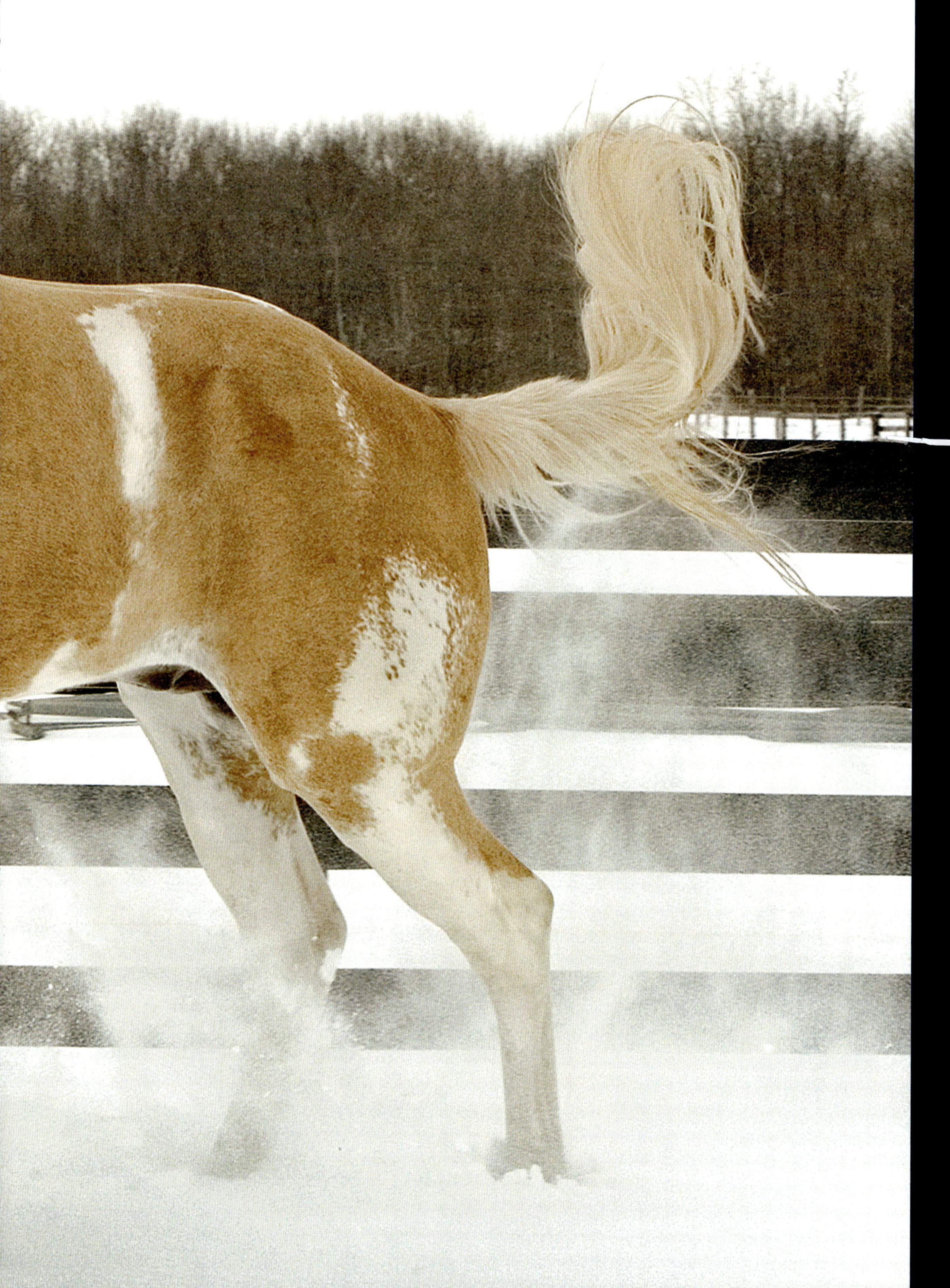

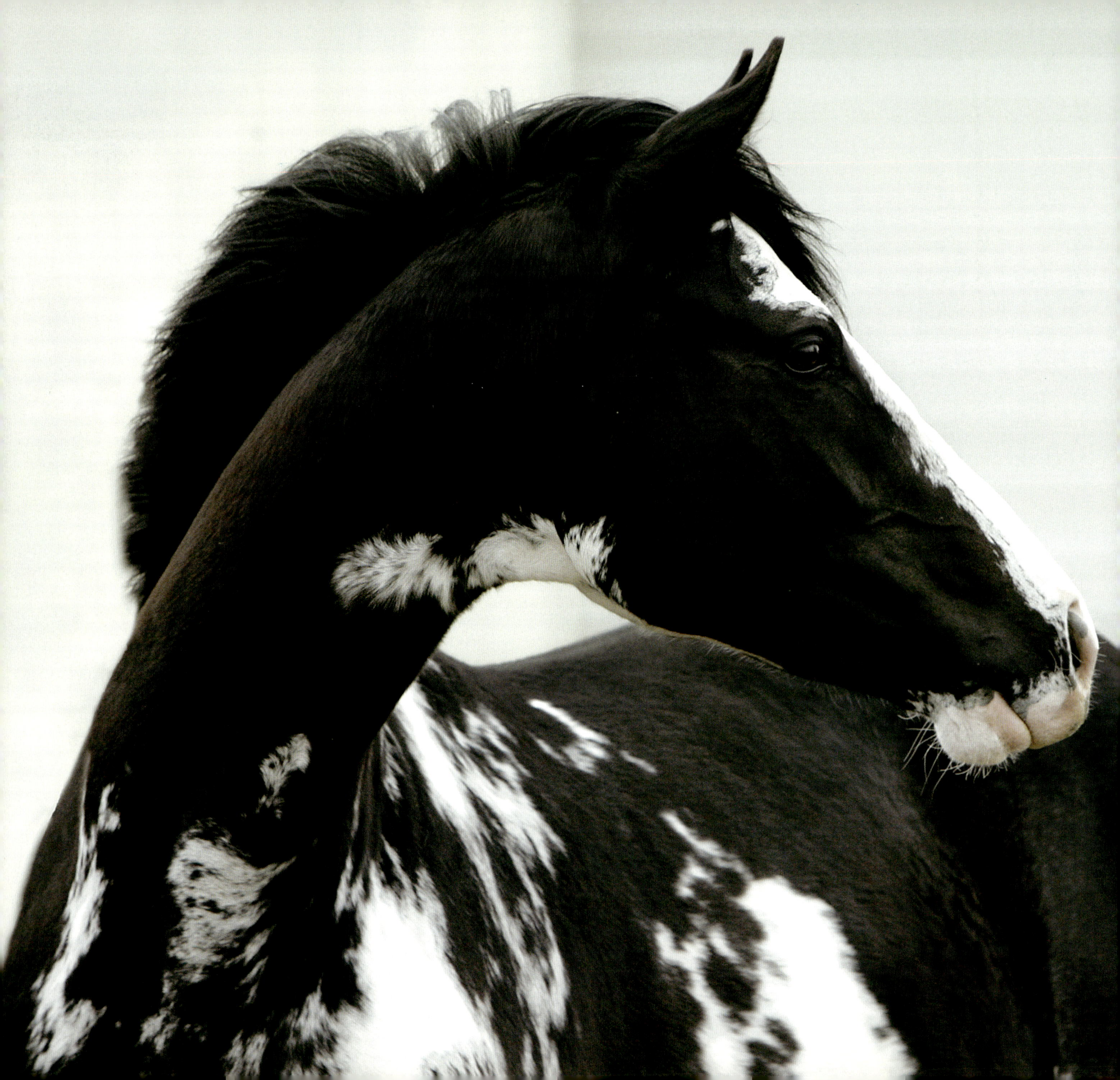

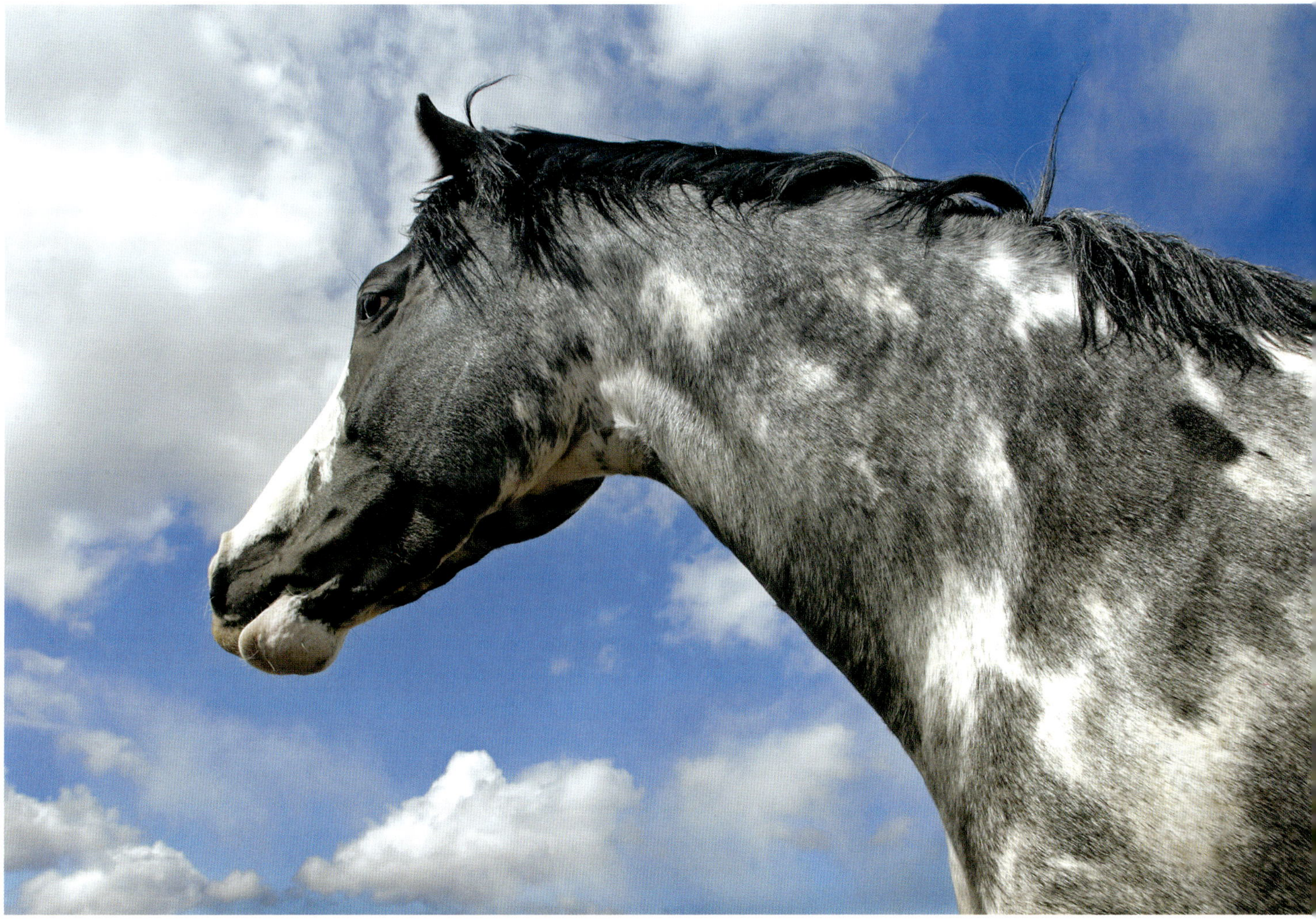

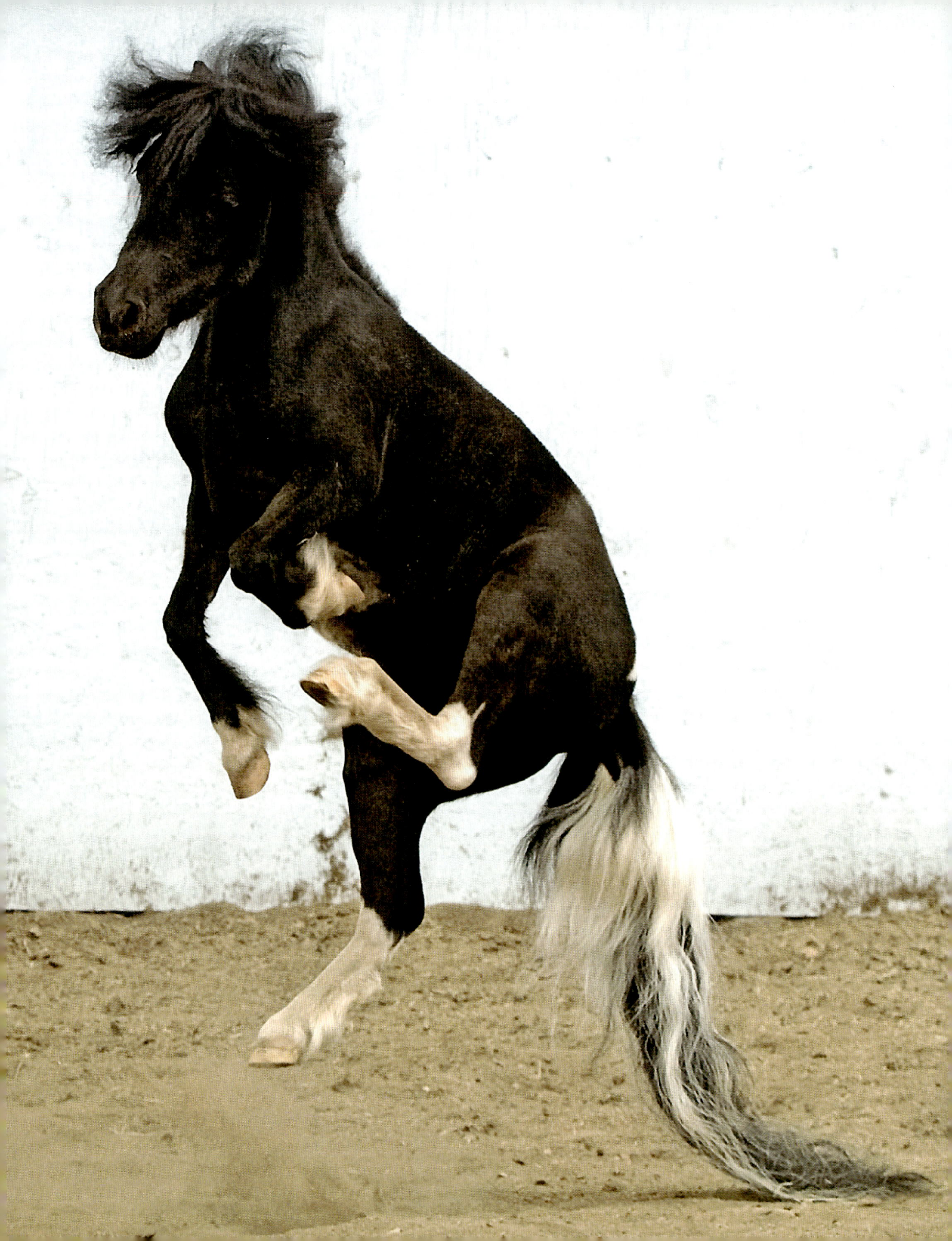

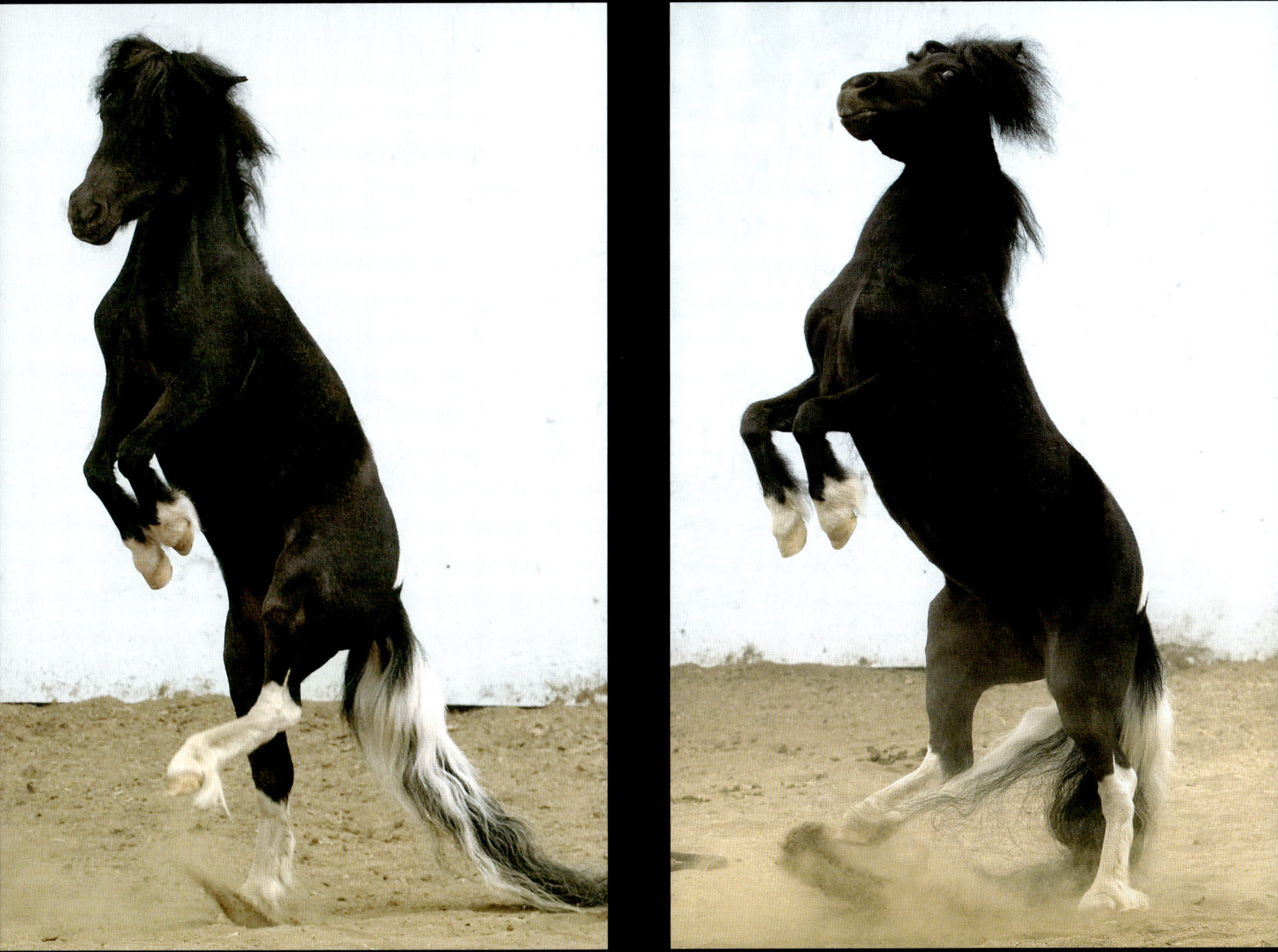

Lady, a Miniature mare, walks willingly for treats. For emphasis, the pint-sized lass even performs an impressive version of "Airs above the ground."

This half-Arabian, a champagne palomino, strikes a memorable pose at Rohara Arabians in Florida.

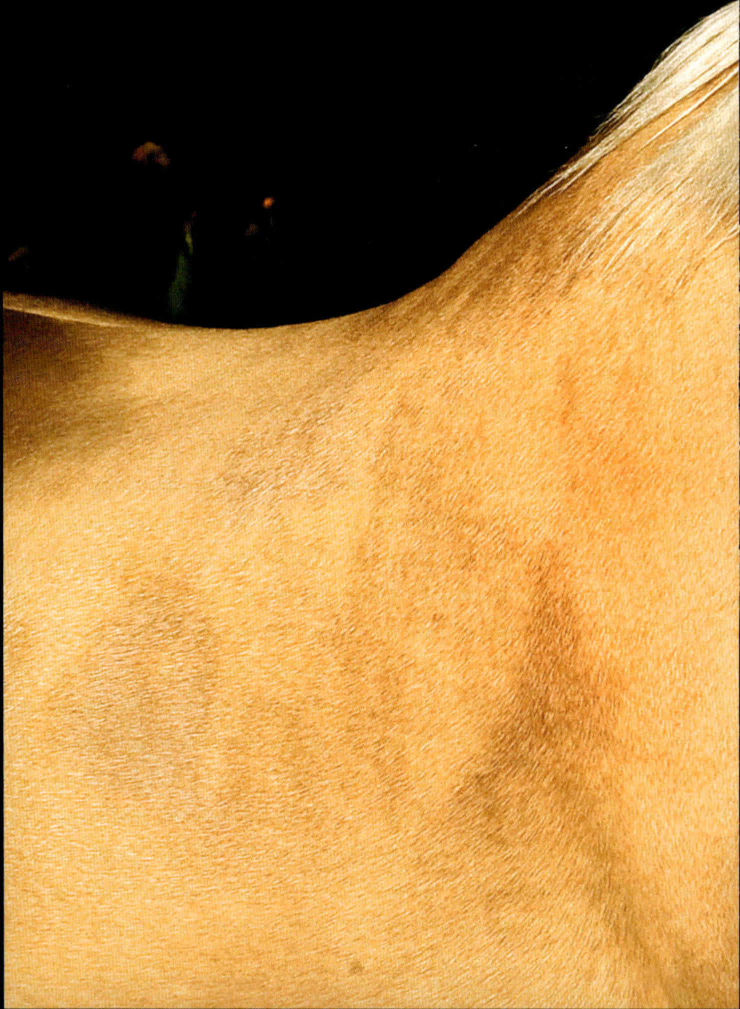

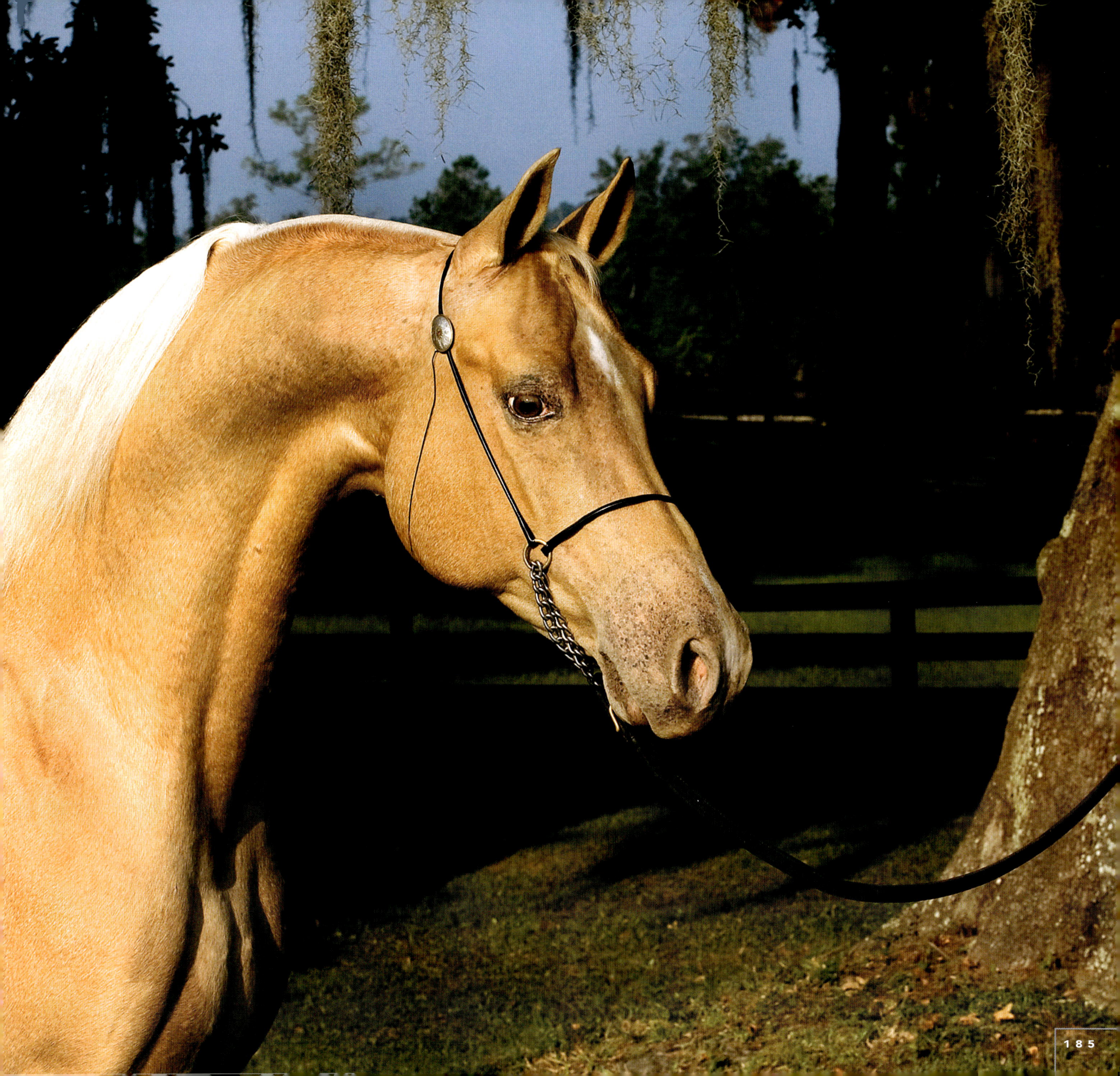

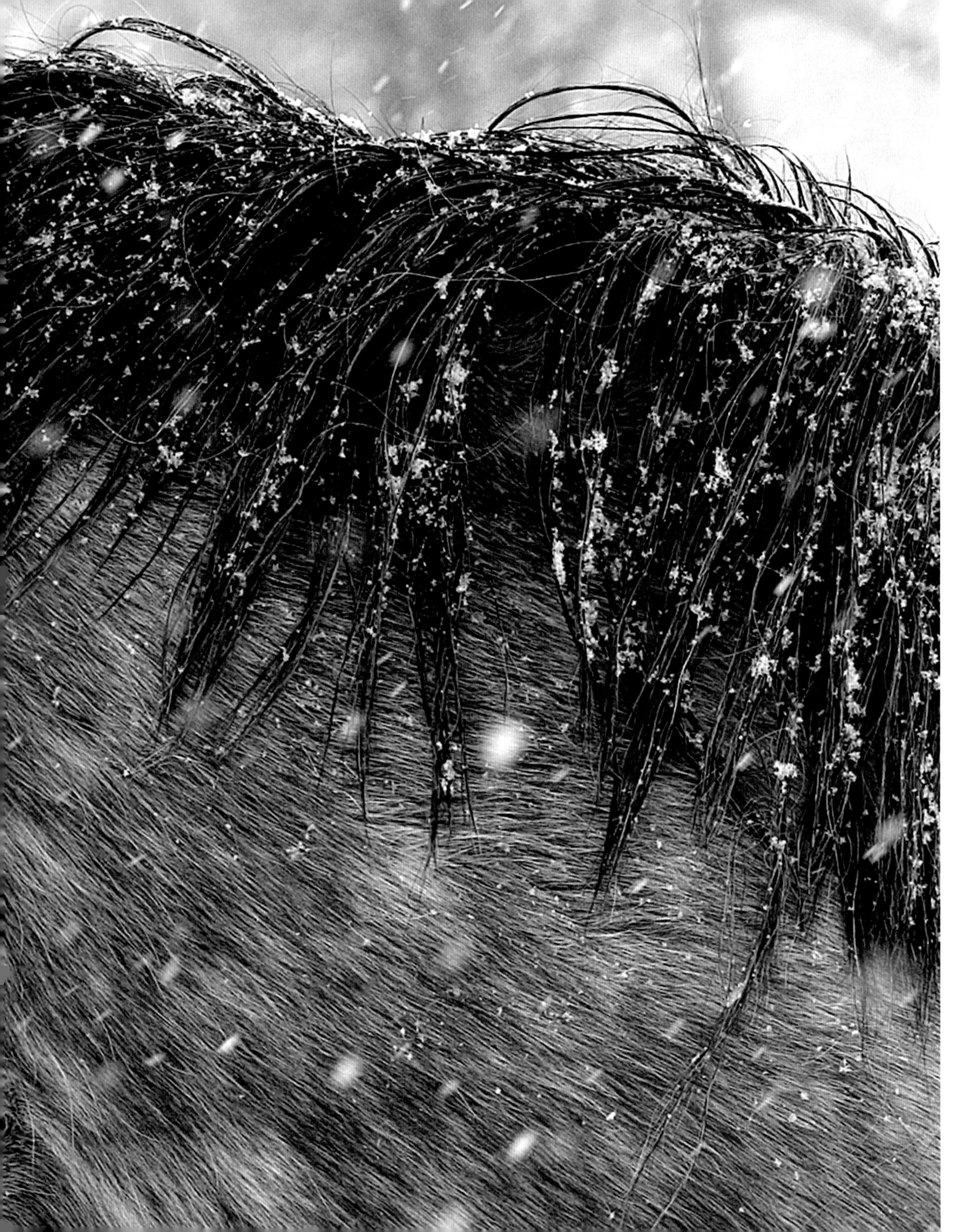

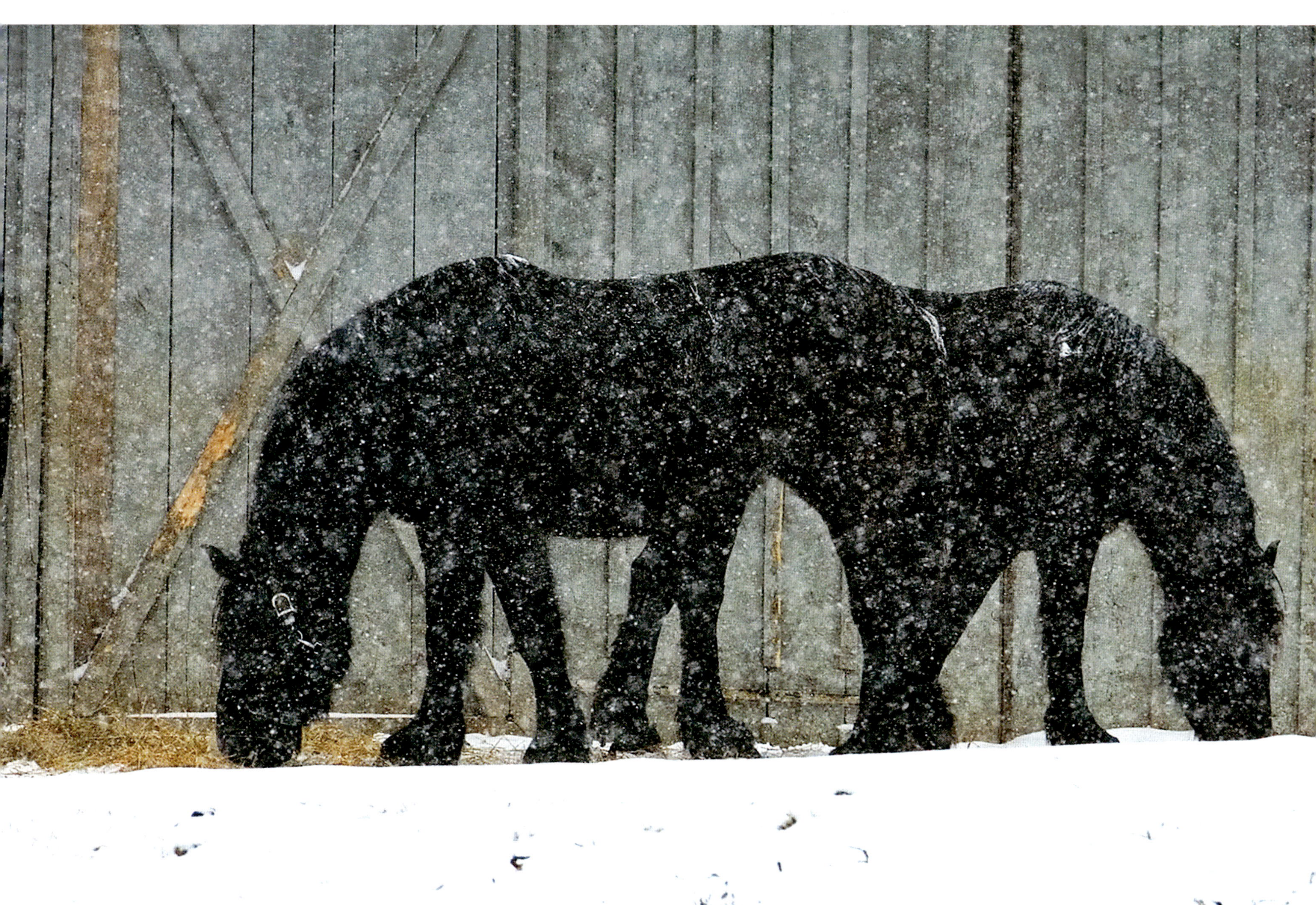

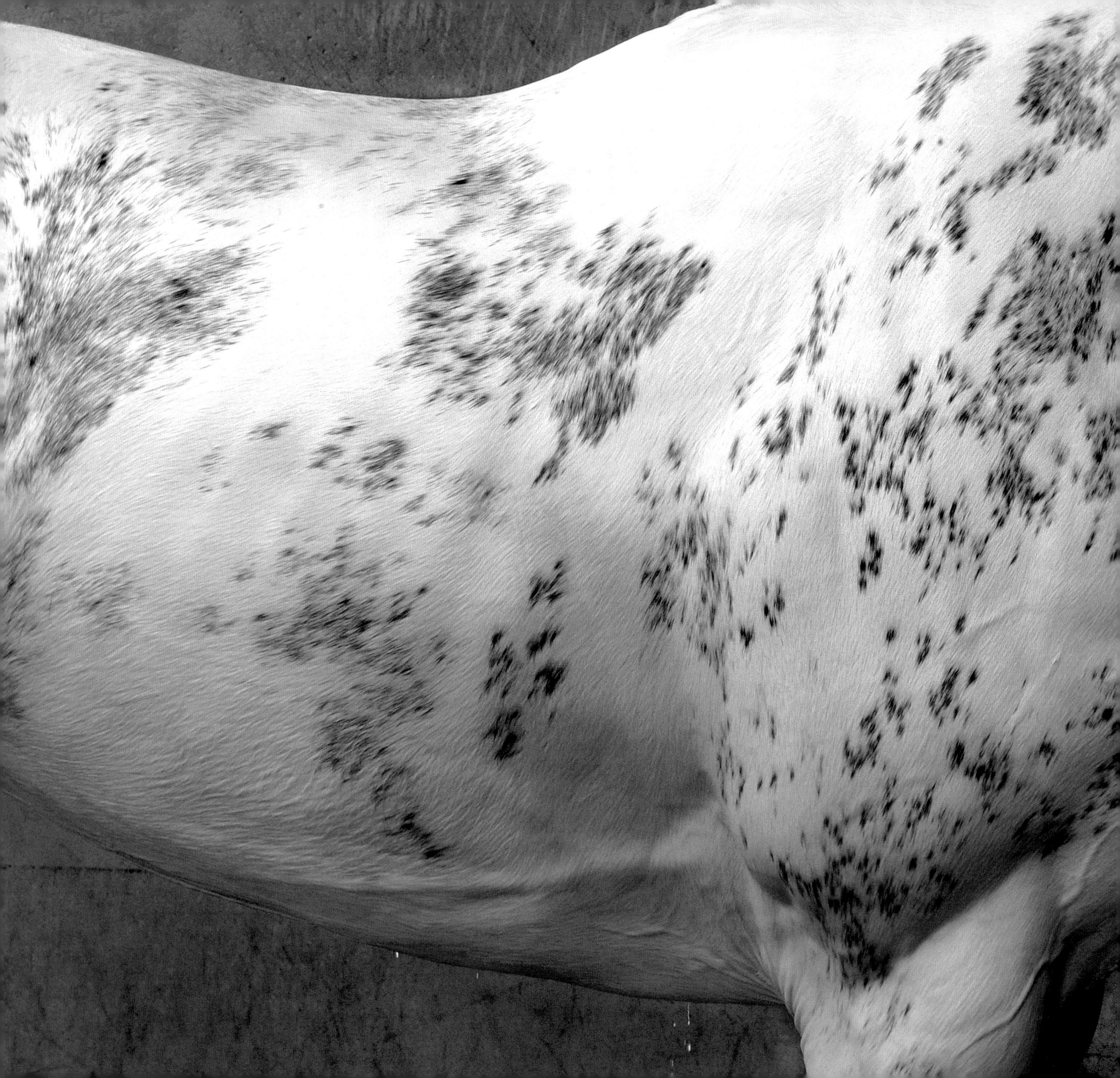

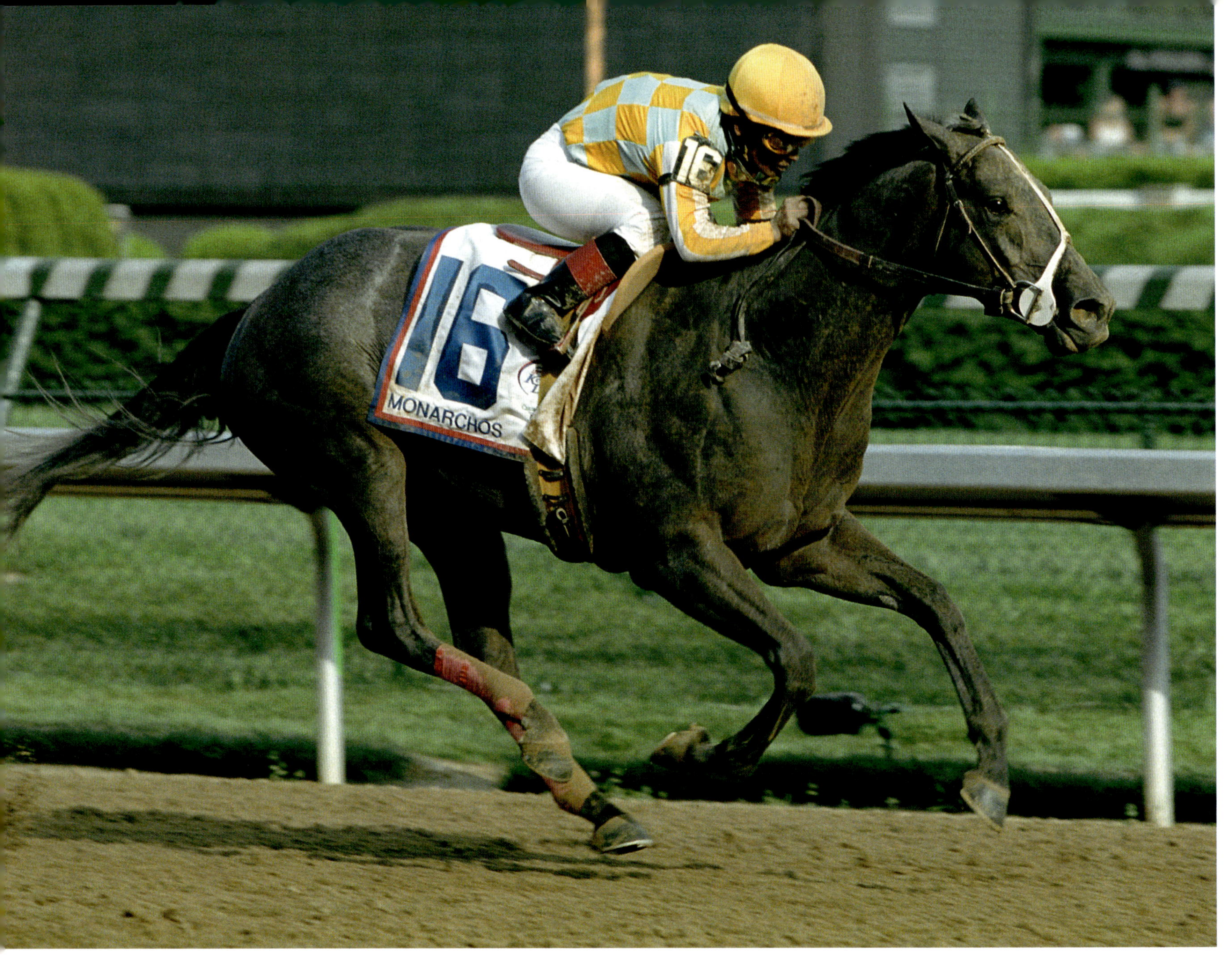

Kentucky Derby winner Monarchos lightened considerably in the eight years between his 2001 Derby victory, above, and 2009, right.

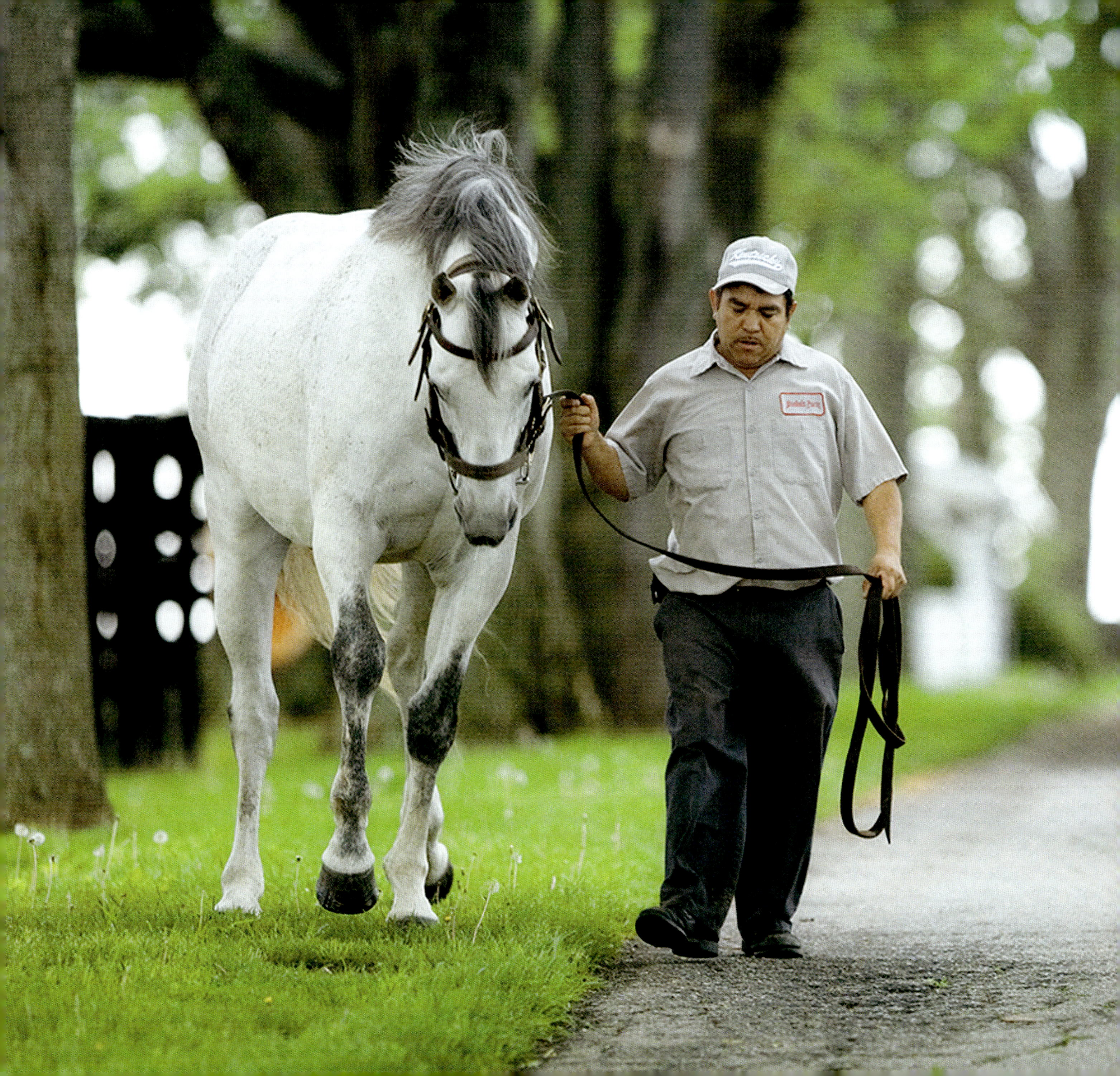

Breed registries occasionally have difficulty with color, especially as more breeders experiment with matings. This Thoroughbred filly is an example. While her breeder considers her a light buttermilk buckskin, The Jockey Club has registered her as bay.

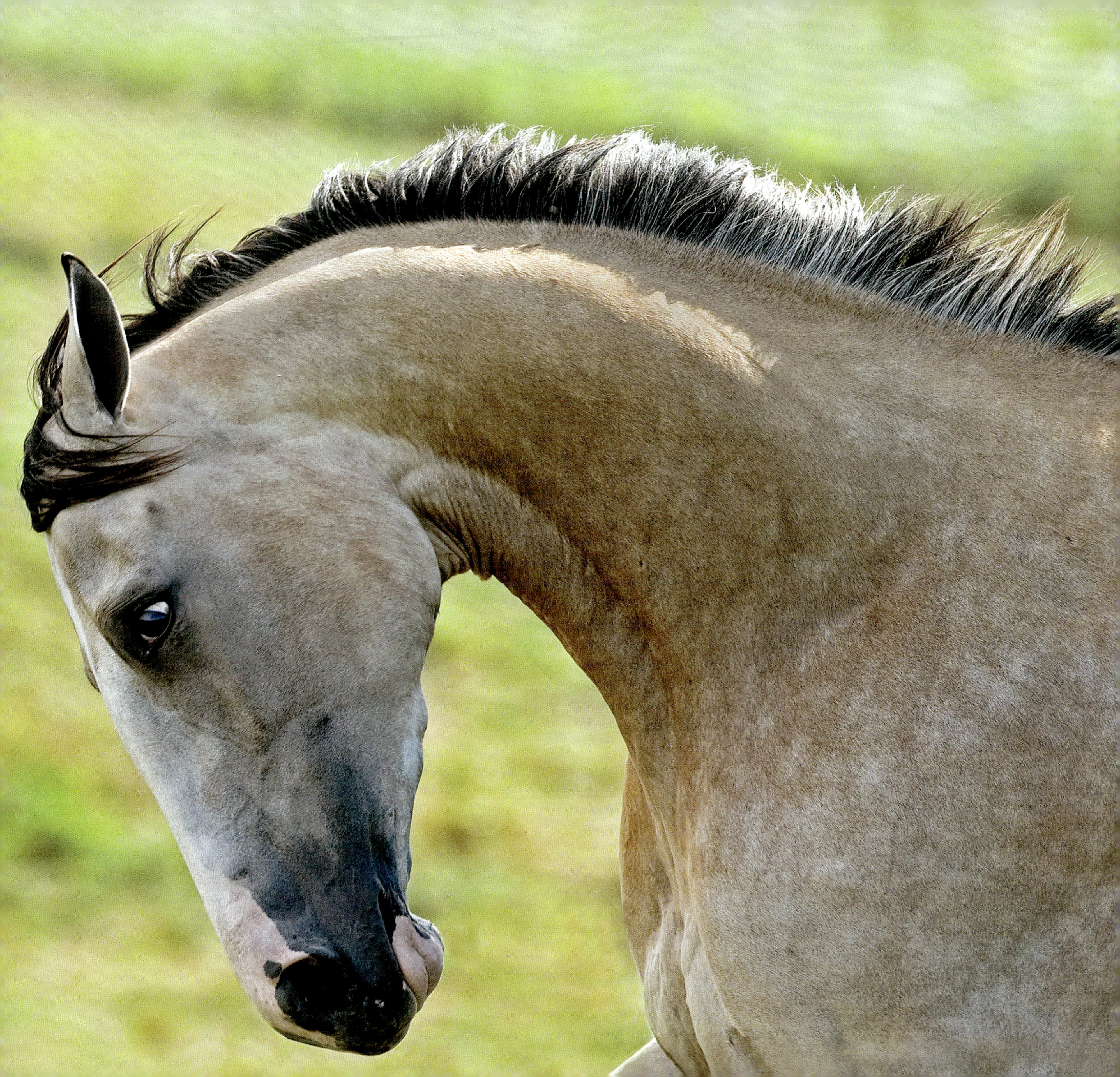

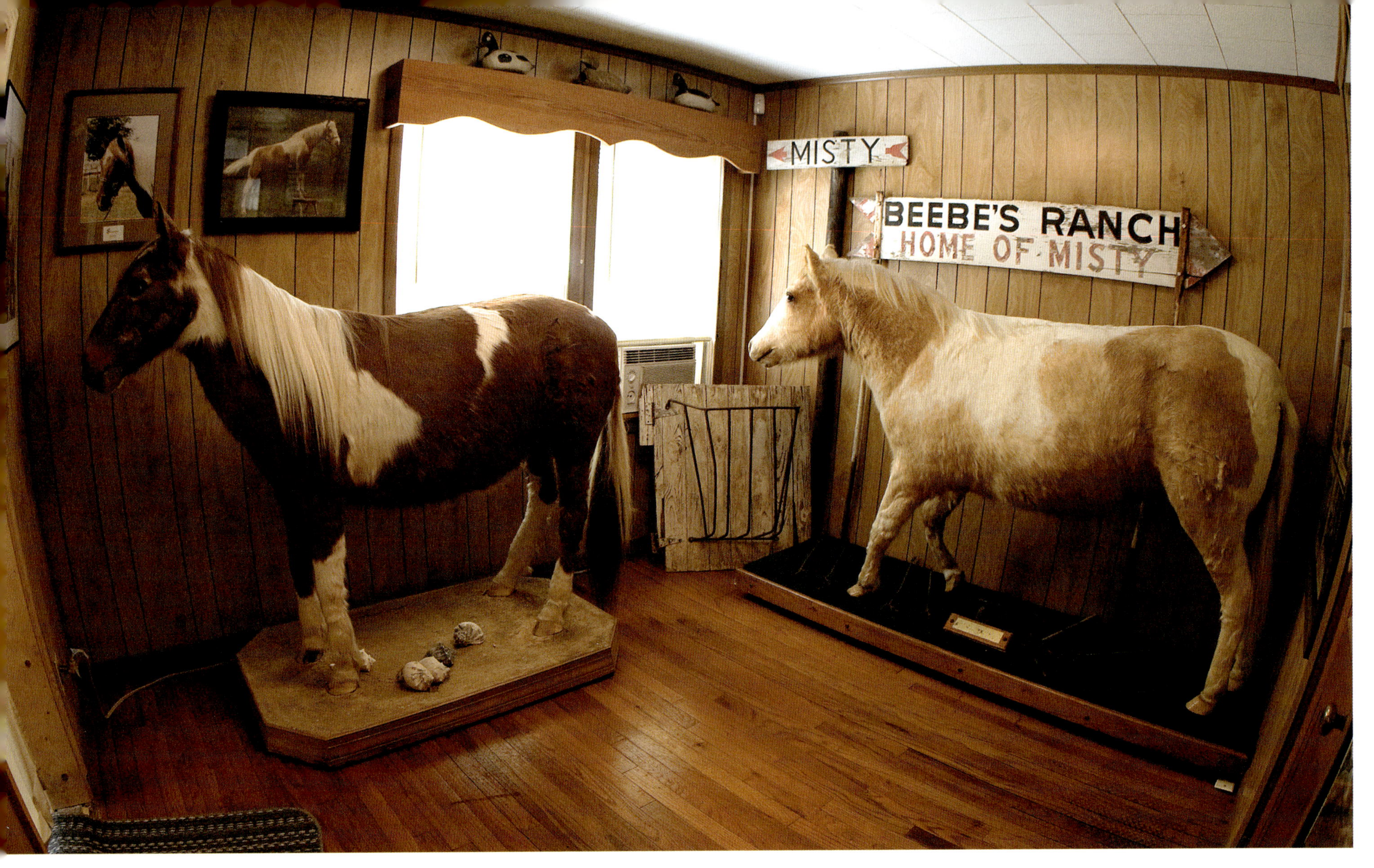

The bodies of Misty of Chincoteague and her daughter Stormy, left, were preserved after their passing. The white marking on Misty's side was said to resemble a map of the United States.

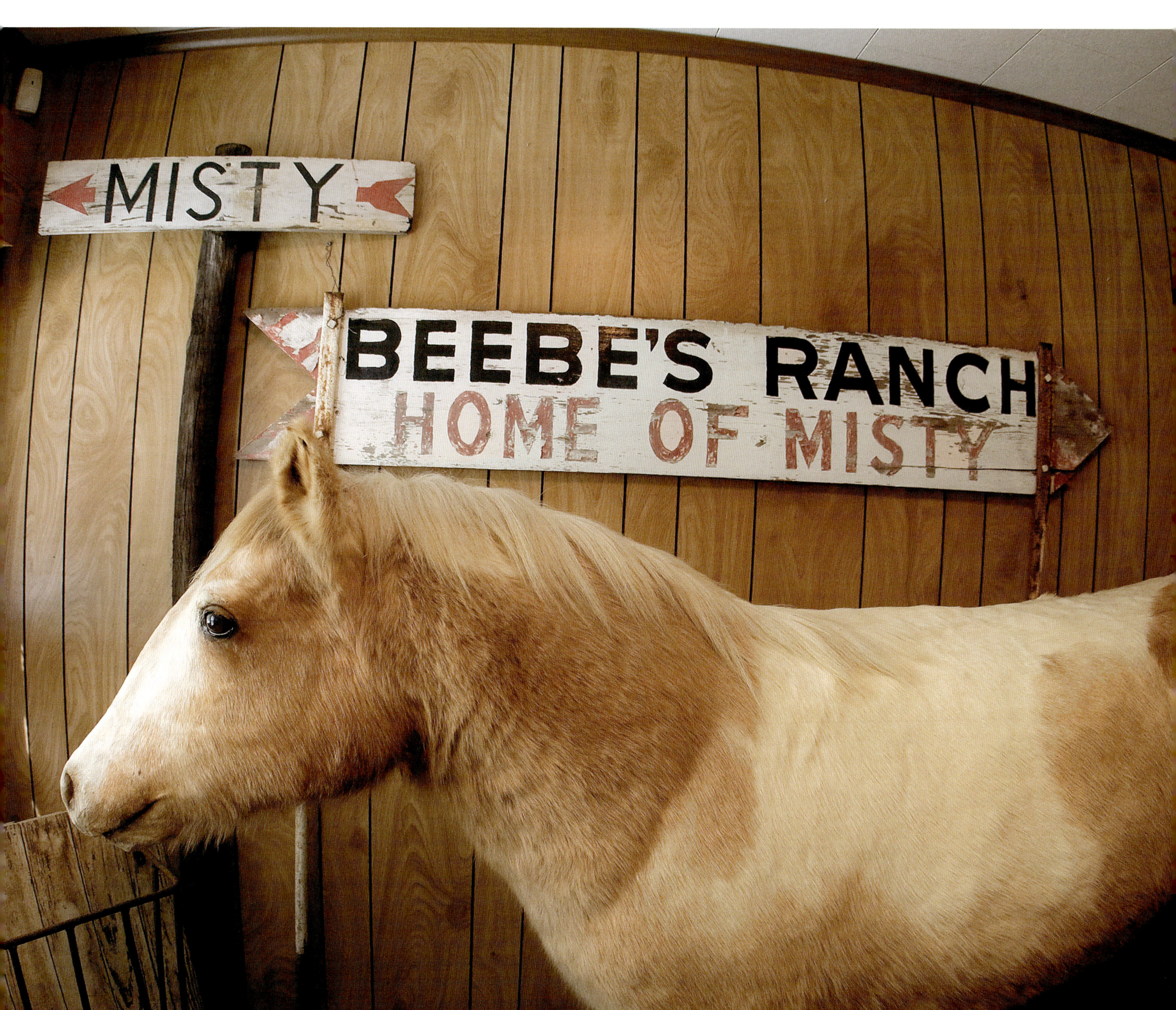
MISTY
BEEBE'S RANCH
HOME OF MISTY

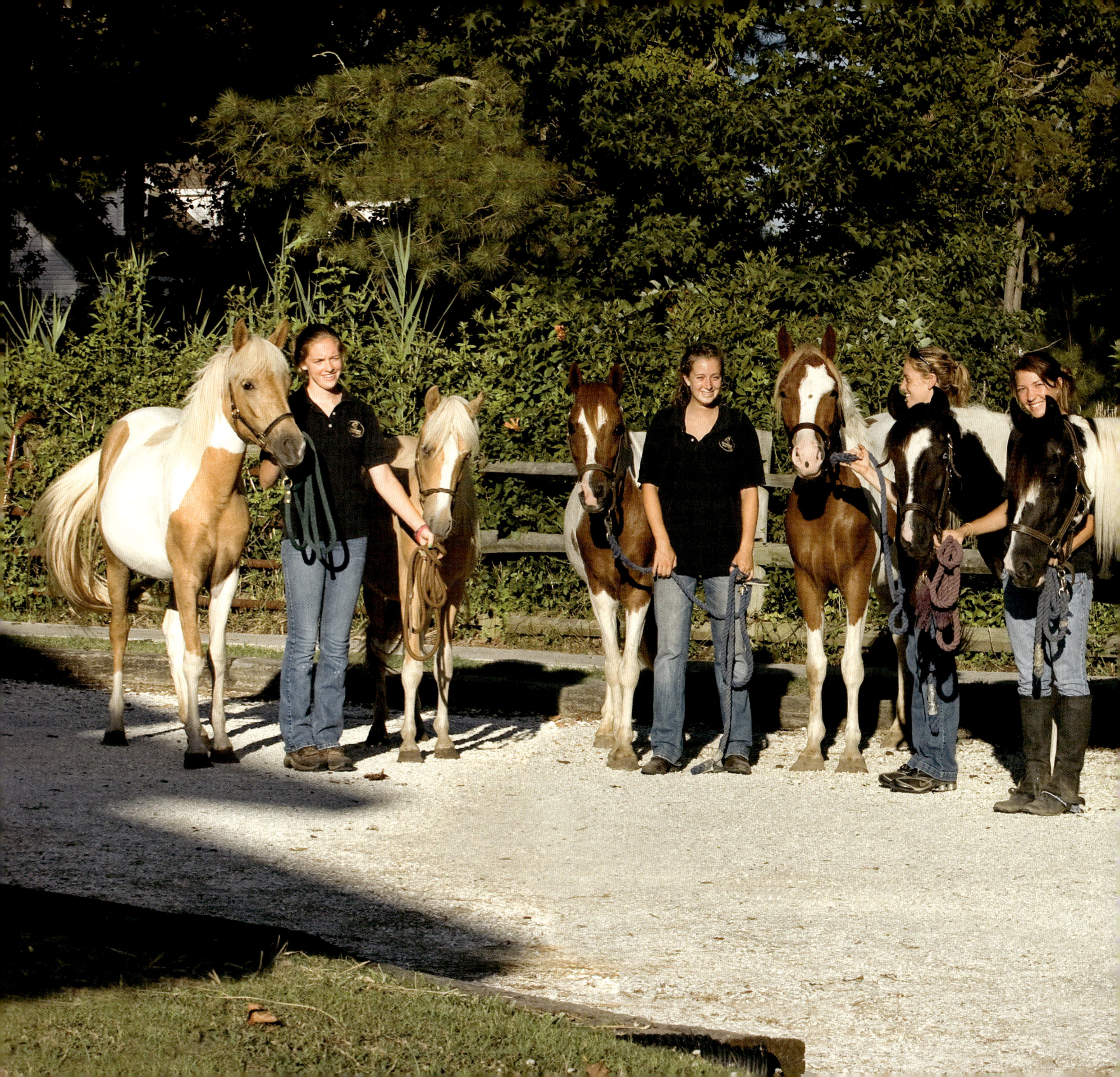

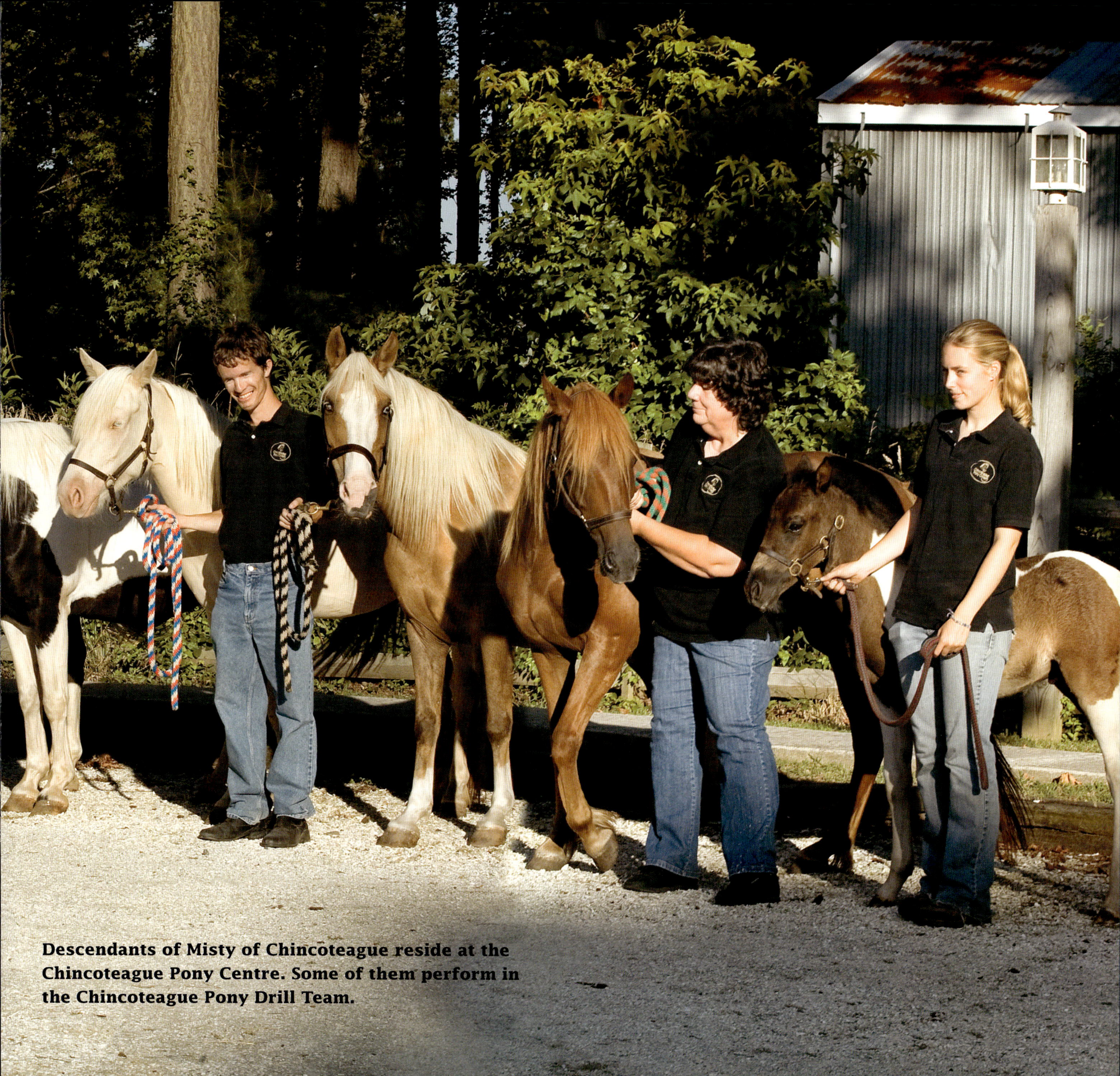

Descendants of Misty of Chincoteague reside at the Chincoteague Pony Centre. Some of them perform in the Chincoteague Pony Drill Team.

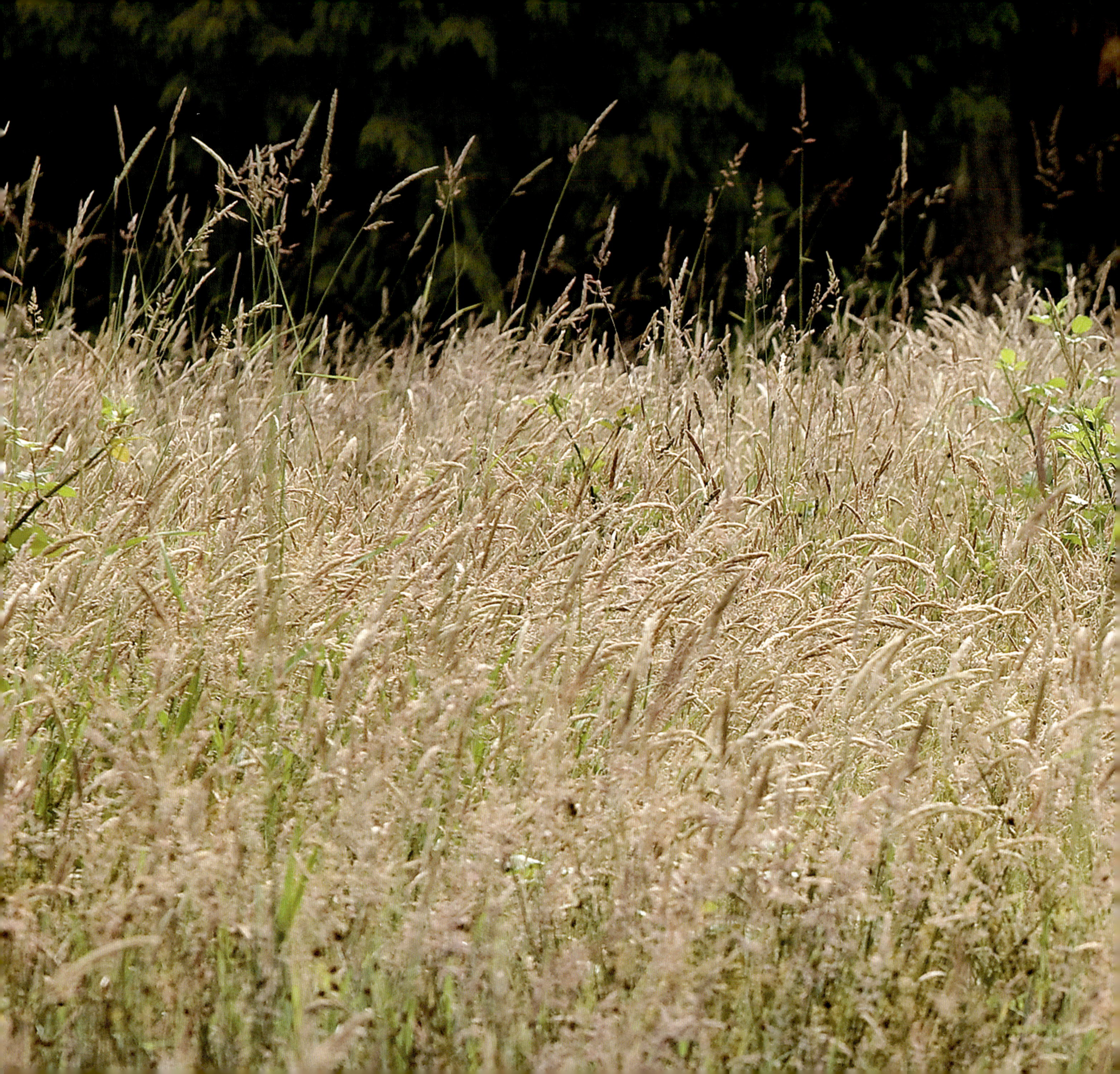

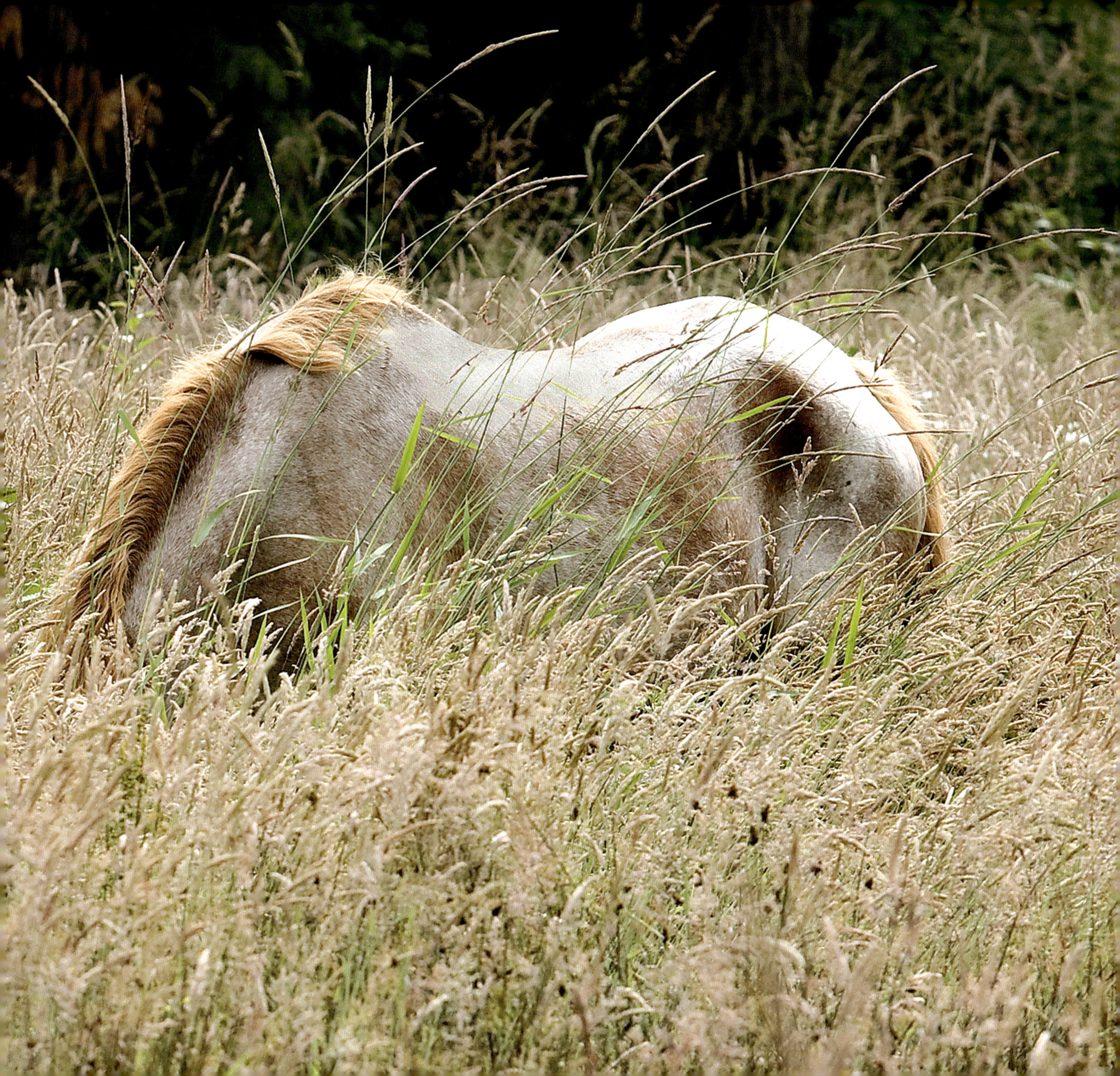

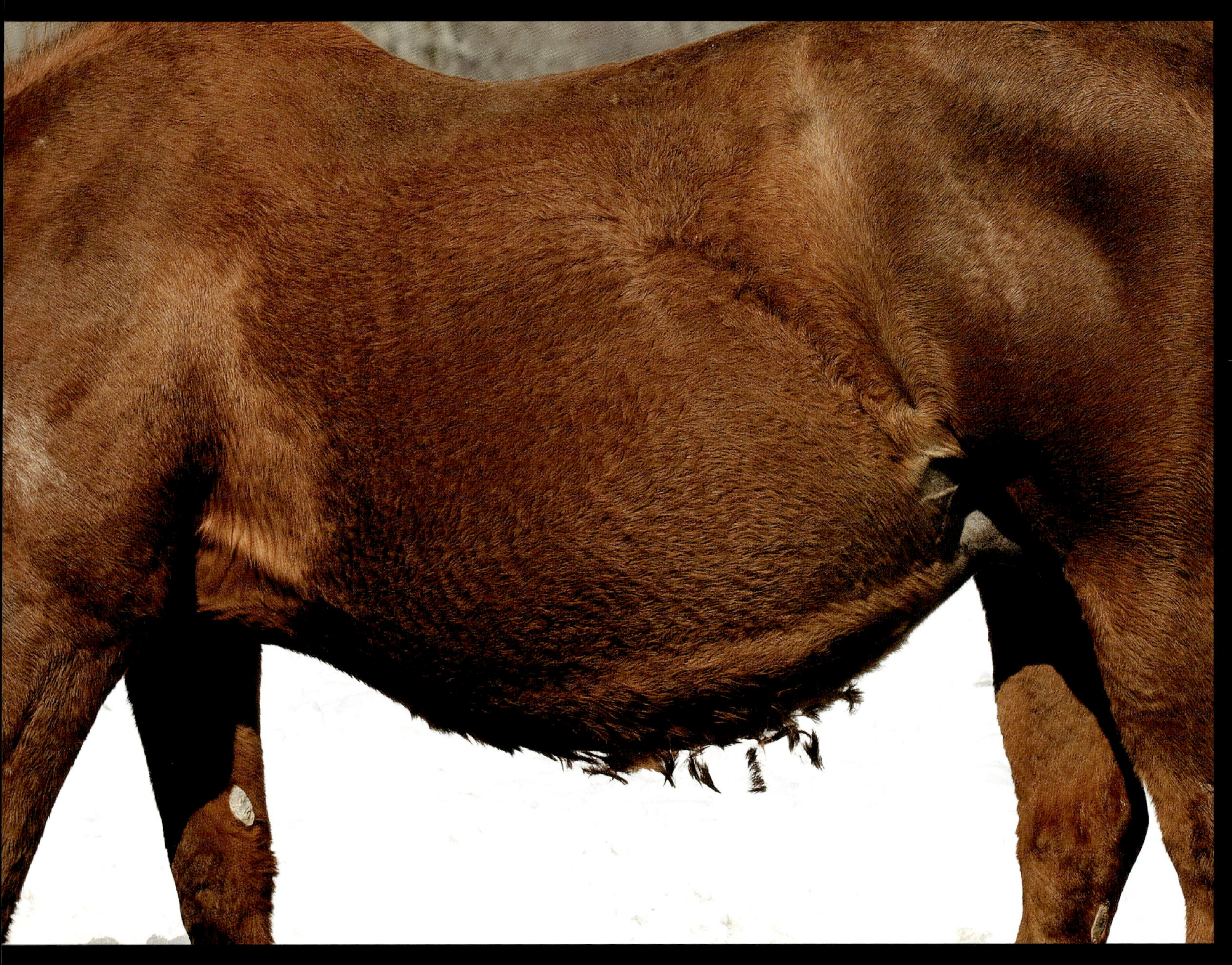

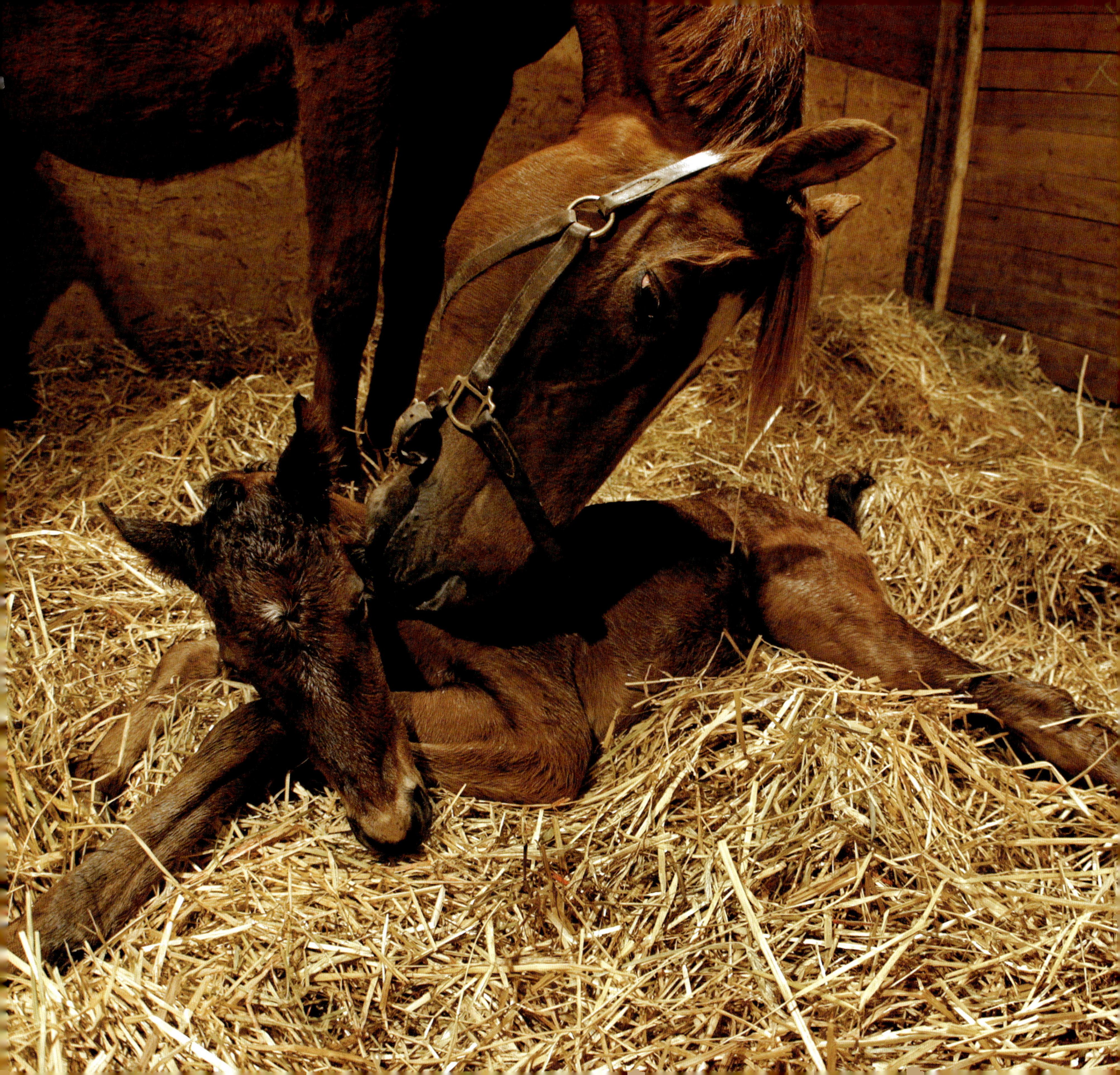

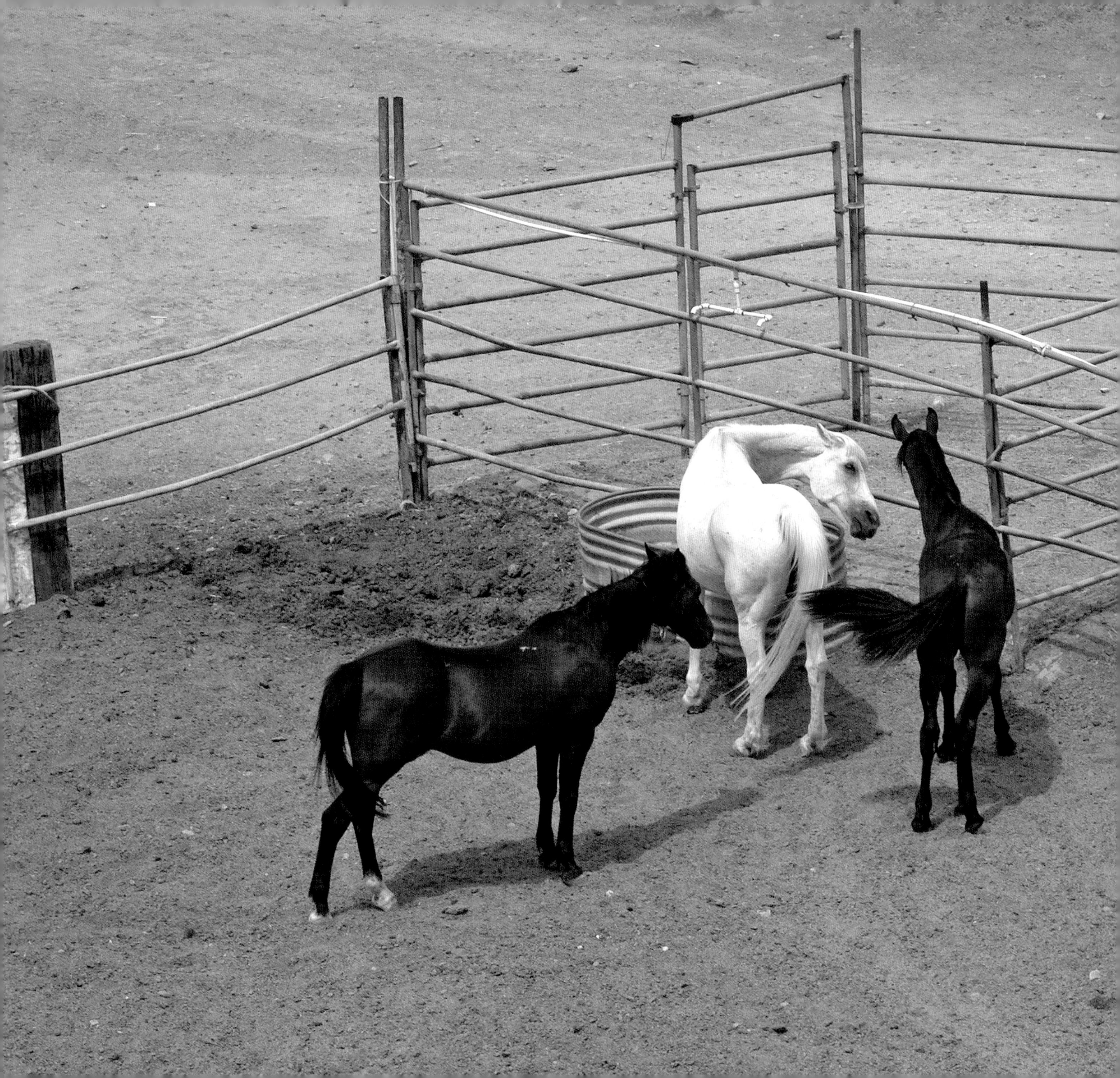

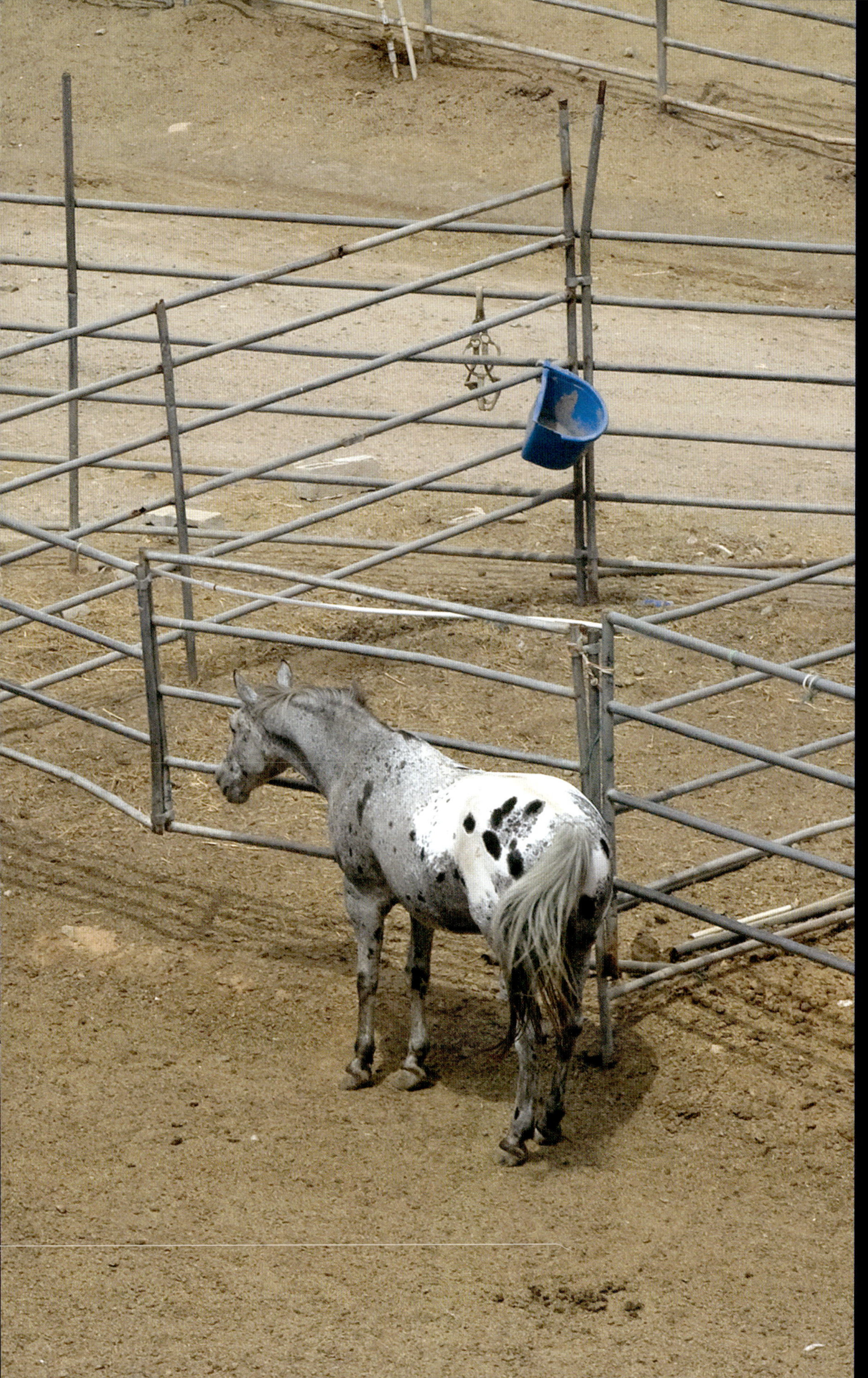

The alpha horse determines who drinks next at Steppin Straight Farms in California.

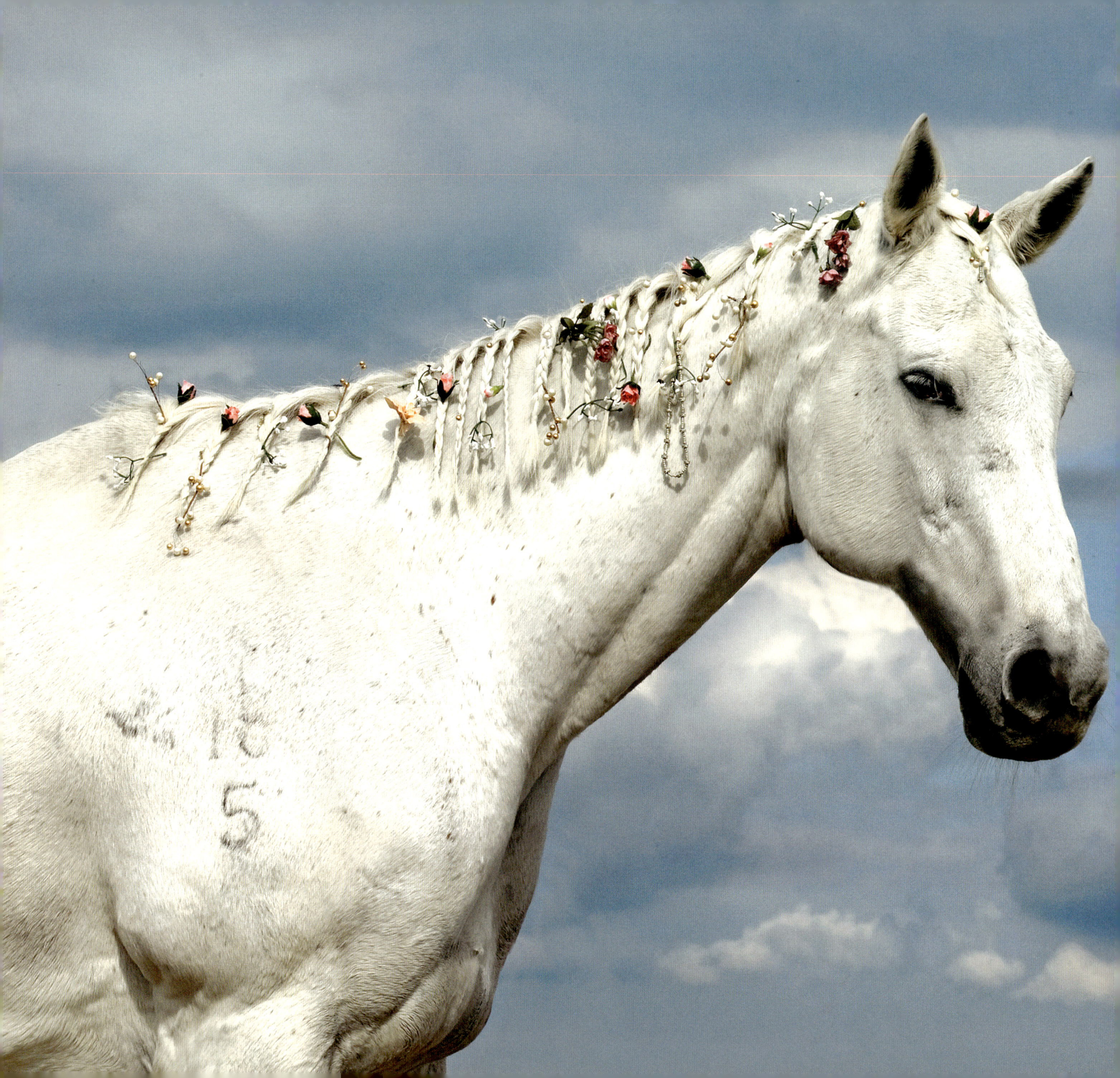

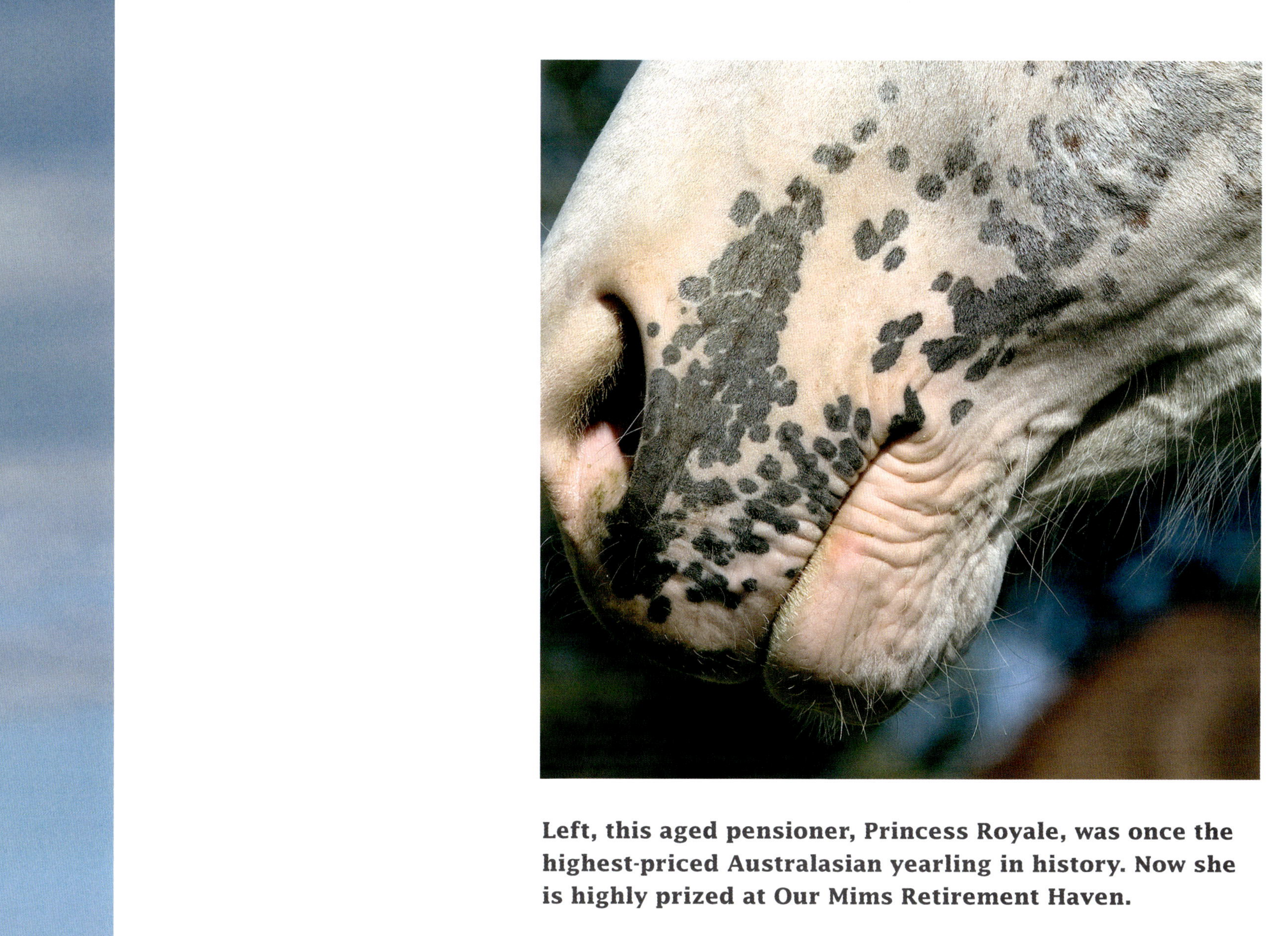

Left, this aged pensioner, Princess Royale, was once the highest-priced Australasian yearling in history. Now she is highly prized at Our Mims Retirement Haven.

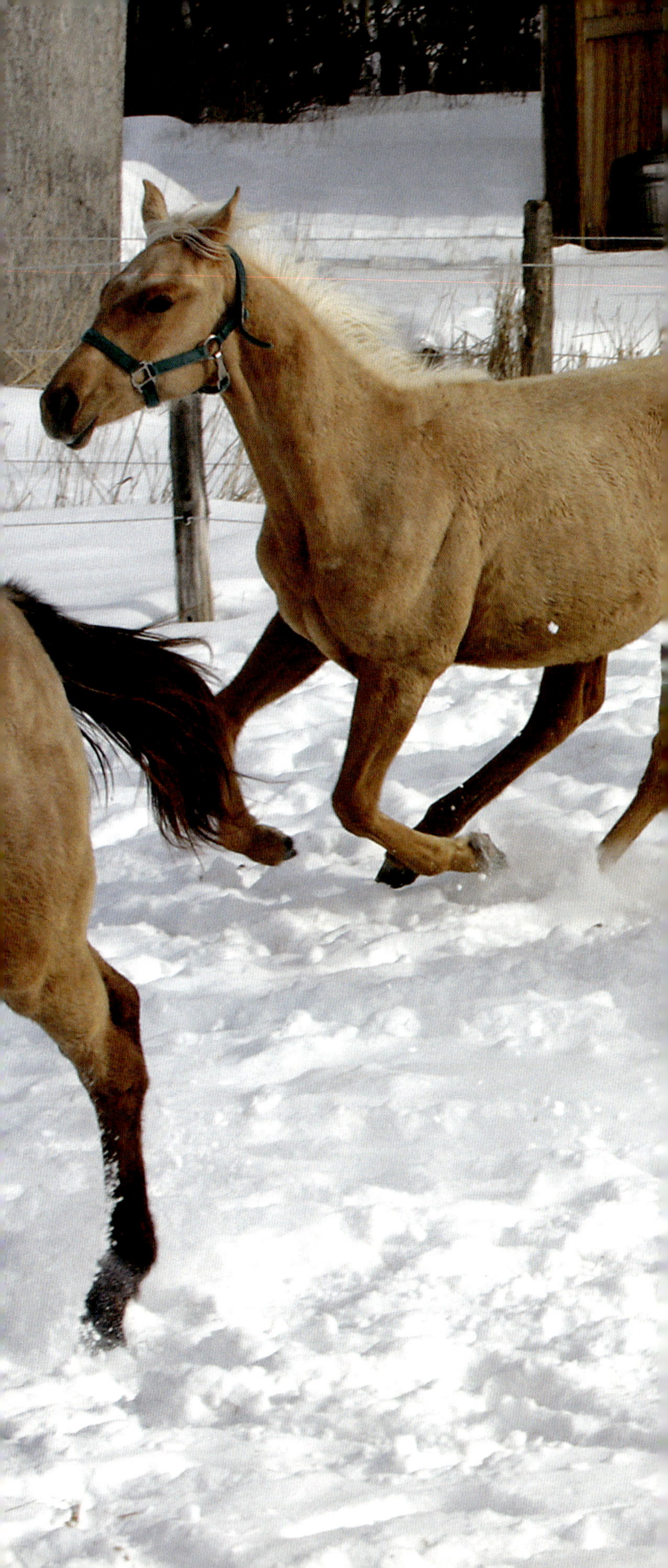

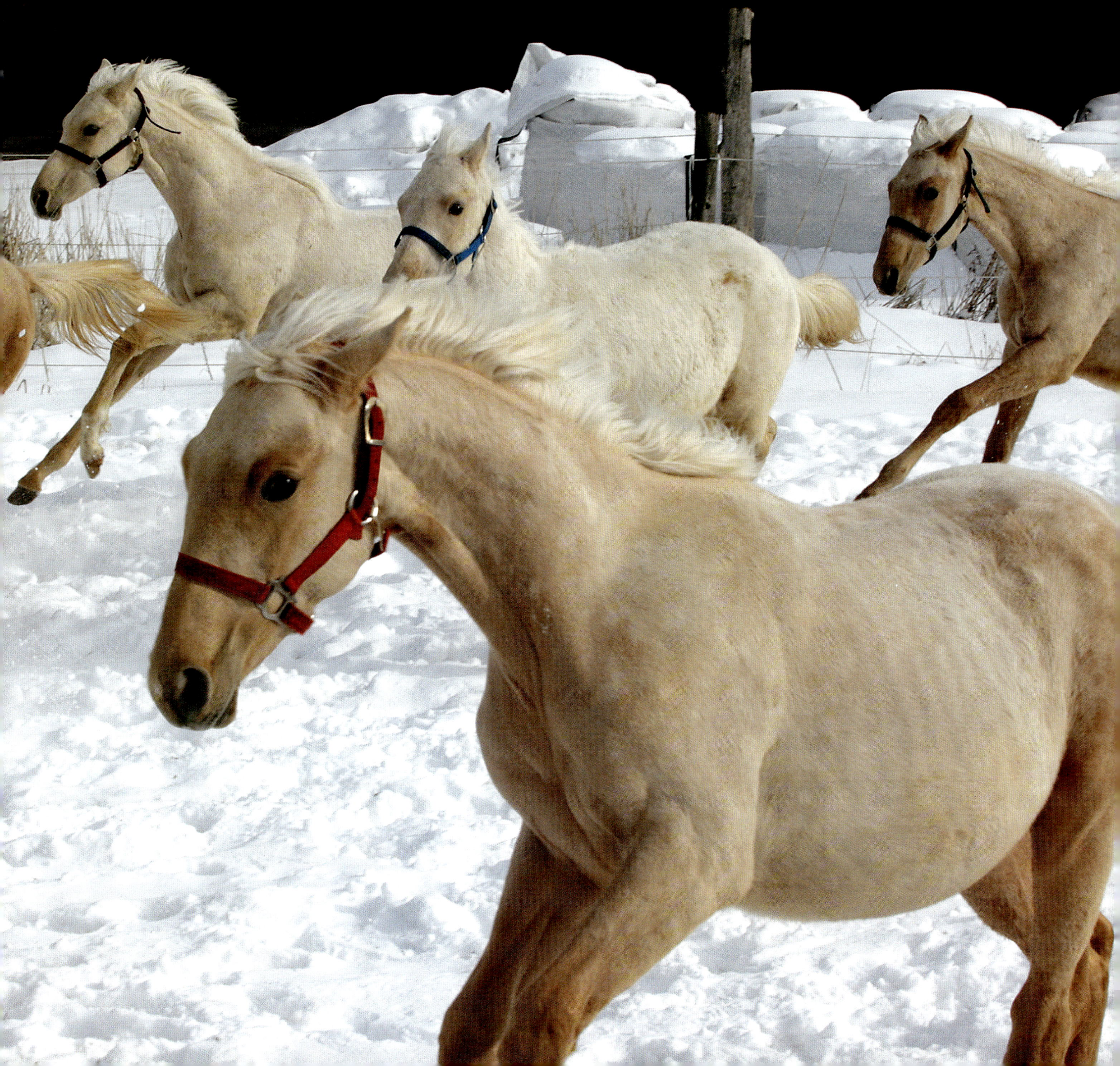

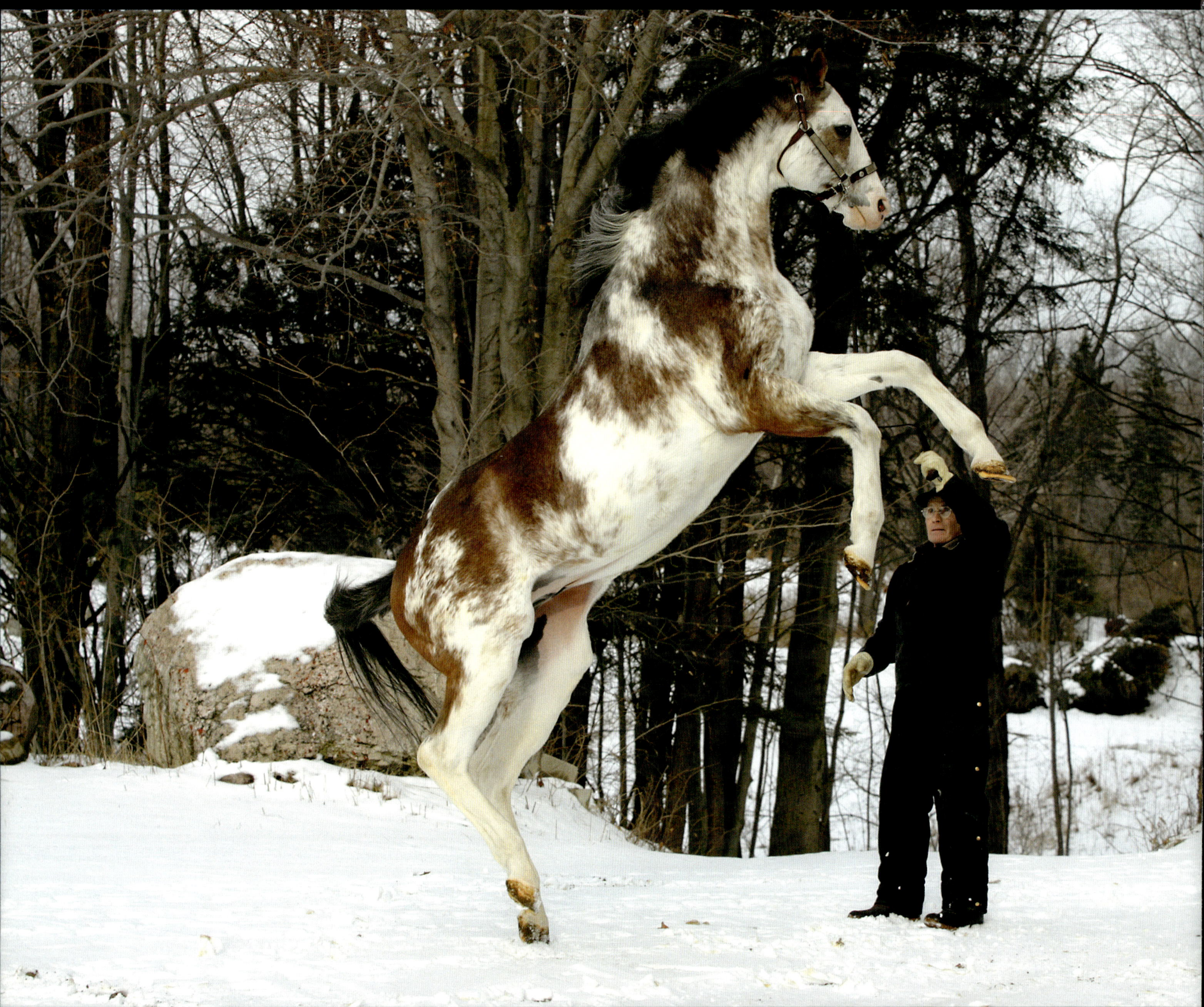

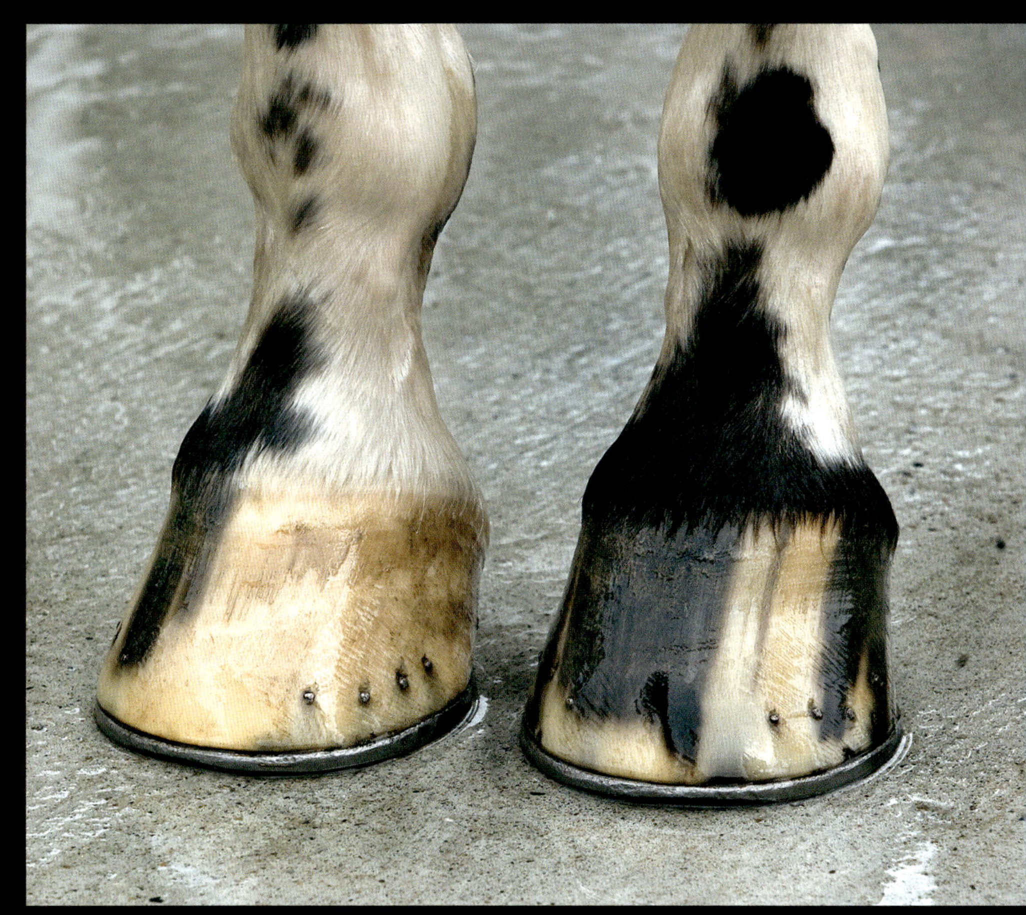

Left, Puchilingui, a Thoroughbred whose coloration shocked The Jockey Club, became a foundation sire of Paint and pinto Thoroughbreds.

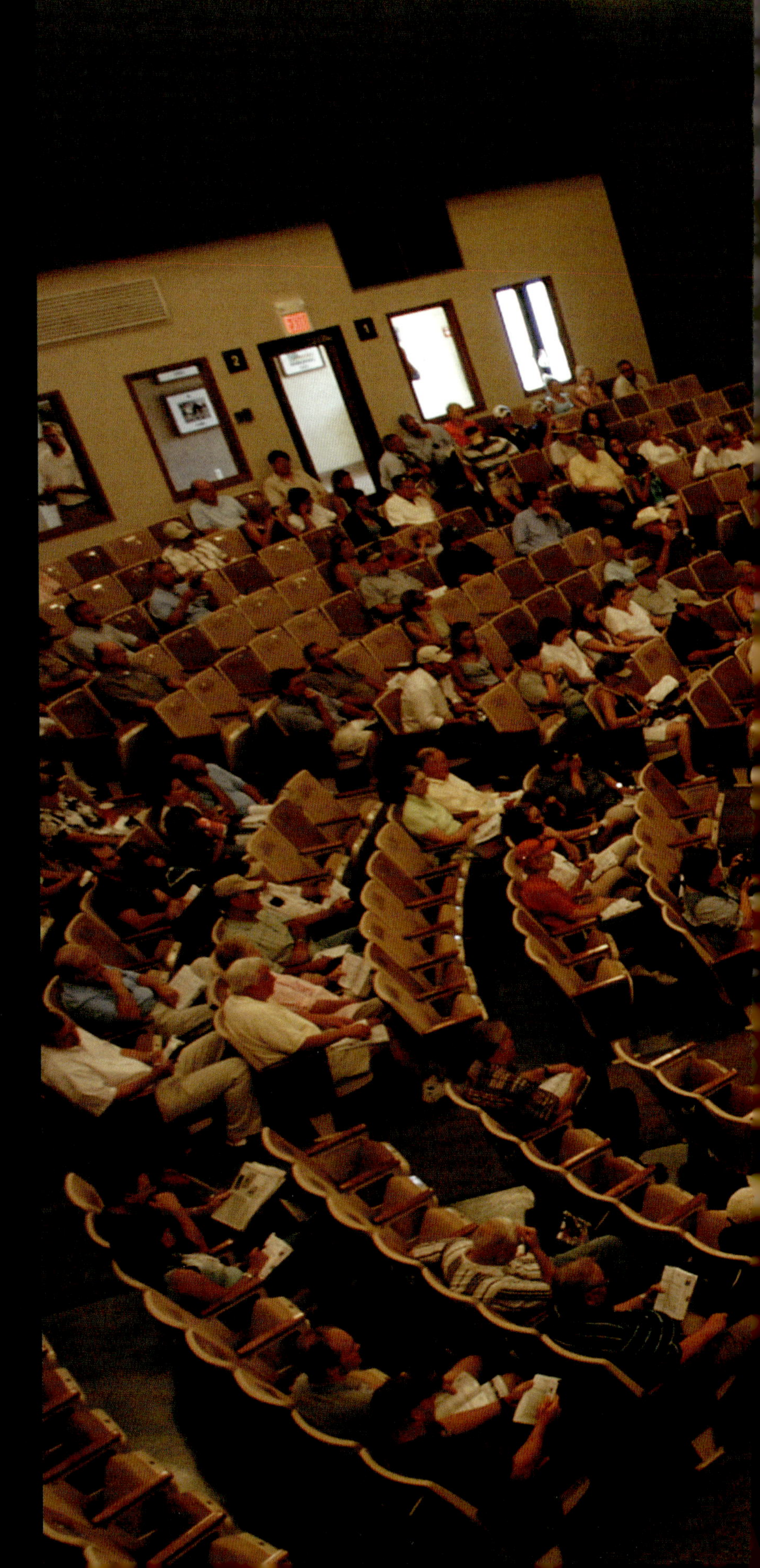

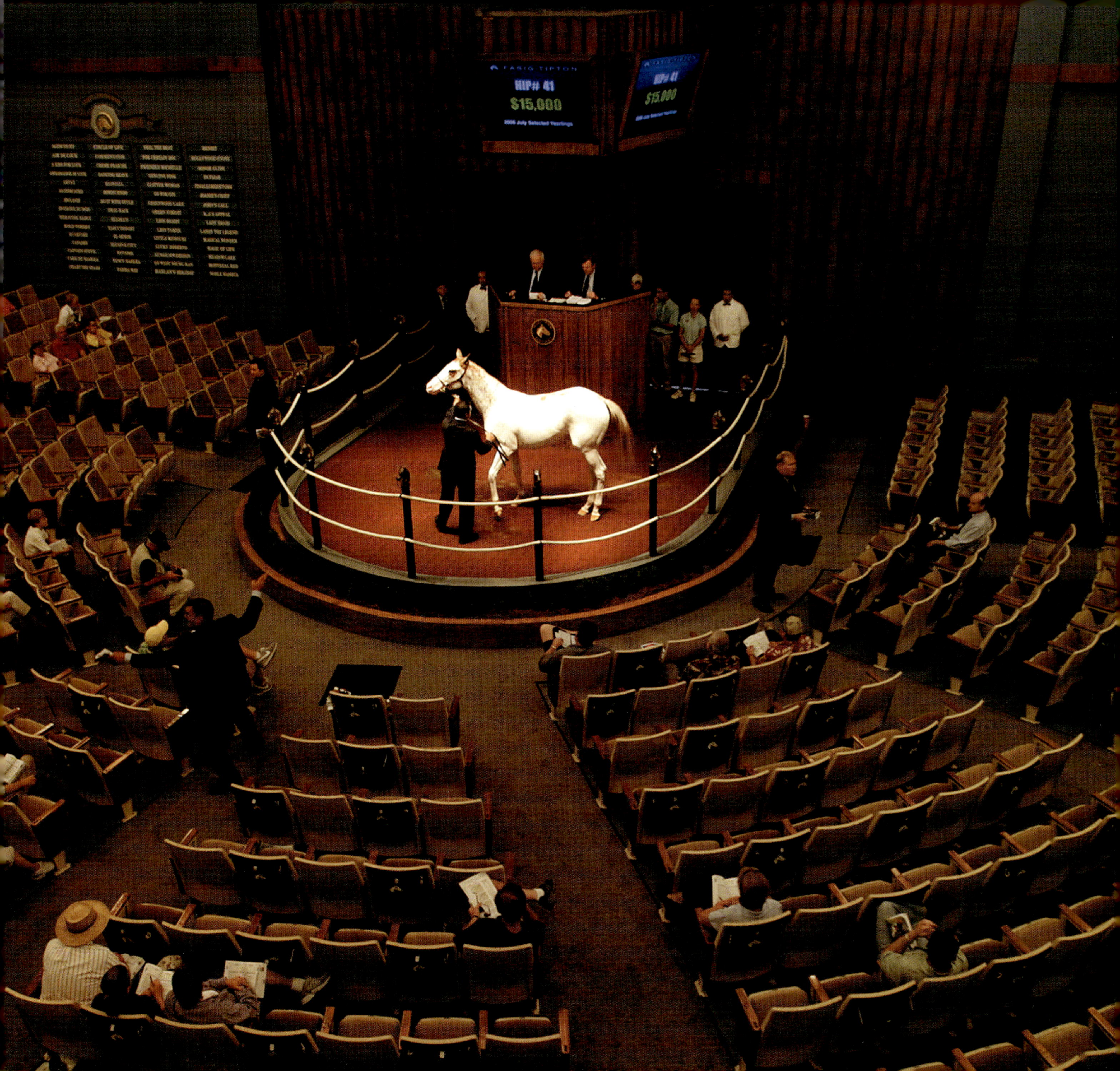
FASIG TIPTON
HIP# 41
$15,000
July Selected Yearlings
HIP# 41
$15,000

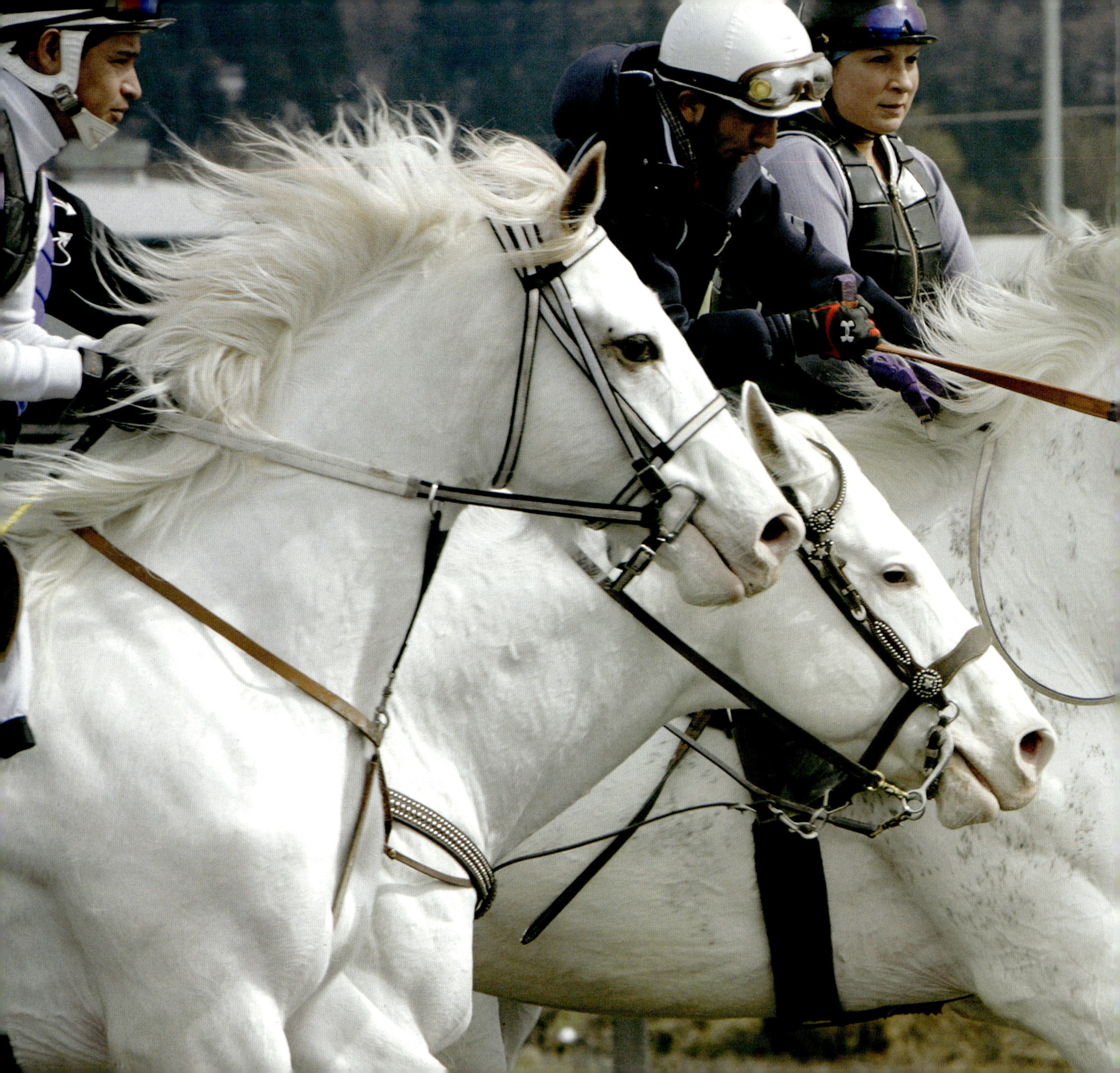

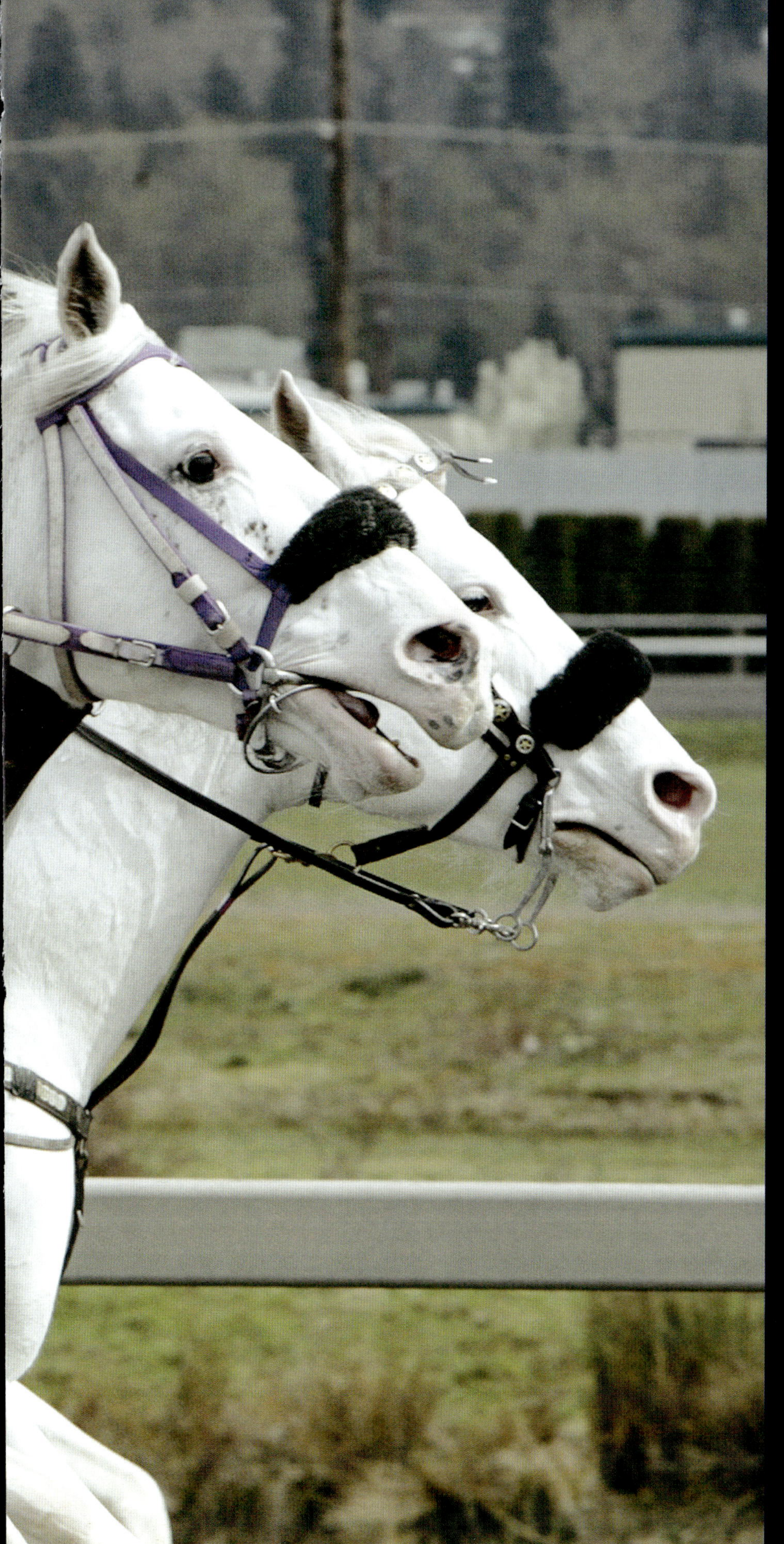

These white horses at Emerald Downs racetrack near Seattle, Washington — three Thoroughbreds and a half-Thoroughbred (on rail) — all descend from the spotted sire Airdrie Apache.

Zebras, while built similarly to horses, are actually quite distant relatives. The most common question about them is this: Are they black with white stripes or white with black stripes? As with so many questions in the world of color genetics, the answer is still open to debate.

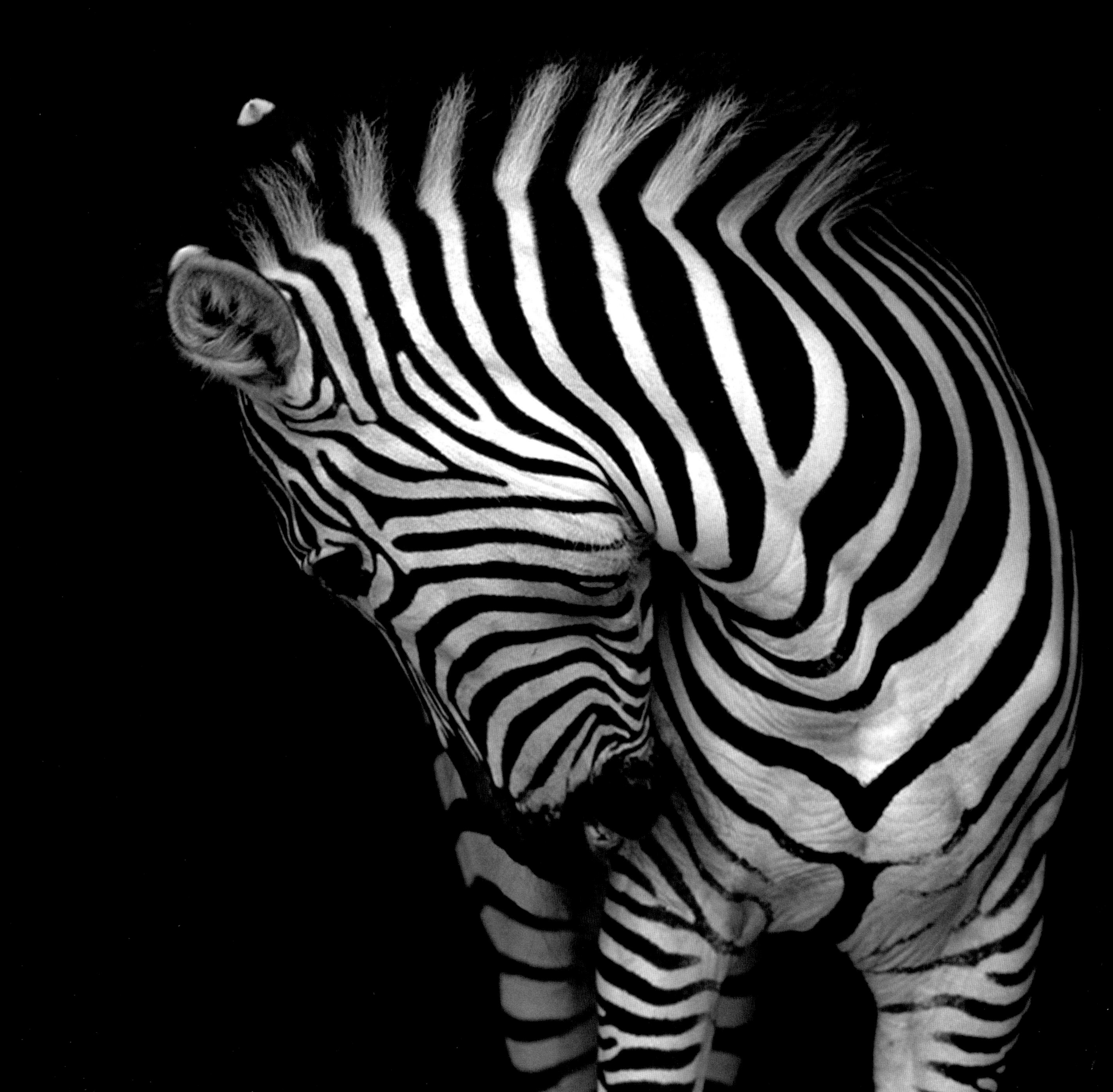

KEYS TO THE COLOR

Some horses included in the book are identified below by their name, breed, and farm/owner. In a few cases, additional information is included.

Where the owner has provided the horse's color it, too, is listed.

Thoroughbreds are listed according to both their Jockey Club-registered color and, if appropriate, by the color the owner says is accurate.

Cover
Knabstrupper mares at LaRen Stud

Pages 6–7
Name: Natal Clasi
Breed: Brazilian Warmblood, also Rheinland Pfalz-Saar International (RPSI) approved in U.S.
Color: White brindling on mahogany bay
Owners: Natal Partners/Ms. Doni Biggs

pp. 8–11
Name: Reply (Jockey Club), Sinatra's Reply (American Paint Horse Association)
Breed: Thoroughbred, Paint, Quarter Horse
Color: Bay overo
Farm/owner: Kestrel Farm/Desiree Williams

p. 12
Name: Snow Robin
Breed: Thoroughbred, Paint (APHA)
Color: White
Owner: Painted Desert Farm

p. 14
Name: Adonis Amber Rose
Breed: Arabian
Color: Chestnut, flaxen mane and tail
Farm/owner: Rohara Arabians/Doug Corp

p. 15
Name: Cookie
Breed: Miniature Horse
Color: Tri-colored paint
Owner: Leslie Ann Hackney

pp. 16–17
Feral pony on Assateague Island

p. 18
Name: Habit of Diamonds
Breed: Thoroughbred, Paint (APHA)
Color: Chestnut (Jockey Club)
Farm: Painted Desert Farm

p. 19
Name: Sheza Firestarter
Breed: Paint (APHA)
Color: Palomino overo
Farm: Painted Desert Farm

pp. 20–22
Name: OYY Salvadore
Breed: American Curly Horse
Color: Bay
Farm: Top O' the Hill Farm

p. 23
Name: OYY Ceda and OYY Sweet Dreams Baby
Breed: American Curly Horse
Color: Buckskin, cremello
Farm: Top O' the Hill Farm

p. 24
Name: VBF's Diamond Venture
Breed: Rocky Mountain Horse
Color: Chocolate with white mane and tail
Farm/owner: Van Bert Farms/Crystal Gait Horses

p. 25
Name: Cool Hand Luke
Breed: Rocky Mountain Horse
Color: Chocolate with white mane and tail
Farm/owner: Van Bert Farms/Mike Charles

pp. 26–27
Name: Silver Wagon
Breed: Thoroughbred
Color: Grey or roan (Jockey Club)
Farm: Empire Stud

pp. 28–29
Name: JF Arwen (mare) with FGF Talitha (filly)
Breed: Gypsy Vanner
Color: Black and white tobiano
Farm: Fields of Gold Farms

pp. 30–31
Feral ponies on Assateague Island

p. 32
Name: Painting Miss Kitty
Breed: Thoroughbred (Jockey Club), Paint (APHA)
Color: Chestnut
Farm: Painted Desert Farm

p. 33
Name: Mesa Queen
Breed: Thoroughbred
Color: Chestnut (Jockey Club)
Farm: Painted Desert Farm

pp. 34–35
Name: Goldmaker
Breed: Thoroughbred (not registered)
Color: Cremello
Farm/owner: Stoneybrooke Farm/Vivian Hill

pp. 36–37
Name: Polka Dot Com
Breed: Unknown
Color: Full spot Leopard
Owner: Mary Jane Nuckols

p. 39
Name: Koriakin of Narnia (a.k.a. Harrison Fjord)
Breed: Norwegian Fjord
Color: Dun
Farm: Cricket Hill

p. 40
Name: Trintje Wytske M.
Breed: Friesian
Color: Black
Owners: Char Hummel and Alan Goldberg

p. 41
Name: Metheringham Upton Isaac
Breed: Shire
Color: Grey
Farm: Ox Kill Shires

pp. 42–43
Breed: Knabstrupper mares
Farm: LaRen Stud

pp. 44–45
Name: Sheik af Hallundbaek
Breed: Knabstrupper
Color: Black leopard
Farm: LaRen Stud
Miscellaneous: Represented by a Breyer model

pp. 46–47
Name: Snow White (Candy), left, and White Pharaoh (Casper)
Breed: Thoroughbred, Paint (APHA)
Color: Cremello maximum sabino (Snow White), palomino maximum sabino (White Pharaoh)
Farm/owner: Blazing Colours Farm/April Wayenberg
Miscellaneous: Blue eyes on cremello, dark eyes on palomino

p. 48
Name: El Duque De Bel Terra (Duncan)
Breed: Andalusian/Arabian
Color: Grey
Farm/owner: Boarded at Four Chicks Farm/Erin Ryder

pp. 49–50
Name: Spots 'N Stripes Zantazia
Breed: Zorse (sire, zebra; dam, red dun Quarter Horse)
Color: Base color red dun
Farm: Spots 'N Stripes Ranch

p. 51
Name: Spots 'N Stripes Zane
Breed: Zonkey (sire, zebra; dam, donkey)
Color: Base color caramel
Farm: Spots 'N Stripes Ranch

p. 52
Name: RE Autumn Gold
Breed: Colonial Spanish Horse
Color: Buckskin dun sabino/splash white
Farm: Rainbow's End Farm

p. 53
Name: Mirabeau
Breed: German Warmblood
Color: Cremello
Farm/owner: Blazing Colours Farm/April Wayenberg

pp. 54–55
Name: Big Chex To Cash
Breed: Quarter Horse (AQHA), palomino (APHA)
Color: Palomino overo
Farm: Fappani Performance Horses
Miscellaneous: Breyer model

p. 58
Name: Clononeen Isolde
Breed: Gypsy Cob
Color: Black and white tobiano
Farm/owner: Rose Canyon Ranch/Paul and Jennifer Godward

p. 59
Feral stallion on Assateague Island

pp. 60–61
Name: GPs Krugerrand (Andy)
Breed: Thoroughbred
Color: Palomino with Birdcatcher and Bend Or spots
Farm/owner (2007): Symmetry Ranch/Peggy Kohn

p. 62
Name: Sky
Breed: Oldenburg, registered German Oldenburg Verband
Color: Tobiano black/dark bay pinto
Farm/owner: Silverwood Farm/Elizabeth Potter Hall

p. 63
Name: Star Magnitude
Breed: Thoroughbred
Color: Chestnut
Farm: Juddmonte Farms

p. 64
Name: Unnamed 2009 foal by Maybry's Boy out of Point Spread
Breed: Thoroughbred
Color: Grey, color not yet listed with Jockey Club
Farm/owner: Highcliff Farm/Flying Zee Stables

p. 65, left
Name: Armonk
Breed: Thoroughbred
Color: Grey or roan (Jockey Club), with blood mark
Farm: Juddmonte Farms

p. 65, right
Name: Wayward Wind
Breed: Colonial Spanish Horse
Color: Bay sabino/splash white
Farm: Rainbow's End Farm
Miscellaneous: 20 years of age, 14½ hands high, easily jumps 4'

p. 66, left
Name: A Mir Foolish Fool (Gambol)
Breed: Sporthorse, unregistered
Color: Black with spotted blanket, 2 partial blue eyes
Farm/owner: Twin Creeks Farm/Angela Farr

p. 66, right
Name: Gizmo
Breed: Unknown
Owner: Leah Gyarmati

p. 67
Name: RE Promise of Gold
Breed: Colonial Spanish Horse
Color: Perlino dun
Farm: Rainbow's End Farm

pp. 72–73
Name: Windigo's Crimson Warlock
Breed: Tennessee Walking Horse and Spotted Saddle Horse (TWHBEA and ASHA)
Color: Chestnut sabino
Farm/owner: Windigo Farms/Pauline Rounds

p. 74
Name: Seahorse Dance
Breed: Paint (APHA)
Color: Black and white overo
Farm: Painted Desert Farm

p. 75
Name: Bo
Breed: Miniature Horse
Color: Black and white tobiano
Farm/owner: Mountain View Miniatures/ Leslie Ann Hackney

p. 76
Name: Nycomi Cadillac Kid
Breed: Paint (APHA)
Color: Tovero, with badger face
Farm: Heavy Horse Farm

p. 77
Name: Spectacular Tabasco
Breed: Paint
Farm: Painted Desert Farm

pp. 78–79
Name: A Mir Foolish Fool (Gambol) (see page 66, left)

p. 80
Name: Cheyenne
Breed: American Miniature Horse
Color: Sorrel and white
Owner: Sharon and Gary Sergeant

p. 81, left
Name: Raiders Little Jessie
Breed: American Miniature Horse
Color: Sorrel
Farm/owner: Miniature Ventures/Larry or Maryann Cerullo

p. 81, right
Name: Bond Brown Betty
Breed: American Miniature Horse (AMHA)
Color: Bay
Farm/owner: Miniature Ventures/Larry or Maryann Cerullo
Miscellaneous: All three examples of lacing are Miniatures descended from AMHA stallion Bond Showboy

pp. 82–83
Name: Leo
Breed: Miniature Horse
Color: Black silver varnish roan (appaloosa)
Farm: Maxon Farm

pp. 84-87
Name: RE Painted Lilly
Breed: Colonial Spanish Horse
Color: Grulla sabino/frame overo, one brown eye, one blue eye
Farm: Rainbow's End Farm

pp. 88–89
Breed: Colonial Spanish Horses
Farm: Rainbow's End Farm

pp. 90–91
Name: Payana von Rosenof
Breed: Knabstrupper
Color: Black/white full leopard
Farm: Cedar Creek Stables

pp. 92–95
Name: Cayuse Gold
Breed: Colonial Spanish Horse
Color: Buckskin Dun
Farm: Rainbow's End Farm

pp. 96–97
Name: Myrewyn Sophisticated Lady (Diana)
Breed: Thoroughbred x Swedish Warmblood
Color: Palomino
Farm/owner: Myrewyn Equestrian/Sara Bosch

pp. 98–99
Name: Arctic Cielo
Breed: Thoroughbred
Color: White
Farm/owner (2007): Derby Lyn Farms/ Katie Clark

p. 100
Name: Bonfire Glo
Breed: Thoroughbred
Color: Palomino
Farm/owner (2007): Symmetry Ranch/ Peggy Kohn

pp. 102–103
Name: Say Florida Sandy, Say Florida Sandy weanlings
Breed: Thoroughbred
Color: Dark bay or brown
Farm/owner (Say Florida Sandy): Boarded at Buckridge Farm/Walter Downey

pp. 104–105
Name: Natal Clasi (see pp. 6-7)

pp. 106–107
Name: Jamra
Breed: Thoroughbred
Color: Flea-bitten grey
Farm: Our Mims Retirement Haven

pp. 108–109
Name: AC's Painted Lace
Breed: Quarter Horse or Paint
Color: Flaxen chestnut overo (see expanded definition of color in introduction)
Owners: C. Reid & Audry Crosby McLellan

p. 110
Name: Sheela vom Nordstern
Breed: Knabstrupper
Color: Bay based full leopard
Farm: Cedar Creek Stables

p. 111
Name: Pekiwatha
Breed: American Miniature Horse
Color: Pintaloosa (pinto, appaloosa), also lacing
Farm: Spots 'N Stripes Ranch

p. 112
Name: Gold Marquesa
Breed: Thoroughbred
Color: Palomino (Jockey Club); cremello (according to Symmetry Ranch)
Farm/owner (2007): Symmetry Ranch/ Peggy Kohn

p. 113
Name: Sato
Breed: Thoroughbred, Paint (APHA)
Color: Palomino sabino
Farm/owner: Blazing Colours Farm/April Wayenberg

pp. 114–115
Name: Windigo's Crimson Warlock (see pp. 72–73)

p. 116
Name: PDF Silversmoke
Breed: Thoroughbred, Paint (APHA)
Color: White
Farm: Painted Desert Farm

p. 117
Name: Chet DT
Breed: Thoroughbred, Paint (APHA)
Color: White (Jockey Club); red roan overo (APHA)
Farm/owner: Double Tree Paint Farm/ Jerry and Nancy Tyler

pp. 118–119
Name: Mona Lisa (left) and Lady Godiva
Breed: Gypsy Vanner
Farm/owner: Vanner Valley Farm/Mort and Brigitte Kozak

p. 120
Name: Patchen Beauty and her foal The White Fox
Breed: Thoroughbred
Color: White
Farm: Patchen Wilkes Farm

p. 121
Name: Thunder Kitty, and her Count Me In foal
Breed: Thoroughbred
Color: Dark bay or brown (Jockey Club); black (according to Painted Desert Farm)
Farm: Painted Desert Farm

pp. 122–123
Name: Fletcher's Gold (Caesar)
Breed: Appaloosa (APHC)
Color: Cremello, with blue eyes and snow cap blanket
Owner: Dr. Amy M. Gill

pp. 124–125
Name: Willspynow
Breed: Thoroughbred
Color: Bay with Birdcatcher spots

p. 126
Name: Wayward Wind (see page 65)

p. 127
St. Clement's horse show participant, Saratoga Springs, NY

pp. 128–129
Name: Cartwheel
Breed: Miniature Horse
Color: Bay tobiano/sabino
Farm: Maxon Farm

pp. 130–131
Maxon Farm – various breeds and colors

p. 132
Name: Jo Jo
Breed: Clydesdale
Color: White and bay
Farm/owner: Birsh Family Farm/Charlotte and Nickoli Birsch

p. 133
Name: Windsheer
Breed: Thoroughbred
Color: Chestnut
Farm: Painted Desert Farm

pp. 134–135
Name: Blue Eyed Streaker
Breed: Thoroughbred, Paint (APHA)
Color: Frame and sabino overo
Farm: Echo Hill Farm

p. 136
Name: Hailey
Breed: Clydesdale
Color: Bay
Farm: Birsh Family Farm

p. 137
Feral pony on Assateague Island

pp. 138–139
Name: El Duque De Bel Terra (Duncan) (see page 48)

p. 140
Name: Splish Splash
Breed: Uncertain/appaloosa cross
Farm/owner: Cornerstone Equestrian/ Linda Worley

p. 141
Name: Chex Nu Jewel
Breed: Quarter Horse, Palomino (Palomino Horse Breeders of America)
Color: Sooty palomino
Farm: McBride Quarter Horses

pp. 142–143
Name: Sharp Trilogy
Breed: Quarter Horse, also member of National Foundation Quarter Horse Association
Color: Red dun brindle, greying per grey dam
Farm/owner: Owl Glen/Denise Charpilloz

p. 144
Name: Barbaro
Breed: Thoroughbred
Color: Bay
Owner: Roy and Gretchen Jackson

p. 146
Name: Blue Apache Wind
Breed: Paint (APHA)
Color: Overo sabino
Farm: Heavy Horse Farm

p. 147
Name: RE Promise of Gold (see page 67)

p. 150
Name: Thunder Snow
Breed: North American Spotted Draft Horse
Color: Black and white tobiano
Farm: Heavy Horse Farm
Miscellaneous: 17.2 hands

p. 151
Name: Flashy Bull
Breed: Thoroughbred
Color: Grey or roan (Jockey Club)
Owner: West Point Thoroughbreds

pp. 152–153
Name: Kiger Eclipse, and her 2009 colt by Silver Bullet
Breed: Kiger Mustang
Color: Grulla
Farm/owner: Spanish Sage Ranch/Diane Pinney

KEYS TO THE COLOR

pp. 154–155
Name: Good Thunder
Breed: Arabian
Color: Bay
Farm/owner: Rohara Arabians/Marikate Matthews

pp. 156–157
Name: Chex Nu Jewel (see page 141)

pp. 158–159
Name: Nikolai
Breed: Przewalski's Horse stallion

p. 160
Name: Argos Quest
Breed: Thoroughbred
Color: Palomino
Farm/owner (2007): Symmetry Ranch/ Peggy Kohn

p. 161
Name: Thor
Breed: Brabant
Color: Blue roan
Farm: Heavy Horse Farm

pp. 162–163
Name: Sharp One
Breed: Quarter Horse, also member of International Buckskin Horse Association and Brindle and Striped Equine International
Color: Red dun brindle
Farm/owner: Owl Glen/Denise Charpilloz

p. 164
Name: Charmander
Breed: Thoroughbred
Color: Grey or roan (Jockey Club), with 'bloody shoulder' mark
Farm: Needham–Betz Thoroughbreds

p. 165
Name: Arctic Shadow
Breed: Thoroughbred
Color: White
Farm: Painted Desert Farm

pp. 166–167
Three white Thoroughbred mares owned by Painted Desert Farm

pp. 168–169
Pastoral scene near Three Sisters volcanoes, Cascade Mountain range, Oregon

pp. 170–171
Name: Kiowa's Breeze
Breed: Colonial Spanish Horse
Color: Grulla sabino/splash white
Farm: Rainbow's End Farm
And her foal:
Name: RE Shenandoah
Breed: Colonial Spanish Horse
Color: Smokey black sabino/splash white (probable)
Farm: Rainbow's End Farm

pp. 172–173
Name: Lightning
Breed: Unknown
Color: Chestnut, with some white hairs in body
Owner: Magic Forest

pp. 174–175
Name: North Forks Tickle Your Fancy
Breed: Welsh Pony of Cob Type (Welsh Section C), also a First Premium American Sportpony
Color: Flaxen chestnut sabino mare
Farm/owner: Myrewyn Equestrian/Sara Bosch

pp. 176–177
Feral ponies on Assateague Island

pp. 178–179
Name: Sato (see page 113)

pp. 180–181
Full sister and brother:

Name: Painting Shadows
Breed: Thoroughbred, Paint (APHA)
Color: Black (Jockey Club); black overo (APHA)
Farm: Painted Desert Farm

Name: Painting Freedom
Breed: Thoroughbred, Paint (APHA)
Color: Dark bay/brown (Jockey Club); black overo (APHA); black (according to Painted Desert Farm)
Farm: Painted Desert Farm

pp. 182–183
Name: Spots 'N Stripes First Lady
Breed: American Miniature Horse
Color: Black and white pinto, minimal tobiano
Farm: Spots 'N Stripes Ranch

pp. 184–185
Name: Golden Providence
Breed: Half Arabian – National Show Horse
Color: Champagne palomino
Owner: Laurie and David Menard

p. 186
Grey mare on a snowy day at Mill Creek Farm

pp. 188–189
Name: Allamystique
Breed: Thoroughbred
Color: White
Farm: Painted Desert Farm

pp. 190–191
Name: Monarchos
Breed: Thoroughbred
Color: Grey or roan (Jockey Club)
Farm/owner: Nuckols Farm/John and Debby Oxley

pp. 192–193
Name: Faux Finish
Breed: Thoroughbred, Paint (APHA)
Color: Bay (Jockey Club); light buttermilk buckskin (according to True Colours Farm)
Farm: True Colours Farm

pp. 194–195
Name: Misty of Chincoteague (right) and her daughter Stormy
Breed: Chincoteague Pony
Owner: Beebe Ranch

pp. 196–197
Misty descendants at the Chincoteague Pony Centre, with members of the Chincoteague Pony Drill Team

Names: Misty III, Misty's September Stardust, Misty II's Henry, Misty's Heart of the Storm, Misty's Morning Glory, Misty's Black Mist, Misty's Icicle, Misty's Heat Wave, Misty's Desert Sun, Misty's Smoke N' Mist
Breed: Chincoteague Pony

p. 201
Name: Sucre Sucre with her Desert Warrior colt
Breed: Thoroughbred
Color: Chestnut; foal color bay
Farm/owner: McMahon of Saratoga Thoroughbreds

pp. 202–203
The Water Trough. Farm scene at Steppin Straight Farms.

p. 204
Name: *Princess Royale
Breed: Thoroughbred
Color: Grey
Farm: Our Mims Retirement Haven

p. 205
Name: Snow Dancing
Breed: Thoroughbred, Paint (APHA)
Color: Grey or roan (Jockey Club); white, chestnut overo
Farm: Painted Desert Farm

pp. 206–207
A happy winter group: A mixture of Thoroughbreds and Thoroughbred crosses (Warmblood, Anglo Arab, and buckskin) at Flying Colours Farm

p. 208
Name: Puchilingui
Breed: Thoroughbred
Color: Grey or roan (Jockey Club)
Farm/owner: Double Tree Paint Farm, Jerry and Nancy Tyler

p. 209
Name: Gizmo (see page 66)

pp. 210–211
Name: Turf Club
Breed: Thoroughbred
Color: White
Venue: Fasig–Tipton

pp. 212–213
Names: Snow Robin (Thoroughbred), Arctic North (Thoroughbred), Allamystique (Thoroughbred), Arctic Dash (half-Thoroughbred, half-Paint)
Color: White
Farm: Painted Desert Farm

pp. 214–215
Name: Spots 'N Stripes Zintawa
Breed: Zebra
Farm: Spots 'N Stripes Ranch

ACKNOWLEDGMENTS

Thanks to Michael Tyner, Michael Amoruso, Sandy Zaconick, Anne Castle, and my family for their inspiration and help, and to Tom Hall for his invaluable assistance. Thank you also to Brian Turner, David Young, Alexandra Beckstett, and Jacqueline Duke.

Thanks to Shelley Cummins at Magic Forest, Kendy Allen of the Chincoteague Pony Centre, the Chincoteague Pony Drill Team, Matt DesJardins, Bonnie and Billy Beebe of Beebe Ranch, Mary Morris Collings, Kirsten Wellman of White Horse Productions, and the people of the informative Equine Color Web site. D. Phillip Sponenberg's 2009 book, *Equine Color Genetics*, was very helpful, as was Jeanette Gower's *Horse Color Explained: A Breeder's Perspective*. For those interested in the genetic reasoning behind colorful horses, both are interesting and informative.

Special thanks to Audrey C. Crosby, photographer and student of equine color genetics, for sharing her vast knowledge with me.

Thank you to all of those who allowed me the honor of photographing their beautiful horses.

And, most of all, thank you to Tom Keyser.

ABOUT BARBARA

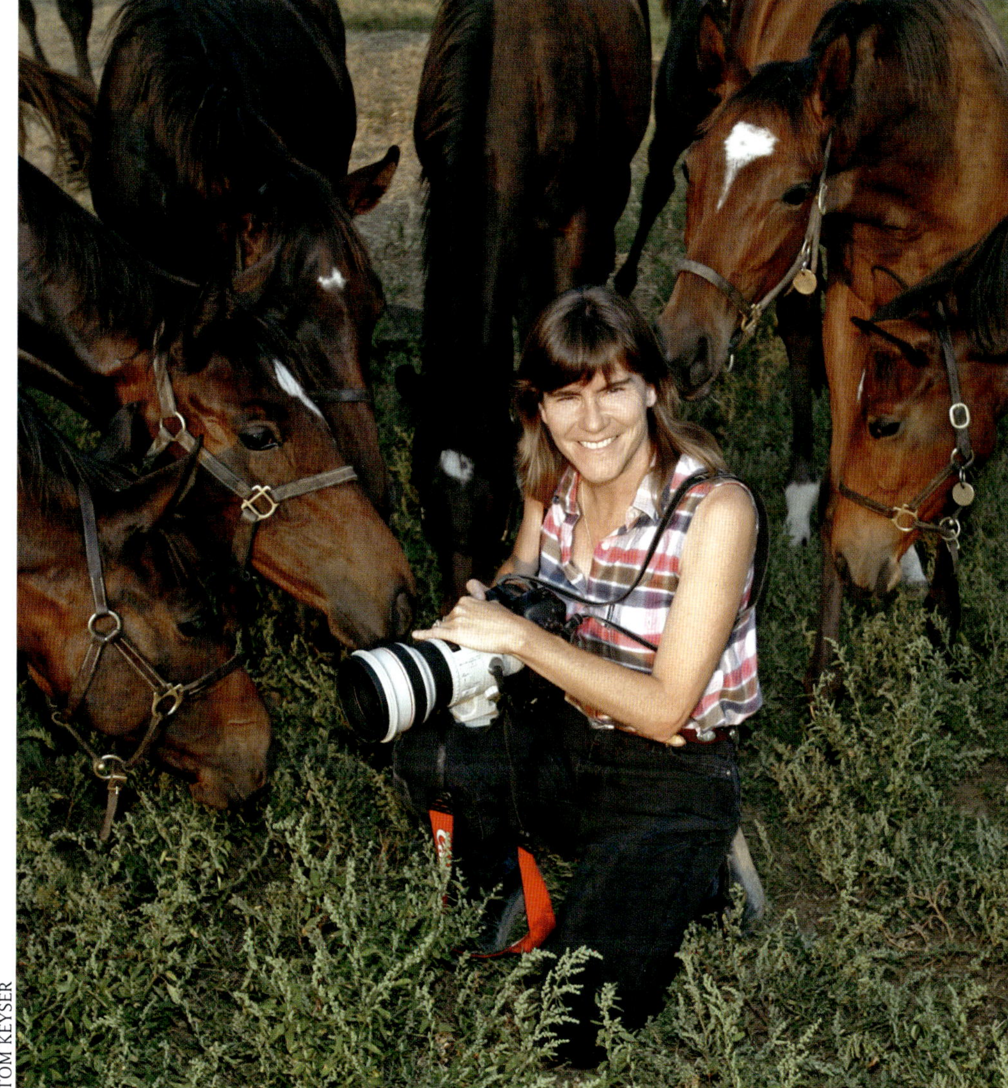
TOM KEYSER

Barbara Livingston, who has been photographing horse racing for more than thirty-five years, is widely recognized as one of the sport's top photographers. She has twice been recognized with racing's highest honor, the Eclipse Award for Outstanding Photography.

Barbara is a photographer for *Daily Racing Form*. Additionally, her work has graced the covers of countless racing books and mainstream magazines such as *Newsweek*, *People*, *Sports Illustrated* (including their two-page 'Leading Off' spread), *ESPN The Magazine*, *GQ*, and on the cover of *TV Guide*. Her photos have also appeared on MTV, MSNBC, CBS Sunday Morning, ESPN, HBO, and Entertainment Tonight.

Eclipse Press has published four previous books by Barbara: *Four Seasons of Racing* (1998); *Old Friends* (2002); *Barbara Livingston's Saratoga: Images from the Heart* (2005); and *More Old Friends* (2007).

Barbara has her own popular Thoroughbred racing Web site, www.barbaralivingston.com, where examples of her equine biographical work may be viewed in its archives.

Her extensive photographic record spans approximately seventy years. In addition to her own negatives, Barbara owns the negatives (and their rights) of respected Lexington photographer James W. Sames III. Among them are Kentucky Derby images spanning three decades and the last photograph taken of Man o' War alive.

Barbara graduated with a BFA/Experimental Photography from Syracuse University. She lives in Saratoga Springs, New York.